EAST

THE
NEXT
EVEREST

To my parents, Jean and Joe,
for leading me along life's initial trails.

And to my wife, Gloria,
for climbing with me on life's biggest mountains.

ALSO BY JIM DAVIDSON

The Ledge

THE NEXT EVEREST

SURVIVING THE MOUNTAIN'S DEADLIEST DAY AND FINDING THE RESILIENCE TO CLIMB AGAIN

JIM DAVIDSON

St. Martin's Press
New York

First published in the United States by
St. Martin's Press, an imprint of St. Martin's Publishing Group

www.stmartins.com

Endpaper and insert photographs courtesy of Jim Davidson

Design by Michelle McMillian

Library of Congress Cataloging-in-Publication Data

Names: Davidson, Jim (Professional speaker), author.
Title: The next Everest : surviving the mountain's deadliest day and finding the
   resilience to climb again / Jim Davidson.
Description: First edition. | New York, N.Y. : St. Martin's Press, 2021. |
Identifiers: LCCN 2020048604 | ISBN 9781250272294 (hardcover) |
   ISBN 9781250272300 (ebook)
Subjects: LCSH: Mountaineering—Everest, Mount (China and Nepal) |
   Mountaineering accidents—Everest, Mount (China and Nepal) |
   Mountaineering—Psychological aspects. | Davidson, Jim (Professional speaker)
Classification: LCC GV199.44.E85 D394 2021 | DDC 796.522095496—dc23
LC record available at https://lccn.loc.gov/2020048604

First Edition: 2021

10 9 8 7 6 5 4 3 2 1

1

We climbed the deadliest section of Everest at night. The jumbled icefall we struggled through rose more than two thousand vertical feet in a mile as we ascended from base camp to Camp One. PK Sherpa—Pasang Kami Sherpa lived in the village of Phortse, and everyone called him PK—and I threaded our way among thousands of leaning ice pillars as they crept downhill in an endless stream, tumbling and shattering as they went.

Darkness made it harder for us to pick our way through the shifting ice maze. But the deep nighttime cold slowed the Khumbu Glacier's movement, which reduced the chances of frozen walls collapsing on us or avalanches burying us. At least, so we hoped.

I tried to hurry through the Khumbu Icefall but could only lumber uphill like a tired old yak. Whenever I stopped, my achy thigh muscles regained some strength, but after just a few more steps, my pace decreased once again. Even though I was in the best climbing shape of my life, my oxygen-starved legs just couldn't move any faster in the low-density air at nineteen thousand feet.

It was my first day climbing Mount Everest, and already the chaotic landscape and self-doubt had me awash in uncertainty. With a few hours left until we reached Camp One, we pushed deeper into the icefall.

Light from our headlamps bounced off the gleaming ice walls. Dancing shadows sometimes made the glacial blocks look like they were moving. About half of the other fifteen climbers and fifteen Nepali guides, known as sherpas, on our team climbed above us in the tangled icefall; the rest followed behind. A guide moved along with each team member. Most of the climbing sherpas we hired were of actual Sherpa ancestry, but a few came from other ethnic groups, like Bhote.* Including our two senior American guides, thirty-two of us ascended the dark icefall, along with people from other teams. Every few minutes, the jittery sweep of someone's headlamp marked the way ahead.

Even though the night hid some of the danger, ominous evidence of glacial cracks surrounded us. My headlamp beam illuminated a slight sag in the snow that hinted at a crevasse lurking underneath. In many places snow bridges had crumbled into obvious open holes. We passed a few yawning gaps that went as deep as 120 feet into the glacier.

Twenty-three years earlier, when I was descending a glacier on Mount Rainier, in Washington State, a glacial snow bridge had collapsed beneath my feet. I got dropped deep inside an enormous crevasse. Now every glacial crack I stepped over, and every giant chasm we skirted, reminded me of what had happened back then. And what could happen now.

Dawn's arrival converted the black-and-white world around us to color. First the Khumbu Glacier turned purple. Growing daylight shifted the dark clouds toward lighter shades of gray and revealed frosty blue tints inside the glacial ice. When I could make out the dark-red portions of PK's pack, I shut off my headlamp. We kept following the thin climbing rope, which was anchored in place. This fixed line marked the path

---

* In Nepal, a mountain guide is generally described as having the occupation of "sherpa," regardless of that person's heritage. However, a person's name, ethnicity, and spoken language are written here as "Sherpa."

through the frozen labyrinth and served as a safety rope to clip our climbing harnesses into.

The route angled leftward, close to Everest's west shoulder. PK started climbing faster, rushing when he clipped his harness into and out of the lines. After stepping across one open crevasse, he grabbed the fixed nylon rope, scrambled twenty feet up an ice ramp, and disappeared over the top. Instead of his usual momentary stop to make sure I was moving well, he didn't even look back. I chased after him, my chest aching from sucking in the sparse air. Every breath contained less than half the oxygen it would have at sea level. I found PK two minutes later, waiting for me at an anchor point along the ropes. As soon as I arrived, he said, "Hurry. Very bad place."

Still breathless, I couldn't answer. Instead I nodded and pointed a gloved finger forward. PK took off even faster than before. I thought, We must be close to last year's accident site.

One year and one week ago, on the morning of April 18, 2014, sixteen Nepali mountain workers died in this part of the icefall. A glacial block the size of a ten-story building sheared away from an ice ramp hanging a thousand feet above their heads. As the frozen bomb plummeted toward them, it shattered into a barrage of rock-hard shrapnel. All that ice debris collapsed into the icefall and buried the men.

A *National Geographic* cartographer later compared before-and-after satellite photos of the area. He determined that as much as 31 million pounds of frozen debris had fallen on them. Two days of risky search-and-rescue efforts recovered thirteen bodies but could not find the others: Three men remained entombed in the ice somewhere beneath our feet.

I glanced above my left shoulder and saw the white underbellies of several ice fields looming a hundred stories above us. One of them was the culprit.

Thinking of those lost and their families, I wanted to pause and pay some brief respects. But stopping for even a second might give gravity an opening to drop an ice building on us. I hurried after PK as best I could, my pulse pounding in my temples.

Gauzy clouds parted enough to reveal the 25,000-foot-tall ridge ahead.

That long rock wall had kept us in the freezing shade since sunrise. But with the sun now above the ridge crest and the clouds thinning, the morning sunlight cut through. With every passing minute, warm energy loosened up the ice fields hanging over our heads and seeped into the glacier flowing beneath our feet. I needed to move faster.

I traversed a snowy shelf by placing my feet into the bootprints of previous climbers. The metal spikes of my crampons squeaked as they bit into the firm snow. I pushed the snap-link carabiner* of my safety leash along the fixed lines as I climbed. Those community ropes and anchors had been placed earlier in the month by a brave and dedicated sherpa team known as the Icefall Doctors. As I stepped across an open crevasse, the inky abyss underneath my feet plunged far inside the glacier. We clambered among the glacial blocks like ants crawling through a loose pile of ice cubes.

After following the fixed line into a narrow alleyway, I emerged at an alcove ringed on three sides by vertical ice faces. The smooth walls and angular shape of the nook struck me as odd. While earning my geology degrees, I had studied glaciology. When I examined the icy alcove closer, its floor seemed unusually flat, and a thick layer of ice shards covered the ground. I pushed my boot into the loose debris, and the sharp-edged remnants moved freely—they hadn't frozen together yet. All this had just formed. We were standing in a spot that had recently caved in.

PK and two other climbers whom I didn't know stood staring up a tall aluminum ladder. Following their gaze about thirty feet higher, I saw a climber from another team. He ascended the crooked ladder with slow, awkward movements. We were at a full stop in an active collapse zone.

I stood close behind PK. When he looked back at me, his brown cheeks showed a tinge of red sunburn from our past three weeks at high altitude. His face curled into a frown, and he shook his head in frustra-

---

* A carabiner is an oval-shaped link of metal, usually aluminum, that a person can easily open on one side by squeezing a hinged gate with their fingers. Climbers use carabiners to quickly clip themselves into and out of climbing ropes and anchors.

tion. To ask PK if we had to go slowly, I said in broken Nepali: *"Bistarai jane, ho?"*

"Ho," he confirmed.

Though anxious about standing there, I needed the rest. I breathed deeply and tried to slow my heart. The floundering climber finally cleared the ladder, and the next person started up. We waited.

I yanked my right glove off and shoved it inside my thick midlayer jacket to keep it warm. Then I pressed two bare fingers against my left wrist. The skin covering my artery bounced against my fingertips. Two beats per second. Even after a break, my heart still hammered at 120 beats per minute. My resting pulse raced three times faster than back home in Colorado.

Though I was thirsty, I didn't want to be fiddling with gear when my turn came to climb. I unzipped the chest pocket of my outer jacket and pulled out a Hershey bar. Once I unwrapped the frozen chocolate, I broke off half and tried handing it to PK. As usual, he politely declined. But after I insisted the customary three times, he relented and took the candy.

"Thank you, Jim Dai."

At twenty-five, PK was about half my age. When he addressed me, he often included the Nepali honorific for "older brother." We munched away and kept looking up over our left shoulders at the ice cliffs shining brighter as more sunlight fell upon them.

When PK's turn came, he clambered up. His rhythm made the flimsy ladder sway, so I tugged my right glove back on and grabbed the side rails to reduce the bouncing. As my father had taught me on painting jobs four decades earlier, I also pressed the toes of my boots against the ladder's lower legs to stabilize it. PK slowed on the upper portion but soon cleared the wall and stepped onto flat ice. Then he spun around, waved me up, and grabbed the top rails.

With a glance, I detected the ladder leaning rightward to bypass an ice bulge. The ladder's top did not sit directly above the base. To clear the wall, six mismatched ladder pieces had been lashed together end-to-end with old faded climbing cord.

I clamped my sliding rope ascender onto the vertical safety line. Climbing smooth instead of quick seemed like the best plan. First I slid my ascender up the rope with my right hand, then I grabbed the rung above my head with my left. I hefted one heavy boot onto a shin-high rung and started up.

After placing my other boot higher than the first, I paused and took two full breaths. I repeated the pattern and got an efficient rhythm going. Every few steps the stainless-steel crampons that were clamped onto my boots skated sideways along the aluminum rungs. The metal-on-metal screech echoed off the alcove walls.

As I rose higher, the untrustworthy assembly sagged. Now I understood why the others had just struggled. The view down revealed a half-hidden crevasse running along the base of the ice wall. One ladder leg sat less than a foot from the cavern's edge. I moved slower, but as I ascended, the ladder's weaknesses and quirks made it bounce. With no one below me footing the base, I worried the ladder might skitter over the lip and drop me into the black hole.

Though I was attached to the safety rope, the fixed-line anchor points in the icefall usually had only a single ice screw or snow picket. With no backup pieces in place, I didn't trust the anchors. My next step up felt awkward, and my hand overgripped the rung. I kept looking down and thinking too much about falling.

2

1977

A warm breeze skips red oak leaves across the church lawn. Above our heads, the white tower of Saint Bernard's Parish stretches high into the New England sky. To paint the upper belfry, Dad has found the biggest ladder in Massachusetts: a seventy-two-footer borrowed from his steeplejack friend who specializes in high church work. The aluminum ladder is a gigantic three-piece extension version that I have never seen before.

When a task looks tough, Dad likes to joke that it will require "two strong men and a boy." That's precisely what we have today. Dad is forty-five years old and in prime shape from a decade of painting six days a week. His brother Bob is three years younger and still possesses most of the muscle and agility he wielded as a star halfback for the Concord High School football team. At age fourteen I'm the same height as my father, but scrawnier. My fingers are half the thickness of Dad's and aren't covered in calluses like his.

The industrial-strength ladder weighs about 180 pounds—standing it up takes all three of us. Once we have the gray giant pointed skyward,

Dad holds one side rail of the base section and I steady the other side, while Uncle Bob pulls the extension rope with all his might. We extend the intermediate section, then the wobbly third piece. Together we lower the fully-extended ladder toward the steeple, but the leaning weight overpowers our combined strength. The ladder's top crashes hard against the belfry trim board, bounces a few times, then settles down.

"Jeesh, what a monster!" says Dad.

Scuffing his boot on the smooth granite walkway, Uncle Bob says, "I don't like this, Joey."

"Yeah, it's slick as frozen snot," Dad replies.

Bob ties the ladder's dangling pull rope to a steel handrail anchored in the speckled granite staircase, but he still isn't comfortable. "Maybe we should both stay here and send Jimmy up."

Uncle Bob radiates energy, and he's our most nimble high-work man, so he usually goes up. Dad looks at me, then stares at the belfry. He's the more analytical brother. Before joining Bob as co-owner of Lincoln Painting Company back in 1963, Dad worked ten years as an electrical technician for Bell Labs and for a microwave engineering firm.

"You're right," Dad says. "Better to have the weight here at the base."

At 140 pounds, I'm by far the lightest, so I know I'm going up. Along with Dad and Uncle Bob, two of my other uncles also paint for a living. I have been climbing ladders since age eight. This is my seventh summer painting, and I work for them most Saturdays and school vacations too.

I'm comfortable on every ladder we own, including the two-piece forty-eight-footer. But this is different. From a side view, the leaning ladder bows badly in the middle portion and then gets extra steep in the upper third. Dad watches me eyeball the odd curve with a scowl on my face. He says: "The deflection is worked into the design. It's all right."

We don't use backup safety lines because they slow us down. Thinking about the long potential fall to the granite makes me nervous. But Dad and Bob know what they're doing. Besides, I don't want to look bad. So I get ready.

I tie a second overhand knot in both shoelaces. To keep my tools from falling onto my ladder men, I remove the putty knife and screwdriver from the back pocket of my jeans. I pull off my Bruins cap, drop the tools in the hat, and set it all down on the grass.

Earlier we painted most of the belfry by reaching out from the inside. Only the highest boards still need a coat. Uncle Bob hands me a one-gallon pot with a few inches of white paint inside. A four-inch brush hangs off the bucket's lip from a brad nail that's been hammered halfway into the brush's wooden handle and then bent into a rough semicircle. I sling the pot onto my belt with a metal paint-pail hook.

Dad steadies his heel on the ground while placing the toe of his boot on the ladder's lower side rail. He pushes the toe of his boot down the rail, smearing the rubber sole against the ladder's foot. By "footing the ladder" like that, he'll prevent it from skittering across the slippery stone slab. Bob stabilizes the other side rail the same way. I start up and hustle through the lower section, no problem. But when I ease onto the sagging middle piece, the ladder bounces with every step. The built-in deflection feels like it's springing back out of the gyrating side rails. I stop climbing, but the ladder keeps bucking. Gripping tight with both hands, I lean in.

"Hey, take it easy!" Dad yells.

"I feel like it's going to spit me off!"

I look down and see Uncle Bob bracing hard against the base. Dad still has his foot and both hands on the ladder, but he stares up at me. In a softer voice, he says: "Tuck your feet against the rails."

Gradually I slide my paint-splattered sneakers outward to opposite ends of the rung. Wedging the outside edges of my tennis shoes against the side rails helps. I move slower and smoother past the swaying middle section.

"That's better!" Dad shouts.

Though steep, the uppermost "fly" section moves less as its top rests against the church steeple. I peer down to my right and get a bird's-eye view of my hometown. Station wagons and hefty sedans cutting through Concord Center cruise around Monument Square. Mom works two doors away at Sentry Insurance, across from Concord's Colonial Inn. At the Old

Hill Burying Ground, next to the church, tilted slate gravestones carved half a century before the Revolutionary War line up in crooked rows.

I climb until I'm even with the golden crown of a nearby maple tree. As the wind whirls around me, a dozen yellow leaves fly past like panicked warblers. My steps get clunky. Then an upward gust rising from the void below shakes the ladder and jostles me. I clutch a single rung with both hands and halt five feet short of the unpainted board.

My world becomes the open space around me and the long drop to the granite slab. The ladder almost disappears, and my senses scream that I might fall.

On a rising pitch, I yell into midair: "This is creepy!"

"Hey, listen up!" Even though we're farther apart than a minute ago, Dad's voice somehow sounds louder. I glance down and see him cupping his hands alongside his mouth to amplify his voice. He waits until I'm ready to hear him.

I relax my hunched shoulders and stand straighter on the rung. After exhaling hard, I look up and contemplate the climb ahead. Into the air I call out: "I'm listening!"

From the other end of the ladder, Dad's words resonate over my shoulder: "Focus on the climb, not the drop!"

3

I stared at the ice wall ten inches from my nose and slowed my breathing. To loosen my death grip on the snowy rung, I wiggled four gloved fingers. I slid my right boot outward until it hit the side rail. After tucking my left boot against the other rail, I was more stable. I focused on the rungs and kept climbing. The crevasse remained down there, of course, but it felt more remote.

Once I reached the top, I clipped my second harness leash onto the fixed rope above the anchor knot. I unclipped my ascender from the vertical dropline, then stepped over the highest rung to join PK on the flat ice.

"Good job, Dai."

Still panting, I smiled but said nothing.

Over the next hour we crossed dozens of crevasses and ascended several more ladders. The farther we got from the deadly collapse site, the calmer I felt. We scaled the last ladder and escaped over the top lip of the Khumbu Icefall.

An enormous oval amphitheater stretched ahead of us. This uppermost shelf of the Khumbu Glacier was named the Western Cwm (pronounced "*koom*," like "*boom*") by famed British explorer George Mallory.* On that first Everest expedition, a reconnaissance trip in 1921, he used the familiar-to-him Welsh word for a glacial valley closed in by steep sidewalls. His word choice forced yet another colonial name onto a Himalayan wonder. Because the high valley walls block noisy winds, climbers have since nicknamed this place the Valley of Silence.

This ice basin extends for three miles, and although the glacier appears to angle gently uphill, it gains more than 2,000 feet of elevation over its length. The distant head of the ice field rises to 22,000 feet above sea level. I was standing on the highest glacier in the world.

The glacier looked smooth compared with the chaotic icefall we had just left, but I knew from studying topographic maps and aerial photos that its apparent temperate nature was deceptive. Dozens of large crevasses cut visible slot canyons across the glacier's half-mile width—which meant that a hundred more cracks lurked unseen beneath the innocent-looking snow. As the ice ceaselessly flows downhill, new cracks split open and old ones pinch closed. Though its movement is difficult for the human eye to discern, the splintered Khumbu Glacier creeps forward three to four feet per day up here. Gravity constantly pulls ice down the mountain as imperceptibly as a snow leopard stalks its prey. Then, like a pouncing leopard, falling ice plunges in the blink of an eye.

Since leaving base camp around three in the morning, we'd spent the last five hours down in the confines of the icefall. With the basin open before us, I could finally see far ahead. A dozen climbers from various expeditions were in front of us, working their way toward Camp One, about forty minutes away.

We would spend two nights on the glacier at Camp One to partially adapt our bodies to the 19,700-foot elevation. Then we planned to move up to Camp Two, near the far end of the basin. Adapting to

---

* George Mallory and his teammates explored the lower reaches of Mount Everest on the Tibet side in 1921. He spotted the Western Cwm (also spelled "coombe" or "coomb") while peering off the Pumori-Lingtren ridge, about 3,000 vertical feet above what would later become the Nepal base camp location, which is still used today.

the 21,300-foot altitude up there would be a real suffer-fest. Forcing our bodies to acclimatize to ever-lower oxygen levels is always brutal, but that's what we needed to do if we wanted to try for the summit in another month.

High-altitude climbing demands significant hard work, and it inflicts considerable discomfort. Those difficulties, and the inherent dangers, can make wise people in the lowlands wonder why climbers climb. I was first attracted to mountain climbing for its many straightforward benefits: exercise, excitement, nature, scenery, and so on. But those pleasures can also be obtained by easier and safer activities, such as hiking or adventure travel. There are deeper reasons to climb.

Most mountaineers I know, especially those who stick with it for many years, are moved by passion and the desire for continual self-improvement. My climbing partners and I share a mutual commitment to keep one another safe and to help one another achieve our dreams. That camaraderie is powerful.

In Himalayan teahouses and noisy mountain taverns, I've had deep conversations with fellow climbers about what drives us. We often speak reverently about peacefulness, spirituality, and connection with the earth. Long alpine days bring satisfying exhaustion to my body and quietness to my mind. Mountaineering is a form of moving meditation.

While some people seek their passion through music or marathons, for me it's mountains. Climbing not only allows me to nurture those meaningful aspects of life, but it also lets me experience personal growth while traveling through some of the most magnificent wild places on the planet. The high mountains exemplify immensity, intensity, and inspiration. In essence, I climb to seek awe.

Since age ten, when I first saw a black-and-white photograph of the mountain's soaring summit in my parents' encyclopedia, I've been captivated by Mount Everest. The promise of that wonder encouraged me to keep climbing through three decades, even while juggling the responsibilities of education, career, and family. My search for awe had finally brought me to Mount Everest.

. . .

The upper Khumbu Glacier pressed tight against the basin's three soaring sidewalls. To the left, Everest's west shoulder rose 4,000 feet above us. On our right, a steep rock face sprouting from the glacier's edge soared a vertical mile up to the 25,791-foot summit of Nuptse (pronounced "*nup-say*"). Three miles ahead, the upper end of the Khumbu Glacier met the foot of the Lhotse (pronounced "*loat-say*," like "*boat bay*") Face. That steep ice wall angled up 6,000 feet to Lhotse's summit—the world's fourth-highest at 27,940 feet.

On our mid-May summit push, we planned to ascend half of the Lhotse Face, then turn left at about 24,500 feet. From there, we'd traverse north over the famed crumbling rock of the Yellow Band and then angle toward the elevated pass known as the South Col. The upper pyramid of Everest remained hidden from view off to our left. From our stance just below Camp One, the 29,029-foot summit still loomed almost two vertical miles above our heads.

The expansive Western Cwm, its beauty, and my amazement at standing in that magnificent spot left me speechless. Four decades after Dad encouraged me to read my first book about Mount Everest, I was actually there.

I started climbing in 1982, and back then only a few elite athletes went to the world's highest peak. When I was twenty years old, Everest represented the loftiest goal I could imagine. Even getting to the base of the mountain would require me to do more and become more than I ever had before.

Talking about Everest with climbing buddies was fun and inspiring, but for a nonathletic kid like me from flatland Massachusetts, scaling it sounded implausible. I couldn't even run a mile during high school physical education tests. Turning myself into a climber would demand fitness and focus. The intensity of that rigorous commitment invigorated me.

And it scared me, too. In college I began seeking challenges that could gradually craft me into a person who might someday earn a shot at a big mountain, maybe even Everest. I learned, trained, and climbed.

I moved to Colorado in 1986 to be near the Rocky Mountains. For the first twelve years I scaled hundreds of technical routes and summited dozens of peaks more than 14,000 feet tall, known to Coloradans as "fourteeners." I scoured mountaineering books and sought out people who could teach me more about the high mountains. Over the next decade I teamed up with dedicated climbing partners on a dozen expeditions across North America, South America, and Asia. I narrowed my attention to extreme-altitude trips beginning in 2009. That year I summited the sixth-highest peak in the world, Cho Oyu (26,906 feet), and then aimed higher. On April 25, 2015, after thirty-three years of mountaineering, I had finally started climbing Mount Everest.

We only had two hundred vertical feet left until we reached Camp One, and the trail along the fixed lines cut back and forth across huge, irregular blocks of glacier fragments. PK led the way along the zigzagging lines as we bypassed one gigantic crack after another. These 150-foot-deep slots nearly surrounded each glacial pillar, revealing the immense strain the glacier was under as it squeezed between the narrowing rock walls and accelerated into the icefall below us.

As sunlight transmits through a glacier, the dense ice selectively absorbs red and yellow wavelengths, leaving only blue light behind. The deeper the crevasse, the bluer it gets. These eerie cracks glowed vibrant blue as if a pent-up energy source lay hidden within the earth. They were the biggest and bluest I had ever seen.

Camp was only twenty minutes ahead, but I needed water and sunscreen. Although tempted to ignore my needs and just push on, I had promised myself on this expedition to maintain extra diligent self-care. Stumbling into camp dehydrated and sunburned was unacceptable. I intended to last long enough on the mountain to make a summit attempt.

Once we reached the middle of the ice-block island we were crossing, I called a halt. I removed my outer shell jacket and stuffed it in my pack.

As we sipped water, a pair of our teammates trudged past. I silently exchanged a thumbs-up with my friend Bart Williams and his Nepali guide, Lakpa Bhote, as they went by.

A moment later I was rubbing white sun cream into my cheeks when I thought I saw two climbers from another team moving above us while unclipped from the fixed lines. I squinted and stared. Sure enough, the front man stepped across a narrow crevasse without needing to remove or reclip any safety leash. Then the second climber did the same: They were crossing the glacier untethered.

I had a clear side view of the block they were traversing, and I could see a deep crevasse four yards to their right. While the flat terrain looked straightforward, with crevasses everywhere and the fixed line right beside them, the risk they took to save a few minutes seemed unnecessary. Watching them meander unroped among the open slots flushed an anxious surge of prickly heat through me.

PK and I finished our short break, shouldered our packs, and started the final segment. We pulled into the relative safety of camp at about eight-thirty in the morning. Bart stood near the orange cook tent, waiting to greet us. Pausing between each step to breathe, I moved toward him and then stopped two feet away. Bart grinned. "Welcome to Camp One."

Hardworking sherpas and guides from our expedition company, International Mountain Guides (IMG), had already established camp several days before our arrival. Besides the cook tent and an orange storage tent, our site contained thirteen yellow sleeping tents placed in a rough oval about eighty feet long and forty feet wide. Giant open crevasses transected the glacier just a few yards above and below our campsite. There would be no wandering around.

Knee-high bamboo wands stuck into the snow marked the perimeter of camp. Small, stiff marker flags made from red duct tape projected sideways from the wand tops. With a dozen other expeditions settled nearby, about a hundred people occupied our little glacier community.

Camp One was hemmed in by the west shoulder of Everest several hundred yards north, and by the Nuptse wall about a thousand feet south. Almost every south-side expedition since the Swiss in 1952 had camped in this same midglacier area.

Bart led me twenty yards across camp to our tent. We'd also shared a tent for five days last week when we climbed a 20,000-foot peak, Lobuche East, for acclimatization. At age sixty, Bart had a gentle manner and an easygoing friendliness. A senior financial adviser, he was smart and a pleasant conversationalist, even after long hours confined in a cold tent. Bart was a committed family man who smiled whenever he talked about his four children and seven grandchildren.

I dropped my climbing pack upright into the snow with a grunt. I unloaded gear from my backpack one item at a time and handed it to Bart inside our tent. Even this minor activity increased my respiration rate and pulse. I reminded myself to move slower than usual.

From the cook tent across camp, PK strolled toward me carrying a plastic cup in each hand. He passed one to me and said: "Lemon juice."

I sipped the tangy lemonade and then sighed. "Thank you, PK."

Everest can be viciously cold and then unbearably hot just a few hours later. The thin atmosphere allows the intense sun to fry us, and the white snow surface reflects those sun rays in all directions. Unwary climbers can get sunburned under their chins by the upward-reflected sunlight. I've even heard of glacier climbers who sunburned the roofs of their mouths because they panted openmouthed for too long.

The white bowl landscape of the Western Cwm seems to bounce the warm energy repeatedly until it builds to stifling levels. Most spring days a thick afternoon cloud bank traps all that heat and makes climbers swelter. Diligent rehydration is critical at altitude, so I paused from unpacking to slurp down the sweet drink. Between sips I admired the view westward over the icefall. Half hidden by clouds, the nearby peaks of Pumori and Lingtren rose a vertical mile directly behind base camp.

"PK, thanks for leading us through the icefall today."

"No problem," he said with a grin.

The lack of sleep and the strenuous climb left me tired. But my thoughts were clear, and I was excited to be up there—both great signs at altitude. After a dozen previous trips to this height, I felt the best I ever had at nearly 20,000 feet. All this confirmed to me that I'd been on the right path to climb Mount Everest for a long time.

I crawled inside our yellow dome tent and organized my gear. Every few minutes a new teammate arrived in camp, along with their sherpa partner. When I heard them enter our campsite, I usually stuck my head through the tent doorway and shouted out a welcome. Most of the climbers looked fatigued but happy. The Nepali guides seemed unfazed. Since they and their ancestors had lived in these high valleys for more than six hundred years, the Sherpa people inherently functioned better at altitude than the rest of us. Our Nepali guides had also carried loads of food and equipment up here several times over the past week, so they were fit and acclimatized. Each time I looked outside, the clouds built thicker over the mountain and filled the Khumbu Valley below us.

My wife, Gloria, had been worried about my first trip through the crumbling icefall. To ease her concerns, I dug out my global positioning system (GPS) device that could also send and receive text messages via the GPS network. At 10:51 a.m., I wrote:*

Safe at camp 1. Feel real good. By moving steady I got here fast in 5 hrs.

With visibility clamped down and lunch still two hours away, Bart and I settled in for a nap. I struggled to remove one of my oversize triple boots. After a minute of panting, I recovered enough to wrestle off the second one. I removed my outer clothing and slid into my sleeping bag. The thick down loft felt cozy and coaxed me to sleep.

---

* All texts, emails, letters, and journal entries are quoted as they were written, with only minor edits made for clarity and brevity.

. . .

Through a drowsy haze I sensed the hard, glacial ice stabbing my right hip. I flopped onto my back and my sleeping bag swished against the thin nylon tent wall. Just rolling over at this altitude made my heart race. I gasped for air.

Next to me, Bart still seemed to be napping. Camp sounded quiet. The unhurried rest was luxurious.

A low rumbling noise came from my right. Still sleepy, I thought Bart must be bumping into his side of the tent. But the sound seemed too loud and sustained. The rumble built and moved closer as if coming from outside. That's strange, I thought.

I lifted my head out of the sleeping bag to listen. Bart stirred.

"Avalanche?" he asked.

"Yeah. I think so."

We had heard avalanches daily down in base camp over the last week. They were usually miles away and headed in a different direction—they didn't pose much risk. Most avalanche noises faded away quickly. But this growling continued.

An image flashed through my mind of the ice fields dangling high above us. From beyond the paper-thin tent fabric, the rumble deepened and grew louder. My chest tightened.

"Whoa, that's close!" Bart said.

He and I sat up. As if trying to see beyond the yellow tent wall, we both stared rightward toward Nuptse.

A colossal boom sounded from the left. Our heads snapped around toward the new noise. In an instant, the sound swelled to a thunderous roar. Another avalanche on a different slope.

"Something's wrong!" I shouted. "Grab your hat and beacon, then get out!"

Over the rising din, Bart yelled: "I don't have an avalanche beacon."

"Then get out, get out!"

Bart thrashed to escape his sleeping bag. I lunged toward the tent door and reached for the zipper, but I missed when our tent jumped violently. We, the tent, and the thousand-foot-thick glacier underneath us all lifted half a foot into the air.

My stomach lurched.

A second later we dropped back down.

The tent heaved up again. We hovered there for about two seconds, then fell back once more.

Inside the tent Bart and I rose and sank in unison, as if we were riding a lifeboat over rolling ocean swells.

"Not good!" I yelled.

"What is it?!" screamed Bart.

The vertical heaving paused for a moment, and then the glacier shuddered hard beneath us.

What was happening?

Maybe two massive avalanches had crashed onto the glacier with so much force that the entire ice field was vibrating like a drum. But that didn't seem right.

Why the shaking and two separate avalanches all at the same time?

Then I got it.

Earthquake!

4

The ground trembled faster, and both avalanches thundered louder.

If we were still inside when they arrived, the tent's large surface area could drag us under the debris wave like a sea anchor. Being outside gave us the best chance for survival so we could try to swim atop the flowing avalanche.

Get out fast!

Bart crawled toward the exit. I finally unzipped the door, and he scurried outside. I tore out of my sleeping bag to race out behind him.

Before abandoning the tent, I scanned the gear for anything that might help. I saw my avalanche transceiver and wondered if I should put it on. If I got buried, the beacon could help others find me before I suffocated. Even if I died, the locating signal would let them pinpoint my body. Recovering my corpse quickly would be safer for the rescuers and easier on my family than if I were left on the mountain.

I grabbed the palm-size device from the tent's mesh side pouch. After pressing down the plastic safety latch, I slid the power switch up. My beacon always needed five seconds for a system check before it functioned. I stared at the tiny screen, willing the electronics to work faster.

The avalanches outside grew deafening. I hoped that lingering inside the tent for precious seconds wouldn't prove fatal.

Finally the beacon beeped once and flashed an orange light. I considered just holding on to the transceiver and rushing outside to save a few seconds, but the beacon had to be strapped tight against my chest so it would stay on if the avalanche tossed me about. I slipped the shoulder loop over my left arm and head, then pulled the nylon strap around my waist. I rose onto my knees and clicked the black buckle closed.

Through the tent floor the glacier quivered against my kneecaps. The longer the ground shakes, the bigger the earthquake.

My small GoPro camera lay nearby. If we all died, a recording could document what happened. And if I lived—well, I'd have an amazing video. I hit the Power button and crawled out of the tent, camera in hand.

Stay on top of the slide, no matter what.

When I emerged, most of my teammates were standing nearby. They were all looking south toward the avalanche coming at us from Nuptse. I turned that way too but saw only a veil of thick clouds.

I pivoted and looked toward the sound of the second avalanche. More clouds. We couldn't tell if the slides were coming at us.

No one ran because we had nowhere to run. With camp almost surrounded by crevasses, the only safe way out was north, toward Everest's west shoulder. But fleeing that way would send us directly toward the second avalanche.

So we stood there, stared into the clouds, and waited. I wondered which avalanche might be big enough to charge across the glacier and overrun our camp. Maybe neither. Maybe both. My eyes darted back and forth. I tried guessing which side we'd be hit from first.

A mighty wind blasted my face, and I instinctively put my back to the gale. I stumbled a half step forward. When my foot slammed onto the hard ice, pain shot up from my toes. I looked down and saw my feet clad only in socks.

No boots. *Stupid!*

An even bigger gust crashed into me from a different angle. Sudden violent winds from two different sides seemed bizarre. Then a memory surfaced from the Snow Dynamics and Avalanche class I once took: Big avalanches push away the air in front of them as they charge downslope. Those sideways winds weren't caused by weather—they were compressed waves of air being bulldozed ahead of the avalanches. Both slides were heading straight for us.

The second air blast carried hard-driven ice particles. A white squall wrapped around my shoulders and stung my cheeks like frozen beach sand tossed into my face. In an instant visibility dropped from a hundred feet to only a few yards. Most of the team disappeared—I didn't *think* they'd been blown away, but I wasn't sure.

A gust shoved me hard from behind. I feared the wind might knock me off my feet and sweep me into a crevasse. I considered lying down. But being prone would increase the chance of getting buried when the rushing debris arrived.

I dropped to one knee as a compromise and hunched my shoulders against the wind. This put my face close to the video camera, still grasped in my right hand. A steady red light indicated the camera was powered up but not yet recording. By forgetting to push Record, I had missed capturing the start of the mayhem. *Shit!*

As a geologist, I figured I should document the quake and avalanches so somebody could figure out later what the hell had happened. Besides, there was little else I could do. I hit the Record button.

Lifting my head from the camera, I watched my two nearest teammates disappear behind swirling whiteness. Visibility was now zero.

Ice dust thickened the air. When I inhaled, frozen sludge choked my windpipe. I gagged and gasped hard, which sent even more ice daggers down my throat. They scratched and burned and chilled my airway.

Wanting to block out the thickening particles, I jammed the crook of my left elbow against my nose. I tried sneaking a mouthful of air from underneath my arm. When I sucked in a gulp of the thick slurry, it felt like inhaling a milk shake.

Can't breathe!

Panic rose.

Can't stay outside!

When I thrust my right arm out blindly, it smacked against the tent. I crawled in and tried opening my eyes. Wind and ice powder swirled around inside the tent. I shut my eyes again and fumbled with both hands to close the tent's outer door. Once the zipper was mostly shut, the wind inside decreased. I opened my eyelids but only had a blurry view from the ice dust and water droplets covering my eyeballs. Blinking a few times cleared my vision. I was alone.

"Bart! Bart, where are you?!" I yelled.

I could hardly hear myself over the roaring winds. The Valley of Silence was no longer silent.

The tent stopped gyrating. I sat taller and thought, Is it over?

Then, an even stronger gale slammed into the north side of the tent where the second avalanche was still cascading down. At any moment the airborne crystals could give way to bouncing ice blocks the size of microwaves, refrigerators, or even houses.

I had been hoping that maybe the avalanches would veer away from us, but the unceasing powder blasts proved they were still coming our way. Everyone in camp could be buried in another minute. Gloria and the kids flashed through my mind. I put my left hand on my chest and clutched the avalanche beacon against me.

Fine ice particles washed over the tent in waves as the winds ebbed and flowed. Each pulse of pulverized ice dust skidded across the nylon tent fly with a loud hiss. The white static noise rose in volume and pitch whenever bigger air blasts hit the tent.

Outside our tent, the wind walls collided and tussled for dominance. Avalanche winds sweeping off Everest's west shoulder made the tent lean southward. Then a powder blast from Nuptse squashed the dome back in the other direction. The tent walls spasmed as the opposing gales chased each other in circles. Two great beasts fought to claim Camp One and all of us who cowered there.

I glanced one way, then the other, at whichever direction the loudest roar came from. To stay as far away from the walls as possible, I huddled in the middle of the tent. I hadn't closed the door completely, so tiny ice crystals streamed through the opening. White dust whirled around the tent like an indoor snowstorm. Powder piled up a quarter-inch deep around my sock-covered feet.

Then I remembered the still-running GoPro camera I had tossed next to me. I picked it up, and although the lens was coated in half-melted snow, I pointed it at myself and began talking.

"There was a—"

Beep. Beep. A sharp electronic warning interrupted me. I started over. "There was a huge avalanche and a huge powder blast."

A loud *whoosh* outside the tent indicated that the raging wind battle had shifted again. "Here comes another one!" I said.

The annoying beeps squawked once per second.

"There might have been two avalanches. Can't tell."

My eyes wide, I listened intently as the swirling winds and hissing snow grew louder. "Shit!"

I zipped the door tighter, then looked back at the camera. "I'm wearing my beacon."

The beacon, of course. At first I had thought the camera was emitting the beeps, but finally I realized the sound was coming from my avalanche transceiver. I looked down at the beacon, but without my reading glasses, I couldn't see the small markings well. After putting down my camera, I spent a moment fidgeting with the beacon. Why's it beeping?

As my flustered mind focused, I realized that in my scared rush to activate the transceiver, I had mistakenly pushed the selection switch past Transmit all the way over to Search mode. It wasn't transmitting after all. If I'd gotten buried, the beacon would've done me no good. *Crap—no more mistakes!*

The steady beeps while in Search mode meant I'd been receiving a signal broadcast from a nearby beacon. Somebody else was transmitting their position too. Even though I had thirty-one teammates within sixty feet of me, I felt isolated in the tent. At least the beeping put me in remote contact with someone.

After putting my reading glasses on, I could see well enough to move the control switch from Search to Transmit. The beeping stopped. Finally the beacon was protecting me.

Cold stung my wet face. I clenched my eyes tight and grimaced. Although there was no way to know if anyone might ever find my camera, I wanted to keep recording the video log as long as possible, just in case. Realizing that Gloria and our two children, Jess and Nick, might see it someday, I thought, Don't make them feel bad by seeing me afraid at the end.

I drew in a breath and tried talking calmly to the camera: "It's swirling around the basin in circles. The avalanches happened almost two minutes ago."

The winds began quieting down. Other outside sounds filtered through the tent wall, but they were hard to hear over my panting. I fought to slow my breathing. Long seconds passed before I told the camera: "It's stopping now, I think. I gotta get some better clothes on and get outside."

I pushed the top button of the videocam. The recording ceased, but the camera stayed powered up. I dropped it onto my sleeping pad and looked around, trying to determine my next move. The powdery snow covering me from head to toe began to melt, so I brushed it off. I reached for one of my mountain boots. After pulling it on, I yanked the inner laces tight but fumbled with the simple overhand knot.

As I continued putting on my boot, I wondered what I might find outside. Maybe everything was okay, or maybe I'd find someone buried. Maybe *everyone* was buried. A pulse of hot adrenaline rushed through me: What if I'm the only one left?

I yelled: "Bart, are you outside?!"

No answer.

My shaking hands made it hard to adjust the straps of the outer boot. Someone outside squatted near our tent, unzipped the door, and poked his head through. White snow blotches stuck to his black hair—PK.

"Is everybody accounted for?" I asked.

"Everything okay."

Seeing him was a relief, but I had the feeling he was giving me general assurance, not actually answering my question.

"You all right, PK?"

"Yeah. Don't worry, I'm here."

Nearby a radio erupted rapid words in either Nepali or Sherpa language. PK and I both fell quiet and listened. Kneeling in the doorway, PK's position blocked my view as he looked around camp. I wondered if anyone had been buried or blown into a crevasse.

I said, "We'd better count—"

PK spoke over me in Nepali, but I didn't understand. He stood up outside the tent door, then hustled off across camp. With the doorway clear, I saw a few teammates scurrying back and forth.

From farther away I heard other voices, some in Nepali, some in English. People began emerging from their tents. PK seemed pretty calm, so everything in camp must not be too bad. Five minutes had passed since the avalanches started and two minutes since the wind blasts ceased. I stared at the tent floor, unsure of what to do next. Things were less chaotic, but so much remained unclear.

A red light flashed from the camera in my hand. Apparently I had restarted the recording when PK opened the tent door. I pulled in three measured breaths, then looked into the water-coated lens and said: "We're going to have to do a count-off and make sure everyone's accounted for."

The enormity of what just happened began sinking in. With two simultaneous avalanches and the glacier bouncing beneath us, there must have been a giant earthquake. I knew that people outside a building can feel quakes that are larger than a modest 4.0 moment magnitude.* This was way bigger than that.

---

* Moment magnitude measures the size of an earthquake. It is the preferred measuring system used by seismologists instead of the outdated Richter scale, which had limitations. Because the moment magnitude uses a logarithmic scale, a 7.0 tremor would be ten times larger than one measuring 6.0 magnitude and it would release about thirty-two times as much energy. The largest earthquake ever measured was 9.5 magnitude.

Feeling the camera's steady presence, I looked into the lens. "Sounded like it rumbled off, uh, Nuptse. But then I thought I heard another one. It's hard to tell. The sound was bouncing around."

I stared at the tent wall and paused. "All right. I gotta get dressed. Stand by."

After I powered off the camera, I stuffed it into my jacket pocket. I grabbed my other boot and tugged it on. Then I laced the inner boot, cinched the midlayer Velcro straps tight, and zipped up the waterproof outer gaiter. Following this routine calmed me and gave me a moment to think. With a quake that big, there would be aftershocks and probably more avalanches. I tapped my hand against my chest and felt the beacon's hard plastic case.

By the time I scrambled from the tent, most of my teammates were back outside, some of them half-dressed. The avalanche winds were gone, but snow drifted down from the sky, perhaps signaling another pending avalanche blast.

I studied the falling snow with suspicion. Delicate flakes floated down and settled gently on my jacket sleeve. It was just regular snow. Relaxing a bit, I stepped toward a cluster of my friends and immediately saw Bart in his orange-red down suit. I exhaled hard, took two strides, and hugged him.

"Where were you?" I asked.

"When the winds hit I dove into the nearest tent. I was in the cook tent with the sherpas. Man, that was scary."

People exchanged hugs. We rattled off the names of teammates and sherpas we knew were okay. After collectively naming all thirty-two people on our Camp One team, we concluded that everyone was accounted for. No one was even hurt. Though this good news brought relief, my friends' faces still showed uncertainty and fear.

We rehashed the last few minutes, everyone talking over one another. My teammate Matt Tammen stood next to me. He'd served in the military and was usually quite even-keeled. Describing the glacier's violent movements, he said: "It was moving back and forth, up and down." He flapped both arms madly like a large bird to mimic the glacier's movements.

I smiled and forced a nervous chuckle to agree with him.

Someone made a small, silly joke, and everyone laughed way too hard. The snowfall increased, and we were all getting wet. There was nothing useful to do outside, so we retreated to our tents to stay dry and wait. Bart lay atop his sleeping bag next to me and stared blankly at the ceiling. I wiggled my lower body into my sleeping bag.

Suddenly the entire tent jerked sideways.

Aftershock!

My chest tightened again. I pressed my palm against the tent floor, trying to feel if the quake's energy was growing. The tent and the three-mile-long glacier beneath us both glided back and forth a few inches. Realizing I could record the moment, I turned the camera on and described what was happening. "The tent just moved again. Another earthquake. This was probably less than a third of the energy of the last one."

After about five seconds of silence, I continued. "It's like pitching a tent on a table and having someone push the table around. I can feel it now a little bit."

As the glacier oscillated beneath us, it struck me that we were perched atop a thousand-foot-thick matrix of fragile ice. If the violent shaking caused the crystalline ice to shatter, we could collapse down into the glacier. I did not want to get dropped inside a glacier, as I once had been long ago.

In a low voice I said, "Jeesh, I hope this glacier holds together."

Bart whispered, "Yeah."

We went quiet and listened for avalanches.

5

As the aftershock continued, the massive ice sheet beneath us kept gliding back and forth like a porch swing. Bart and I kept listening, but we didn't hear any thundering snowslides. Soon, the ground movement dampened, and the earth went back to sleep. For now.

I looked at Bart and shook my head. He exhaled in a single big puff, then fell silent and stared at the yellow tent ceiling. As the aftereffects of adrenaline dispersed through my body, I felt antsy. We couldn't just sit there and wait for the next scary aftershock. There had to be something beneficial we could do.

In case we got wiped out by another quake or avalanche, we could leave behind a detailed log, like shipwreck survivors. Recording a video would be the fastest way. To keep myself from slipping into pessimism or, worse yet, filming some premature farewell to my family and friends, I decided to keep the recording factual and formal. After organizing my thoughts for a moment, I started the camera.

"Hi. It's April 25, about 12:30 in the afternoon, Nepal time. Um, my tentmate Bart and I were just sitting here kind of half-awake from our naps and, all of a sudden, we heard a big crash."

For two minutes I summarized all that had occurred when the quake and avalanches had arrived. Then I began talking about what we knew from radio calls exchanged between our camp and base camp:

"The Ncell towers are out for the cell phones, so that suggests an earthquake. There's been a disturbance the whole way. Tents were flattened at the base of the icefall. So, that could be a powder blast from our two major avalanches, or it could be more collapsing below us. It's still chaotic."

Bart lay on his sleeping bag with his right arm tucked behind his head. I turned the camera on him and asked: "What was your experience?"

After he summarized the quake's arrival, Bart described what happened after we got separated by the powder blast. "I made my way down to the dome tent where all the sherpas were gathering and chanting their Buddhist prayers—" He cleared his throat. "At that time I got a little emotional—"

Bart's voice cracked and he paused. He smiled at me for a second, but then his weak grin dropped away. My typically upbeat friend lifted his lower lip and twisted his mouth into a tight grimace. He blinked and waited.

In a thin, wavering voice, he continued. "I was wondering if it was about to be the end, and how . . . how it might feel to be buried."

He tightened his face again. After a moment he resumed speaking with his voice almost back to its normal timbre.

"But pretty soon things started to quiet down. Then some of the sherpas said: 'It's okay now.' A lot of them kept chanting, and we came out of the tent. Then we all found each other and hugged and were thankful that it hadn't been worse."

To conclude, Bart forced a stoic smile and stayed quiet. I caught his cue and turned the camera back on myself. I said: "It's been about twenty, twenty-five minutes now, and we just did feel a secondary shake."

My inner geologist took over, and I said: "One of our guys here is from California. He said it felt bigger than a 5.0 earthquake. Based on how the glacier and our tents were moving, I was thinking about P waves and secondary S waves.* We're on a glacier, and it's just a big frozen sea of water. So we're like a cork bobbing on the ocean here."

My voice slowed and sounded forlorn. I wanted to be more optimistic, so I changed topics and continued: "It's going to take another hour or two until we start to figure out what's going on. We're staying right here 'cause we're safe. We've just been tested."

I paused for a moment: "A lot of radio chatter's going on. It's about twelve-forty now. Typically there are still people in the icefall about this time of day."

I looked away and pulled back the camera. I shook my head and spoke softly: "We went through some pretty unstable ice today on our way up here . . ."

My voice trailed off. I turned away from Bart and the camera. For a few seconds I froze while imagining what might have happened to any climbers down in the icefall when the quake hit. They might have been crushed by ice, dropped into crevasses, or buried under debris. A wave of horror washed through me, and I felt queasy.

With my eyebrows arched high, I darted my gaze back into the lens. "We'll keep our fingers crossed for all our compatriots . . ."

Blinking, I clenched my mouth shut and silently nodded my head. I fought hard to push out the rest of the sentence. In a quivering, high-pitched voice I finally finished by saying: ". . . down in the icefall."

Instinctively I patted my leg three times to soothe myself. Tears filled my eyes, and I blinked again rapidly as I struggled to stay one step ahead of an emotional flood. In a not-quite-normal pitch and volume, I said: "We'll see what happens over the next few hours."

I shut the GoPro off. Exhausted by my on-camera tussle, I flopped back onto my sleeping bag. With both hands over my eyes, I focused on breathing. I had tried to maintain a veneer of control for the video log, but inside everything roiled.

---

* Earthquakes transmit two types of seismic waves: primary waves (P waves) and secondary waves (S waves). They each cause different forms of earth movement, with S waves often causing more damage.

It was hard to believe we had just ridden out a massive earthquake. As bewildering as the vertically moving glacier and sustained ground tremors were, they were superseded a minute later by the brutal arrival of the powder blasts.

Hearing the slides coming but not being able to see them was like standing on a highway in thick fog and hearing trucks blaring their horns as they closed in on you. There was no way to tell which way to run to save your life.

We had endured half a dozen bizarre and overwhelming experiences in the space of five minutes. My nerves were frazzled. I was also rattled by realizing what significant roles luck and randomness play during a disaster.

I took my hands off my face and stared at the tent ceiling with unfocused eyes. In the numerous articles and books that I had read about Everest, no one ever mentioned the potential hazards of earthquakes.

I said to Bart, "Pretty wild that we're here during a big quake, huh?"

"Yeah. It's amazing nobody here even got hurt."

Setting our tents in the traditional Camp One spot helped save us. It kept us far enough from both sidewalls so the quake-triggered slides didn't reach our campsite. We owed a significant debt of gratitude to earlier generations of climbers who had fine-tuned the best camp placements and passed that knowledge on.

We weren't completely safe, though. Back in 2005 Camp One had been crushed by a massive rock-and-ice avalanche. Almost all the tents in the main camp, about sixty-five of them, got obliterated. Only five tents isolated at the upper end of camp escaped destruction. A few people were injured, but no one died, primarily because it happened in May. By that late in the season, the climbers were acclimatized enough to skip Camp One on their trips between base camp and Camp Two. Hardly anyone was in Camp One when the avalanche arrived. An IMG senior guide, Mark Tucker, wrote about the incident: "The Everest community did not dodge a bullet today, it dodged a bomb."

Their narrow escape, like ours, had included a generous helping of favorable fortune. I wondered how long our good luck would last. After-shocks were inevitable and more avalanches probable. Plus, if the route below us had been destroyed, we might have to craft a new descent route or maybe just solo down. Neither of those seemed wise. Getting off the mountain could degrade into "escape or die trying."

Whatever it took, I had to get down to see Gloria and the kids again. Jess turned twenty-one just before I left for Nepal, and Nick was eighteen. As young adults they didn't require close parental supervision anymore, but we all loved and needed one another. We lived far away from most of our relatives, so the four of us depended on one another to keep our little family unit strong and steady.

The possibility of me dying somehow in this disaster seemed remote, but who knew what might unfold? Anxieties and uncertainties about ever seeing the three of them again began to simmer. But I couldn't give space to those feelings yet—I couldn't let myself get overwhelmed by scary or sad possibilities. From the many medical emergencies and mountain rescues I had helped with, I knew that staying safe and sur-viving demanded that I focus only on the immediate problems and solutions.

Risky climbs and dangerous painting jobs had taught me that if I was afraid of dying, and wanted to see my loved ones again, I should tem-porarily put thoughts of them away. This conscious compartmentaliza-tion doesn't eliminate fear, grant someone superpowers, or turn a person into an unemotional robot: It gives you the best chance of getting through the mess and going home.

Bart and I tried to rest, but I kept fidgeting. I opened the tent door and stuck my head outside. Wary, I scanned camp for any sideways-blowing snow. Fat flakes floated down innocently from overhead clouds. None of the surrounding slopes were visible through the white-gray gloom.

I pulled my head back inside and brushed snow off my unkempt hair. "It's coming down harder."

"Yeah, we're not going anywhere today," Bart said.

Muffled conversations emanated from nearby tents. Our team leader, Emily Johnston, huddled two tents away, talking over the radio to her co-leaders in the other two IMG camps. As a veteran expedition leader and emergency medicine physician, Emily always communicated in clear, succinct statements.

We heard pieces of the incoming radio calls. Our IMG teammates in Camp Two, about 1,500 feet above us, got rattled by the quake and avalanches, but no one was killed or hurt. My good friend Alan Arnette was also up at Camp Two acclimatizing for his ascent of Lhotse. I worried about him, but the IMG climbing leader said that no slides had reached Camp Two.

About seventy climbers from various teams were camped at that communal site alongside the Khumbu Glacier. Since April 25 was still early in the climbing season, the fixed lines only reached Camp Two. No one was higher on the mountain.

Our IMG climbers and staff in base camp had also escaped harm. But frenzied radio calls from other teams down there came through in a mélange of four or five languages. We couldn't sort many details from the frantic chatter, but their anxiety was high. Something was very wrong down in base camp.

They spoke rapidly about avalanches, rockfalls, and injuries. Many tents had been destroyed. Urgent calls went out again and again for doctors or anyone with medical skills who could help triage and treat the many wounded. Trained as a wilderness first responder, I wanted to assist, but of course remained powerless to aid them from Camp One. As an emergency medicine doctor, Emily was precisely what they needed, but she too could only listen to the plaintive calls.

Like everyone else, I wanted more details. But I knew that this early in the emergency, the base-camp leaders would be scrambling to get a handle on the situation. Bugging them for answers they didn't have yet would only be a hindrance. We had to sit tight for a while and take care of ourselves.

Though not hungry, Bart and I forced down snacks and water to stay strong. With the ground no longer moving and the surrounding slopes quiet, our immediate environment appeared about the same as it had one hour earlier. And yet everything had changed.

Climbers flocked to Everest because tectonic forces had built the mountain into the planet's highest peak. We all understood that over long periods of geologic time, continents collide and mountains move. But being on a high peak when the geologic clock jumped forward a big, uneven tick gave me a new perspective. Everest is even more dangerous than it looks. Things can change at any time. Like it or not, we were going to have to change too.

From the first expedition in 1921, the climbing history of Everest overflows with difficult and tragic circumstances. The famous 1996 storm and the resulting eleven deaths that season were well documented in numerous books. Another infamous event was the icefall collapse in 2014, which killed sixteen Nepali people.

But, on April 25, 2015, we found ourselves in a unique predicament— trapped partway up Everest by massive earthquakes and avalanches. We were in uncharted territory. My gut told me that our climb of Everest was over. After thirty-three years of preparation, my dream might have ended just nine hours after leaving base camp.

More radio reports arrived from below. One distraught voice said: "Base camp has been obliterated." Numerous calls stated that people had been hurt by flying debris. And a few callers speculated that the glacier underneath part of base camp had collapsed. Hearing about possible ground failure increased my nagging concern about the glacier beneath our camp caving in. Crevasses, meltwater channels, or weaknesses in the ice might give way if the Khumbu Glacier got rattled hard enough.

We learned that the quake had not only rocked Everest but the entire

Khumbu Valley below the mountain. Reports relayed from mountaineers west of us even suggested that much of Nepal had been shaken.

With far-flung stories trickling in, our news would soon reach the outside world. I had to tell my family I was okay before an early report implied that we were hurt or dead. Though I had been holding back for some hopeful developments before notifying Gloria, with the bad news piling higher, I couldn't wait any longer.

I dug out my GPS. The orange-and-black plastic case felt familiar in my hand. Every day for the last month, I had used it to post social media updates and to text family and friends.

Once the screen came to life, I noted the battery level exceeded 90 percent. That was enough juice to send and receive messages for days. With careful conservation I could stretch the battery for almost a week.

I didn't want to worry Gloria too much, so I tried to craft a positive message. At 2:04 p.m. Nepal time, I texted her:

We r still safe. probable earthquake here. some avi [avalanches] nearby but our camp is well placed so we r fine. More info later. Luv yas.

As a night nurse, Gloria got off work at midnight, which was about two hours ago back home. She would be sleeping and wouldn't see my message for hours. Jess and Nick had to be asleep too. Because I wanted Gloria to be the one to tell the kids that I was all right, I didn't write them for now.

I pondered whom else to notify, and who could maybe help me from afar. The obvious answer was my best friend and longtime climbing partner, Rodney Ley. We had co-led five international expeditions together, taking college students up high mountains. Back in 1998 we led students to the top of Imja Tse (aka "Island Peak"), a 20,000-footer located just six miles southeast of Camp One. Over seventeen years, we had hiked, skied, and climbed hundreds of days together. When things got tough in

the mountains, there was no one I trusted more than Rodney. I shared a
bit more with him than I had told Gloria:

**I am safe at camp one. Apparent earthquake. Big avi nearby.
Powder blast in our camp. Glacier cave in under some base
camp possible. Staying put.**

An all-around climber since 1970, Rodney was an expert in every
aspect of mountaineering and mountain safety. Perhaps more important, he understood me as a climber better than anyone else. He knew my
background, skills, and the way my mind worked.

When Rodney saw my message, he'd kick into full-blown support
mode back in Colorado. He would work the phones, the internet, and
the vast climber network we both belonged to. I knew he'd gather vital
information and get back to me ASAP. Having Gloria and Rodney watching my back made it a bit easier to remain optimistic when the situation
seemed so grim.

As a speaker and writer, I also had people following me on social media, including friends, family, clients, colleagues, and climbing partners.
Many followers were strangers, though; there was no telling who might
post what online. Previous emergencies I had helped with showed me
that once the emotional rumor mill gets rolling, information and misin-
formation both spread fast. To get in front of all that, I posted an update
on social media repeating what I wrote to Rodney.

The afternoon dragged on, and intermittent radio calls flowed out
from the base-camp turmoil. Over time the stories converged to indicate
that there had not been a glacier collapse under camp after all. Instead it
appeared that a massive avalanche had struck. Driven by hurricane-force
winds, a giant debris cloud filled with airborne rocks and ice chunks had
blasted through the middle of base camp. People were hurt. People were
dead.

6

The quake had struck three hours ago, and so far all we had done was wait. Rough weather kept us pinned in our tent. I lounged atop my sleeping bag and stared up at the universe of small yellow squares woven into the tent fabric. To distract myself, I contemplated trying to count the tiny boxes, but that seemed useless.

When I glanced over at Bart, he was gaping at the ceiling, too. I sat up and looked outside again. Clouds and snowfall limited visibility to about fifteen yards. I closed the tent zippers.

Bart propped himself up on one elbow, his short-cropped gray hair tousled from removing his hat. During the entire expedition, Bart had worn a disarming smile. That gentle grin matched his calm demeanor so well that talking with Bart felt like a warm chat with your favorite uncle—the one who saw the best in everyone and always had something positive to say.

But Bart had hardly smiled since the quake. His salt-and-pepper eyebrows drooped with worry, which made him look older. During three rugged weeks on the trail and seven uncomfortable nights sharing a tent, I had never seen Bart upset. The somber guy facing me changed that.

"So, Mr. Geologist, what do you know about earthquakes?" Bart asked.

"I've been trying to remember. I studied them in college, but it's been about thirty years. Mostly I've been thinking about aftershocks."

"And?"

"The biggest tremor almost always comes first, and the aftershocks tend to decline in size over time. So there's a good chance that we already had the biggest one."

"Well, that's good."

"Yeah, but once in a while the first quake isn't the biggest." I arched my eyebrows high at Bart.

He tightened his lips and nodded slowly.

I said, "We'll definitely get more aftershocks, and some will be big."

"For how long?"

"We might get big ones for days or weeks. The smaller ones will continue for months, maybe years."

Bart sipped from his water bottle and said nothing. I jabbed my index finger in the air toward Nuptse and said, "I'm concerned about a big one happening while we're still here."

Though he could see only the inside of the tent, Bart looked southward toward the peak. Its mile-high wall of ice fields and cliff bands towered above our campsite.

He dropped his head and stared at the water bottle resting in his lap. After a few quiet seconds, he tilted his head toward me and said, "Then we could get more avalanches."

"Yup. That's what worries me. I've been thinking about telling Emily. I don't want to add more to her plate, though. What do you think?"

"I think you should tell her," Bart said.

I nodded. Reaching into the side pouch of the tent, I grabbed my snack bag. I nibbled on dried apricots to get some food energy into me for the cold trip outside.

Putting on boots, two jackets, gloves, and a hat takes about ten minutes at 19,700 feet. I proceeded even slower than usual while thinking about what to tell Emily. After opening both tent doors, I crawled outside and found three inches of new snowfall on everything. I closed our doors fast and walked toward her tent. The fresh dry snow squeaked as it compacted under my boots. Standing outside her tent, I said, "Knock, knock, Emily."

While she unzipped the inner door, I opened the tent fly. Ducking under the doorway, I crawled in and sat on the floor. Emily lowered the volume of her radio and put it down. I got right to the point.

"I need to share something with you. You know I'm a geologist, right?"

"I remember. What's up?"

"Well, I'm not an earthquake expert, but I know a few things."

She nodded.

"As you probably know, we're going to get more aftershocks. And I need to give you a heads-up—some of them are going to be big."

I waited. Her face showed no visible reaction, but I knew she was thinking it through.

"How big?"

With her training, I could lay out the science.

"The size of aftershocks usually declines asymptotically. My best recollection is that after the initial event, the biggest shocks will be about 90 percent the strength of the original."

Emily blinked but didn't speak. I continued: "There's a small chance of one being even bigger than the original quake, but that's unlikely. For sure, though, we're going to get some very big aftershocks soon."

As an ER doctor, Emily was used to processing bad news fast. She looked calm. Her sun-beaten red cheeks glowed against her long white hair. Emily said: "Okay. Anything else?"

"No, that's it for now. If I think of something important, I'll be sure to tell you."

"Let me know if you need anything."

I paused, forced a small smile, and said, "Just let us know the plan when you're ready, Chief."

All the facts and fears I'd been contemplating for hours ricocheted in my mind. With the bad weather and uncertainty about the route's condition, we couldn't descend. We had enough gear and supplies to hold us at Camp One for a few days. But when the fuel ran out, the precious water and food would stop. We could last only so long. Camping on a fractured and brittle glacier left us vulnerable to the next earthquake. And staying at Camp One kept us near the runout zones of active avalanche paths. With more snow accumulating by the hour, even a modest aftershock might shake it all loose.

Even if we somehow stayed safe for a few days, fleeing Camp One would be tricky too. The three-dimensional chaos of the icefall below us had been rattled. We didn't know if the two-mile-long rope-and-ladder system back to base camp even existed anymore. So the deadliest place on Everest—our only descent route—was even more dangerous now. It seemed like we shouldn't stay, but we couldn't leave.

I needed to know how we were going to get down. I wanted to hear when we were leaving. But I had gone to Emily to share critical information, and to help her if I could. I didn't visit for her to reassure me or for me to point out every uncertainty. Emily already knew all those concerns. If I poured out all my worrisome questions, I'd only be adding to her heavy burden.

After spending the last twenty-six days trekking and climbing with her, I knew that Emily didn't speculate. She and the other expedition leaders were working on a plan. When they had one, she'd tell us.

Back in our tent, Bart and I resumed waiting. He puttered with his gear while I journaled like I always do on expeditions. We took turns trying to lift each other's spirits. Mostly we stared at the tent walls.

I was tempted to turn on my GPS messenger to see if Gloria had written me back, but it was still the middle of the night at home. There was no way she had seen my earthquake message yet. I needed to conserve battery power, so I fought off the urge to check.

Whompf! Whompf!

The booming noise wrenched me alert. *Another* avalanche?

My overworked brain immediately hit the fear button. Hot chemicals flooded my limbs.

"What the hell?!" Bart shouted.

We both bolted upright.

Whompf! Whompf! The sound was softer now, and it came from the west side of camp, where no threatening slopes existed. The muffled bursts blended in with the casual chatter of two teammates talking outside.

"It's only somebody clearing off their tent," Bart said.

There was no avalanche. I slumped back on my sleeping bag and pressed my palm against my forehead. "Shit, give me a break!"

Our teammates continued shaking snow off their tent, rankling my frayed nerves. I forced my tense shoulder muscles to relax and tried slowing my heart rate.

Bart had brought a satellite phone. Though expensive to use at about $1.00 per minute, the ability to call home from anywhere provided a nice luxury and sometimes filled an urgent need. Earlier in the afternoon, Bart had called his wife, Judy, back in Ogden, Utah, to let her know that he was alive. He decided to check in with her again, so he pulled the small black phone from his pack and warmed it inside his down suit.

Judy had trekked with our team for the first two weeks as we approached Everest. A sweet mother and grandmother, she was a fun and flexible travel companion. I had enjoyed hiking and sharing meals with her and Bart during our slow acclimatization journey up the Khumbu Valley.

Expedition life includes many unwritten rules, and one of them is to respect your tentmate's privacy—even when spending night and day six inches from each other.

I asked, "You want me to clear out?"

"No, that's fine. Nothing personal on this call."

I didn't have any music or headphones to distract myself with, so I turned away and focused on journaling to give Bart some privacy.

A few minutes later the phone beeped as Bart powered it off. Then there was a soft plastic click when he pushed the extendable antenna down. Protocol dictated that after their call, I shouldn't comment or ask about their discussion unless Bart shared it with me.

"Judy says hi, and she's really glad we're doing okay."

I withheld comment and let my friend steer the conversation.

"She said the earthquake is all over the news back home. Things look bad across Nepal."

None of this surprised me, but having it confirmed draped a cloak of sadness over us. Bart looked uneasy. Speaking even slower than his usual measured pace, he said: "She heard that the camps on the north side might have been wiped out by avalanches."

I froze. My mind's eye jumped over Everest into Tibet and looked down. I imagined the 10,000-foot-tall north face collapsing in a giant wave of swirling white snow and flying black rocks. Debris, tents, and bodies might be scattered everywhere. I struggled to comprehend.

Bart asked softly, "About how many people is that?"

Because I had followed Everest news and permit numbers for years, I could make a good guess. When the answer came to me, my jaw slackened.

"Maybe three hundred."

"Oh no!" Bart said.

I looked away from Bart's gaze. My eyes panned the tent floor, unfocused. In a rush I asked, "Is Judy certain? Is this right?"

"She doesn't know for sure. She heard it reported, but everything's crazy."

Bart offered to loan me his satellite phone so I could call Gloria. In Nepal the time was 5:30 p.m., but determining the exact time back home always required a bit of thinking.

To exhibit its national sovereignty, Nepal refused to use the same time zones as its much larger neighbors, India and China. Instead this tiny country established Nepal Standard Time. To drive the independence point even further, rather than utilize the standard one-hour increment, Nepal operated a quirky fifteen minutes off most other time zones. That made Colorado eleven hours and forty-five minutes behind Nepal, which meant it was 5:45 a.m. in Fort Collins.

It had been more than five hours since the quake, and the word was spreading around the globe. But Gloria wouldn't wake up for about another hour. Besides, before calling I needed to plan what to say. Of course I would tell her everything that had happened, but I wondered how positive and confident I should be. Increasing Gloria's concern that I still might die on the mountain wouldn't help her or me.

Everest possessed many hazards. My friends and I had worked for years to analyze and reduce the risks through training, technology, and tactics. None of us ever dreamed that a major earthquake would be the biggest danger on the mountain. Even as a geologist, I hadn't worried about it. I shook my head in disbelief. Gloria would soon wake to the news that an earthquake had me trapped on Everest.

7

2014

A warm spring breeze flows into our home through the open back door. Jake wanders outside to poke his Labrador-retriever nose into the bushes. The trilling calls of red-winged blackbirds spill into the kitchen—they must be squabbling over nesting spots in the nearby wetland.

Gloria stands at the sink, hand-washing a saucepan. As she scrubs, her auburn hair swings back and forth, giving me peekaboo side views of her face. I'm sitting at the kitchen table sorting and recycling the week's mail. Our morning chores are winding down, and we don't have much planned for the day. Maybe it's time to bring it up.

For sure, I don't want to discuss something this big at the wrong moment. I sip my tea and think things through. Hockey season wrapped up last week, so for the first Saturday in months, we won't attend one of Nick's games. He drove off an hour ago to fly-fish with his teammate. Jess is at college until spring break, so she's fine too. With both kids busy and us hanging around the house, it's as calm a day as we ever get around here.

Gloria puts the clean pan on the stove to air-dry. She wipes her hands with a red-and-white-checkered dish towel and slides her wedding ring back on. I'm clutching the cup with both hands in front of my face, but not drinking. Glo catches me eyeing her over the teacup rim and says, "What's up?"

My stomach flutters. "You have a minute to talk?"

She raises her eyebrows and smirks. In a drawn-out voice, she says, "Ok-a-a-y. What about?"

"Everest."

The playful smile drops from her face. Her head tilts to the left like it always does when she's agitated. She tosses the towel on the counter and stares at the floor for a moment. Then she walks to the table and sits down across from me.

I say, "We've talked a bunch already. I won't go through the old stuff again unless you want to."

"So why are we discussing it again now?"

"Because it's time to make a final decision."

She hunches both shoulders up, lets them sag back, and exhales with a sigh. I pause to see if she'll speak first. Gloria contracts her eyebrows down toward her nose. "Jim, I . . . I don't know. Why do we have to decide now?"

"Because if I go in 2015, I leave in late March. So we're coming up on one year until departure time. I need to map it all out—work, money, gear. And I have to start training hard."

Jake trots back in and catches the tension. He checks on Gloria, sniffing her hand. She doesn't respond, so he comes to me. I slowly rub his smooth black fur until he sits on the hardwood floor. Jake stares at me while Gloria and I stare at each other.

"What are your thoughts?" she asks.

I try to sound matter-of-fact. "It seems like now is the best time ever for me to go. The kids are older now, and both on a good track. Everything around the house seems fine."

Gloria says nothing.

"I'm not getting any younger, so climbing Everest isn't going to get any easier."

"Who would you want to go with? IMG?"

Though most of my expeditions are with my regular climbing partners, Glo knows that International Mountain Guides is the commercial guiding company I went to Cho Oyu with five years ago. They are highly skilled guides, and they pull together strong teams of sherpas and other high-mountain workers. Because they've led scores of expeditions to the world's highest peaks, they are excellent with complex logistics and permitting.

"They seem like the best choice," I say. "I understand IMG's approach and its systems. And Greg Vernovage will be expedition leader again in 2015, so that's good."

"He led your Tibet trip, right?"

"Yeah. We already know and like each other, which is a big plus. Their Everest groups get kind of big, though. Some years they have about twenty-five climbers, several Western guides, and all the sherpas."

"But I thought you like smaller groups."

"They divide us into three subteams, which helps. Everyone moves on different schedules. So no matter where I am on the mountain, there will usually be people in the camps above me and below me in case I need help. IMG keeps the camps well stocked, so there's always emergency oxygen nearby too."

"What does Alan think?"

Alan Arnette is our close friend and my regular climbing partner. He's been to Everest four times and summited in 2011. As a renowned Everest blogger for thirteen years, Alan knows all the major guide companies and has vast insider knowledge.

"We talked a bunch, and he agrees that IMG is a good match for me."

Gloria narrows her gaze and asks, "Did you already tell Alan you were going?"

Catching her drift, I answer, "No. I told him I had to talk to you first." I smile wide.

"Very good," she says and smirks back.

After twenty-four years of marriage, I know better than to make a significant commitment without Gloria's buy-in. We're both self-sufficient and strong-willed, but we operate as a team when it comes to big decisions. We've had discussions like this before each of my other high-altitude expeditions, but this time it's Everest. The costs, complexities, time away, and risks to life and limb are all at a maximum.

She turns serious and pauses. I put down my teacup and sit taller in my chair.

Gloria leans forward and slowly asks, "What if something goes wrong?"

"The chance of something critical going really wrong is small. Yes, things can go off track. That's why I'm picking one of the best operators to go with. And that's why I'm going to bust my ass for a year to get in the best shape of my life."

"But there's so much you can't control—storms, avalanches, altitude sickness." She pauses a moment and then says the one that's scariest to us both: "Crevasses."

"Yup, they're all there." I pause too. Then I speak in a measured voice. "We both know I can't make those go away. But Glo, I've been getting ready for this for thirty-two years."

"I know, I know."

Gloria looks out the window. Her eyes dart around, focusing on nothing. I bet she's thinking about the risks, us, and the kids. Gloria's dad died when she was just fifteen, so she knows what life is like for a family without a father or husband. Maybe she's thinking about climbing friends of ours who went to the mountains and never returned. I'm sure she's remembering what it was like after our good friend, and my climbing partner, Mike Price, died on Mount Rainier. I barely made it home alive from that trip. There are many twisted strands in this big knot.

I pick up my cup, take quiet sips, and wait.

Her gaze shifts. I move us another step forward: "The good news is that the summit and survival stats in the Himalayan Database show that, based on my age and experience, I'm in a very good spot statistically."

Gloria scowls.

I raise my eyebrows in mock excitement, smile, and ask, "You want to see the numbers?"

"No," she says in a flat voice.

I stop smiling.

Gloria stares at me for a long minute. I gaze back, trying to seem positive and neutral at the same time. Jake's nose bumps my hand, but I wave him off.

Her pursed lips relax. She says softly, "Okay, I agree. You can go."

My pulse quickens. I'm thrilled. I'm scared. I'm going to Everest.

"Thank you, Glo. I'll be careful."

"I know."

I stand up and open my arms wide, asking for a hug.

Each of us moves around our side of the dinner table, and we meet near the bulletin board covered with family photos. We hug and stand still.

Gloria leans her torso back a few inches to open a little space between us. I keep my hands on her hips. Glo looks up at me, and I smile at her. She wiggles her right hand free. Gloria pokes the chest muscle over my heart once, and in a hushed voice say, "You'd better come back."

8

couldn't wait any longer to call Gloria.

Calling Glo so early back home meant I might wake her. But, since I didn't know if she'd seen my text yet, I needed to talk to her before she saw a scary report on TV and assumed the worst. Besides, I needed to hear her voice.

After extending the satellite phone's antenna, I dialed home. Bart rolled toward the tent's far side and turned his back to me. Our kitchen phone rang once before Gloria picked up.

"Hello?"

I heard tension and worry. She knew about the quake.

"Glo, I'm at Camp One. We're all right."

I put the most important information right up front—if the satellite call dropped, at least she would know I wasn't hurt.

"Thank God. Are you okay?"

Before starting every sentence, we each had to pause to allow for the typical one-second delay as the signal traveled halfway around the planet.

"Yeah, I'm fine. Did you get my text?"

"Yes. I'm so sorry this happened."

"So am I. It's unbelievable. Everyone at C1 is fine, but we're stuck for now."

"Your message got here after I went to bed, so I saw it this morning. I woke up early with both phones ringing and one of the neighbors knocking on the door. It's been nuts—everybody's worried sick about you guys."

"You need to let the kids know I'm all right."

"I did as soon as I saw your text. Jess and Nick both know."

"Okay, good. Alan is above me at C2. Most everyone there is okay, but I haven't been able to talk with him directly. Have you heard anything?"

"Yes. Alan's all right. He posted an audio update to his blog a few hours ago."

"If he's blogging, then he's fine. I'll see him somewhere soon. I can't talk long 'cause we're conserving batteries. We'll be here overnight until we figure a way down. The route through the icefall probably got wrecked. Do you know how big the quake was?"

"The news said 7.5 magnitude."

"Whoa! That's huge."

"Yeah, the biggest one in Nepal in eighty-one years, they say."

"There's going to be some serious problems."

"The news footage from Kathmandu looks terrible. It's heartbreaking. Hey, what do you want me to do about the reporters?"

"What do you mean?"

"Reporters and TV stations keep leaving voice mails asking if they can talk to you directly."

"Like who?"

"ABC, NBC, *The Denver Post*—a bunch of them."

"You're kidding!"

"You're one of the only people posting updates from Camp One, so they're following you. A lot of people are."

"Jeesh, I don't know. I guess I can text them, but I'd better let IMG know first. They aren't fond of journalists, usually."

"What should I do?"

"Text their names and contact info to my GPS, please."

There was so much to ask and so much to say. But we needed to save satellite phone minutes and batteries. After agreeing to mostly use text and for me to call her again in twelve hours, we got ready to sign off.

"Stay safe. We'll be sending you white light and love."

"Thanks, Glo. Give the kids my love. I love you."

I felt drained after the call, but better. It was good that we'd had a chance to talk, just in case. I thanked Bart for the phone and promised to repay him later for the costs. He waved his hand in the air dismissively and put the phone into his down-suit pocket.

Ten minutes later, the smooth purring of our tent zipper startled us. When the door flopped partway open, a jacket-clad arm reached inside. It was PK.

"Give me water bottles. I will fill."

The evening hot water was ready. We each passed him two empty bottles. The sherpa guides and support staff had manned two kerosene burners all afternoon to melt snow into water. Providing two quarts each to all thirty-two people on our team demanded melting down a pile of dense snow the size of a living room couch. Expedition staff did this critical work three times a day.

Cold high-altitude air possesses very little moisture, which means we must fight to stay hydrated. Dehydration not only weakens us, but it can also thicken our blood and raise our heart rates. All that increases our chances of frostbite and severe high-altitude illness. And, if you're more than fifty years old, like me, the risks of heart attacks and strokes go up too.

PK soon brought full bottles back along with two semihot "meal in a bag" dinners for us. The precooked food wasn't fancy, but a warm meal provides comfort and a psychological boost. We thanked PK and dug in. Bart ate chicken curry, and I forced down some pasty spaghetti with meat sauce. My meal sure didn't taste like Mom's homemade cooking used to, but at least I got it into my stomach.

After rinsing our bowls and spoons with a little precious warm water, we dumped the sludge into the snow behind our tent. Sunset loomed an hour ahead, so we started the many steps necessary to be in our sleeping bags by dark. When the sun dropped behind the western Himalayas, the temperature would dive far below zero degrees Fahrenheit.

Bart adjusted his clothes and put loose items away. I took a low dose of acetazolamide to help prevent acute mountain sickness.

Outside our tent, Emily announced her arrival and unzipped the door. After scooting inside, she said, "I've got an update."

We paid careful attention.

"If the weather clears tomorrow, we'll send a few guides down into the upper icefall to assess the route."

"Sounds good," said Bart.

"If they can, base camp will send people up at the same time. They'll try to meet in the middle," said Emily.

"How is base camp?" I asked.

She shook her head. "Not good. It looks like they have over sixty wounded. And unfortunately, seventeen people died."

We all fell silent. After hearing bad news spill from the radio all day, we knew there had been deaths. But seventeen? That didn't seem right. They came here to climb, like the rest of us. How could they be dead?

Emily told us that base camp's field hospital had been hit by the slide too. The three doctors escaped with minor injuries, but the avalanche winds scattered and buried the medical supplies. She said our mess tent had been pressed into service as an emergency hospital—they were treating patients on the dining tables. Our IMG teammates, along with hundreds of other climbers and Nepali staff, were helping the wounded as best they could.

As she prepared to leave, Emily wrapped up with a warning: "Since we don't have a clear way off the mountain yet, we need to stay flexible. We might be here awhile."

Bart and I nodded in gloomy agreement. Emily left to have the same difficult conversation with all the other anxious climbers.

Around 6:30 p.m. I checked my GPS for text messages. Rodney had written:

IMG reports no injuries to any clients or staff. Mag 7.5 near Pokhara, looks bad for them (many fatalities). USGS monitoring aftershocks.

Getting outside confirmation that our entire team eluded harm was a relief. And I felt reassured that the U.S. Geological Survey was scrutinizing the earthquakes.* I knew a few senior scientists in the survey, so I could text them if we needed more information.

Rodney and I swapped a few more cryptic messages, and then he signed off with:

Hang in there. Stay the course. You are safe for the moment! . . . another Everest tragedy.

Connecting with Gloria and Rodney was comforting, but it made me miss home even more. I yearned to see them all again. Part of me wanted to reveal my fear and ask them for support. Another portion of me felt obligated to reduce their worry by projecting confidence. After all, I had brought this upon them by deciding to climb Everest. I signed off for the night at 7:30 p.m. with a text to Rodney:

Going to sleep now. Base camp big mess. Will have a plan in 14 hours.

Bart slid into his sleeping bag while I pondered what we would do if another quake or avalanche hit us overnight. Near my head I carefully stacked my gloves and headlamp in case we had to run for our lives

---

* Initial reports stated that the earthquake of April 25, 2015, was 7.5 magnitude. As is common, the estimated value rose over time as more science stations reported their readings. The highest estimate reached 7.9 before data integration produced an official value of 7.8 magnitude for what was later named the Gorkha earthquake.

during the night. Because putting on my big boots takes too long in an emergency, I considered wearing them all night. But they would make the inside of my bag wet and cold. I skipped the boots and compromised by placing them close so I could grab them fast.

At sundown the yellow evening light in our tent faded like life draining away. This day had established a brand-new, terrible record. With seventeen people killed in base camp, it had become the deadliest day on Mount Everest.

9

As I settled in, I pondered wearing my beacon all night in case we got slammed by an avalanche. But ten hours of transmitting would eat up the batteries, and strapping the hard case to my chest would interfere with sleep. I decided not to wear the transceiver and instead hope that the Himalayas didn't tremble while we slept. Hope seemed like scant protection.

I wiggled inside the sleeping bag, still wearing my down suit. With the suit's three inches of feathers and six more inches of down sleeping bag lofted above me, I warmed up fast. Lying motionless on my back and wondering when the next earthquake would arrive made me feel vulnerable. Then I remembered something that would help—the photos. Excited, I turned on my headlamp and dug into my pack lid's most secure pocket, I tugged out a doubled-up plastic bag, opened both ziplocked bags, and pulled out my favorite family pictures.

The first photo showed Jess and me smiling at the summit of Kilimanjaro five months earlier. There was one with Glo and me flanking Nick at the ice rink where he'd played hockey for thirteen years. In his skates Nick towered over us both.

On the next print, lush orange sunlight warmed the faces of Jess, me, and Jake the Wonder Dog. Jessica's twenty-first birthday fell the week before I left for Everest. For her special day, Jess wanted to hike up our local training hill, Horsetooth Mountain, before dawn so we could summit at sunrise. We topped out five minutes before the sun peeked above the Colorado plains.

All those family pictures were recent, but two others were taken long ago. A 1985 reprint of Mom and Dad smiling together in the kitchen of my childhood home made me grin. And the last photo, from 1992, showed my old friend Mike Price.

Mike and I met at Colorado State University during our graduate studies—literature for him, geology for me. Over six years we became close friends and regular climbing partners. Our biggest climb together was the treacherous Liberty Ridge on Mount Rainier, in Washington State. I took that picture of Mike on the second day of our climb, about halfway to the top. Seeing the old photo of him reminded me how his vast experience as a climbing instructor gave Mike a powerful aura of confidence and mountain savvy.

After summiting Rainier, we descended the glacier roped together. I was out front when a hidden snow bridge collapsed beneath my feet and dropped me inside a giant crevasse. The long fall dragged Mike in there with me. Tied to each other, we plummeted eighty feet inside the glacier.

Mike died from the fall into the crevasse.

Devastated at the loss of my friend, and terrified at being trapped down there, I almost gave up. But by digging in with his ice ax, Mike had slowed the first fifty feet of my fall and saved my life—I couldn't just quit because climbing out seemed too hard or too scary. Ice climbing alone up the overhanging crevasse wall demanded more from me than I ever thought I had. After I made it out, park rangers recovered Mike's body.

For the past twenty-three years some of Mike's spirit had gone with me on every climb. In addition to the photo, I also had with me Mike's Colorado Outward Bound pin, which his father had given me after Mike's death. And, deep in my pack, as my secret weapon, I was carrying Mike's superwarm hat that he earned during his season on the Antarctica search-and-rescue team. I was going to need all the strength and protection I could get from Mike, and from all my loved ones, to get off Everest.

I shuffled through the photos again. Seeing them calmed me and reminded me to endure whatever happened and do everything necessary to get home. I had planned on carrying them all to the summit with me. Now it seemed doubtful that they, or I, would be going any higher.

Carefully I slid the photos back into the first plastic bag, closed the seal, and then protected the inner bag with the second clear one. Opening the left chest pocket of my suit, I placed the packet inside and tugged the zipper closed. If I got buried, I'd have them with me.

I stuffed a spare jacket under my head as a pillow. Yanking the drawstrings of my sleeping bag cinched the opening tight around my neck to trap heat. Beneath all that insulation, I pressed the pictures of my loved ones against my chest. Trying to settle my nerves, I told myself everything was going to be okay.

I closed my eyes and hoped for dreamless sleep.

Even though we had left the door flap ajar to vent out our exhaled breath, the water vapor froze overnight to the tent walls and ceiling. By dawn on April 26, the entire inside of our tent was coated with delicate hoarfrost crystals.

My shoulder bumped the sidewall and a bracing ice shower fell on my face. By the time I freed an arm from my sleeping bag to wipe the ice dust off, it had melted to cold water. I was wide awake.

The soft light told me sunrise was half an hour away. Since clear morning skies prevail on Everest in springtime, there was a good chance I could finally see what had happened all around us yesterday.

I geared up and crept from the tent as quietly as possible to avoid waking Bart. The air felt stinging cold, and fresh snow coated all the peaks. Everything in camp hid under six inches of new snowfall.

With my camera I captured a 360-degree panoramic video. The sky was clear except for one heavy cloud bank lingering three miles northwest of us. It straddled the connecting ridge between Pumori and Lingtren—precisely where the avalanche that overran base camp had originated.

Studying Everest's west shoulder above camp, I looked for signs of the avalanches. Most of the evidence had been frosted over by the new snow, but on the glacier near us, there was a wide field of angular ice blocks—they had spilled off the shoulder during the avalanches. Unseen, that slide had plunged thousands of feet through the clouds, then raced toward us. It stopped about four hundred yards from our tents. The chopped-up blocks nearly hit a pair of dome tents pitched recklessly close to the foot of the west shoulder. A low wall of avalanche debris had piled up about fifty feet from their tent doors.

Turning around to face the other side of the Western Cwm, I examined the slopes below the 6,000-foot-tall Nuptse wall. Avalanches had run toward us from that side too. Some large open crevasses between us and the wall had trapped most of the rolling avalanche debris, which limited the slide path's reach. This avalanche had come within three hundred yards of our camp before halting.

Though the slides had pressed close from both sides, we'd been saved by camping in the traditional midglacier spot—and some luck.

Morning alpenglow lit up Nuptse and other high summits, tinting the fresh snow pink and orange. All that beauty projected an air of serenity and gave no hint of the violent shaking, roaring, and blasting that had happened eighteen hours earlier. Everest is as unpredictable as it is unforgiving.

I took photographs and watched the sky brighten behind Lhotse's summit ridge. Several of my teammates and our sherpa partners moved about camp. Direct sunlight would not thaw camp for another hour. I returned to the tent to warm up and check my GPS for messages.

When the device powered up and connected with the satellites, a rising electronic warble announced the arrival of one message, then more. Overnight I had received a dozen texts. I scanned them and saw that most were from friends and family, asking if we were okay and wishing us well. Several inquired about our potential escape plans.

Gloria had sent me contact information for representatives at CNN, NBC News, and *Good Morning America*. They wanted to do phone interviews with me from Camp One. I couldn't accommodate them. The cheap Nepali cell phone I purchased in Kathmandu was useless as long as Ncell service remained down. Even if the system started up soon, the high rock walls surrounding camp meant my cell phone wouldn't get any signal.

Bart and I ate a light breakfast of instant oatmeal. While nursing a cup of hot tea, I checked my messages again. A representative from De-Lorme, the manufacturer of my GPS, texted me that a few more journalists had called them asking for my contact information. My social media posts automatically included that they came from my DeLorme GPS text account. From that, several industrious reporters from ABC and other news outlets had tracked me down. A DeLorme representative sent me the reporters' email addresses.

My cold, fat fingers pecked stiffly at the GPS buttons, writing my responses one slow letter at a time. I sent them each a brief message, trying to arrange a group text interview to avoid having to answer the same questions repeatedly. Night had arrived in the States, which meant I did not expect to hear back from them anytime soon. The GPS chirped with a message from Gloria:

> **Phone ringing off the hook. Lots want to hear from you. I can't believe this is happening. So sad for climbers and Nepalese.**

Jess and Nick sent along warm messages of encouragement and concern. I tried to make my responses sound cautiously optimistic. Shortly before seven, Rodney fed me more critical information:

> **Stay focused. Icefall repair needed. CNN reports (at least) 10 dead at EBC. Alan reported okay but no direct report. Thinking of you constantly.**

The outside-world news was a bit behind what was happening on the mountain, but not by much. I hoped to see Alan soon, either on the mountain or back at base camp.

Bart and I left the confining tent to chat with our teammates. Every time Emily walked by with the radio in her hand, someone asked her for an update. She told us that the emergency at base camp had calmed down some. IMG's three dining tents and our big communication wall tent had been converted to emergency wards. About ten doctors and many volunteers had been caring for dozens of seriously wounded patients for more than twenty hours. Everyone had to be exhausted. The Nepali and Western patients with head wounds, crushed limbs, and fractured pelvises all needed better medical care as soon as possible. A few locally based helicopters reached base camp soon after dawn, and they were airlifting patients down-valley to rural medical clinics.

We heard that a few dozen moderately wounded people had been moved to the nearby Asian Trekking camp, managed by Dawa Steven Sherpa. Another expedition operator, Himalayan Experience, run by the veteran Everest guide Russell Brice, cared for more wounded people and hosted many displaced people whose camps had been destroyed. The base-camp community was helping one another and holding on, but the situation remained tenuous.

Under the blazing sun the temperature rose fast. In three hours we went from shivering in down suits to feeling comfortable in just polypropylene long underwear. We hid beneath hats, sunglasses, and copious sun cream.

"Look!" someone shouted.

Like a dragonfly rising skyward, a sleek red-and-white helicopter appeared over the icefall. As it flew toward us, the engine strained to climb in the ever-thinner air. The chopper stayed about forty feet above the glacier's surface to use the added uplift of its own blade-driven air bouncing up off the ground. The pilot was hugging dangerous terrain just to milk the tiny incremental benefit of this "ground effect." That machine was working near its limit.

The aircraft cruised by and continued three miles farther up the glacier to Camp Two. We knew it had to fly back past us on its descent, so a few people grabbed their cameras. As we watched and waited, Emily emerged from her tent. She knew we were curious. She said, "A guy in C2 has a breathing problem. They've already flown about seventy wounded out of base camp, so now they're lifting him out too."

Five minutes later the chopper descended faster than it had ascended. Some dirty, scared climber was on his way to the hospital and then home. Watching his speedy escape made me a tad envious. I wanted to be free of this stressful place, but high-mountain helicopter rides are risky, and I did not want to be in the back of that barely flying cabin.

Bart and I returned to our tent and tried to be patient. Because his satellite account still contained hundreds of prepaid minutes, Bart offered me his phone to talk with the reporters. I pressed him hard to ensure he felt comfortable extending such a generous offer. He seemed fine with it, so I accepted and insisted on repaying him. Since interviews were now possible, I realized I should clarify my intentions with Emily.

I crawled out of our tent and walked over to hers. "I've gotten several media requests to do interviews," I said. "I know IMG likes us focused on climbing, not journalism. But it feels important to let the world know what's happening up here, so I wanted to ask if that's okay."

She smiled. "Yeah, that's fine, Jim. You'll be a great representative for us."

Emily surprised me by agreeing so fast. I said, "Thanks. I'll be straightforward and respectful of what's going on."

"I'm sure you will."

The sunshine and clear skies continued all morning, so I lingered outside examining the slopes above camp. The three-mile-wide Nuptse wall revealed massive layers of folded metamorphic bedrock topped with scores of hanging ice fields. Last winter had brought big snowfalls to the Everest area, and significant new snow had fallen just a few weeks ago. That had seemed like a good thing then because all the snow blanketed the icefall, making our climbing route smoother and faster. It also glued down the loose rocks onto the high slopes all around us. But standing in Camp One, below a trilogy of mile-high walls plastered with delicate white frosting, I now found myself cursing all that hanging snow for the avalanche risk it posed. More tremors were coming; we had to get out of that basin.

Looking northwest toward the Khumbu Icefall, I thought about our possible descent. If we went back the way we came, we had to pass directly beneath the hanging glacier that collapsed on the sixteen sherpas last year. That cursed spot had to be even riskier now; traversing underneath it would be nuts. But that was the only way to climb down. After sixty-three years of south-side expeditions, no one had found a viable way to avoid the dangerous gauntlet of the Khumbu Icefall.

Even on a good day, climbing among the shifting ice blocks was a drawn-out game of chance where you put your life on the line for hours at a time. After the quakes, the icefall towers had to be even more unstable. I wondered how the hell we were going to get off the mountain.

I looked across camp and saw one of the IMG guides, Justin, putting on his gear. He stepped into his harness one skinny leg at a time. Next to him was Dawa Sherpa, the lead climbing sherpa for our team. Dawa had vast Everest experience, and though he stood a foot shorter than Justin, he was every bit as strong. From the butterfly knots Justin had tied in the climbing rope, I could tell they were preparing to cross the glacier roped together.

As they loaded their packs and donned their helmets, Damian Benegas showed up from a nearby camp. Damian had guided Everest and other high peaks for fifteen years, often accompanied by his equally skilled twin brother, Willie. It seemed like almost everyone on the mountain knew these flamboyant Argentine siblings. After clipping into the rope, the three of them walked out of camp, each carrying an ice ax. They adjusted their pace to keep the climbing rope snug between them as they traversed the crevassed terrain. Once they merged onto the existing trail stomped into the snow, the rope team turned left and began descending into the upper Khumbu Icefall.

Emily walked up to our cluster of watching climbers and said: "They're going down to scout the route."

"Think they'll find any ropes and ladders left?" someone asked.

"We'll see," Emily said.

Like clockwork, thick clouds began filling the Khumbu Valley as midday approached. A few of us milled around outside, trading snippets of information about the earthquake damage across Nepal and in the neighboring countries. We watched the growing cloud bank gradually roll up and over the icefall, coming toward Camp One like a gigantic floating cotton ball.

By noon we grew tired of talking and staring at the white wall around us. We all retreated to our tents. I ate a crunchy granola bar and thought about how we might craft a route off the mountain. About 110 climbers were trapped at Camp One, and around 70 more mountaineers hunkered at Camp Two. All 180 people were fit, focused, and highly motivated. Every one of them was a world-class guide, an experienced sherpa, or a climber who had scaled high peaks all over the world. We certainly had enough people and skills.

What we did not have were replacement ropes and ladders to rebuild a route through the icefall. The path between base camp and Camp One required dozens of aluminum ladders and several miles of zigzagged fixed rope. There wasn't that much extra gear available within fifty miles. Even if we had that equipment standing by, building the route through the always-moving glacier takes a week or more of effort. And now the whole unstable pile had been shaken by Nepal's biggest earthquake in eight decades. The icefall had to be a mess—geology and gravity guaranteed it.

Besides, we didn't have a week. We needed a plan that we could implement fast, and that would minimize our exposure time in the icefall. No sane person would want to be down there toiling away when the inevitable aftershocks hit. Everything depended on how bad things were in the ice-fall and how much longer the mountain stayed stable.

If we needed more rope, we could go up the mountain to dig out and cut away old lines abandoned by previous expeditions. Those battered ropes would be weak and untrustworthy after years of exposure to the harsh ultraviolet light that breaks down nylon at high altitude. But we needed the system to last only a day or two until everyone from Camps One and Two reached base camp.

Maybe we could string together enough rope to at least sneak through the most precarious parts of the icefall. We'd have to take our chances and just climb unroped over the rest. With some spare ropes carried to us by chopper and a team building the lower route upward from base camp, perhaps we could string enough together to jerry-rig our way out in a few days. When the scouting team—

A deep rumble emanated from Nuptse. My head snapped up, and I stared toward the mountain. Then, just like yesterday, a second avalanche growled at us from the west shoulder of Everest.

The glacier started shaking again.

10

Over the growing rumble I yelled: "Another avalanche! Another tremor!"

My heart pounded against my rib cage. Bart lunged for the tent door and said: "Oh no!"

I sat up, grabbed my GoPro, powered up the camera, and hit Record. The flashing red light assured me it was working. My boots were already on, so I ducked outside right behind Bart. Clouds hid the avalanches from us just like the day before, but having seen the debris paths earlier in the morning, this time I had a good mental map of where the slides might come from. I scanned the gray mist for any movement.

Emily stood by the cook tent next to Jason Ahlan and his wife, Caroline Le Jour. I pointed the camera at them; they looked nervous but not panicked. So far the avalanches weren't as loud as the others had been, and it didn't seem as scary. Also, this time we knew what was happening. We were getting used to the chaos.

The ground didn't buck vertically like last time—instead, it twitched gently like a sleeping dog's leg. I looked down at my feet. Inside my boots I curled my toes and pressed them downward as if trying to read the earth's next move. The glacier jerked once, then the massive ice sheet swayed back and forth. All the motions felt gentler than the previous day's violent earthquake. I hoped it meant that the tremor was smaller. A strong wind gust hit me from the right side and several snowflakes flew past my face.

I yelled, "Here comes the powder blast!" With the camera still running, I stepped backward two strides to position the tent as a protective wind block. Pulverized ice crystals from the west shoulder swirled through camp.

Caroline was clad only in a long-underwear top and bottom, so she sprinted to her tent. Jason and Emily were wearing better clothing for the pending onslaught. They walked toward shelter, but before they got inside, a white powder wave rolled into camp.

I squatted down behind the tent. Grabbing the hood of my black midlayer, I flipped it over my head and waited. The amount of blowing powder and its impact on my cheeks was smaller than the previous avalanche. After a minute the powder blast died down and the glacier's oscillations petered out. As the avalanche rumblings stopped, the valley returned to silence. We'd made it through another round.

Exhaling deeply, I tried to slow my heart rate. A glance at my watch showed that it was 12:28 p.m. I said into the camera, "Today's quake was almost exactly twenty-four hours after the last one. Oh boy!" Then I shut it off.

People trickled back outside, and we discussed the tremor. We were glad this one had been less powerful. Our quake-savvy Californian, Don Harbart, guessed that this one would measure about 6.0 magnitude. Scientists later assessed the aftershock at 6.8.

Emily's radio crackled to life—the guys! Our scouting team had been down in the icefall when the quake hit. With thousands of crevasses and ice blocks surrounding them, the icefall was the worst place to be in an earthquake. Emily talked rapidly to Justin over her radio. Then she lifted her arm above her head, turned her palm toward us, and waved gently. They were all right.

We waited until she signed off, then we circled around her. "They got rattled, but they're fine," she said. "They're coming back up."

"What did they see down there?" Don asked.

"They said the route's wrecked. Most of the ropes and ladders are missing."

My shoulders drooped. Though I thought it unlikely, I'd been hoping that if the ropes were somehow intact, we could blitz through the icefall and be off this mountain in a few hours. With our only route back to base camp gone, we were truly stuck. My teammates wore concerned looks as they pondered the bad news. One by one, people drifted back to their tents.

With the mountains covered by clouds, there'd be no more helicopters flying for the rest of the day. We lay in our sleeping bags for an hour, hardly moving. There was nowhere to go and nothing to do. So we did nothing. Other than the occasional hacking cough from a tent close by, camp was quiet.

An hour later the smooth growl of a zipper told us that someone nearby was exiting their tent. Heavy boots crunched past our door and then faded across camp.

"Hey, the latrine's full!" Emily yelled.

Our toilet was a five-gallon bucket outfitted with a thick plastic bag. The full liner bag had to be hefted out and tossed into a deep crevasse. Tossing trash away, especially a plastic bag of feces, didn't sit right with me. Carrying down the human waste would be much better. As part of Leave No Trace practices, climbers often use individual bags to carry their waste out of wilderness areas. My teammates and I carried our waste off other mountains, using the double-plastic-bag method on Mount Rainier and "clean mountain cans"—portable, lightweight toilet canisters —on Denali. After several field seasons of messy failure and process refinement, those two government-managed systems worked well. Such community approaches required careful planning and reliable funding to create, and they needed diligent administration to work. All of these were in short supply in a resource-limited country like Nepal.

Complex handling systems to collect, transport, separate, and process human waste didn't exist in mountainous Nepal. Many mountain valley residents used an outhouse. Waste management often meant drying yak dung to heat homes and putting raw human poop on vegetable gardens as fertilizer. Bringing human waste down Everest every day via hundreds of bags or dozens of sealed buckets would only help if a sophisticated handling system stood ready to receive them, but it didn't. For the time being, crevassing the poop was all we could do.

After a moment had gone by, Emily called out: "Someone's gotta change the poop bag."

To hear better, I pushed my hat off my ears. Everyone stayed quiet. We all knew what that latrine was like. Vicious foreign microbes fighting prepackaged meals inside our beleaguered bowels meant that half the camp had diarrhea. Fumbling with three layers of restrictive clothing during midnight toilet visits meant people's backside aim was off. The bucket-and-liner-bag combo was a poop-splattered mess. Changing the bag was a filthy, and possibly unhealthy, job that no one wanted.

I assumed that the awful task was someone's assigned job, so I stayed horizontal. I guess I supposed somebody else would take care of the mess. Along with my teammates at Camp One, I'd contributed my daily share to the latrine. But emptying it didn't seem like my job.

11

1978

'm sitting atop an empty five-gallon paint pail on a warm summer day. We have a big contract to paint several dozen houses on the Pease Air Force Base in New Hampshire. Our summer crew—the college kids, as Dad calls them—are strong young men. But as temporary help, they aren't really painters.

Though I'm only fifteen, by now I'm familiar with every aspect of commercial painting. I started out scraping off peeling paint and cleaning brushes with toxic thinner at age eight. Dad taught me how to operate a spray gun at age twelve. I don't have my driver's license yet, but I can operate a sixty-foot-tall man-lift crane and deftly position the two-man basket among an angling network of steel beams.

With so many houses to paint here, we're operating three spray guns. We've been runnin' and gunnin' all morning, and now we're out of paint. Dad had to drive off base to the gas station payphone to find out when the truck will deliver our four hundred gallons of military gray. The five college kids and I are lounging around the shop until he gets back.

I slouch on the upside-down metal bucket with my ankles crossed in front of me. The backs of my hands are covered in gray drops, so I pick dried paint from my nailbeds. Three college kids sit against the shop walls sipping coffee. Two others splay out on the floor near the doorway nursing Marlboros, the acrid smoke curling above their heads.

Just then our foreman, Rocco Ciraso, walks in. His cut-off sleeves reveal bulging, tattooed biceps. One arm has the classic broken heart with "Mother" written inside, while the other sports a colorful replica of "Taz," the Tasmanian Devil cartoon character. The brawny little creature bears an oversize barrel chest and a mean, mischievous grin. He and Rocco could be brothers.

In a thick Boston accent, Rocco asks, "What are ya doin'?"

"Nothing," I say. "We're out of paint."

Rocco has worked for Dad and Uncle Bob for thirteen years. I grew up watching him come and go from the painting barn in our yard. Although I'm not usually afraid of him, I know from the stories about his two long stints in the joint that underneath his quiet, middle-aged exterior still lurks a motorcycle-gang member. Rocco makes most people nervous, but he's totally loyal to Dad, so I like and trust him. Mostly.

Rocco strolls across the paint shop, stops in front of me, and softly says, "Get up."

I stand, and he gives my empty paint pail seat a mighty kick. It sails across the shop and bounces head-high off the concrete wall. The metal can crashes to the floor with a violent *clang*. I flinch, and three of the guys jump to their feet.

"Hey! What's that for?" I ask.

"Get to work."

I back up one step and scowl at Rocco. A filterless Lucky Strike hangs from his mouth. The stub has a quarter inch left before the smoldering end will scorch his walrus mustache. I look around the shop for support. The college kids are all standing now, but they're quiet and wide-eyed, watching Rocco and me.

My cheeks feel warm, and I'm not sure what to do. I wave my arm at the crowded paint shop. "There's no paint. What do you want us to do?"

"I don't give a shit. Wash brushes. Sweep the friggin' floor!"

In a rising voice, I say, "Sweep the floor?"

Rocco steps toward me. "Just get off your ass and do somethin'."

"What are you yelling at just me for?"

He leans six inches closer. Gray beard stubble gives his cheeks the texture of eighty-grit sandpaper. The sweet smell of burnt tobacco mixes with the harsh stink of singed mustache hair.

"You've been at this a while. You know better than to sit and do nothin'."

12

Somebody, let's go," Emily said louder.

Someone needed to do something. I sat up, grabbed my inner boots, and pulled them on.

"You going?" Bart asked.

"Yup."

I laced the liners fast and hustled outside. Emily stood thirty feet away on the small trail to the latrine. "I got it," I said.

Emily nodded once. "Thank you."

"Which direction do you want me to take the bag?"

She pointed to the south edge of camp. "That way." Then she headed off toward the kitchen tent.

I walked to the latrine and took a good look. The bucket was chock-full. I pushed my sleeves up my forearms to keep them from getting dirty. Using two fingers of each hand, I pulled the top edges of the bag upward and gathered the plastic together. Then I gently twisted the bag top into a tight bundle and tied an overhand knot. I held my breath but still caught the stench. When I lifted the liner from the pail, the weight surprised me: sixty pounds of liquids and solids. My tight grip got me more skin contact than I wanted, but I needed to make sure I didn't drop the bulging bag. In my mind I heard Dad say: "Knuckle onto it!"

Walking twenty paces to the disposal crevasse while holding the filthy weight at arm's length took all of my upper-body strength. The consequences of spilling the contents all over the snow, or me, seemed too awful to imagine. I moved two strides outside the designated camp perimeter toward a ragged hole in the snow. The previous night's snowfall meant I couldn't tell where the glacier ended and the crevasse began. I didn't want to get too near the edge, wherever it was, but I needed to stand close enough so that when I tossed the bag, it didn't miss the hole. If the waste bag fell short, I would have to move even closer to the crevasse edge to push it in.

I took another tentative step so that I was five feet from the visible opening—that was close enough. When I peered into the crevasse, I saw that its black gullet plunged at least eighty feet into the glacier's guts.

To build momentum, I swung the bag in front of me and then back. On my next forward swing, I stared at the black target and tossed the bag hard. The sack hit a bit short, but the edge of the thin snow bridge broke off and widened the hole. Without a sound, the bag slipped into the crevasse. Instinctively I counted time to estimate the slot's depth. I reached four seconds but heard no impact.

Down there the waste would freeze and meld into the glacier. Perhaps it would grind to bits as it got carried down the mountain by the slow glacial flow. Our collective frozen shit stain would creep downhill for centuries to come.

I walked back inside the safety of camp, staring at my hands. Right on cue PK came from the kitchen tent carrying a saucepan of steaming water. Wanting to know if the water was boiling, I asked in Nepali, *"Pani umaleko cha?"*

"No, only hot. It's okay."

PK poured the water over my hands. Using fuel and water for hygiene was an outrageous expenditure at 19,700 feet. As he splashed more precious liquid onto my open hands, I noticed several of our teammates standing nearby. All the activity had drawn them out of their tent co-coons to watch and lend moral support. We'd all been pulled from our lethargy.

Darren stepped forward and handed me a mini–soap bar worth its weight in gold at that moment. As I rubbed my hands together, a reas-suring lather formed. Another warm rinse from PK's water pan and I felt okay, though I still studied my hands, thinking about microbes. My buddy Fred hustled over holding a clear plastic bottle of hand sanitizer. He squeezed a blob of clear alcohol gel into one hand and I rubbed my palms together. My hands felt clean.

Throughout the afternoon Emily's radio provided updates about base camp. Helicopters finished evacuating all the injured people before the midday clouds moved in. Carrying two or three passengers per flight, the choppers flew them down-valley to modest medical outposts in the villages of Pheriche, Lukla, and Namche Bazaar. The walking wounded had been treated in base camp. Due to the relentless efforts of so many volunteers, the medical emergency finally seemed to be over after twenty-four hours.

During the clear morning conditions a few hours earlier, base-camp residents had gotten their first good view of the shattered landscape around them. They'd pieced together an initial understanding of what had happened the previous day.

The avalanche started on the tenuous ridge crest that connected 23,494-foot Pumori to the adjacent peak, Lingtren. That fragile spine of rock towers and ice blocks stretched a mile long and ran behind the full length of base camp. When the quake rattled the ridge, massive debris chunks broke loose and hurtled 3,000 vertical feet down the steep moun-tain face. Cloudy weather prevented people in base camp from seeing the start of the avalanche and most of its initial approach. But the earth-shaking thunder from behind the clouds gave everyone a few precious seconds of warning to run and hide.

As it tumbled down, the debris wall picked up more rocks, ice, and snow along the way. When that giant wave of rubble splashed onto the valley floor, a portion of it deflected laterally and rushed across the basin like a mountain tsunami. That shock wave of hurricane-force winds and flying debris then bulldozed through the middle of base camp.

The rushing debris cloud contained angular rock and ice chunks ranging from golf ball–size to as big as microwave ovens. They shot through base camp like cannon fire. Roaring winds flattened dozens of tents and tore others from the ground—anything, or anyone, inside got carried away. All those flying objects were hurled several hundred yards east across the glacier. Duffel bags, barrels, and people were scattered across acres of rock fields and ice pinnacles.

Even a day later the radio reports said that searchers continued to comb the debris field for more dead or injured people. Details about the seventeen known deaths were still sketchy. The dead included both Nepali staff and foreign climbers. The well-known Adventure Consultants group and a team led by British climber Tim Mosedale each lost several people. We heard that Madison Mountaineering had a fatality too. A burst of worry flashed through my mind because my friend Alan was climbing with them. But he'd left base camp a day ahead of me, so he had to be at Camp Two.

Through satellite calls and text messages, we also received sporadic updates from the outside world. The early reports about climbers dying on Everest's north side were utterly incorrect. We were relieved. That early reporting error showed us the difficulty of sorting fact from fiction as a disaster unfolds. Worldwide media attention had turned to Nepal, and videos were emerging of collapsed buildings in Kathmandu. The news reports said that thousands of people died because of the quakes, avalanches, and landslides.

Such an enormous tragedy would strain even well-resourced countries, and Nepal was among the poorest nations in the world. The Nepali government, infrastructure, and citizens would be totally overwhelmed. We couldn't count on much outside help, either for the expeditions or the local residents. The Everest community would have to figure things out on its own.

With the rope-and-ladder system through the icefall destroyed and aftershocks looming, base-camp leaders were considering a helicopter lift for us to escape Camp One. If the weather stayed favorable, perhaps the choppers could return. But there wasn't much time, as several days of bad weather were predicted. The expedition leaders in base camp arranged for nearby helicopters to arrive the next day, and the leaders in Camp One devised a fair method for the teams to take turns.

If the plan worked, choppers would extract the 110 of us at Camp One first. The 70 people in Camp Two would descend a few hours on foot to the snowpacked helipads at Camp One. Flying them out from a lower altitude of 19,700 feet—instead of 21,300 feet at Camp Two— would enhance the choppers' limited lift capacities. This tiny power increase improved flight safety by a slim margin. If we kept squeezing a drop of improvement out of everything possible, maybe we could pull it off.

The prospect of escape infused us with energy, but many uncertainties remained. Emily told us to load a small pack of critical gear to take with us. To save space on the helicopters, our less-important equipment would be left at Camp One. People first, things last.

Bart and I sorted gear inside our tent. Back home I'd worked hard researching, buying, and testing high-altitude gear. I spent hundreds of hours assembling the best equipment possible. Now tossing gear into a white rice bag to stay behind took about five minutes. How strange to suddenly abandon all that precious equipment, but the stakes were so high that it felt easy. Maybe we would get our abandoned gear back later, maybe not.

We all knew the evacuation plan could be delayed or scrapped at a moment's notice. I recognized that we shouldn't become mentally or emotionally attached to the idea of escaping the mountain in the morning. In order to avoid getting discouraged later if the plan failed, I tried to stay optimistic but realistic.

Flying in Nepal is unpredictable even under normal circumstances. Localized bad weather in one spot can halt air travel even when the sky remains crystal clear at the flight path's other end. Clouds and fog often stop mountain flights in the Himalayas for days and even weeks. Flying through rugged mountain terrain demands clear skies. Nepali pilots like to say: "We don't fly through clouds because in Nepal, the clouds have rocks in them."

Around four in the afternoon, my text device started sounding off. It was before dawn back home, so I knew the messages weren't from Gloria. On the East Coast of the United States, the time was nearing six in the morning, which meant the national news shows were looking for interviews. I texted several producers back, and we set phone appointments for later.

After an early dinner Emily confirmed that tomorrow's airlift was on. We had to get up at 5:00 a.m., dress and pack by 6:00. To go through all that work and hassle in the vicious predawn cold, we needed to trust that base camp would send the helicopters on time. And for them to take on the difficulty, expense, and risk, our leaders and the pilots had to know that we'd be ready when the first flight arrived.

Evacuating the Camp Two climbers added more complexity. The plan called for them to break camp early and descend while the Camp One climbers were being flown out. If timed well, they would arrive just as the final Camp One climbers departed. The many pieces of this intricate plan were held together by a glue of mutual trust and commitment. Each person had to know and believe that everyone else would do their piece, on time and without fail, no matter what. When resilient people focus their efforts, amazing things can get accomplished.

To me, the helicopter evacuation seemed like the last good option to move everyone down quickly and safely. I really didn't want us to still be there when the next aftershock and avalanche one-two punch arrived. With bad weather grounding the choppers much of the time, we were going to need a gift from the weather gods. The plan was set: The helicopters would arrive at first light.

. . .

Our second cold night at Camp One began. Everyone settled in to sleep, but I was gearing up for interviews. I mentally reviewed the media training I'd done during my career as an environmental geologist and expert witness. Part of me dreaded the upcoming calls because I knew we would discuss all the tragic deaths. It's hard describing the impacts and uncertainties of a disaster when you're still living it.

The rising pitch of an electronic warble announced an incoming text. I pushed the stiff buttons of the cold GPS and read a confirmation message about speaking with ABC News. I didn't want producers and reporters calling in the middle of the night, so I wrote each network that I would phone them instead. To avoid disturbing Bart with my chatter, I planned to make the calls outside.

After putting on my boots, I zipped my down suit and slipped on two pairs of gloves. I grabbed the GPS, satellite phone, and my glasses. When I crawled outside into the night, the cold bit my cheeks hard; the temperature had dropped below zero.

Refusing to leave the safety of camp, I could move no farther away from everyone than the latrine. I walked fifty feet west, beyond the last tents, and stopped on the hand-dug toilet platform. The latrine bucket sat in the middle of the four-foot-by-four-foot space. I stood right next to the waste pail and dialed, keeping my thin liner gloves on while pressing the buttons.

I got through to ABC and said: "This is Jim Davidson calling from Camp One at Mount Everest."

"Oh, wow! That's incredible. Hold on while I patch you through," the producer said.

Random electronic noises sounded over the line. The connection seemed weak. Someone at ABC picked up, but neither of us could understand the other. The usual one-second delay for our signals to travel in each direction made matters worse. Through the noise I heard them say they were tying my call into the control booth. There was a sharp beep, then silence. Somewhere along the way, the call got dropped.

I exhaled hard and hung up, frustrated. To protect my fingers from frostbite, I had to shove my hands inside my down suit for five minutes. Once my hands felt normal, I started over again. A second attempt also ended with an abrupt disconnect before we got very far. The enormous walls of the Western Cwm hemmed me in on three sides, reducing the phone's access to satellite signals. The mountains' dark silhouettes constrained the overhead sky into a skinny strip of stars.

On my next attempt to connect with ABC, I adjusted the direction I faced while calling. Facing open sky to the northwest helped some, but the third try failed, too. This exasperating process ate up thirty minutes. Even though we never did an interview, I had to give up and get ready for my next scheduled call. Standing in one spot for so long had let the cold night air seep through my down suit, so I hustled back to our tent.

Half awake, Bart asked: "Are you done?"

"No. I'm just warming up for a bit."

I burrowed my legs deep into the sleeping bag and waited. To save batteries I shut off my headlamp. Sitting in the cold darkness soon became boring, so I checked my GPS. New messages arrived as everyone awoke back home. Texts came in from friends, journalists, and unknown numbers—probably more reporters. When the next interview time approached, I trudged out into the night for a second round on the glorious latrine stage.

My tired eyes struggled to focus as I dialed the CNN newsroom. After waiting and being passed along the communication chain, I finally spoke to the host, Poppy Harlow. During the interview she said, "Take me back to the moment of the quake—what was that like?" I tried painting a verbal picture of the earthquake and avalanches at Camp One. She asked how we planned to get down. I told her we might fly out by helicopter in the early morning. After a few more questions, she wished us well and ended the call. The interview went fine, but discussing death and destruction wore down my spirits. When I returned to the tent, Bart was snoring. He was smart to rest.

In my down suit and big boots, I struggled to clamber over my tent-mate without bumping him. We usually didn't wear boots inside the tent to avoid tracking in snow, but taking mine off seemed like a lot of work only to put them on again soon. I sat down, faced the open doorway, and stuck my lower legs back outside. Holding both feet aloft, I smashed my boot soles together to knock off the snow. Banging the bright-green boots against each other reminded me of young Dorothy far away in Oz. By clicking the heels of her ruby-red slippers, she could go straight home. I envied her.

I draped my open sleeping bag over my legs and waited. Feeling drained, I wasn't looking forward to this last interview. Tomorrow at dawn we had to be ready to go, ready for anything. And instead of resting I was wearing myself out and letting media people squeeze out of me everything that I knew and felt. I realized that if I kept the GPS and phone powered up, they could keep contacting me, and this tennis match would continue all night. This had to be my last interview.

The time came to call NBC, so I pushed myself back outside. Following my bobbing headlamp beam, I tramped down the snowy trail and returned to my toilet office. While on hold waiting for the interviewer, I shone my headlamp into the latrine bucket—not very full. Good. I hoped we'd be gone before that had to be emptied again. When I realized how unglamorous this moment was, I chuckled aloud.

During the interview I adjusted my head position in tiny increments to find the best satellite phone angle. A leftward head tilt worked best. The NBC reporter asked about the safety of several hundred climbers on Everest's north side. Their Tibetan campsites were only a few miles northeast of us, but we couldn't see over the Himalayan divide, of course. Because we had no communication with them, I had no firsthand information. She pressed for an opinion about their status, inviting me to speculate. During my long science career, I'd learned how to stand firm when insistent people pushed for answers that didn't yet exist. Guessing was inappropriate—that's how false rumors got started. She dropped the topic and wished us luck getting off the mountain. I commented that so many others in Nepal were facing far worse conditions. We thanked each other and signed off. Finally finished, I shuffled back to our tent.

Right as I plopped down on my sleeping pad, the satellite phone rang. This surprised me, as few people had the number. "Hello, this is Jim."

"Hi, Jim. This is CNN calling. Can you do an interview with us?"

"I did one for you an hour ago."

"That was for the newsroom show. I work with Breaking News—they gave us your number. Anderson Cooper would like to talk to you."

I knew very little pop culture. I didn't watch much television, and I never recognized the people who won a Grammy, Emmy, or any other entertainment award. But I knew Anderson Cooper. I could even picture his well-groomed white hair. It was already 9:30 p.m., which was the latest I'd stayed up throughout a month of expedition life. I didn't want to talk anymore; I wanted to shut off the electronics and lie down.

As I struggled to decide what to do, my expedition partner Rodney flashed into my mind. He'd be ticked off if he knew I wasn't taking care of myself on the mountain merely to accommodate strangers in the media. He was probably right. But I agreed to the interview. To justify my decision, I thought, This'll be the last one for sure. Keep it short and get inside the bag soon.

Anderson was on his way to the studio, so we set a call time of 10:00 p.m. When I crawled back outside, camp was quiet. Back by the latrine, I tried dialing CNN. The fat fingers of my thick glove forced me to remove the right one and dial the icy phone clad in only a liner glove. A cold sting burned my dialing finger. Frostbite was just one small mistake away. After connecting, I slid my chilled right hand into my down suit and shoved the fingers deep into my armpit. Warmth returned slowly while I stayed on hold. The producer jumped on and off the call, making technical arrangements. I was too tired to remember her name.

Having my down suit partially unzipped let cold air infiltrate my clothing. I put my thick right glove back on, zipped my suit closed, and walked in place for two minutes to create heat.

"Mr. Davidson, Anderson is still in transit. It will be another five minutes."

My left hand began tingling. I switched the phone to my right hand and fought to rewarm my left one. Of course, moving disturbed the delicate phone connection. To find the best satellite signal, I shuffled around the tiny toilet platform, my right hand holding the phone against my ear, always facing northwest toward Cho Oyu. Sidestep right, one step back. Sidestep left, one step forward. If one of my teammates had looked outside their tent, they might have thought I was square-dancing around the poop bucket.

When I found the best phone and body orientations, I stood rock-still to stay connected. I shut off my headlamp. As my eyes adjusted to the darkness, more stars appeared in the narrow band of heaven above me. The phone's hungry cold gnawed through my glove. I swapped the device back to my left hand, and the connection wavered. My torso muscles started twitching. Hypothermia was setting in. I resumed walking in place for warmth. My heavy legs protested, so I stopped a minute later. Standing so much after a stressful day tired me, and my knees felt weak. Desperate for relief, I knelt in the snow. The cramped space forced me against the outer edge of the snowpacked platform as my boots clunked behind me against the dirty pail.

The down under my knees compressed and lost insulation value. My kneecaps began burning with cold. Kneeling close to the snow surface gave my locked-ahead eyes a new sight. Nearby I saw the feathery edge of a snow bridge hanging out over an inky black crevasse. The menacing hole waited a poop-bag toss away. What if I tripped? What if another aftershock hit and I slipped inside? With everyone asleep, no one would ever know what had happened to me; I would simply be gone when my teammates woke up.

This is dangerous. This has to stop. Rodney would be furious with me.

"Hi, Mr. Davidson. I'm really sorry, but Anderson is talking with someone in the studio. It's going to be another ten minutes."

"I'm sorry, but I can't wait anymore. Let's forget this."

"What? You won't wait a few more minutes to talk to Anderson Cooper?"

"Lady, do you know where I *am*?!"

"No."

"I'm on a glacier at nearly twenty thousand feet on Mount Everest. It's an active earthquake and avalanche zone. If anything goes wrong, I'm dead. So, no—I can't wait anymore."

"Oh gosh! Sorry."

"Tell Anderson I said good night." I hung up.

I could finally crawl inside that sleeping bag. If our luck held out, the helicopters would arrive in seven hours.

13

My exhaled breath turned white in the frosty morning air. That water vapor would freeze into another layer of ice feathers on the tent ceiling. I checked my watch for the third time. The alarm would go off in another two minutes. I lay quiet while Bart slept.

Beep-beep. I hit the alarm's Stop button and sat up with my blue sleeping bag still around me. Bart unzipped his bag and crawled to our tent door. He yanked the zipper open and looked outside. "Clear as a bell."

"Yes!" I said.

With a flurry of gloved hands, we packed up our last items. I accidentally bumped the tent wall with my right elbow, releasing a squall of ice flakes onto everything in the tent.

"Damn! Sorry, Bart."

"I don't care as long as we get out of here today." We both laughed, and I nodded while stuffing my sleeping bag into my pack.

Five minutes later PK stuck his head through our tent-bound vapor cloud. "Morning. No hot water today. Helicopters coming."

"We'll be ready," I said.

The camp noise increased as everyone scurried about. I thought,

Please give us a few hours of clear skies. Ten minutes before the 6:00 a.m. deadline, Bart and I were standing outside our tent in our down suits. Almost everyone waited outside, too, anxious to leave. Emily moved about camp alternately conferring with Dawa and then talking into the radio. She walked into the camp's central open space and said: "The first chopper's on its way."

A small cheer went up. I gritted my teeth and squeezed my fist in a muted celebration. I wanted to stay controlled in case the plans had to be canceled.

Two of our guides, Justin and Phinjo Sherpa, moved closer to the temporary helipad stomped into the snow. They would manage the line of climbers and sherpas waiting to board the helicopter. Emily later told me that she chose these two large men because she wanted some muscle guarding the landing pad in case there was a mad rush toward the helicopters. But no such panic ever happened.

Our expedition leader Greg had insisted that the helicopters must carry out Nepali citizens and foreigners at equal rates to keep it fair. Emily picked out two team members and two sherpas to send in the first waves. Then she turned in our direction and said, "Some of you guys will be next."

I grabbed my pack as if a starting gun had just fired. Emily thrust the palm of her gloved hand toward us and said: "Hold on. It'll be about fifteen minutes."

Bart exhaled with a chest heave and clapped me once on the upper arm. I returned my pack to the ground, my heart rate dropping halfway back toward normal.

"Stay in camp until Max leads you over there," Emily said. Then she left to direct operations at the helipad.

I checked our tent a final time and took one last glance at the two gear bags we were leaving behind. The tents had to stay too, so I zipped our door shut. Several people marched in small circles while others stomped one foot on the ground and then the other. It was fifteen below zero, and with no food energy in us, we chilled down fast. Though the biting cold made the morning unpleasant, we welcomed it. The denser air would give the twirling rotor blades a better bite as the helicopter clawed its way through the weak atmosphere.

In a few minutes a rhythmic thumping noise rose toward us from below. A glossy black chopper popped above the lip of the icefall, blasting us with the full volume of its screaming engine. The helicopter stayed low to milk the marginal uplift of air bouncing back up off the glacier's surface. At our campsite, and at every cluster of tents nearby, all heads turned as it flew past. Instead of continuing three miles farther to Camp Two like the one had yesterday, this time the pilot cut a sharp U-turn and gently set the skids down on the snow seventy yards from our camp. The evacuation was on.

From our safe vantage point, we watched Emily and another guide approach the helicopter to be the ground crew. Wearing her blue down suit, Emily waved two waiting climbers forward. They started toward the open side door. Moving fast at 19,700 feet is nearly impossible. What looked to me like two fluffy people waddling lazily across the snow probably seemed like an anaerobic sprint to them. Although the helicopter could normally seat six people, up that high it could lift only three: the pilot and two evacuees.

The two passengers momentarily disappeared into a whirling ground blizzard of snow kicked up by the still spinning rotors. It looked like we were going to board the faster and riskier way, called "hot loading." Keeping the engine and rotors running while passengers climb aboard puts the aircraft and everyone nearby in greater danger, but it saves a little time. Shaving a minute or two off every load cycle could make the difference in getting everyone off the mountain before the weather closed in.

Once the door closed, the loaded helicopter struggled ten feet off the ground and sluggishly moved away. When the tail rotor cleared the upper lip of the icefall, the pilot tilted the nose down. The chopper rushed forward and downward simultaneously, like a canoe going over a waterfall. Then it disappeared from view. Base camp sat 2,300 feet lower and less than two miles away as the helicopter flies, so the round trip would take about ten minutes.

One minute later, however, I was surprised to hear the thumping of a rising helicopter. I wondered if they were coming back, or if something was wrong. When the chopper rose up from the icefall, its rescue-red paint stood out against the deep-blue sky. This was a different helicopter—we had more than one flying. The pilot circled above camp and landed at the makeshift helipad. Two more climbers from the standby line hurried over, and the loading process played out again.

To understand exactly what Bart and I had to do in a few minutes, I studied all the synchronized moves. I memorized the sequence, just like when I watched my rock-climbing partner execute the crux moves on a tough route. To keep myself and everyone near me safe, I had to do it right.

Once the red helicopter left, Max looked at six of us standing by and said, "Let's go!"

As a fit guide with no backpack weighing him down, Max set a fast pace out of camp, and the five of us followed behind. Our leaders apparently chose the calculated risk of having us shuffle about two hundred feet across the glacier without roping up. Tying in as a team for glacier travel would take time and add complexities. Plus, once we reached the landing pad, we'd spend even more time untying it all. And with helicopters rushing in and out, we couldn't risk letting any loose rope get sucked into the rotors. So, we left camp untethered for our five-minute walk across the glacier. This was one of those times in the mountains when speed was safety.

Walking unroped on the glacier for even a few minutes felt hazardous, like sprinting across a busy highway. I scanned the ground warily for signs of crevasses. We passed an open black hole five yards to our left, and I watched the menace from the corner of my eye. I wondered if the quake had opened any new crevasses underneath the snow.

The waiting area near the landing pad consisted of a flat-topped serac, or block of glacial ice, bordered by crevasses on three sides. We stood in the shallow snow trough that the previous passengers had stomped in. Justin gestured for us to wait while he went to the helipad ten yards away to talk with Emily. I looked for any malicious clouds that might slam the weather window shut at the last minute. The sky remained crystal blue.

Standing at the icefall's upper lip, we could hear the helicopter returning. The heavy *thunk-thunk-thunk* of the rotors echoed off the rock walls and filled my ears like a Pink Floyd concert. The black chopper stayed close to the west shoulder, flew past the helipad by about a hundred feet, turned, and landed ten yards in front of Emily. The rushing winds from its blades washed over us in an icy stream.

After two sherpas climbed aboard with packs, the aircraft labored a few feet into the air. The engine let out a high-pitched whine as the machine strained against the four hundred extra pounds that had crawled into its belly a moment ago. Once they pulled away, the chopper angled down the fall line of the icefall and accelerated. It skimmed about forty feet above the tilted glacier and flew away over the shattered icefall. Then it skirted around a few protruding ice towers and faded from view. Echoes of the pounding rotors assured us that it remained airborne.

My usually reserved teammate, Don, stared in its direction, shook his head, and said, "Holy shit!"

Because Don had randomly lined up in front of me, he and I would go next. Andy paired up with Nic, another of our teammates. Bart would fly with a sherpa that he did not know. I cinched all my pack straps tight and tucked the dangling ends away. The rotors on these choppers usually spun safely a few feet above our heads, but the uneven ground might raise us higher than expected. I couldn't risk any loose straps getting sucked into the whirring blades.

I'd volunteered on several mountain rescues involving helicopters, so I knew the rotor wash would be more ferocious when we got close. To prevent ice shards from being driven into my eyes, I pulled snow goggles from my pack and positioned them on my forehead. I silently thanked my hard-skiing son, Nick, who'd loaned me his excellent pair in case of windstorms. I'd planned to use them on summit day.

Emily waved her arm to beckon us closer, so Don and I walked ten yards forward. Five minutes later we heard a chopper returning. We held our backpacks next to us; carrying them was safer than wearing the packs and then taking them off while under the blades. Emily aimed one finger skyward and thrust her hand toward us. One minute. She knelt in the snow, so we did too.

I took the GoPro from my chest pocket and powered it up. The red-and-white helicopter completed its U-turn and approached the helipad. I hit the camera's second button and it began recording just as I slid my goggles down over my eyes. My left hand held the camera while I clasped my pack under my right arm. Both of my legs twitched like I was about to run for my life, but I knew that a controlled boarding was better than a fast, disastrous one. Calm down, I thought.

The pilot eased the aircraft lower until the two skids touched the snow-packed glacier. The helipad crewman grabbed the handle of the side door. Emily stood halfway into a hunched position and stayed low to remind us that we should too. Don leaned forward from the waist and scrambled toward the chopper. I stood in a low crouch and started after him. I saw Emily mouthing words, but I only heard a vibrating roar as the pilot kept the engine revved high. As I passed by Emily on the narrow approach path, I got her point. She waved her hand frantically toward the ground: Keep your head down so it doesn't get taken off.

I hurried as fast as I could in my heavy boots and bulky suit. Don tossed his pack through the helicopter's hatchway and scooted inside in one smooth move. To prevent me from throwing my pack onto Don, the ground man gestured for me to hand it to him. I did and then slid in next to Don. Our ground man shoved my bag toward me and slammed the door shut. The noise level dropped by half. Getting aboard felt like it took a long time, but my video later revealed that only twenty-eight seconds passed between the helicopter landing and the door closing.

A glance around the cabin revealed that the passenger seats had been taken out to save weight. No seats meant no seatbelts. Don and I sprawled on the floor behind the pilot and hoped for the best. The Nepali aviator focused on his instruments and never acknowledged our presence. Five seconds later he applied all the power he had. The cabin floor shuddered, and then we floated up a few feet.

I pointed the running video camera through the closed window at about fifteen people lined up on the glacier. They gathered near a second snow helipad about eighty yards to the south, waiting their turn to escape.

Our chopper wallowed about thirty feet forward past the icefall's upper lip. For an instant we hovered directly over a gaping blue crevasse. I stared straight down the dragon's throat. Once the tail rotor cleared the ice behind us, the nose dipped a few degrees and we glided away from the helipad.

I looked to my right at Don. A white stream of exhaled vapor poured from his mouth into the icy cabin. Wearing a forced smile, he said in a soft voice, "Hey."

The helicopter nose tipped steeper, and we accelerated like a roller coaster plunging into the first drop. We seemed to be half flying and half falling as gravity pulled us down the mountain. As we descended into the ever-thickening air, the engine gathered more power, which the pilot used to rush ahead even faster.

I stared out the window, mesmerized. Beneath us a hundred exposed crevasses slid by in the first thirty seconds. Crumbling ice castles leaned over the dark openings. Many of the crevasse lips and ice blocks looked old, with worn edges rounded by sun, wind, and time. But several straight-line fractures looked clean and angular. Their sharp edges still held slender ice swords that protruded into the air against gravity. Such delicate features must have been freshly formed by the quake and its aftershocks.

We skimmed fifty feet above the glacier. I looked for ladders and any of the two miles of rope between base camp and Camp One. Two days ago all of it had formed a ludicrous but usable pathway through the Khumbu Icefall. Now I saw nothing but crumpled ice.

About five hundred vertical feet below Camp One, the rock walls on both sides squeezed toward each other. This constriction accelerated the Khumbu Glacier ahead at a quick four feet per day and shattered the ice into its most tumultuous mess. With no lateral space for the flowing ice to go, the shifting blocks either got shoved up or dropped down. Protruding ice towers and yawning crevasse holes sheared past one another every few yards. The jagged openings below us looked like the gaping mouths of a hundred hungry dragons. We whizzed past, fifty feet above them, like tiny prey passing by just out of reach.

Flying over the icefall was a rare thing. Until twenty years ago, helicopters weren't powerful enough to carry passengers at this altitude. Even though modern choppers now can, the extreme risks discourage most mountain pilots from even trying. And since Everest sits in a national park, the Nepali government limited flights above base camp to emergencies only. It flashed through my mind that I might be one of the only geologists ever to have such an amazing perspective of the icefall. I tried studying the frozen landscape as a glaciologist, but it's tough to make meaningful observations when the observing scientist lies sprawled on a helicopter floor, terrified by the savage terrain zipping past.

At the icefall's narrowest constriction, we flew so near the wall that I couldn't see any blue sky. The side window revealed only dark rock and gray ice. My close-up view of a protruding ice tower revealed fresh fractures cutting through it in all directions, probably from the earthquake. That ancient glacial block had grown over ten millennia as microscopic snowflakes coalesced. It had splintered in a single moment when continental plates collided.

Halfway down the icefall, the steady chorus of engine and rotors humming was suddenly joined by a deep, rumbling vibration and the helicopter shook hard. I darted my eyes around the cabin looking for any problems. Nothing seemed amiss, and the daring pilot remained composed. I hoped it was just the rising temperature or thickening air at lower altitude that made the chopper shake so much.

14

The pilot veered left. My throat squeezed tight. Then I realized he was probably making room for the other helicopter headed back to Camp One. My window continued to provide a closer-than-I-wanted view of the adjacent rock wall. Our distance from the mountain face looked to be about seventy feet. It was enough for the blades not to hit the cliff, as long as we didn't fly into shifting air currents.

We turned southwest, toward open air space. I relaxed a bit when blue sky filled my window again. As I recognized a hanging glacier on Nuptse's west face, I realized we'd cleared the icefall. Below us the glacier flattened out on the valley floor. I spotted the ice pinnacles we'd trained on a week earlier, but among the white pillars, some bright-colored objects lay scattered about. As the chopper dipped lower, I identified one purple blob as a sleeping bag. Nearby the yellow remains of a shredded tent draped across the ice. Then I noticed hundreds of other colorful possessions strewn all over the glacier. Blue barrels. Green pants. Suddenly I realized that the rainbow of mangled equipment must have been blasted out of base camp by the avalanche. Dread filled my stomach.

Our helicopter flew past camp's southern edge. I wondered if the pilot planned to take us farther down the valley. Then the chopper cut a wide rightward U-turn about sixty feet above the ground and headed back toward our base camp. When I identified the main IMG dining tent nearby, I felt as excited as a small child recognizing its own neighborhood out of the car window. We were going to make it.

Captivated by the promise of safe ground, I flinched when three loud beeps emanated from my right hand. The video camera battery had died. A spike of annoyance flashed through me as I realized I wouldn't record any landing footage, but it was for the best. Exiting a whirling helicopter presented as many opportunities for mishap as climbing aboard, especially when the passengers were as overwrought as we were. A safe exit was better than more video. I dropped the camera into my chest pocket and prepared to land.

The chopper slowed, and the ground rose to meet us. Out the left-side window I recognized Greg, all six foot five inches of him, in his jeans and blue down jacket. Three much shorter men stood by his side.

With a slight bump we landed at base camp. The Nepali ground crew next to Greg rushed forward. One opened the door, and a second man forcefully took the backpack from my arms, probably to make sure I didn't lift it above my shoulder out of habit while still underneath the blades. As I stepped onto the ground, the third attendant came to the helicopter's side holding a rectangular five-gallon can. I smelled jet fuel. Spending twenty years cleaning up petroleum spills meant that my nose could readily identify fuel types. With us still exiting and the blades spinning full speed above our heads, the Nepali man began sloshing fuel into the chopper's tank. Loading flammable fuel like that was extremely dangerous, but the gamble saved a few more valuable minutes. The noise, the rotor wash, and the sharp smell of fuel being hot-loaded an arm's length away made for an overwhelming first five seconds in base camp.

I kept my head down and moved out from under the blades with Don a few strides behind. Greg stepped forward and gave me a quick welcome hug. Then he pointed wordlessly toward the main dining tent. I walked partway there and then looked back at the helipad. After loading a few gallons on board, the refueler stepped back. Apparently he didn't refill the whole tank but instead added only enough fuel for another round trip to the Western Cwm. Flying with a partially empty tank gave the machine a little more power and maneuverability. They were cutting every corner to make this airlift work.

For two days my worries about the glacier possibly collapsing out from underneath us had gnawed at me. Now pebbles grinding beneath my feet suggested that we were back on what should be solid ground. But with the recent quakes, the earth no longer seemed as trustworthy as it once had.

I pushed open the dining tent door flap and stepped inside. After ten days of sharing meals and companionship in there, it had become the closest thing to a family kitchen that we had. Alone, I exhaled with relief and flopped into a dark-blue camp chair. My arms drooped to the sides and my legs splayed wide on the frozen dirt floor. Slumped and still, I gazed at an orange coffee cup with unfocused eyes. I couldn't believe we'd made it off the mountain.

The door flap rustled and in came Kaji Sherpa, from Kerung, carrying a small plate of food. Kaji served as our head cook, and we knew each other from our Tibet expedition six years earlier. He looked troubled but grinned a little when our eyes met. I stood up and smiled at his friendly face. When I gave Kaji a hug, he put his free arm around my shoulders. We stood still for a moment, our foreheads touching.

Outside, the helicopter engine screamed while revving for takeoff. Kaji put the plate on the table and gestured for me to eat. To thank him, I put my palms and fingers together in front of my chin and lowered my head to him. He returned the bow and left. The helicopter shrieked away, and the dining tent fell silent.

Base camp seemed about thirty degrees warmer than the glacier had just five minutes earlier. Already overheating, I unzipped the down suit to my waist. I sat down, slathered fake butter on the cold pancakes, and doused the stack with the sickly-sweet brown goo that passed for pancake syrup. The phony sugar sludge I'd disdained for weeks now tasted like exquisite maple syrup tapped from New England's finest trees. I closed my eyes, thankful for the food and the gift of another day.

The familiar food and shelter made me feel safer. But with the deadly avalanche having missed our tents by less than a hundred yards, I knew that base camp wasn't safe. After all, the deaths had happened at the foot of the mountain, not up high where Everest fatalities usually occur. We were still a long way from being safe, but when PK, Bart, and the rest of the team got down, at least we'd all be together.

My friend Andrew Towne ducked his head under the doorway and stepped inside. His thin frame and lack of a down suit made him half as wide as me.

"Jim!"

"Andrew, it's damn good to see you!"

"You too. We're glad you guys were okay up there. Is everyone coming down?"

"Yeah, it'll take a while because they're only carrying two at a time."

While picking at the pancakes, I asked, "How was it here?"

Andrew's smile dropped. He opened his mouth to say something, paused a moment, and then closed it again. Finally he said, "It was pretty bad. People kept bringing the injured here. We threw all the dining tables and chairs outside, and this became a hospital tent."

We fell silent. I looked around and noticed that the dining tent contents had been shuffled around since a few days ago. It must have been awful inside this unheated tent with walking wounded staggering in and bleeding patients being carried through the doorway. What had been done to save them? What about the ones they couldn't save? I dared not ask the haunted man sitting before me.

Later, we discussed those terrible base camp events in detail. Andrew and many other volunteers carried, comforted, and cared for dozens of wounded people all day and all night. During the nearly twenty-four-hour incident, the volunteers had different jobs asked of them. Initially,

Andrew acted as what he described as a "traffic cop," directing the seriously wounded over to our communications tent, where several doctors worked frantically. Less seriously injured people, like those with broken limbs, got steered to one of our three dining tents being used as hospital wards.

Andrew also directed the placement of corpses next to our outdoor stone altar. He personally helped carry several of the deceased to the spot as "the line of bodies kept getting longer."

All night, Andrew and the others fought to keep the patients warm by distributing hot-water bottles and sleeping bags that had been scavenged from IMG tents and neighboring teams. After the wounded were flown off to more definitive medical care on April 26, Andrew and a few stoic volunteers used bleach and water to scrub blood off the dining tent walls. The suffering and sacrifice endured in base camp after the quake seemed overwhelming. Similar survival scenes, and worse, played out all over Nepal. That morning in our reassembled main dining tent, Andrew's sharp jawline clenched tight and his eyes lingered on the table. After a moment, he lifted his head and said, "I hope I never go through that again."

"Where are they all now?" I asked.

"Most got flown to Pheriche and then Lukla. Some of the worst went on to Kathmandu."

"What's the plan for us?"

"We're just waiting for all you guys to get down, then we'll see."

Another helicopter landing nearby made the tent walls quiver and filled the air with thumping noise. A minute later Bart walked into the mess tent, looking odd in his high-altitude boots and bulky down suit. He seemed stunned and relieved to be standing there. We poured him a cup of water and he plunked down into a chair. I rose to go call Gloria.

Andrew said, "Before you go to your tent, during the medical emergency, we needed foam pads and other things for the wounded. We took gear from wherever we could grab it. Some of your stuff may be missing."

He shrugged in a small gesture of apology. Someone said, "No worries—it's just stuff. Good job taking care of everyone."

Andrew squeezed his lips together and nodded slowly. As I left he told me that several doctors from the medical camp were temporarily staying in our communications (comms) tent.

Bright light stabbed my eyes when I stepped outside. I smiled because the sun's presence meant the helicopter evacuations would continue. With almost one hundred people waiting at Camp One when I left and seventy more soon arriving there from Camp Two, we really needed the weather to hold. Over the icefall I heard the heavy *whap-whap-whap* of a helicopter heading back up. I thought, Keep 'em flying, boys.

In my clunky boots I plodded down the rocky footpath toward my tent. I'd walked the familiar trail a hundred times since arriving in base camp two weeks ago, so when I spotted an unfamiliar object, I stopped. It was a tangled pile of clothing frozen into the mud alongside the trail. We always kept a tidy camp, so that shouldn't have been there. My eyes locked on red-brown smears staining the sleeves of a white shirt. Blood. I wondered if the shirt's owner survived. Then I realized that the mangled clothes were a warning of how different camp had become.

I looked around as if I'd suddenly noticed that someone had moved things around inside my house. Near my tent I spied a bigger debris pile. I crept cautiously down the trail and stopped in front of a rubbish heap containing three foam mattress pads. Since they were half-covered beneath yesterday's snowfall, I couldn't tell how much of the brown staining on them was glacial mud and how much was dried blood.

After taking three strides toward my tent I zipped it open. Half expecting that my gear had been taken to help patients, I was surprised to see things undisturbed. I sat in the tent with my legs protruding outside and stared at the discarded mattresses eight feet away. The sleeping pads didn't look familiar, so I presumed they came from another expedition whose members had used them as impromptu stretchers to carry wounded people into our camp.

I thought about discarding the bloody sleeping pads, but where? Maybe I could clean them and return them to their owners. But among hundreds of scattered base-camp residents, I wouldn't be able to determine who owned them. The owners might be waiting at Camp One, leaving base camp, or lying in a Kathmandu hospital. Feeling sluggish and confused, I flopped onto the tent floor. I closed my eyes and imagined echoes of the mad crisis that had erupted around my tent two days ago. With all those people hurt and killed, it must have been terrifying chaos.

Gloria knew we planned on flying out, and she hadn't heard from me in a few hours. She'd be worried. Although I could text her, that wouldn't cut it—she would want to hear my voice. And I needed to hear hers. Without bothering to remove my down suit, I stood up and walked fifteen yards to Bart's tent to borrow the phone. Then I hustled across camp holding it.

One of my teammates five tents away saw me and shouted, "Hey, Jim! Glad you're down!"

I waved but kept walking. For the best reception, I climbed a small hill at the edge of camp. I extended the antenna and powered up the phone. Facing toward Colorado, I dialed. When Gloria answered, I immediately felt a little better.

"Glo, I'm safe. We're back in base camp."

"Oh thank God! It's a miracle you're off the mountain."

I paused and swallowed hard. "Yeah. I feel very lucky."

"Is everyone down yet?" she asked.

"They're working on it. It'll take a few hours."

"Then I'll keep praying for good weather there."

"Glo, I wanted to let you know I'm down, but I can't talk long."

"I understand."

"I'm roasting from standing here in my down suit."

"Okay. Go take care of yourself."

"My foot hurts too—my toes."

"Why?"

"Standing still in the cold last night for three damn hours doing interviews. I think I might have frostnipped it."

"Oh no. Go check your foot and let me know."

With a promise to talk soon, we signed off and I returned to my tent.

The rising temperature inside made me swelter. I tore off my down suit like it was on fire. Then I stripped off my stinky inner layers and put on dirty base-camp clothes that were a little less smelly.

I examined my right foot. The tips of three toes were blanched white. When I poked them, I felt a tingly sensation mixed with mild numbness. Thankfully there was no visible frostbite or frostnip. One after another, I pinched all five toenail beds and watched them slowly resume their healthy pink color. My capillary refill was slow but adequate. They would recover. My left foot checked out fine too. During thirty-three winters of ice climbing, I'd never gotten serious frostbite. Ever since I turned fifty, though, my peripheral circulation wasn't as good.

I pulled out the GPS and sent Gloria a text:

Feet are ok.

She wrote back:

Oh great! Thank goodness. I am relieved! Take care of your heart and soul.

Unfamiliar female voices emanated from the comms tent twenty feet away. After putting on dry socks and hiking boots, I grabbed my GPS and went over to the olive-green canvas tent. After I yelled a greeting, one of the voices invited me inside. I pulled the heavy fabric door flap aside and stepped in. Before my eyes adjusted to the dark interior, a woman asked, "Do you need help?"

"No, I'm fine."

The two women inside introduced themselves as Meg and Rachel. Dr. Megan Walmsley was an Australian anesthesiologist, and Dr. Rachel Tullet, from England, worked as an emergency room physician in New Zealand. Along with a young Nepali doctor, Aditya Tiwari, and support staff, they were volunteering their skills at the "Everest ER"—a field clinic run by the Himalayan Rescue Association, or HRA, which operated in base camp every spring climbing season. It served the medical needs of the roughly nine hundred people in the south-side base camp. Foreign climbers paid an up-front fee for the season plus a small charge for any medical supplies they needed. Nepali citizens were treated for free. When anyone in the Everest community had a medical need—big or small, day or night—as the lead mountain-medicine doctors, the HRA team was on the front line. During the avalanche disaster, they were not only on the front line, they were also under it.

The HRA camp had been overrun by wind- and avalanche-driven debris. In the first hour of the crisis, they had grabbed what medical gear they could from their wrecked tents, gathered their flock of wounded patients (which was growing by the minute), and abandoned their collapsed field hospital. The HRA team sent less severely injured patients to the Himalayan Experience base camp and then reopened their medical clinic at the IMG base camp. Then they managed the mass-casualty incident for twenty-four hours. Now Meg and Rachel were living in our musty comms tent.

Many physicians and medically trained people volunteered to help treat the wounded. As the official doctors for base camp, the HRA staff had probably taken the worst cases and made the hardest triage decisions.

"Thanks for helping so many people," I said.

"That's what we're here for," Rachel replied.

The avalanche wrecked their personal tents, so they had few possessions left. With their laptops gone, they had been unable to contact their families. I offered them the use of my GPS texting device. With wide eyes, Megan said, "That'd be great!"

Once I gave them a lesson on how to send a message, I stepped outside. Helicopter noise filled the air. Many incoming flights landed at the flat hilltop near our camp while others set down on raised helipads farther away. Those makeshift structures were circular dirt mounds supported by sidewalls of hand-stacked rocks. Several helipads scattered across base camp provided close access to most areas. I looked skyward and counted four helicopters working the tight air space between base camp and Camp One. More choppers had joined the airlift.

While waiting for Meg to send her messages, I looked around camp. Base camp sits on an outside curve of the Khumbu Glacier. The glacier's hilly western edge is mostly covered by mud, rocks, and boulders so that only small sections of the gray glacial ice are exposed. Beneath its rocky covering the glacier melts and moves, so the terrain looks a bit different every year. Transient meltwater ponds form on the glacier's surface only to drain and collapse later. Hundreds of colorful tents were pitched along nearly a mile of undulating terrain.

Base camp's midpoint, where the crushed HRA facilities were, was at an elevation of about 17,600 feet. The upper part of camp rose a few hundred feet higher than that, while the lower end, where the IMG tents sat, extended down to about 17,400 feet. The glacier's velocity decreased as it flowed down the gently inclined valley floor, and that dwindling momentum meant that base camp didn't usually move at a rate perceptible by humans. But after several quakes, and with more aftershocks coming, the old norms might no longer apply.

Meg exited the tent and returned the GPS to me with a hearty thanks. I headed off to check with Bart. When I walked past exposed patches of glacial ice, I studied them for any fresh cracks or other signs of movement. The superficial ice looked fine, but it was like trying to judge how dangerous a resting snow leopard might be by glancing at a few hairs on its back.

I found Bart draping damp clothes on his tent lines to dry in the sun. "Base camp sure feels different, huh?" I said.

"Yeah. Everyone's pretty somber."

"I know not everyone's down from C1 yet, but it still seems too quiet," I said.

"Most of the sherpas are gone. Greg let 'em go home to check on their families."

Bart and I talked about my use of his satellite phone. Since the prepaid phone minutes were running low, I offered to buy us five hundred dollars' worth of additional airtime. Bart placed the order electronically, but it was Sunday night back home, so he wasn't sure how soon the time credits would appear in the account. He told me that I could hang on to the phone to call Gloria again.

I headed past the comms tent and back up the hill. With base camp nestled at the far northern end of the Khumbu Valley, it was hemmed in tight on three sides by mountains that towered 2,000 to 11,000 feet overhead. I faced southwest toward the open sky. From my high vantage, I saw climbers, sherpas, and a few yaks leaving camp. The instinct to flee this deadly place was strong.

Gloria answered and soon asked, "How safe is base camp?"

I turned toward Pumori and Lintgren. My eyes scanned the high ridge where the avalanche had come from. "That's a good question. Hard to say right now."

"How bad is everything?"

"Our camp is fine, but everyone's shook up and nervous. I haven't seen the wrecked area yet, so I don't know about that."

"The news now says there are eighteen dead in base camp," Gloria said.

"Eighteen? I thought it was seventeen!"

"The count keeps going up."

Another death. It felt like a punch in the stomach. With the evacuation going well, I'd hoped we had turned a corner, that things would improve from here. But just a few hundred yards away, someone else lay dead.

I sat in the dirt. The phone crackled.

"Are you there?" Gloria asked.

"Yeah. Still here."

"I'm so sorry, hon."

I looked over my right shoulder toward the middle of base camp where the avalanche had torn through. Intervening hills of rock-covered glacier blocked my view, but I knew the destruction was not far away. Static hissed in my ear. To keep connected, I instinctively stood up.

"What are you going to do now?" Gloria asked.

"I need to check on Alan, but they have to descend from C2 to C1 before flying out. So he won't get down for a while."

"Are you all right?"

"I don't know, Glo."

Ten yards away I saw several of my teammates huddling with Meg by the comms tent. I kept making conversation with Gloria, but I was lost in thought about the new death and distracted by my friends gathering nearby. Another person walked to the group carrying a long-handled shovel. Something was up.

"Hold on, Glo."

I moved the phone away from my face and yelled to the gang, "Hey, what's going on?!"

Someone shouted back, "We're going to the field hospital to dig. We're looking for medical equipment."

A charge shot through me. I could help. If we recovered enough medical supplies, maybe the dying would stop.

"When are you going?" I asked.

"Now. Join us."

The electricity flowing through me doubled. This was something we could do to make a difference. Putting the phone back to my ear, I said, "Glo, I need to help dig out buried medical supplies. I have to go."

"Now?"

"Yeah, they're rallying up right now."

"Jim, wait. If it's medical supplies, there'll be sharps mixed in. Don't get stuck by a needle."

As a nurse, Gloria was right, of course. "I'll be careful and wear thick gloves," I said.

We exchanged fast good-byes, and I charged down the hill before my finger had fully depressed the End Call button. I rifled my tent looking for my leather summit gloves. Then I slathered a glob of sun cream across half my face. After slamming down a big slug of water, I grabbed my camera and sunhat.

I jogged over to Bart's tent. He wasn't there, so I tucked the satellite phone inside it. To make sure the group didn't leave without me, I ran faster toward the comms tent. I arrived breathless, partly from sprinting at high altitude but mostly because we were finally going to do something to help.

15

Six of us, including Andrew, waited while one of our guys went to borrow a pickax from our sherpas, who normally used it to carve flattish tent platforms into base camp's frozen dirt. In five minutes he returned carrying the heavy tool on his shoulder.

Rachel led our seven-person team toward the destroyed HRA camp. I walked right behind her carrying the spade shovel, while Andrew and the rest followed me. We took the gradual uphill trail that skirted base camp's eastern edge close to the white glacier. I watched Rachel's stiff-legged limp: Flying debris from the wind blast had slammed her into a rock, which smashed her kneecap and split open the flesh. She later stitched her own knee shut without anesthesia.

Ten minutes of slow walking—painful limping for her—brought us to an area with tattered gear strewn about. Twisted clothing and water-logged paper littered the ground. Bent kitchenware and a crooked ski pole protruded from the dirt. A single red boot lay submerged in a meltwater stream flowing alongside the trail. One hundred yards farther along, I noticed a laptop leaning against a dishwasher-size boulder. I stepped off the path to pick it up but stopped when I saw that the computer was folded like a taco. We all saw the destruction around us, but no one said much.

Another fifty yards up the path, so much debris covered the ground that the main trail was hard to discern. Only a few tents were standing. At one former campsite, shredded tent fabric draped off bent poles like meat strips hanging from a butchered yak's ribs. We were deep inside the avalanche runout zone.

We stopped for a moment while Rachel decided which way to lead us. I looked across the glacier toward the lower icefall. Out among the ice pinnacles, about a hundred yards away, several people were moving about. No one was climbing the mountain anymore, so I wondered what they were doing. I watched them meander slowly in one direction and then back the other way. Their heads were bent forward, and they rarely looked up. It seemed like they were searching the debris field for something, or someone. They reminded me of shell-shocked tornado survivors picking through a leveled neighborhood.

Rachel hobbled her way up a small rise, and we stopped at a flat bench. I was surprised to see the white hospital tent still partially standing. A bright-red cross on the side gave me a little flash of hope. The tent was built around a series of strong metal poles shaped into sturdy arches that were anchored to the ground. This must have allowed the shelter to withstand the blasting wind and flying debris that crushed the medical supply tent and sleeping tents nearby.

"We want to recover any useable medical supplies we can," Rachel said. "The supply tent stood right about here." She pointed at the debris-covered ground.

Our dig team moved in the down-blast direction a few feet and spread out. Two people started pulling half-buried items from the dirt. One climber swung the pickax while someone else manned the shovel. With thick gloves protecting my hands, I picked up broken glass and put it in a pile. Then I switched to moving big rocks out of the way. After a while we'd pulled thirty or forty objects from the rubble, but most of them were ruined. A broken plastic container held two dozen white pills coated in dirty snow. Two cardboard boxes of bandages seemed promising but were contaminated with mud.

When I found a sealed plastic bag containing a salvageable mask and hose, I smiled like I'd won a raffle prize. We switched jobs often to maintain momentum. My turn swinging the pickax soon reminded me that base-camp air contained about half the oxygen found at sea level. I took a shift digging with the spade, but each hard-fought stab of the metal spade produced only a handful of rocky soil.

The HRA staff spread a plastic tarp on the ground for us to put potentially usable items on. All the rest we tossed into a trash heap. After an hour of digging and poking, we'd salvaged about two armloads of supplies. Our trash pile had grown as big as a dome tent.

Toward the end of the second hour, our efforts became more futile. Digging any deeper meant that four of us stood idle while two people scratched away with our only tools. Moving our dig holes farther away from where the HRA tents once stood meant we found fewer medical items. Based on the debris patterns, I suspected that we'd begun to encroach into the overlapping debris field of another campsite. Our productivity declined, and the small pile of recovered items wasn't growing.

Finally I admitted to Rachel, "We're just not being effective anymore." Though we recovered some medical gear, and helped clean up a bit, it felt like we hadn't achieved much.

Rachel stayed to work with the HRA staff, and the rest of us trudged back toward IMG. As we returned along the streambed trail, I saw the same laptop again. Someone had placed it atop a waist-high boulder to make the computer more visible. Perhaps the rightful owner might find it.

When the path wandered close to the ice pinnacles, I stopped by a truck-size boulder. Spread across the rock was a salvaged tent, drying in the sun, with the usual assortment of wrecked gear scattered about. The boulder's overhanging west face formed a small grotto, and in that tiny cave stood a black cross.

It was handmade from scrap wood and bore no inscription. Someone had intentionally placed it upright in the undisturbed snow. I presumed it marked a special and sad spot. I'd brought my camera to the HRA dig, but I'd been too busy to take many photos. I snapped a digital image of the cross beneath the boulder. Later another climber who had been in base camp during the avalanche told me it marked where one of the four American bodies was found.

After a somber moment, my teammates returned to our campsite. With my camera in hand, I lingered to document the destruction. I snapped a few pictures of tattered gear and mangled tents. When I squatted down to take a side shot of wet clothing piled up against a rock, I suddenly felt uneasy. These were someone's belongings. Maybe that person was out looking for their clothes, or maybe they weren't even in base camp anymore. They could be alive or dead. Either way, taking pictures of their misfortune seemed wrong. I powered off the camera and put it away.

Going to and from the destroyed HRA campsite had only taken me along the edge of the impact zone. I felt obliged to see the worst of it, to bear witness. So I left the trail and angled rightward into the core of the avalanche path. The debris layer thickened. One battered piece of equipment rested atop the next. Walking without stepping on damaged gear seemed impossible. I skirted around the larger items, but I couldn't avoid tromping my muddy boots on people's tattered stuff.

After fifty yards of halting progress, I noticed that the higher ridges contained less debris, probably because the roaring blast winds had swept them clear. I snaked along the elevated ridgelines and skirted around shallow swales filled with the detritus from a hundred uprooted tents.

I kept moving westward, back along the flow path where the avalanche shock wave had raced through camp. No tents stood. A few naked tent poles stuck into the air like the bare bones of a fallen dinosaur. Man-made debris mixed with mud and rocks as if a bulldozer had churned through camp. The destroyed zone was several hundred yards wide. I was at ground zero.

Overwhelmed, I struggled to comprehend what had occurred. I wondered whose green jacket lay in that puddle, where the victims were standing as the blast approached, and what they were thinking when flying rocks arrived. I could scarcely imagine the horror and pandemonium. Trying to make sense of the senseless, I leaned on my science skills. Maybe if I studied the landscape, examined it, I could understand what had happened. So I started looking at the evidence.

Off to both sides of the destruction stretched a transition area of partial damage about fifty yards wide. Some tents still stood there, and I saw people milling about. My untouched tent was another hundred yards past the transition zone. Had the avalanche struck four hundred feet farther south, the IMG camp would have been pulverized. Subtle factors of geology, topography, and luck made the landslide a scary near-miss for some teams and a deadly direct hit for others.

In a few places I noted cobbles the size of grapefruits sitting on punctured tent fabric. The geologic principle of superposition—which says that the uppermost deposits are the most recent—meant that the avalanche blast had transported deadly rocks through the air and onto the tents. I looked farther west toward where the avalanche entered camp, but a high hill blocked my view. That hilltop would be the best viewpoint, so I trudged over there. As I walked, my feet sometimes skidded across wet, slippery gear, so I watched my footing closely. Nepalese rupees, American dollars, and bills from another currency I didn't recognize lay scattered on the ground.

From the hilltop the full extent of the avalanche impact zone was visible as a big triangle of wrecked gear and flattened tents. That razed triangle was about 1,500 feet in length from the upstream end, where it started, to the far-downstream edge near the ice pinnacles. The far end was about 600 feet wide. Altogether the avalanche blasted about ten hilly acres of base camp.

I slowly turned 180 degrees and faced due west, where the avalanche began. The starting zone hid 3,000 feet above me and a mile west. Much closer, though, was a sinuous ridge called a lateral moraine, which is an elongated pile of silt, sand, and crushed rock that got deposited alongside the Khumbu Glacier's edge. The moraine formed when the advancing ice shoved aside glacial debris over thousands of years. Stretching for miles down the Khumbu Valley, the ridge of rocky debris was hundreds of feet wide and rose two hundred feet higher than all the tents. Though that substantial berm usually protected base camp from debris falling eastward off Pumori and Lingtren, this time it wasn't enough.

Several base-camp residents who had seen the fast-approaching debris cloud agreed that just before it arrived, it shot over the moraine behind camp. Looking across the avalanche-blasted terrain, I examined the zone where the blast had overtopped the moraine. As I studied the top profile of the moraine ridge, a deep chill ran through me. The high protective ridgeline had a gap about fifty feet deep and a hundred feet wide. This low dip carved out of the moraine aligned precisely with the head of the avalanche debris fan. And both edges of the avalanche-flattened zone converged right toward the snowy notch. That shallow U-shaped groove may have been where the air-blast tsunami burst through.

Squinting, I studied the side of the moraine closest to me. The area right below the notch's curved lip was plastered with enormous tendrils of snow and ice. Their sharp edges and precarious positioning meant they must be recent, or else the intense sun would have melted them away. Nowhere else along the moraine exhibited these icy traces, only the notch. It looked like that residual frozen debris got smeared across the lip as the slide blasted through the gap. The geologic killer had left a frozen fingerprint right where it burst into camp.

Based on the mounting evidence, I concluded that the low, snowy notch must have been where the avalanche launched over the moraine. "Shit!" I said under my breath.

I tried imagining the mechanics of a liquefied wave of air and debris shooting through that opening. By constricting the flow, the notch's small outlet area had funneled and accelerated the flying debris. That increased velocity allowed the lethal avalanche to fly even farther across base camp and hit so many people. The notch's geometry acted like a pouring spout, aiming the avalanche blast right at base camp.

All the terrible geological pieces fit together. The earthquake, the collapsing wall, the slope, the notch, and base camp's position had all been in tragic alignment. Together they had focused the avalanche force, amplified it, and shot it right into camp.

"Dammit!" I yelled.

My feeble cry echoed off the rocky terrain. Alone on the hilltop, with seven football fields of devastation around me, I thought of the dead, the wounded, and the tens of thousands of people impacted across Nepal. We were minuscule before the Himalayas.

After a few minutes I gathered myself and headed south toward my tent. I walked slower than before, skirting around one destroyed camp after another. I passed two climbers chatting while spreading muddy clothes on rocks. Since I didn't recognize their language, I said the common greeting "*Namaste.*" In return they both replied, "*Namaste*," which means "I salute the god within you."

When I was about ten minutes from the IMG camp, I heard the frantic shuffling of feet scuffing loose rocks. I looked back and saw a scrum of six sherpas scooting along the trail. They walked in two parallel lines of three men each, and the faces of the front two men showed great strain. One barked something in Nepali to the others behind him.

The group was fifteen feet away and coming toward me fast. I needed to move out of their way, so I stepped off the trail. As they passed me, I saw that the six men struggled to carry an orange tarp. On that carrying tarp was a wrapped human body. A second tarp, a bright-blue one, tightly encased the dead person. Brown twine secured the tarp around the corpse. Although the body was hidden, I easily discerned the shape of the person's head, torso, and legs.

When they hustled by me, the rapid stutter-step of twelve feet revealed how hard they were working. After they went past, I saw the bottom of the victim's boots. Black soles. Worn.

I had volunteered several times over the years to help evacuate injured hikers and climbers from the mountains. Carrying even a well-designed rescue litter over rough ground is tremendously difficult. Stepping around boulders and stumbling over loose cobbles keeps shifting the load in unpredictable ways, which makes the work harder. Carrying someone on an improvised litter like a tarp is harder still. The lack of structural support makes the wounded patient, or deceased victim, sag. No carrying handles mean that the only way to get a grip on the tarp is to roll the loose material into a bunch and grab the lumpy wad tight in your fist. Hand strength gives out fast, especially when another rescuer loses his grip and you suddenly find yourself carrying a double load. Two steps more, another rock obstruction, and the whole load shifts again. After carrying a patient even a hundred feet, the carriers might need a break, but no one wants to quit. So the team stumbles on, struggling to rush an injured person toward medical care or to solemnly carry a dead person off the mountain.

Two yards past me, they turned right onto a narrow side trail. The skinny path meant that none of the six was walking on the trail. They had to step over, on, and between the loose rocks lining both sides. One of the rear carriers tripped, and the victim's blue-wrapped legs slid across the slick carrying tarp. It looked like the body might slip off.

I rushed forward and grabbed the back of the slumping tarp. With my limited Nepali, I told him it was mine by saying, "*Mero.*"

As he resumed his spot along the carrying tarp, the sherpa who had stumbled nodded at me and said an affirmative "*Ho.*"

They were moving fast, and I didn't know how to ask in Nepali if they wanted me to keep helping. So I held up the tarp on both sides of the victim's feet and scurried along with them. Being centered in the back meant that I was positioned over the trail, so the footing was better for me than for the others. I mostly carried the weight of the lower legs, so my load seemed light. But whenever someone else stumbled, the corpse shifted, and I momentarily had a big share of the weight. I clenched my teeth and gripped the smooth tarp harder.

I had no idea where we were going or why. I didn't know who we were carrying or where they were from. And between the frantic pace and the language barrier, I couldn't communicate much with my new teammates.

None of that mattered. We were carrying a fellow climber, one of our own, away from the mountain.

By the time we had hustled twenty-five yards, I was breathing heavily. At the fifty-yard mark I was wondering how much longer I could continue. From coordinated rescues I had been on, I knew that the designated team leader should be near the victim's head. The leader should monitor the team's performance, think about everyone's needs, and call a halt when they needed rest. Then we could all change positions to utilize different muscles before someone gave out. I sensed that this was an impromptu body recovery, though, and none of that applied. We weren't stopping.

I stared down at my weakening hands. The soles of the person's boots were six inches from my wrists. When we started up a small hill, more of the weight shifted toward me. Our pace was slower, but the work felt harder. The front carriers were higher than we were in the back, so the body angled downhill. About halfway up the slope, the corpse slid a few inches down the orange carrying tarp toward me. My load share doubled. One of the two carriers at the legs said something in clipped Nepali, and I instinctively shouted in English, "Watch it!"

At the top of the short hill we slowed. I felt relieved that we were about to put the person down on the ground. But instead someone spoke Nepali, and the head end of the orange tarp got raised about eighteen inches. Apparently we were lifting the victim onto a high stone platform. With the head higher than the feet, a rush of bloody fluids suddenly poured from the folds of the tarp. A pint of watery red liquid flowed out between the victim's ankles.

Instinctively I jerked my torso back while still holding the orange tarp at arm's length. I danced my feet out of the way as the death fluids ran off the tarp and onto the ground. I was more scared about possibly dropping the victim than about the infectious liquids, so I kept my grip on the tarp.

One last grunt, and the corpse was settled atop the high rock wall. Everyone let go and stepped back. Only then could I see that we'd lifted the body onto a stone-walled helipad.

I was dizzy. Only a few minutes had passed since I'd intuitively grabbed hold of the tarp, but those moments had absorbed me. I still didn't have a sense of what was next. Suddenly the sherpas stepped around me, and one said in English, "Thanks." Then they walked off in the direction from which we'd just come. I tried to find the Nepali words to ask what was happening, but I came up empty. By the time my dull mind considered English, they were far down the trail. They'd left me alone with the body.

Scared and confused, I watched them hustle away. Should I follow them, or stay here? I looked toward the victim's face, hidden beneath blue plastic, for an answer. My gut told me to stay. No one should be left alone in the mountains, alive or dead.

The departing sherpa crew passed the trail junction where I had jumped in, and then they kept going. I assumed they would return soon because they must have known I didn't understand what to do. I sat on the wall next to the victim. We would wait together.

16

The patient is lying in the snow ten feet ahead. He's not moving. Up this high it must be fifteen degrees below zero. Now that we've stopped climbing, we're going to chill down fast. I pull my down coat on over my other four layers to trap in all the body heat I can, but I never take my eyes off the patient.

My partner Rodney Ley hands our radio to one of the three rescuers standing over the sick climber. "My name's Rodney. You can use our radio."

"Good. I am Thomas," says the redheaded man. His English is excellent, but I detect a slight accent. "We found him two hours ago, lying in the snow."

"He's not climbing with you?" I ask.

"No. We exited the Messner Couloir and saw him there alone."

"Where's his partner?" asks Rodney.

Thomas shrugs. "No partner. No rope. No pack."

I ponder those strange facts. How could this man be alone, high on

Denali, with no gear? I glance toward the 20,320-foot summit, about 1,200 feet above us. Was his partner still out there somewhere?

I point at Rodney and tell Thomas, "He's a Wilderness First Responder, and so am I."

Thomas says, "Good. I'm a trained guide." He points at the black-bearded man standing next to him and says, "He's a doctor."

I'm relieved that their medical knowledge exceeds ours. I ask, "Do you know what's wrong with the guy?"

Thomas speaks in fast German to his partner, Stefan Voelzke, and to the Austrian doctor. Then Thomas turns to us and says, "The patient has water in his lungs and in his head. The doctor already injected the man with high-altitude drugs for his swollen brain, but he's not responding."

Crap. With both pulmonary and cerebral edema, we'll never get him to walk. If we aren't careful, this guy's problems could get us all killed.

Thomas moves to the cliff edge for better transmission and talks on the radio. I hear him repeating himself over and over. It's not a good sign. A moment later he returns to our small group and says, "It's not working."

I look at my other partner. "Terry?"

"I'm on it, Jimmy," says Terry.

Terry Parker is an electrical engineer. If anyone can get the radio going, it's him. Terry sits on a dark rock and starts fiddling with the radio, wearing only thin liner gloves between him and the biting-cold metal. I'm scared for my friend's fingers. A momentary lapse up here could get him frostbitten. Frozen fingers mean you can't work your hands or adjust your clothing. Soon you're hypothermic and in big trouble. Then the whole team's at risk.

With twenty-five years of climbing, Terry knows how to be cautious in the cold. We're all going to have to be careful during this rescue. Before coming to Alaska, I read many stories about the vicious cold and unrelenting storms on Denali. There have been a few amazing rescues up this high, but also a few terrible tragedies when volunteer rescuers had been hurt or killed too. In the first-aid and rescue classes we'd taken, the first rule was "Don't turn rescuers into patients."

During the Alaskan summer climbing season, Denali National Park keeps rescue rangers standing by at the 14,000-foot camp. But they're a vertical mile below us and a full day of roped glacier travel away. It's good to let them know we have a serious problem up here, but they may not be able to help us for a while.

I point at the sick climber and ask Thomas, "What's his name?"

"I don't know. We cannot understand him. We dragged him down from 19,700 feet and now we're very tired. He's American, your country-man. Go talk to him."

Standing still for five minutes has let me recover some, but walking ten yards through the crusty snow sends my heart rate soaring again. I lower myself to the ground, but it's more like dropping to my knees. I am near the patient's head. His eyes are shut and his face is puffy, like a boxer who's just lost a match. He has peripheral edema, from long exposure to high altitude.

The heroic German and Austrian team have the patient stuffed into a red-and-purple nylon bivy sack, like an uninsulated sleeping bag cover, for warmth. The patient's yellow jacket hood is pulled over his forehead. I lean over him. "Hey, buddy. Talk to me. What's your name?"

He moans. I lean closer so he can hear me over the wind gusts. His breath smells fruity, like bubble gum. He might be in acidosis, which means he's critical. "We want to help you. What's your name?"

No answer. Rodney comes over to me and asks, "Anything?"

I shake my head at him. "No."

Rodney turns to his pack and starts picking through our meager sup-plies. We're on our summit push, so our tent and sleeping bags are two thousand feet lower, back at high camp. We're carrying emergency gear, though: a snow shovel, a stove, and a small aluminum cook pot.

"Better get some water going," Rodney says. "We're going to be here awhile."

He's right, as usual. At fifty-one, eleven years older than me, with three decades of climbing under his harness, Rodney is a mountain veteran. He runs the Outdoor Adventure Program at Colorado State University, so his skills, knowledge, and instincts are well honed. Including our 1998 Nepal and 2000 Bolivia trips, this is our third expedition together, and I have never seen him lose his cool. The man's unflappable, even when everything's going to hell.

We don't have a plan yet, but nothing's going to happen fast. From previous rescues I've been on, I'm certain that things are going to get worse before they get better. Reaching the park service and getting a helicopter would be the fastest way to move the patient down. But even if we get through on the radio, will a chopper be available, and can it reach this high? I look at my wrist altimeter: 19,100 feet. That's about the altitude limit for the small bubble helicopter that the park leases during the climbing season.

If the chopper can't get here, we'll have to try bringing the man down ourselves. There's no way the six of us can carry him very far at this altitude. With our rope we could drag him partway down, but when we reach Denali Pass at 18,200 feet, we'll encounter one thousand feet of steep, angling descent through heavily crevassed terrain. We don't have the manpower or gear for that risky traverse. Ascending the two thousand feet from our 17,000-foot camp to here took us five hours of hard work today. Trying a technical evacuation back the way we came with our tired team might take all day or longer. We definitely do not want to be out in the open when the nighttime cold strangles the mountain.

I move over to Rodney and kneel next to him to see if I can help. I block the wind with my hands and body while Rodney lights the stove. He pours a little starter water from his insulated bottle into the dented pan to keep it from scorching. As he drops in small bits of snow, I notice that his gray beard has gotten scraggly after twelve days on the mountain. Excess lip balm hangs off his cracked lips, and his glasses are a little iced over. We both stare at the melting slush. After five minutes a few ounces of icy water wet the bottom of the pan.

Rodney slides his nearly empty pack under his knees to insulate himself from the snow. It looks like he's settled in to man the stove for us.

Using Rodney's shoulder to steady myself, I straighten my stiff legs and stand.

"I'm going to check on the others," I say, and then I hobble fifteen yards over to them. To improve the radio transmission, they're perched as close as they dare to the top edge of the rock-and-ice wall. Thomas is talking to the National Park Service on the radio. I ask Terry, "You got it going?"

"Yeah, I warmed our spare batteries inside my jacket. When I put them in the radio, they worked."

I clap his down coat–covered shoulder and say, "Good job, Parker!"

We exchange smiles. I lift my head and look toward the summit. The crown of North America is about two hours above us. During my twenty years as a mountaineer, I had dreamed about standing there someday. We'd been moving well before the rescue even though I'd felt lethargic from mild altitude sickness.

Rodney had craftily solved my problem, though. Instead of letting me plod along on the back of the rope, thinking about being tired, he made me get out front. He knows me so well that he figured my enthusiasm for the summit would overcome my body's reluctance. After twenty sluggish minutes, I found a sustainable pace and settled in. I felt better, and my mood improved. Energetic music by the Rolling Stones pounded away inside my head. I turned to Terry and Rodney, strung out behind me on our orange 165-foot rope, and happily shouted: "I can do this all day, boys. We're heading for the top!" The guys cheered in response.

All that had happened an hour ago, right before we'd stumbled into the rescue. There would be no summit now. How this guy got himself into this situation, we had no idea. But regardless, he's somebody's son, maybe somebody's brother. And that family back home would give anything for us to save him. The summit is unimportant compared to getting him down.

After Terry and I move back over to the patient, Terry kneels near the guy's head. I kneel close to Terry with my left side touching his right, all the way from our shoulders to our calves. We can share a little body heat and block the wind for each other.

Terry talks to the patient, to keep him conscious. "Where's your partner?"

No answer.

"Where are you from?" Terry asks.

The patient flutters his eyes and slurs out some words. When Terry asks another question, the man thrusts his arm out of the bivy bag's top opening and swipes at the air as if trying to hit us. We both grab his forearm, and as he struggles against us, his mitten slips off. His hand stops right in front of my face. His fingers are puffy, white, and frozen. They look like freezer-burned hot dogs. Thomas had told me that when they found the man he was wearing only one mitten. He has deep frostbite.

The man's strength runs out fast, and Terry and I slip the mitten back on him and easily shove his arm back inside the bivy bag. Though we do it to protect the patient and ourselves, I'm glad not to have to see his damaged hand again. We can't thaw his fingers while we're out in the open, so there's not much we can do for his hand right now. Besides, his fingers are the least of his dire problems.

Our patient spews out nonsense sounds with an aggressive tone like we've made him mad. It's his swollen brain: High-altitude cerebral edema makes water pool in the brain, but since there's no excess space in the head, the brain gets squished hard against the skull and doesn't function well. The confused mind senses things are very wrong but isn't sure why. Sometimes the struggling brain will blame the confusion and fear on anyone nearby, including the rescuers.

I say, "Take it easy."

In a calm voice Terry says, "I know you're hurting, but we're going to help you. Just slow down."

The patient stops thrashing and mumbles some unintelligible words. His eyes flutter, so Terry asks, "What's your name?"

"Jothf," he slurs.

I look at Terry to see if he caught it. He scowls and shakes his head.

"Tell us again," I say.

"Joth!" he says louder.

"John?" I ask.

"Josh!" the patient says in an angry burst.

"Josh?"

He answers softly, "Yeah." Then his shoulders relax.

"Okay, Josh," I say.

"Great!" says Terry with a grin.

Getting his first name seems like a major accomplishment. We're not even going to ask for his last name right now.

I walk over to where Thomas is talking energetically on the radio. There is some discussion about a helicopter, but there's no definitive plan yet. I trudge back over to Terry and tell him that Thomas is talking to the rangers. Though nothing is certain yet, Terry seems relieved that a solution to this dangerous mess might be forming. To raise the patient's spirits, I turn to him and say, "Josh, we're trying to get you a lift off the mountain."

With great energy, Josh slurs out some words. I lean closer and ask him to say it again. He opens his eyes wide and stares at the sky. Though still slurring a bit, in a loud voice he says, "I wanna go home."

These are the first clear words to come from him, and I'm stunned. Though he can't think well or say much, instinct has kicked in. In a drawn-out plea, he says over and over, "I wanna go home. I wanna go home!"

17

The avalanche victim's feet protruded from beneath the blue tarp just an arm's length from my right hip. I wondered if I should sit that close, so I slid twelve inches farther along the stone wall. Then I thought that maybe this would insult the dead person, so I moved back to where I sat before. My heart kept beating fast.

With my right hand resting on my lap, my elbow poked a few inches closer to the body, right about at the person's knees. Avoiding any thoughts about what the corpse looked like under the tarp, I wondered what had happened to the person. Trying to pass the time together, I struggled to make respectful conversation in my mind with the stranger.

I looked toward his torso and thought, I'm sorry this happened to you.

For a moment I glanced up to where the person's eyes must have been behind the electric-blue wrap. Does your family know yet?

I looked away nervously. Then I studied the icefall, a half mile away. An awkward minute passed. All we wanted to do was climb Everest, right?

A shuffling sound came from my left; the body recovery team was coming back. They were already at the base of the hill. I stood up, but before I could decide how to help, they charged up while emitting loud grunts. They were carrying a second body.

I stepped out of the way, and they placed another tarp-wrapped human shape on the helipad next to the first. All six men gasped for breath. I felt in the way, so I moved back. I didn't need to remain so close to my companion. They weren't alone anymore.

A new sherpa arrived with a radio in his hand. He spoke into it in rapid Nepali while looking into the southwestern sky. Then he shouted over to a nearby tent, and a minute later three more Nepali men ambled close to the helipad. Being the only Westerner waiting with them, I wondered if one, or both, of the bodies, were Nepalis. Was I intruding? Should I leave?

No, I was part of it now. I decided to stay until the body of my fleeting acquaintance was flown away. To give everyone some space, I descended ten feet down the hill. We all stood quietly for a few minutes, waiting. In the distance, I heard a *thwop-thwop-thwop* getting louder. Everyone cleared off the pad and prepared for the wind. I pulled my sunhat off and shoved it in my back pocket. With my right index finger I pushed my dark glacier glasses firmly against the bridge of my nose. They needed to seal tight against my face to keep the grit out of my eyes.

The shiny black helicopter banked a low U-turn over destroyed tents and settled on the raised helipad. I didn't have to duck, as the entire chopper was far above me. The man with the radio opened the side door and stepped forward to talk in the pilot's ear. The six body-recovery sherpas surged forward, keeping their heads down. They hefted the most recently arrived victim aboard first. Then they grabbed the person we'd carried together. As their backs arched, in my mind I heard the command Lift. My shoulders twitched.

They slid the blue-covered body into the back of the helicopter. As the radioman prepared to close the cabin door, I looked one last time at my companion's boot soles: Peace to you and your family back home.

The engine roared, and the helicopter lifted. I blinked the water from my eyes so I could witness the chopper leaving. Once he was fifty feet out from the pad, the pilot found the right trajectory and the chopper flew straight away from us. It passed out of the shattered avalanche zone and breezed over a dozen expedition campsites. The helicopter accelerated past IMG, where all my teammates would be gathered. Moving ever faster, it disappeared into the lower Khumbu Valley as it carried the two passengers toward home.

After the helicopter noise faded, my solemn duty was done. In ones and twos, the sherpas drifted off to the right. My campsite was in the other direction. It was time to part ways. I stalled for a moment, watching more sherpas leave the helipad area. One of the recovery team noticed me standing there. He turned to face me from about forty feet away. Placing his palms together in front of his face, he bent slightly from the waist, then bowed his head and hands toward me.

I faced him and bowed, returning the blessing. When I stood upright, I could barely see through the tears pooling behind my glacier glasses. I turned toward camp and walked half-blind a few steps down the trail. I lifted my glacier glasses off my nose toward my forehead. Salty water trickled down my dusty cheeks, washing small grains of Mount Everest into my mouth.

I plodded along the camp trail, stepping over tent-pole trip wires and fabric flaps protruding from the ground. When I exited the southern edge of the debris field, the terrain resumed its normal appearance: rocks and dirt, ice and snow. The landscape ahead gave few indications that anything bad had happened, yet acres of wreckage stretched behind me. Over my shoulder I felt chaos looming the way a beachgoer senses a dangerous wave swelling from behind.

Once I reached camp I stopped at my tent and checked my GPS for messages from Gloria, the kids, or my friends. It was the middle of the night back home, though, so there weren't any texts from loved ones. My in-box contained a half-dozen interview requests from news outlets. Too drained to deal with the media, I stuffed the device into my duffel bag. I sat inside my tent with my legs protruding outside and stared at my boots.

The rhythmic clanging of a soup ladle being drummed against an empty cook pot startled me. Our kitchen staff was announcing lunch. Tent zippers purred nearby, and hiking boots scuffled along the hard-packed trail as my teammates gathered. I dragged myself toward our dining tent, more for friendship than for food.

Inside the mess hall about a dozen of our climbers sat in folding chairs on both sides of the long kitchen table. People mixed hot drinks and passed tin plates of food down the line. Lunch consisted of fried potatoes, steamed cauliflower, and a slice of canned meat that sort of resembled Spam. Not fancy, but no one complained. The somber atmosphere suppressed our noise level, but everyone huddled with their neighbors, trading updates. Bart and I discussed how numerous teams were already breaking down their camps to leave. Someone shared a rumor that the nearest airstrip, in Lukla, and the Kathmandu airport remained closed. It was unclear how the exiting teams would manage to reach the capital.

One of us at the far end of the table had heard a firm number on how many people had died in base camp. Like a big, boisterous family, people along the table hushed one another and asked for the information to be repeated. Once the side conversations settled down, a lone voice carried across the mess tent: "The death toll's still eighteen."

After a few quiet seconds someone else repeated an internet report they'd read: Three more sherpas had supposedly died earlier in the day while trying to reestablish the route back up the icefall. None of us had heard that around base camp, though. With the upper mountain being evacuated by helicopters, why would they have been rebuilding the route? After a short debate, we wrote off the rumor as unfounded. Though media reports varied on how many people had died in Everest base camp, the most accurate number appeared to be eighteen.*

---

* Initial media reports between April 25 and April 29, 2015, listed the number of people killed in the south-side Everest base camp as ranging from "more than 10" up to "at least 24." Early reports

Ten minutes later Greg walked into the mess tent, and our chatter faded fast. Everyone wanted the latest official news. He stood at the head of the dining table, and with all of us seated, his towering height seemed even greater. Our sherpa team manager, Phunuru Sherpa, from Phortse, flanked Greg on the right. Greg paused and said, "All our climbers and sherpas from C1 and C2 are off the mountain."

A small cheer erupted. But with so many problems still looming, the positive energy evaporated fast. Quiet returned. Greg said, "The choppers got almost everyone down today, including the Camp Two climbers who'd descended to C1. There's a few left from a team that wanted to stay for now, but they'll probably fly down tomorrow."

A murmur of relief percolated from the group. Greg continued, "You need to keep taking care of yourselves and each other. We're not sure what the plan is yet, so we're staying here until we figure out our best move."

Phunuru added, "Maybe we'll go to Phortse. Some buildings are wrecked in the village, but not too bad."

During our month in Nepal, the IMG guides and sherpas always had well-defined plans for us. Their uncertainty about what to do seemed strange. But managing so many injuries and deaths while dealing with an earthquake posed new challenges.

I shoveled another bite of cold food into my mouth and left the dining tent. With all the Camp Two climbers evacuated, Alan should be down. Madison Mountaineering's tents sat a bit higher than ours, near the middle of base camp, so rushing uphill made my heart pound. Crossing into the destruction zone brought a heavy air of solemnness. I slowed my pace.

---

were understandably on the low side. Once the names, ages, gender, nationalities, and expedition companies of the deceased were confirmed, the most accurate information indicates that seventeen people died April 25. An eighteenth body was recovered on April 27. Reported death estimates of twenty or more seem to include the erroneous initial report of three sherpa deaths in the icefall on April 27. I confirmed with the person who made that initial field report that those three reported sherpa deaths did not occur. While the error was an honest mistake that emerged from the fog of disaster, it sparked some confusion about how many deaths had occurred.

Though I'd visited Alan five days earlier, nothing in Madison's camp looked familiar. They'd been hit hard. The avalanche's bulldozing air blast had knocked almost everything down, churned the gear with rocks and snow, and then smeared the remains eastward across the rugged glacier. Twenty yards away I saw my friend sitting on a boulder. My chest sagged as I exhaled hard. He was okay.

One end of his yellow sleeping tent remained propped up while all the other tents nearby lay flattened. Alan didn't see me; he was typing into his phone. I snapped a picture of him sitting among the wreckage. It was like documenting a weary soldier on the battlefield after the fighting had ceased.

I approached slowly. "Alan."

He looked up with tense face muscles and clamped-down eyebrows. Then his eyes widened and his jaw relaxed. "Jim!"

Alan jumped to his feet as I rushed forward. We hugged. My voice cracked as I said, "I'm glad you're okay, buddy."

We both stepped back but hung on to each other's jacket sleeve for a moment. Alan's short-cropped hair looked even whiter than usual against his tan face. His gray beard made him look a bit bedraggled, but he seemed okay. I asked, "When did you get down?"

"About an hour ago. We walked down to Camp One then waited our turn to fly out."

"How bad was it at C2?"

"The glacier shook pretty hard and we heard big avalanches, but nothing came close. We were just approaching camp when the quake struck."

I turned my head and surveyed his team's smashed base camp. "This is horrible."

Alan pointed at their chest-high stone altar and said, "Look."

The four-inch-thick wooden pole that had once held their sacred prayer flags aloft over camp had been snapped in two. A few inches above the base, remnant splinters pointed skyward, but the tall wooden pole and the long strands of colorful prayer flags were nowhere to be seen.

We sat on the ground. Then, in a soft voice, Alan told me that the base camp avalanche had killed one of his teammates, twenty-eight-year-old Eve Girawong. Though not a climber, Eve worked as a physician assistant in the emergency department of a New Jersey hospital, so she served as the expedition's doctor. While Madison's climbers made their first rotation to acclimatize at Camps One and Two, Eve remained in base camp with a few other team members and the kitchen staff.

When the quake triggered the avalanche along the Pumori-Lingtren ridge, though the slide was obscured by thick clouds, it roared down the 3,000-foot-wall. Eve and the others went outside to see what was happening. As the wave of wind and debris closed in on base camp, people ran in different directions to hide behind boulders or inside tents. The ferocious winds plucked poor Eve off her feet and catapulted her away.

Nepali staff members soon found Eve and tried to care for her, but there was little they could do for her severe head injury. When she died later, they radioed the news to Garrett Madison at Camp Two. Worse yet, Alan said that Garrett and Eve were dating, and that Garrett had invited her on the expedition. Garrett was devastated, and the Madison team was in mourning. Alan pointed to where Eve's tent had stood. Mauled camping gear stuck out from under the rocks and snow left behind by the blast.

About twenty-five of the thirty Madison tents were flattened or gone. Alan's shelter was one of the few still standing. He explained that he and his guide, Kami Sherpa, had moved Alan's tent a few days earlier to a quieter spot away from the mess tent. By pure luck they'd placed it behind a small hill that had protected Alan's tent from the avalanche winds and flying debris. With a teammate lost, their camp wrecked, and so much gear missing, the Madison team planned to leave base camp in a few hours.

Alan and I discussed catching up with each other in a few days farther down-valley, and then we exchanged temporary good-byes. I shuffled back to IMG thinking about Eve and feeling sad for the loss of someone I'd never met. It didn't seem fair. The vagaries of weather and scheduling had placed Alan and me in the relative safety of the upper mountain, while others happened to be in base camp when the earthquake struck.

Of those caught in the avalanche's path, some zigged to a safe spot, while others zagged to a place that turned deadly. Randomness played a big part in what was destroyed and who was killed.

IMG's electrical generator hummed away, so we took turns recharging our cell phones, satellite phones, and laptops. The Nepali Ncell phone service was still out, but the base-camp internet worked half the time. Our increased access to information gradually revealed the terrible scope of the quake's impact across Nepal. At least four thousand people had been killed, and the number kept rising. Many homes and schools had collapsed all over the country. Nepal pleaded for international aid, and other countries were responding.

Inside my tent I closed my eyes and tried to sort my swirling emotions. The deaths in base camp were terrible, yet the national loss was far more significant. Everest remained mired in fear, sadness, and uncertainty, but in contrast to many parts of the country, we were lucky. A small, scared part of me wanted to flee to somewhere safe. But with aftershocks on the way, it was hard to know where safe might be.

I checked the missed-call list on Bart's satellite phone. CNN, CBS, and ABC had the number from our previous conversations, and they'd all called me again. GPS text messages from Gloria gave me the names and phone numbers of anxious producers from *Good Morning America*, the *Today* show, the Weather Channel, and more. I scribbled the contact information into my journal and pondered whether to return the calls. The earlier interviews at Camp One had shown me how difficult those discussions were to arrange and how exhausting they were to do. But the world seemed desperate for firsthand news about the earthquake. Maybe sharing what had occurred would bring increased attention and more emergency relief to Nepal.

It was three in the afternoon, which made it almost five in the morning along the Eastern Seaboard. I started calling back news shows. Through a barrage of incoming and outgoing phone calls, I worked my way down the list. I tried not to move my head or body during the on-air calls so the connection wouldn't drop. Between interviews I walked laps around our stone altar to loosen up and fight off fatigue. As always, I made sure to circumnavigate in a clockwise direction to follow the Buddhist tradition of keeping my "clean" right side toward the altar.

The interviews continued until the metal clanging of the dinner bell forced me to stop. After eating, I put on two more layers of clothes, grabbed my headlamp, and hiked back up the hill to resume making calls. Night's bitter chill crept through my down jacket. I took notes and tried to keep track of who I was talking with. In spite of my best efforts, I missed a call from Anderson Cooper's producer at 9:22 p.m. Then *Good Morning America* called me four times between 9:30 and 10:00 p.m. I missed them all because I was already conducting another interview. With my foggy mind and cold-stiffened fingers, I tried dialing CNN. Then, with a double beep, the phone's keypad flashed a message at me: OUT OF SATELLITE MINUTES.

In frustration, I tilted my head back and let out a small growl. Clouds had settled over base camp, and I suddenly realized how late it was. I staggered to my tent and got ready for bed. As I put my gear away, I considered wearing my helmet in case another avalanche happened during the night. I put it on and lay down, but the helmet's bulk bent my head at an uncomfortable angle. I'd never sleep. I removed the helmet and shoved it into my orange duffel. That big bag and the even larger gray duffel bag took up a lot of tent space.

Then I had the idea to use the enormous duffels as protection. Inside my tent I arranged them into a V-shaped wedge pointed westward at Pumori, where the avalanche had originated. Sleeping with my head and torso tucked behind the berm would give me partial protection from flying rocks if an aftershock shook loose another landslide. Of course the barrier would work only if the next slide came from the same direction as the last. There was no way to know.

I placed my packet of family photos in my jacket's chest pocket, curled into as small a ball as I could, and hid behind the bags. It would have to do.

18

Thanks to the high slopes encircling base camp, the morning sky turned light long before any warm sun rays touched my tent. I hunkered under my sleeping bag's thick down loft and watched my exhaled breath chill into white clouds. An hour before breakfast, I trudged up "phone call hill" and turned on my GPS and cell phone. Along with interview requests from the Associated Press and Reuters, I read a short text from my daughter, Jess, urging me to call her soon. She understood how tumultuous everything remained here, so something was up.

When she answered the phone, we each made sure the other was okay, and then she said, "My friend Claire, from school, contacted me. She said her sister, Charlotte, was trekking in the Khumbu and they haven't heard from her in days."

"Jess, thousands of people in the valley are fine but still out of touch. Odds are she's safe."

"I know, but she was supposed to reach base camp on the twenty-fifth."

I paused. Thinking out loud, I said, "So if she hiked up from Gorak

Shep or Lobuche, like most trekkers, then she'd have gotten here in the late morning, around the time of the quake. Crap!"

"Her family's worried. Can you please check, Dad?"

After Jess and I wrapped up our call, I thought about where Charlotte might be. Trekkers and tourists are not allowed to stay overnight in base camp. So if she escaped injury, she'd have walked down-valley three days ago. If she'd been hurt, she would've been flown to one of several clinics and probably moved somewhere else later. Either way, I'd never track her down. I would find her only if she was still in base camp. If she was dead.

I went to our former comms tent and asked Doctors Walmsley and Tullet if they knew of any unidentified female bodies in base camp. They didn't, which was a good sign. Next, I decided to ask Emily if there was a list of the names and nationalities of the deceased. I walked into the middle of camp and found Emily standing outside our cook tent in her big puffy coat. Steam clouds from the hot cook pots billowed out the open tent doorway and dissipated above her head. A small vapor tendril rose from the coffee mug she held in her hand.

We moved a few yards away to escape the clattering pans, roaring burners, and instructions shouted among the kitchen staff. I explained the situation. Emily offered to make a radio call to the Himalayan Experience camp to see which bodies had been identified.

She soon returned and told me that four of the eighteen people killed in base camp were American. Three were male, and only one was female: Eve Girawong, from Alan's team. Emily also said that no female bodies remained unidentified. I returned to my tent and crafted a text to Jess saying that her friend's sister was not among the dead in base camp. After hitting Send, I exhaled hard. One more unsettling task was completed. Later in the day Jess told me over the phone that Charlotte had checked in with her family back home—she was unhurt.

Breakfast time had arrived, so I headed back to the dining tent. As always, before entering I washed my hands with liquid soap and ice-cold water from the community wash bucket near the doorway. There was a small pink towel for drying off, but I never used it. Touched by a hundred hands per day, the moist rag seemed like an excellent breeding ground for germs. Instead I shook my hands and let them air-dry. By the time I sat down inside, my damp fingers had gone numb.

Few on the IMG team thought we would resume climbing, but since we were still in base camp, theoretically it was possible. Over breakfast, my end of the table discussed whether rebuilding the route back up the mountain was even possible. The Icefall Doctors, whose job it was to keep the rope and ladder route open, had already departed. When the landslide crushed their camp, the survivors had immediately descended to the nearest village, Gorak Shep. A few people in base camp were upset that they had left so fast instead of staying and trying to rebuild the route up to the 180 of us trapped on the mountain. But they'd just survived a near-miss, and they needed to make sure their families were safe. Who could blame them?

With the primary rope fixers gone, some people thought we could rebuild the route if enough climbers and guides joined forces. But even if we gathered enough manpower, critical time had been lost and there was a significant shortage of ropes and ladders. The plan just wouldn't work. Besides, we knew that aftershocks were on their way.

Greg entered the mess tent toward the end of breakfast. He wore a polite smile but didn't exude his typical upbeat energy. Once he had everyone's attention, Greg said, "The expedition's canceled."

The tent fell quiet. After a few seconds, someone started talking, but I didn't take in their words. Instead I lowered my head and stared at my greasy fork. Forty years had passed since expedition books from the Concord library had first sparked my distant dream to possibly climb Everest. I'd focused thirty-three years on mountaineering to prepare. In the last year alone, I'd spent a thousand hours training and preparing. But the climb ended just nine hours after I left base camp. It was hard to believe that my one chance to climb Everest had crumbled so fast. My dream was over.

I kept looking at the dirty utensil in my hand. Even though I'd figured we were going to leave, hearing it said aloud by our expedition leader made it real. It was the only option. Besides, amid this disaster, climbing a mountain didn't seem important. How could we frivolously climb for fun when there was so much suffering going on? Our Nepali teammates were needed at home to dig out and somehow start recovering. With people dead and buildings collapsed all over the country, recreational climbing seemed disrespectful.

Greg told us that the Chinese were closing the north side of the mountain as well. So, 2015 would become the first year since 1974 that no one would summit Mount Everest. I'd picked one hell of a year to go.

In my tent I aimlessly sorted gear. Our team would leave base camp the next morning. We planned to walk two days down to Phortse, where many of our sherpas lived. We'd stay in that town full of friends and see what happened next. Other expeditions had already left the mountain for their uncertain journey toward Kathmandu, but commercial planes weren't flying yet. If scheduled flights didn't resume, we might have to walk to the nearest road, which was 115 rugged trail miles away.

Back in 1992 Gloria and I trekked from the upper Khumbu all the way out to that distant dirt road. We chose hiking instead of flying to have a more in-depth cultural experience. The twelve-day walk crossed many ridges and valleys, so the big elevation gains and losses each day wore us down. When we reached where the road started in Jiri, we hired a local car to drive us six hours along treacherous roads to reach Kathmandu. The IMG team was fit, but if we had to trek all the way to Jiri, it would be a long, discouraging retreat.

Walking between Jiri and base camp was once an integral part of all Everest expeditions. Then, after Sir Edmund Hillary spearheaded the 1964 construction of the dirt runway in Lukla, climbers and trekkers could fly over the lower part of the approach. Among the IMG clients and Western guides, it seemed that I was the only one who had exited the Khumbu Valley the old-fashioned way.

Of course our older sherpas had walked to Jiri before. Our head cook,

Kaji, once told me that he'd done the route many times back in the 1980s when he worked as an expedition mail runner between base camp and Kathmandu. Old-school knowledge becomes valuable when modern systems fail.

Even our safety at Camp One was attributable to the mountain wisdom we inherited from previous expeditions. Six decades of climbing through the Western Cwm had shown the Everest community the safest place to set Camp One. Each generation of climbers and sherpas taught the next where to pitch tents to minimize exposure to the avalanches that tumble off both Nuptse and the west shoulder of Everest. By applying that hard-won institutional knowledge, all 110 of us at Camp One had stayed safe when the earthquake-triggered slides rushed at us from both sides.

Another phone interview was scheduled, so I trudged up the hill. I tried answering the reporter's questions about the situation on Everest while redirecting the discussion to the bigger issue of all the impacts on Nepal. With thirty minutes until my next interview, I moseyed over to the mess tent for tea. There I ran into Willie Benegas, whose twin brother, Damian, had bravely checked out the upper icefall from Camp One two days earlier. The flamboyant Argentine brothers often helped out during mountain mishaps.

Willie was guiding two younger climbers I knew from Colorado, Jim Walkley and Matt Moniz. They'd arrived at base camp just before the avalanche struck. As an experienced rescuer, Willie helped with the wounded and the dead. To verify Emily's earlier findings, I asked Willie if he knew about any unidentified young bodies anywhere in camp. He didn't. Good. But our frank conversation apparently encouraged Willie to ask if I wanted to help him package a corpse. I balked. I didn't want to; it would be gruesome; horrifying, even.

Willie broke the silence and cut through the awful imaginings in my mind. "The dead man's American. I need help," he said.

The deceased climber was my fellow citizen. We were far from home, and the only way to work ourselves out of this mess was for everyone to pitch in. Willie had already volunteered for the grisly task; why not me? In a soft voice I said, "Sure, I'll help."

Willie shook my hand. Then he gave me directions to a helipad on the upper end of the avalanche zone and told me to meet him there in an hour. I tried rallying my energy for the next media call, but in my distracted state, I provided only clipped answers. Thankfully the call ended soon, and I steeled myself to help Willie. From my limited clothing supply, I put on items that I could throw out just in case my clothes got ruined.

On my third trip into the destruction zone, I took a slightly different trail from before. A lot of teams who had already left, or were preparing to leave, tried cleaning up the mess. They carried down what they could and stacked the broken remains into piles. I presumed the trash would be picked up later by the local environmental oversight organization, the Sagarmatha Pollution Control Committee, but I wasn't sure.

When I reached the far side of the destroyed zone where I thought Willie had directed me to meet him, there was no body at the helipad and no Willie. I walked several minutes to a different helicopter landing spot but still didn't find them. Willie's description and directions proved almost meaningless among the jumbled mess. I asked random climbers if they'd seen Willie or knew where a body might be lying, but no one could help. After an hour of checking other promising spots, I began a more systematic search by walking the rough terrain in an ever-expanding outward spiral. I couldn't find Willie or a corpse. By then it was almost two hours past the intended meeting time. I concluded that our work together wasn't going to happen. Either the plans had changed or Willie and I had missed each other.

My broad search led me into camp's upper portion, more than a half mile up the glacier from IMG. Colorado climber Jon Kedrowski was camped in that area, so I checked on him. I found his tent. Jon told me that he was in base camp when the avalanche hit. Like the other avalanche witnesses I spoke with, he said it roared like a hurricane as it descended. As a geographer, Jon estimated that the black-and-white rolling cloud towered several hundred feet high when it slammed into camp.

I left Jon and traversed west along the very upper edge of base camp, a place I hadn't been to before. The Lho La pass leading into Tibet—once part of the regular trade route for the mountain people and Tibetan nomads—sat a mere three-quarters of a mile above me. I scrambled up a rock-covered ice mound of the Khumbu Glacier to stand at about 17,800 feet.

The high vantage point gave me a good side view of where the avalanche had run. It coursed down steep slopes that carried the debris almost three thousand feet vertically and nearly a full mile laterally. Even after the debris wave smashed into the relatively flat valley floor, the wind, rocks, and ice continued another half mile horizontally toward base camp. The projectiles entrained in the cloud sailed across deep landscape depressions and bumpy morainal ground that should have swallowed the advancing wave. It was hard to understand how the debris had been transported a total of almost one and a half miles sideways.

Just before the rushing debris encountered the protective moraine ridge near base camp, there sat an enormous natural bowl that was about a quarter mile across. Instead of being filled to the brim with new debris, the bowl remained oddly empty. This suggested that the advancing landslide might have been riding on a layer of compressed air trapped beneath the rubble. That bed of air smoothed the otherwise rough ground surface and allowed the debris wave to travel far across the uneven terrain. Once the air blast spread out across the valley floor, it must have slowed down and dropped its load of rocks and ice right onto base camp.

19

The walk back toward IMG took a while as my mind kept considering the directions, details, and massive forces involved in the catastrophe. I returned to the main trail along camp's eastern edge, near the white glacial ice. To my left, large duffel bags and waist-high blue-plastic gear barrels remained scattered across the Khumbu Glacier several hundred yards from camp. I tried imagining the energy required to hurl such heavy objects through the air as far as three or four football fields.

By the time I reached our mess tent, lunch had already started. I'd aimed to be punctual throughout the entire trip, so I was embarrassed to arrive late. I walked in just as Greg started speaking. He said, "Now that everyone is finally here . . . " and then looked my way with a pretend scowl.

"Finish packing your gear this afternoon," he continued. "Carry only what you absolutely need in your pack. Put the rest in your duffel bags. We'll try to find enough yaks to bring everything with us, but we aren't sure that's possible, so you may get separated from your bags."

"We'll get them back later, though, right?" someone asked.

"Well, that's the plan, but hey—who knows?" said Greg as he shrugged.

Earlier in the day, helicopters had extracted the last climbers from Camp One and recovered the equipment we were forced to abandon there. I was glad that everyone was off the mountain and relieved to have my rice bag of gear back. Those of us who got our stuff back were more fortunate than the Camp Two climbers. When they descended for the helicopter evacuation at Camp One, they couldn't carry most of their gear. Their abandoned equipment and tents would have to remain at 21,300 feet for the cutting winter winds to tear through and the raven-like gorak birds to pick apart. Though it was unfortunate to have to leave their expensive equipment behind, it seemed a small price to pay to escape the mountain.

When I returned to my tent, I loaded my most valued things into my pack: communication gear, warm clothes, family photos, and my journals. Everything else went into either the gray climbing duffel or the orange trekking duffel: clothes, gear, books. I put aside items that I would give to PK as part of his tip. I pondered what hard-to-afford item might help him the most. One of my two down sleeping bags might serve him well up on the hill and back home during the long Himalayan winter. I added it to PK's pile.

The harsh conditions and high altitudes on Everest make eating difficult, so climbers lose significant body weight. To fight off that debilitating problem, I'd brought an extensive collection of snacks, candy, and energy drinks—enough to cram an extra six hundred calories down my throat every day for two months. All those snacks together weighed about fifteen pounds. Since we were leaving a month early, I had plenty left over. In case we had to walk all the way to Jiri, I put twelve days' worth of trail snacks into my pack. I placed the rest in PK's pile.

Later in the afternoon, the local internet provider, Everest Link, restored full wireless service to base camp. My laptop downloaded scores of messages and good wishes from family, friends, and strangers alike. Scattered in there were two dozen media requests, some of them three days old. I'd learned over the last few days that responding to a journalist, setting up the interview, and completing the call could take one or two hours. It all depended on how many time zones separated us and how many frustrating communication disconnects plagued our conversation. Many media outlets also asked for photos or videos. Getting back to all these journalists would take days of free time and piles of personal energy, neither of which I had to spare.

Social media were even more overwhelming, with hundreds of messages stacked up on five different platforms. The spirit of all that support and empathy uplifted me. But the thought of responding even to a portion of them seemed daunting. I only answered messages from those closest to me. The rest would have to wait.

After dinner I completed more phone interviews with CNN and CBS. I'd spread the word about Nepal's plight enough for a while, so I stopped when the sun went down. After bundling up for the night cold, I turned to a more critical call. Gloria, Jess, and Nick had been urging me to get away from Everest as soon as possible. They knew we were nearly surrounded by steep walls and that more aftershocks were imminent. I called the house phone and Nick answered. When I revealed the unknowns and uncertainties that could hamper our journey home, he tried to encourage me. I think I heard my previous advice to him echo back when he said, "Stay strong and keep the team positive."

I admitted my worry about unstable slopes dropping rocks on us as we trekked out. Nick quoted the old hockey adage about staying alert for approaching danger: "Keep your head on a swivel, Dad."

He passed the phone to Gloria, and I shared our initial retreat plans with her. She said, "I can't wait for you to get out of base camp."

"Just ten more hours, Glo."

Back in my tent, I slid into my sleeping bag and called Rodney. He said Alan had written a blog post about how Pheriche, one day's walk below us, was rumored to be flattened. But when Alan arrived there, he found that most of the village remained standing. After I described our team's exit strategy, Rodney said, "I don't hear any holes in your plan. And I don't sense any cracks in you."

My partner always called it how he saw it, so his comment reassured me that I was analyzing things clearly and facing reality. I told him, "In case the planes don't fly and there's no food along the way, I'm carrying enough calories with me to walk all the way to Jiri."

Rodney replied, "That's the Jim I know."

Even though I had stayed up until midnight, I exited my sleeping bag at dawn on April 29. The IMG camp soon buzzed with all twenty-five of our climbers and most of our sherpas packing to leave. I invited PK to my tent so I could tip him. After thanking him for his hard work, I gave him the sleeping bag and food, and then I handed him cash. PK nodded, smiled, and said: "*Dhanybad.* Thank you, Jim Dai."

Since he was staying longer to break down base camp, we would move down-valley on different schedules. He and I might not see each other again. PK looked solemn and said, "Sorry for bad expedition."

There was nothing he, or anyone, could have done to predict or prevent what happened. I put a smile on and, using the Nepali honorific for "younger brother," I said, "PK *Bhai,* you're a very good sherpa. You are strong and safe." We hugged briefly, then I patted his upper arm. I told him I considered him my friend by saying, "*Mero sathi ho.*"

After PK left I dropped my duffel bags outside the mess tent. Our skeleton crew of sherpas would weigh and stack them with fifty other big bags waiting until two dozen yaks could be rounded up. The stone retaining walls that usually kept the ornery beasts corralled in their fields had tumbled over during the quake. Up and down the Khumbu, no one was sure where all the wandering yaks were.

Though not hungry, at breakfast I forced down three overcooked fried eggs to get some calories on board. I returned to my empty tent. Facing our impending departure, I scribbled in my journal:

> *I'm anxious to get going home, but not to leave Everest. When I do it's an acknowledgment that the Dream of Everest is indeed over. I doubt I'll try to climb Everest again.*

I started listing the reasons why I wouldn't return:

Too unstable now. Too much cold & altitude suffering. Too much health stress.

The list continued:

Too much money. Too much time. Too much time away from Glo and the kids.

After another six reasons, I drew an arrow and concluded:

Just not worth it.

Before hitting the trail, I activated the tracker option on my GPS. This allowed friends and strangers alike to follow my descent in real time via an online map. While fiddling with it, I noticed a new message from Peter Sachs, the general manager of LOWA Boots in the United States. I'd worn their products for more than two decades and credited their boots with saving my toes more than once. LOWA partially sponsored my Everest trip, and Peter had become a friend over the years. As two crusty old New Englanders, we relished making jokes at each other's expense. But at this juncture Peter wrote:

When you leave the mountain, feel proud. You gave it your best.

I crawled from my tent, stood, and studied the sky. A continuous cloud layer hid the sun and gave the mountains a gray, dreary look. Intense energy still penetrated the clouds, so I slipped my dark glacier glasses on and pulled my hat visor low over my forehead. The coverings would protect me from the sun and, if necessary, hide my tears.

Over by the mess tent, my teammates and a few sherpas stood together, removing their outer jackets and slathering on sun cream. I knelt and took one last look inside my empty tent—my temporary base-camp home. Then I zipped the fabric door shut. Our base-camp crew would take the tents down later.

I hefted my heavy pack onto my shoulders and joined the team. A few of us traded one-word greetings, but no one said much. Jason and Caroline, the married couple from Canada, were hugging each other. Once everyone joined the group, Emily said, "Okay, guys. Let's start rolling."

The team began trickling out of the IMG compound. We exchanged waves with our camp crew, who would join us later. I stepped off the trail and looked toward the mountain. The summit of Everest can't be seen from base camp because the protruding prow of the west shoulder blocks the view. It seemed a shame not to get one last look at the peak, but it was just as well. Seeing the unreachable summit would only make me feel worse. I tried hard to be grateful, to be positive somehow. All I could muster was to think, Thank you for letting us come here and try. Thank you for letting us go home.

I turned to follow my quiet teammates down the trail. A few inches of melting snow covered the ground, so I took measured steps to avoid slipping. I stepped over loose rocks along the path and tapped my trekking poles on the ground with each stride.

The trail cut westward and rose up the flank of the lateral moraine. Maybe this higher vantage point would let me see Everest's upper slopes. I considered peering over my shoulder for one last glance. Like a parent who's just dropped off a young child on the first day of school, I felt torn. Regret and longing urged me to turn around, but both my desire to leave and my gut instinct warned me not to. Sadness and guilt and disappointment clouded my thinking.

I stared straight down the trail and tried to focus on home, almost eight thousand miles away. Don't look back. My legs kept churning forward, carrying me away from Everest.

20

Hundreds of prayer flags—blue, white, red, green, and yellow—fluttering alongside the trail delineated the outer perimeter of camp. Beneath the colorful flag strands sat several gray stones marked with handwritten dates and names. Some inked rocks commemorated people who perished nearby in previous years. Others were made by visitors who marred the landscape by scribbling their names and other graffiti onto the rocks.

Half a dozen climbers from another team lingered by the markers. Among those gathered stood the veteran American climbing guide, Charley Mace. At five foot eleven inches, Charley's lean frame hinted at his fitness while thirty-plus years of high-altitude sun and wind had turned his facial skin craggy. During the quake he had been serving as a senior Everest guide for Adventure Consultants, based in New Zealand.

Charley stood watch over two Western climbers about ten yards away. They huddled near a rock slab hand-carved with Tibetan script that proclaimed the ubiquitous Buddhist compassion mantra: *Om mani padme hum*. It is believed that when repeated often, those six syllables help purify the body, speech, and mind.

A middle-aged man knelt before the engraved *mani* stone and sobbed. A younger climber squatted next to him with his arm wrapped around the grieving man's shoulder. I stopped and quietly made my presence known. "Hi, Charley."

"Oh, hi, Jim."

On our trek to base camp last month, Greg Vernovage had introduced me to Charley at a teahouse in Pheriche. Charley and I had chatted a few times since then. Long ago, I had seen him give a slide presentation at a Fort Collins climbing shop called Eastern Mountain Sports. He shared stories from his 1992 ascent of K2 with his teammates, Ed Viesturs and Scott Fischer. As the second-highest peak in the world, K2 is one of the famed fourteen peaks whose summits soar higher than 26,000 feet. In metric units, that's about 8,000 meters tall, so climbers refer to them as "eight-thousand-meter" peaks. When I saw Charley's presentation around 1993, I was thrilled to hear firsthand stories from someone who had actually climbed an eight-thousand-meter peak.

I lifted my trekking pole from the ground a few inches, pointed the tip toward the two men, and asked Charley, "Need any help?"

"No. We'll be okay in a bit."

I asked, "Did he lose someone?"

"Yeah, but not here." Charley canted his finger toward the distraught man and continued, "That's my client. He brought his friend's ashes from home and had wanted to take them to the top, but . . ."

I closed my eyes and nodded my head twice. After a moment I asked, "How's your team overall?"

He tilted his head toward the ground, waited a few seconds, then looked at me and said, "We got hit hard. We lost five sherpas from our team."

"Oh, Charley, I'm so sorry."

"One of our other guys, Jangbu Sherpa, is in the hospital in Kathmandu." He paused and then said, "It doesn't look good for him."

A muffled sob came from the climber kneeling by the *mani* stone. Charley and I fell silent. The man's sadness over a past loss mingled with our present collective grief. Charley's words about Jangbu hinted at even more loss to come.

His group needed their space, so I whispered, "See you down the trail." Charley nodded, and I set off after my departed teammates. A rough path along the spine of the lateral moraine led me downhill. Next to me the Khumbu Glacier's melting remains sputtered their last few miles down-valley.

After descending for an hour, I reached the valley's highest village, Gorak Shep. I took a trailside break there with Jason and Caroline. We chewed dried apricots, and they chatted about the remaining descent to Pheriche. I stayed quiet, seeking the right words to explain how I would be veering off alone for the afternoon. Other than our expedition leader, Greg, I had not yet told anyone about my plan.

As my friends prepared to leave, I spoke up. "You two go ahead without me. I'm turning off on a side trip for a few hours."

Jason glanced at his wife, then turned to me and said, "Huh? What's up, Jim?"

"It has to do with my old partner, Mike Price."

My friends already knew about Mike. A copy of *The Ledge*, the book that I coauthored about the Rainier incident, was in our expedition's ad hoc library. And I had told parts of the story to several of our team over the last month. But neither of my hiking companions realized that a sacred place tied to that accident sat just a mile from where the three of us stood.

I explained how Gloria and I had traveled to the Khumbu Valley twenty-three years earlier to commemorate our friend Mike. On a cloudy morning in October 1992, our Nepali trekking guide, Prem Lakpa Sherpa, led us through a small and somber ceremony, a *puja*. The three of us stood near the craggy summit of Kala Patthar and hung five-colored prayer flags that had been specially printed for us at the nearby Tengbo-che Monastery. Prem Lakpa chanted Buddhist prayers and showed Gloria and me how to cast into the scattering winds the blessed rice we had brought. We sought to honor Mike's memory and help his spirit move forward. Inwardly I also hoped the ceremony would provide me a way to let him go.

During the three hazy months before we made that pilgrimage, Gloria had patiently supported me and nudged me forward through daily life. Other family and friends helped me, too, including the Prices, who warmly welcomed me to connect with them. Though I had been doing okay, survivor guilt and post-traumatic stress meant that some of my head, and much of my heart, remained trapped in that crevasse on Mount Rainier. If I were going to recover and reengage with all the life that I had ahead of me at age thirty, I desperately needed to find a way to move on. I needed a place to put Mike's memory and all the sadness. The summit of Kala Patthar became that place.

Standing at the foot of the 18,519-foot peak with Jason and Caroline, I knew it was time to go back. I needed to pay my respects and to see how the place felt to me twenty-three years later. I needed to check on Mike.

After I explained the heavy history and my mission, my friends offered to accompany me. I said, "Thanks, but I need to go by myself."

They understood but expressed concern about me hiking alone at altitude. I told them how I had cleared my plans with Greg before leaving base camp. He initially insisted that a sherpa accompany me, but when I told him the personal significance of my side trip, he agreed to let me go alone as long as I took a radio, which I did. After exchanging hugs with my two friends, we went separate ways. They followed the main trail south to Pheriche, and I turned northwest.

Several thousand trekkers hike up Kala Patthar each year, so the dirt track was easy to follow. The trail presents no technical difficulty but gains about 1,500 feet in little more than a mile. Partly acclimatized hikers sometimes need two or three hours to reach the top from Gorak Shep. After my two recent trips to almost 20,000 feet, I expected to cruise up, but my energy level felt low. Maybe it was from altitude, exhaustion, or emotion.

On the approach trek a few weeks earlier, I had purchased a string of prayer flags and a ceremonial silk scarf, a *kata*, at the Tengboche Monastery. I planned to hang them atop Kala Patthar to honor Mike. Beyond that, I didn't have a clear plan for when I got there. For certain, I couldn't re-create the spiritual energy from our *puja* long ago. I just intended to revisit that turning place in my life and experience whatever the mountain brought me. After all this time, the wrenching angst since Mike died had softened to fond remembrance and gentle sadness.

Hiking uphill at a steady pace, I thought about Mike the whole way. My memory kept pulling up snippets from the fun times we had shared as if I were flipping through an old photo album. Exuberant days climbing granite cliffs in Rocky Mountain National Park. Late nights swilling keg beer with our grad school buddies.

After ninety minutes I neared the summit area. There's not a distinct top to Kala Patthar, though, as it's not an independent mountain. What the map calls Kala Patthar is actually just a prominent bump along the rising southern ridge of Pumori. The deadly landslide four days ago had rushed down Pumori's east face.

I stopped twenty feet below the high point, suddenly agitated. I was close to the place where we had held the *puja*, but I couldn't recall exactly where. Then I recognized the white-colored bedrock of the triangular summit block, with its tricky scramble up the last few meters. Yes, I recalled making a food offering there by putting out some of the trail snacks we had with us that day. We made the offering to the mountain gods, but I imagine that goraks, which seem to soar over every Himalayan ridge top, ate the food after we left.

Powerful memories of the *puja* burst forth like a sudden glacial surge. I recalled how we had hung prayer flags about fifty feet farther south, where the ridge flattened. I turned south, and the memory was confirmed—yes, Prem Lakpa tied one end of the flag string to a man-size pile of rocks over there. Then Gloria and I anchored the other end to a boulder—that one! It all happened right here.

I looked about—so many memories. Prem Lakpa's chants. My quivering voice wishing Mike eternal peace. Gloria rubbing my back as I cried. Airborne goraks, squawking as they waited to claim the snacks.

It was long ago when I'd last sensed Mike's strong presence atop Kala Patthar. I wondered if some of his spirit still lingered. I said aloud, "Mike. It's me!"

Only the gentle wind made any sound. Empowered by knowing that no other human could hear me, in a louder voice, I asked, "Are you here, buddy?"

I heard no answer. So I strained to sense what my friend would be saying back. I imagined him saying, "Hey, Jim. Good to see you."

It felt weird, even a bit nuts, but I yielded to instinct and let a two-way conversation flow: me speaking aloud, and Mike answering in my mind. I remembered his Okie accent and the two-second pause before he spoke. Letting go of logical thought, I gave myself free rein just to feel what he'd say. I tried not to craft answers for him, but instead to let his words come to me.

I said, "It's been a long time, Mikey. So much has happened."

"I know. You've done a lot. You even got to Everest, like we talked about."

"I wish that, somehow, we could have evenly split the extra life that I got after Rainier. Half of the years for you, half for me."

"Yeah, but it doesn't work that way."

"It was really tough after you were gone, Mike."

"It's okay now, though."

My smile dropped. "I still miss you, buddy."

"It's okay, Jim."

I slipped off my loaded pack and dropped it to the ground. Then I sat on a flattish gray rock. I sensed Mike saying, "Your pack's huge. What're you carrying in that monster?"

"Gear, food for the walkout, my laptop, cameras, a GPS—"

"What's all that crap for? I thought you were climbing!"

Picturing his mischievous grin, I smiled too. Once he got on a roll teasing me, Mike would always pile it on.

"I watched you come up—you hike like an old man!"

I laughed out loud and said, "I *am* an old man now!"

Looking northeast, I had a tremendous view of Everest poking up among the clouds. Whatever summit view that base camp lacked, Kala Patthar made up for in spades. Its height, position, and the angled perspective it offered right over base camp all combined to reveal Mount Everest's spectacular upper pyramid. The West Ridge of Everest formed the left skyline of the triangle. In the middle stood the 7,000-foot-tall southwest face with its half dozen technical climbing routes. The summit pyramid's upper right shoulder revealed the last section of the southeast ridge route, the way we had hoped to go.

Jet-stream winds blasted a snow plume off the summit. The ejected ice crystals formed a tattered white triangle that stretched across the sky deep into Tibet. My mind sifted through all that had transpired in the last five days. And it skipped back through the years, landing on memories of good things and bad that had happened since I last visited with Mike atop Kala Patthar.

I tied one end of the prayer-flag strand to a high boulder, being sure to use the customary end that featured a blue flag, to honor the sky. Then I attached the other end to one of the many existing flag strings left by earlier visitors. Tying a girth hitch, I added Mike's white *kata* to the string. I stepped back and admired the flags fluttering in the breeze and carrying prayers aloft.

From my food bag I fished a handful of almonds. I ate half, and then put the rest on a high rock spike next to me for Mike, the gods, and the birds. After chugging down a few cold sips of silty base-camp water from my bottle, I choked down some dry yak cheese, then left most of it next to the almonds.

Afternoon clouds had begun rolling up the valley below me; they would only get thicker. If I didn't leave soon, I might wind up hiking down in a snowstorm.

I wasn't quite sure how to wrap up our visit. But I knew that I had to be honest. I said, "I'm leaving soon, Mike. And I don't think I'll ever come back to Everest."

Not sensing any response, I continued, "So I might not ever get back here to see you again."

"That's fine, Jim."

When I had left the summit of Kala Patthar back in 1992, I buried one of Mike's carabiners near the top. I dropped it into a deep bedrock crack, then poured sand and gravel into the crevice to hide it in place.

I stood up and glanced over at the outcrop where I had buried it. "Your biner's still here, right?"

"You bet."

I hefted my pack back on, then snapped a few photos of the summit area. Then I said, "I gotta go now. But I'll talk to you again sometime." Though I listened and felt, I sensed little. I smiled and said, "See you, Mike."

Two seconds later I heard Mike's drawl in my mind. "See you, Jim."

With gravity working for me, I descended Kala Patthar in about forty-five minutes. I reached the valley floor at about 16,900 feet just in time to get enveloped by a snow squall. My watch indicated it was 2:30 p.m. I'd have to hustle to reach Pheriche before dark.

21

The trail was almost devoid of people. My teammates, and everyone else who had left base camp that morning, had descended hours earlier. Even stranger, almost no one was moving up-valley. On April 29 the trekking season should have been in full swing, with thousands of hikers spread up and down the Khumbu as they streamed toward base camp to see Everest and its gorgeous neighbors. But over several hours I passed only two small groups. The disastrous quake and aftershocks must have stopped everyone and turned them around. Although enjoyable, the solitude felt eerie.

Snow squalls and cloud banks pulsed through the valley and hid the landscape as I descended. During one lull, the clouds thinned enough to reveal the soaring peak of Lobuche (pronounced "*low-boo-shay*") about one and a half miles off to my right. Fourteen days earlier, our team had climbed Lobuche East (20,075 feet) up to the false summit, a prominent high point that is lower than the dangerous true summit, as part of our acclimatization.

The descent trail cut through the bedraggled village of Lobuche, where life is harsh and hygiene difficult. Snowmelt water running in a ditch carried trash bits and flowed around excrement piles from yaks and humans. When Rodney and I led an expedition of college students through the area in 1998, we spent a rough night at the outpost. Many of the students became ill overnight with violent vomiting and explosive diarrhea, sometimes both at once. In our group journal, one jokester wrote a short poem commemorating our literal gut-wrenching misery there. (Seventeen years later I still recalled the rhyming punch line: "Lobuche, where out of my ass it did spray.")

I hustled straight through town, too afraid of its sherpa-strong microbes even to consider stopping. Two miles off-trail to my left stood the 19,049-foot-tall rocky summit of Pokalde. In 1998, after our CSU Outdoor Adventure Program team shook off the Lobuche illness, we went on to climb Pokalde and another high peak, Imja Tse, five miles farther east. The peak's first-ascent party, in 1953, attached another name to the 20,305-foot-tall mountain—Island Peak—because of the way it sticks up like an island surrounded by a sea of ice. Along with Ang Furi Sherpa, our sirdar, or lead managing sherpa, Rodney and I led all ten of our student climbers to Imja Tse's icy summit. That trip had pulled me back to climbing after the Rainier accident. Rodney's invitation for me to be his co-leader also provided my first expedition leadership experience, which opened up the high-altitude climbing world for me.

A mile past Lobuche village, I stopped at the somber collection of climber memorials. Dozens of stone monuments and metal plaques sprawl across a windswept landscape to commemorate some of the 275 people who have died on Mount Everest. It was not a graveyard, as most of their bodies remained high upon Everest's frozen slopes. Recovering heavy bodies from high-altitude was too difficult and dangerous.

Some simple memorials consisted of a dishwasher-size pile of field-stones, with one rock slab bearing a name. The more elaborate monuments approached the size and shape of refrigerators and they were made from concrete, stone, or stucco. Some were capped with artistic roofs. They incorporated symbolic Buddhist elements and were called chortens, or stupas. Chorten designs vary widely. In the climbers' memorial field, they often included hand-carved *mani* stones, or even elegant metal plates etched with the dead climber's likeness.

Perhaps the most recognized chorten was the one built for Scott Fischer. Along with faded prayer flags, the memorial sported black-and-white accents painted around mantras chiseled into a large boulder. The ground in front of the memorial was crowded by a collection of rocks left there by passing trekkers, friends, and fans.

I spent twenty minutes wandering around the pillars, reading the names and dates. As a climber, I wondered what had gone wrong for each person and how much they suffered toward the end. But when I surveyed the entire stupa complex, with all those gray structures stretching into the distance, the family man in me thought about their dreams that died with them, and the anguish suffered by their loved ones left behind.

Moisture-laden clouds closed in again, and soon the mist clung to my jacket and pooled into droplets that ran off my sleeves. An up-valley wind blew low-hanging cloud tendrils between the chortens, which made my anxious imagination think about ghosts wandering the alpine.

I turned on the radio and called Greg to conduct another check-in and to hear a human voice. Getting to Pheriche would take at least another hour. Greg told me that the teahouse we had stayed in on our approach to Everest had caved in. Other lodges remained serviceable, but to avoid being inside when the next aftershock hit, our team camped out. Greg described the location of the yak field that the IMG tents occupied.

A ten-minute walk from the memorials, two main trails and several informal sidetracks crossed one another within a short distance. I hiked fifty yards down one path before my instinct told me it angled in the wrong direction. So, I backtracked to the main intersection, studied the options again, and then chose the proper trail toward Pheriche. Having spent several days there during each of my three Khumbu trips, I knew where the village had to be, even though the valley was filled with clouds.

Darkness had overtaken day by the time I reached the outer edge of Pheriche. I noted several stone fences had fallen over from the quake, as Alan reported. Two hundred yards ahead, light spilled from a lodge and illuminated several rows of yellow dome tents pitched in a fallow field. It had to be my team.

At about six-thirty I scraped my muddy boots upon the lodge's stone steps. I pushed the heavy wooden door open, which let warmth, light, and noise leap into my face. About thirty-five of our sherpas and climbers filled every chair and bench in the cozy central room. My teammate and fellow New Englander, Fred, yelled, "Jim!" and a dozen beer bottles lifted in salute. After seven hours of solitude and remembrance along the trail, their joyful energy made me smile.

Several people on a bench squeezed in tighter to make space for me. I peeled off my wet boots, and before I could open my water bottle, someone handed me a warm Tuborg beer. I hefted the green bottle skyward toward my friends, tilted it back, and took a big sip.

I had not consumed any alcohol since arriving in Nepal four weeks earlier and not much in the month before that. By the time I downed a third swallow of beer, the first one had already settled in my temples. Several weeks of mountaineering weariness and five days of earthquake worries stepped back for a bit while giddiness and fogginess took over. The noise level in the lodge rose as tension gradually boiled off from the group. I ate a decent dinner and drank a quart of water before calling it quits at the outrageously late hour of 10:00 p.m.

Morning dawned under a blazing blue sky. The atmosphere at 14,000 feet was luxuriously thick, and my body relished the abundant oxygen. Other than a slight headache, I felt the best I had in weeks.

We broke camp, ate breakfast, and continued our march down-valley. Moving in shifting packs of two or three hikers, we accordioned our way along the trail. We followed an ancient path carved into the steep hillsides two thousand feet above the roaring river waters of the Imja Khola. Our route took us along the west side of the valley, so we did not walk near the revered Tengboche Monastery, which we had visited on our way to Everest. That important religious center had been totally destroyed by the

1934 earthquake, so everyone was anxious about its condition this time. From across the valley, our west-side trail brought us about level with Tengboche's 12,700-foot-high position in midafternoon.

The monastery had also been destroyed by fire in 1989. Gloria and I watched the painters put the final touches on the rebuilt structure in October 1992. Whatever its current condition, I felt confident the monastery would be all right in the long run. Its previous destructions seemed to exemplify the Buddhist belief in impermanence. And the monastery's multiple incarnations mimicked the repeating cycles of death and rebirth. Through the scattered trees and thick rhododendron bushes we could make out the main temple and several satellite buildings still standing.

We reached Phortse around four and pitched our tents in a field owned by the family of one of our guides, Mingma Dorje Sherpa. He had worked with IMG for years and had been one of our guides on Cho Oyu six years earlier. A calm and happy man, Mingma Dorje went from tent to tent, making sure we were settled in.

To enhance team dynamics, we rotated tentmates every so often. I moved in with Andy Land from Wisconsin. Andy stood a few inches taller than me, had blond and gray hair, and had three teenage children. Employed as a hospice nurse, Andy had guided thousands of people from life to death. He was a wise man, so I looked forward to tenting with him for a few days.

Evening's approach in Nepal signaled the start of the workday on the other side of the planet. That meant I could respond to media requests that I couldn't address while we were on the move. I called the Weather Channel on my Nepali cell phone, which was finally connecting well. To my surprise, the producer said, "We're good for now, but we'll call you if we need anything." It was almost as if the earthquake story was no longer a priority for them. His reply seemed so odd that I wrote it in my journal.

During a later phone call with Rodney, I shared the producer's strange response, and Rodney said it wasn't just the Weather Channel. He told me how many news outlets had bumped the quake from the lead spot of every broadcast, down to the third or fourth position. I was confused.

How could the world media move on, as if the disaster was over, when the many problems on the ground were still growing?

We ate a simple dinner of vegetable fried rice in a Phortse lodge that night, and afterward Greg gave us an update. No planes were departing Lukla and about 1,200 people were backed up there, trying to get out. From previous experiences with Lukla's tiny airstrip, I knew the airport had to be a mad scene. Such a giant backlog would take days to clear, even under optimal conditions. We might not fly out for quite a while.

Rather than descend into the chaos, Greg said that we would wait until the logjam started to clear. Our sherpa friends lived in Phortse and we were safe in this quiet little side valley, so we'd wait a few days. Since we had time and strength, we would assemble work parties in the morning to help Phortse start recovering from the earthquake.

I went to bed early to prepare for our workday. Outside the tent, I brushed my teeth and looked into the night. A few modest lights powered by Phortse's small hydroelectric plant cast a dim glow, but beyond them was only darkness and a universe of stars. After the busyness of Everest and the chaos of the quake, tranquil Phortse felt like a real-world Shangri-La.

The next morning I put on the same filthy work clothes that I had worn when we dug through the field-hospital debris. After breakfast I joined the volunteer group heading over to Paldan Tashi Sherpa's house. He worked for IMG but I did not know him well. His house partially collapsed during the quake. Fortunately his family escaped without injury. IMG guide Mike Hamill led a dozen of us across the village to Paldan's house, five minutes away. We followed narrow dirt trails, worn deep into the ground, as the paths right-angled their way around each family's rectangular fields. A second work team of IMG climbers and sherpas went uphill to help clean up the earthquake mess at the village's small monastery.

Paldan's home sat on a steep hillside, just a few yards upslope from the neighbors. We saw Paldan's wife working with pans, plates, and other kitchen items under a tarp erected in the yard. The family was living outside. With the annual monsoon due in a few weeks, torrential rains would soon arrive and stay for months. There was no time to waste.

Their house walls were made from stacked fieldstones held in place with hand-packed mortar of soil and yak dung. The lack of cement and reinforcement rods to support those heavy stones was made clear by the two end walls, which sagged a foot out of alignment. They leaned precariously in toward the middle of the home.

The roof's original construction was less apparent because it had been destroyed. Given the broken materials left behind, the roof had consisted of log main beams, some crosspoles, and multiple rows of hand-cut slate slabs. Each irregular rock slice was about three or four feet square and an inch thick. Every piece had to weigh fifty pounds or more, and hundreds of them had collapsed into the house during the tremor five days earlier. Paldan had recovered most of the slabs already and stacked them next to the leaning walls. But some heavy slate pieces remained embedded in the packed dirt floor, where they had landed after their fifteen-foot drop into the building. With Phunuru acting as interpreter, Paldan told us his wife and two young children had run outside just seconds before all those roof rocks collapsed inside their home.

My old contractor's eye immediately concluded that the two end walls had to be torn down and then rebuilt before a roof could be put back onto the house. And before that could happen, the heavy main beams had to be removed. That's where we came in.

One log beam was about eight inches in diameter at its base and tapered to six inches across at the far end of its forty-foot length. The log probably weighed five hundred pounds. The other beam was about half as long and half the weight. They protruded out over the collapsed home, and we had to figure out how to take them down without breaking them, causing further wall damage, or getting anyone crushed. Our only resources were an old climbing rope, some smaller logs, a dozen calculating brains, and twenty-four strong hands itching to get something accomplished.

After moving the family's precious firewood supply out of the way, we spent an hour removing several rows of stones from the teetering end walls. I walked atop the high, crumbling wall and handed the removed stones down to my teammates below. With no handrail or safety lines, it was like working a job site with my dad and uncles.

We spent a half hour thinking, pointing, and debating the best way to move the dangerous main beams. With several pull lines and guide poles in place, we prepared to yank the main beam from its airy perch. Using our combined strength, we dragged the groaning log across the top of the stone wall until it rolled down and crashed safely to the ground next to the house. A small cloud of dust floated into the air, along with a few cheers.

We followed the same process to remove the shorter main beam in just a few minutes. Everyone seemed pleased with the success and our teamwork. As an old crew chief, I felt relieved that we got the job done, and that no one got hurt. Paldan was smiling broadly. Soon he could start rebuilding.

As we prepared to depart, Paldan spoke to Phunuru in rapid Nepali and then scurried across his backyard. Phunuru told us, "We will wait for a minute."

A moment later Paldan returned with his two children. He sat on the stone wall near the exit point of his yard. Then he positioned his two-year-old son in front of him and sat his eleven-month-old baby on his lap. Both kids were bundled up against the cold and had dusty hands from playing in the yard as we worked. Paldan used his hands to bring the baby's hands together, palm-to-palm. holding them forward. As each member of the work crew left his yard, he bowed his head and, on behalf of himself and the baby, said, "Namaste."

The two-year-old copied his father by giving the gesture of thanks to some of my departing teammates. When my turn came, I smiled and exchanged the greeting with the family trio. Then I stepped across the low stone wall and followed my teammates back to our tents, swallowing the lump in my throat as I went.

Back at camp, we cleaned up. I journaled in our tent while Andy made friends with a young Phortse girl who seemed curious about all the strangers camped near her home. Andy showed the girl, who was about seven, some photographs on his phone. The two sat close together on the ground and leaned against a stone wall while she scrolled through the pictures. They chatted at one another, he in English, she in Nepali, or maybe in the Sherpa language—I couldn't tell. I snapped a few photos of them.

Later in the afternoon, I sent text updates to Gloria, who had flown to Cleveland to visit her sick mother. I contacted a few more media outlets, including *Men's Journal*, CBS Radio, and IHeartRadio. Just in case our situation went bad, I also contacted the wilderness rescue insurance provider with which I had a policy, Global Rescue. I told them my name, location, and that I was safe with IMG. Since I was a policyholder, if I were trapped or hurt they would have sent a helicopter to evacuate me at their expense. But since I was not in an imminent emergency, I didn't need rescue. They said if anything changed, they had four representatives assisting people on the ground in Lukla, a two-day walk from Phortse. Five of my teammates also had insurance with Global Rescue, while other people on our team had similar policies with other firms. But none of us requested evacuation.

In a phone call Rodney told me that Alan's blog said that U.S. Special Forces were stationed in Lukla in case any Americans needed extraction. Rodney also said that a journalist had criticized the use of helicopters to evacuate us all from Camp One instead of being used to rescue Nepalis elsewhere. It seemed an odd viewpoint, as about half the people evacuated from Everest's slopes were Nepali.

The base-camp wounded were flown to better medical care on April 26, over the course of six hours before bad weather stopped the flights. The next clear-weather window occurred on the morning of April 27, when four helicopters extricated at-risk people—the 180 of us above the icefall. That sequence complied with standard rescue triage protocol. Also, the airlift to base camp was done only after expedition leaders determined that rapid ground evacuation through the damaged and aftershock-threatened icefall wasn't safe or realistic. To the best of my knowledge, once the 180 or so stranded Nepalis and climbers reached base camp, we later left camp not by chopper but by walking down-valley.

Seven frontline doctors who treated the scores of wounded at Everest base camp (EBC) later published a journal article in *Wilderness and Environmental Medicine*. Their paper detailed the complex triage, treatment, and transport of patients that occurred during the disaster. Those physicians, who represented medical institutions from Nepal and five other countries, wrote:

> *At the time of the evacuation, little was known about conditions in the most severely affected areas of Nepal. Communications were very limited. Weather conditions on the day of the quake and the next few days made reconnaissance flights too risky in most of the hard-hit areas. Damaged roads prevented access by ground to assess the needs for medical evacuation. The evacuations of EBC did not delay rescue efforts elsewhere in Nepal.*

After seven hard days in a row, IMG declared May 2 a rest day. People showered, scrubbed clothes, and communicated with the outside world. Phortse had no public internet, but through texts and phone calls, we received various news summaries.

We learned that two days earlier, on April 30, a massive avalanche fell from the west shoulder of Everest. It crashed into the icefall and tossed a powder cloud of ice crystals toward base camp. Because there had been no climbing for the five previous days, no one was hurt or killed. We knew that a few teams and individuals had remained at base camp in the vague hope that they still might climb Everest. To me that plan seemed dangerous and disrespectful. The new avalanche and continuing aftershocks had finally persuaded the diehards to quit.

With the last expeditions leaving base camp, a Nepali government official oddly declared that Everest remained open for climbing. That statement sounded way out of touch with reality. We speculated that the announcement might be a positioning ploy so that Nepal would not potentially have to refund our climbing permits, which cost eleven thousand dollars per person.

We also heard an update about Jangbu Sherpa, the guide working for Adventure Consultants who had been injured during the avalanche. After several days in a Kathmandu hospital, he died on May 1, 2015. With his sad death, the total toll of people who died as a result of the earthquake on Everest had reached nineteen.

Several news reports indicated that international assistance had arrived from dozens of countries. Military teams from the UK, India, the United States, and other nations were helping Nepal find and recover survivors. International aid agencies brought cargo planes of emergency relief. That help (and more) was desperately needed, but already Nepal's limited infrastructure had caused bottlenecks in processing the aid. The country had only one international airport—Kathmandu. The runways, air traffic control, and parking spaces for planes were already overwhelmed. A rumor alleged that a heavily loaded military plane had damaged the main runway. We also heard that although the weather between Kathmandu and Lukla was fine, no planes could leave the Khumbu because of the snarled air traffic.

With outside help, Nepal kept working to mobilize into the impacted rural regions. Some areas had been out of communication for days. Sadly, the slow progress might have contributed to the counts of dead and injured. When I did an interview with the BBC that afternoon, the producer told me the death toll had risen to a terrible number—7,000 people—with approximately 14,000 others injured.

Many of the sherpas hired by IMG weren't around anymore because they were attending to their homes and families. Our continued presence in Nepal kept them employed, but the work hampered them from taking care of their own pressing needs and those of their communities. I was uncertain whether we could help more by staying in Nepal or leaving.

During that night's dinner, we learned some good news--planes had begun flying from Lukla. But the update also came with an unproven rumor about criminal elements shaking down tourists for "tips" to get on departing planes. To me that just didn't sound like Nepal, so I dismissed the story.

In our work and walks around Phortse, besides damaged private homes, we'd seen public buildings with problems: ground-to-roofline cracks in the two-story community center, crumpled school walls, and holes in the library wall big enough to pass a desk through. Once the residents had more time to inspect, they'd likely find additional impacts. At breakfast the next day I asked our IMG leaders if we could pass the hat among the team to collect money for the town's public needs. With their enthusiastic agreement, I then asked Phunuru if he could guarantee that the money would be put to good and fair use to benefit everyone in Phortse. He assured me that would happen. I trusted him implicitly; I think we all did.

As breakfast wrapped up on May 3, I stood in the lodge's dining room and made a short plea to my friends about thanking the community that had sheltered us by giving Phortse a boost as we left town. I pulled a preplaced wad of cash from my pants pocket and tossed it into my wool hat. Circling the dining room with my cap held out, I chatted up my teammates and thanked them as they tossed significant cash into the hat. Then we gave the money to Phunuru for the village.

We hiked out of Phortse at about eight-thirty in the morning. Our group stopped at the large, square chorten on the edge of town. New cracks from the quake cut across the chorten's base, and half of the decorative stucco had fallen away. This left the hand-painted images of Buddha with only one eye on the south side, and no face at all on the east side of the chorten.

New snow had fallen overnight above 13,000 feet, so the high alpine slopes looked white and pure. The 700-foot descent to the valley floor took us below the snow line and into lush, green vegetation along the Dudh Kosi River coming down from Gokyo. I sat dumbfounded at the water's edge, listening to songbirds chirping in the underbrush and admiring white flower blossoms.

A mile farther along the trail, we crossed paths with two tahrs, wild Himalayan goats. They sported brown wool coats, still thick and shaggy from winter. The male's curved horns were larger than those of the female but were still not enough to fend off the snow leopards that prey upon the tahrs. We hiked past pink explosions of rhododendron blooms. The crystal-blue sky stretched overhead, and sunlight kissed the shining white summit of an 18,901-foot mountain called Khumbila. Said to be the home of the "god of Khumbu," it is a very sacred peak to the Sherpas, so it has reportedly never been climbed. The beautiful spring morning gave me the peaceful impression that everything was fine in the world. To me, it was like a final stroll through our own little Shangri-La.

But that pleasant fantasy did not last long. After ascending 1,200 feet, and then descending 1,000 feet along two miles of secondary track, we merged back onto the main west-side Khumbu Valley trail. Fresh landslide debris had covered the path in places with piles of dirt and rocks. In a few spots the trail was gone, slumped away toward the distant valley floor. We kicked small steps into the moist soil as we traversed above the short missing sections. In less than two hours, we would see how the region's economic hub, Namche Bazaar, had fared in the historic quake.

22

Namche Bazaar has served for centuries as a trading post where Nepali people swapped goods with Tibetan traders. In the last seventy years the village had grown and prospered as tourism, trekking, and expedition support became economic drivers in the region. Many terraced potato fields and yak-grazing areas were converted into lucrative lodges, but the town still retained an ancient feel. When visitors wandered the busy Saturday market, saw the farm crops carried in by yaks, and heard noisy goats offered for sale, the sensory mixture seemed to echo from a time long past. During the busy autumn peak season, the town's narrow stone walkways often bustled with Namche's two thousand residents and about twice that many travelers headed to the high country.

But on May 3, 2015, Namche looked like a ghost town. We pitched our camp in a field at about 11,500 feet and then descended several hundred hand-carved stone steps into central Namche. Most lodges and trekking stores remained standing, but we saw almost no foreigners in town besides us. Tired of the expedition's repetitious menu, I went to lunch in a restaurant with my Australian teammate Fraser McKenzie. We were the only customers in the place. In excellent English the owner told us,

"After you leave town, we will close for the season. No more people are coming."

I stepped outside for better phone reception and texted my travel agent in Colorado. Since IMG hoped to secure us seats on outgoing mountain flights from Lukla in two days, I asked her to start arranging my international flights home after that. The plan was speculative, though, so I needed to temper my enthusiasm. With one or two unexpected changes, we still might find ourselves marching toward Kathmandu for ten more days.

When I went back inside, I saw Fraser sitting across the table from a Nepali man who looked familiar. The man held his two hands forward with his fingers intertwined as if he were praying. He and Fraser leaned toward each other, engaged in intense conversation. I heard the man speaking English and fighting back sobs while Fraser patted his forearm and listened.

Unsure what was happening, I sat across the room at an empty table to give them privacy. They talked for a bit, then Fraser handed his companion cash. The Nepali man thanked Fraser, shook his hand energetically, and soon left. When I rejoined my friend, he told me that the man had been his sherpa guide over the past few weeks. Since Fraser was on a different IMG subteam, I had not seen his guide very often, so I hadn't recognized him. Fraser explained that his guide's aunt had been killed by the quake up in Thame, a village above Namche. The man had been upset as he could not afford her funeral. Fraser had provided the necessary funds.

When we finished lunch, the lodge owner thanked us, put the bill on the table, and walked away. Fraser said, "We might be his last customers for quite a while."

I nodded and said, "Yeah, tourists don't vacation in disaster zones."

We both placed more bills on the table as a giant tip. On our walk through Namche, we stopped in a few stores and bought locally made gift items. We really weren't interested in shopping; we just wanted to spend additional money in town. Fraser and I made fast purchases and did not indulge in the usual good-natured haggling. We paid whatever the shopkeepers asked.

. . .

After breakfast the next morning, the IMG team departed early. We started the day's trek by descending through Namche's quiet core, then followed the main trail east out of town. On the right, several men worked on a multistory lodge that had partially collapsed. Crisp morning air carried the sharp *tink-tink-tink!* of a mason's metal hammer as he chipped round rocks into rectangular building stones. Though modest and slow, the recovery had begun.

We descended the infamous Namche Hill far faster than we had hiked up it five weeks earlier. With every step downhill, the air grew thicker and our fit bodies moved effortlessly. We crossed a strong metal suspension bridge that spanned a steep river gorge. Over eons, the relentless Dudh Kosi River had eroded deep into the bedrock. The river water, fresh from high-mountain glaciers, ran milky white due to its heavy load of fine-grained glacial silt. The torrent raged past as we and the bridge swayed in the wind two hundred feet above. Long strings of prayer flags fluttered from the steel cable handrail on each side.

In the nearly twenty-three years since Gloria and I first visited the area, international aid groups had helped the community install those metal suspension bridges to replace the old wooden ones. The wood deck boards of the rickety bridges could become as slick as frozen snot when rain or snowmelt made them wet. During especially hard winters, desperate local people sometimes removed every other board from the bridges for firewood. Crossing those Swiss-cheese bridges used to provide nerve-racking views of the dangerous water churning below.

Spring blanketed the lower slopes with green vegetation and peppered the valley with colorful flowers. About two hours below Namche, we started across a low suspension bridge that stretched a hundred feet to the other bank. I walked a few strides onto the span, then noticed a yak coming at me from the other side. The number one rule of bridge crossings is that yaks have the right of way. I turned around, returned to shore, and stepped behind a tree so the yak would not run into me, by accident or on purpose.

As the shaggy creature lumbered closer, I realized that at our modest elevation of 10,000 feet, it might be a *dzo* (pronounced *"zo,"* like "so"), a cross between a yak and a cow. Those crossbreeds look similar, at least to my untrained eyes, but they fared better in the warm, low valleys than the cold-loving yaks. Far across the bridge, twenty more beasts of burden followed the first. This was the first yak train I had seen going up-valley in six days. Even more surprising, they all carried full standard loads, about 120 pounds each.

The lead animal plodded past and eyed me wearily. Its pointed horns wavered about eighteen inches from my face. Four white sacks made from knitted plastic fiber were lashed to its back, and each bag bore the message: "Rice. Emergency aid—not for sale." Help was on the way.

Although those were the first humanitarian food supplies I saw on the ground, a worldwide relief effort had been building since the earthquake hit nine days earlier. Within the first five days at least twenty-seven countries had shipped supplies and personnel to Nepal. By the ninth day after the quake, the list of help had grown to at least fifty-three nations and six intergovernmental organizations, like the United Nations. They sent money as well as planeloads of food and equipment. Thousands of people from dozens of other countries were working across Nepal, including soldiers, medical professionals, and rescue teams.

In addition, dozens of major relief organizations had already shipped enormous amounts of aid supplies to the Kathmandu airport. All that assistance was seeping into the countryside through transport chains, both planned and improvised. But such a massive and complex process takes time and lots of human energy. Complex logistics, sluggish bureaucracies, and human error all slow things down. Shipments can get delayed due to language barriers, cultural differences, and miscommunications. Many remote areas of Nepal are hard to get to even under normal circumstances, so the spontaneous relief efforts were slow to reach some locales.

We heard that the Kathmandu airport tarmac was so jammed with planes that air traffic control had to wave off several incoming aid flights. Reportedly the supplies already on the ground were backlogged at customs clearance and overflowing from nearby warehouses. Yet desperate pleas for help still came from local government officials and remote villages. To a hungry person living under a ripped tarp, a week is a long time to wait.

We stopped to rest in the village of Monjo, about one-third of the way from Namche to Lukla. I had sent Glo a message telling her we still planned on flying out the next day. She told me that our old Colorado friend, Jill Rawlins, wanted to speak to me soon about helping her donate significant money to Nepal. We had first met Jill at Colorado State University back in 1986, before she founded an outdoor education program for kids called the Wild Bear Nature Center.

When I called Jill, she expressed relief that my team and I were well, and she thanked us for volunteering in base camp and Phortse. Her small mountain community of Nederland, Colorado, was home to many ex-pat Nepalis. Jill surprised me by saying that in only a few days they had raised $15,000 in cash donations. Then she asked if she could wire me the money so I could deliver it in person to a Nepali charity they liked on the outskirts of Kathmandu.

Nervousness flushed through me, and I paused before answering. I was honored that Jill and people whom I had never met would entrust me with the money. But I had no idea if I could find the charity's office location, let alone connect with the right person to hand over the money. If they were not there when I arrived, what would I do? Even if I made it to Kathmandu soon, I expected a collapsed place of chaos and confusion. While I wanted to help, wandering through a jumbled city looking to deliver fifteen grand to a stranger could prove problematic.

I suggested they donate the money to a well-known relief organization, like the International Red Cross. But she told me some donors were hesitant to do so, as substantial amounts of relief money donated for the 2010 Haiti earthquake had gone missing. Rather than risk having their donation disappear as it moved through an international organization, and then trickled back down through the convoluted Nepali government systems, Jill said they wanted to make sure their donations went directly to help people on the ground. I needed to reach the capital first, and then see if I had the time and resources to find the charity.

After a tea break, we continued down-valley for an hour. My teammates kept going, but I stopped in Cheplung village to visit the relatives of my deceased friend, Ang Furi Sherpa. After he worked with our 1998 CSU expedition, Furi had later spent two nights with Gloria and me in Fort Collins. He died of tuberculosis years later, but I had stayed in touch with Furi's family. His in-laws lived in Cheplung, so I found their teahouse and introduced myself. Their restaurant suffered only minor quake damage, and they were unharmed. We sipped tea and shared memories of Furi. After our short visit, they put a traditional *kata* around my neck to wish me well on my journey. I continued on to Lukla with the orange scarf protecting me.

At the outer edge of Lukla, a stone *mani* wall along the trail was covered with paper signs. Two typewritten notices taped to the stones instructed Australian and British citizens how to ask their governments for help with departing Nepal. But what caught my eye was a handwritten sign, scribbled on two sheets of unlined paper. Together they read: "MISSING PERSONS—Names people looking for."

Below that header sign was sheet after sheet of lined paper, each one torn from a notebook and duct-taped in place. On each piece, in hand-printed block letters, were the names of several missing people and their last known whereabouts:

Joseph . . . Last seen near Namche Bazaar
Dr. William . . . and Dr. Janice . . . Last seen in Dingboche
Spencer . . . Moving toward base camp
Manfred . . . Descending from EBC?
The names of the missing stretched far down the wall.*

---

* Last names redacted for privacy.

Lukla had modest earthquake destruction, though I heard later that the medical clinic had been hit hard. Businesses were open, and people milled about. The airstrip dominates the center of town, so I walked around the small airport complex and headed toward the lodge where IMG had reserved rooms.

We ate dinner in a busy restaurant, and then I returned to the room I shared with Bart. Gloria was in transit from Cleveland back to Colorado, so we swapped text messages. For ten days we had both been counting down how much longer until I could exit the Khumbu. At 9:20 p.m. in Nepal, I wrote to her about our flight to Kathmandu:

Looks good to fly in 9 hours.

She responded:

Praying it all goes well. . . . Good luck. Sending white light and positive energy!

Although Gloria wrote me back in one minute, I did not stay awake to see her message. I fell asleep in my filthy trekking clothes, lying on top of the blankets. Five hours later, I awoke cold, with gritty, unbrushed teeth. The GPS text device remained cradled in my hands, and the blinking light indicated that a few incoming messages had arrived. Once my vision unblurred, I found Gloria's response, as well as seven new texts from my travel agent. She had found me a flight out of Kathmandu in two days for a reasonable fee. After no response from me about her first four messages, the fifth urgently asked:

Should I issue the new tickets?

That text was more than four hours old. Scared that I had missed the opportunity to grab a flight out, I rushed to write back. Within the hour I had a confirmed flight out on May 7.

. . .

When daylight arrived, the IMG team was waiting in the tiny airport and hoping our flights would depart. Our senior sherpa staff debated the harried airline employees about the excess baggage fees we owed. We each took one big duffel bag with us, and we had to leave one behind—maybe to be seen later, maybe not.

Around six-fifteen a small plane landed, then three more arrived in quick succession. Aircraft often fly to and from Lukla in a multi-plane wave. If the lead plane can get through safely, the others follow close on the first one's tail. Not many passengers stepped off, though a lot of emergency supplies were unloaded. The energy level in the crowded terminal soared when about sixty mountain travelers grabbed their oversize carry-on backpacks and lined up.

Some subtle signal was given, and fourteen of us walked outside to board. Direct sunlight had not hit town yet, but the high mountaintops surrounding Lukla burned with pink-and-orange alpenglow. We stopped twenty yards short of our plane to wait while airline workers finished off-loading the remaining cargo. Dozens of identical gray duffels, each about the size and shape of a golf bag, were stacked on the tarmac near the plane. When we finally lined up outside the airplane's door, I read the labels printed on each waterproof sack. They read: "HUMANITARIAN AID—German Red Cross. Family tent, all-weather frame."

I hoped the all-weather claim was valid, as dozens of families might be living in them for the entire monsoon season, which ended in late September.

Inside the aircraft we all sat down. Our plane, like every flight out of Lukla, was at less than full capacity. That's because if there was a passenger in every seat, and full cargo holds below, the airplane would be too heavy to take off in the thin air. The crisply dressed flight attendant said hello and extended a small tray bearing the customary hard candies and cotton balls. I smiled at her, took a lemon-flavored sweet, and selected two thick cotton wads. Then I stuffed one cotton ball into each ear to provide modest hearing protection from engine noise during the forty-minute flight to Kathmandu.

The propellers roared louder and the plane taxied to the short runway's northern end. Lukla's runway is not flat. The paved strip slopes downhill about 200 feet over its 1,729-foot length. That steep 11.7 percent downward pitch lets departing planes build enough speed to get airborne. That's especially important because about 100 feet past the runway's terminus, the ground drops steeply away about 2,000 vertical feet to the valley floor. If an aircraft isn't aloft by the edge of the cliff, it's a long drop to the Dudh Kosi River.

All that is just one set of challenges for flying out of Lukla. Its 9,300-foot elevation, the lousy weather, and complex terrain all add to the risk. Year after year the Lukla airport ranks as one of the most dangerous in the world.

Our pilot revved the engines to full capacity. Twin screaming noises drilled through the cotton and into my eardrums. The Nepali copilot released the aircraft's brakes, and the plane leaped forward. Our speed built fast, but we were still on the ground when we had rolled far past the halfway point. The end of the runway loomed seconds away.

Through the plane's tiny windshield, no more pavement was visible, only the open air that dropped to the river. We raced forward ever faster. Then the rumbling beneath the tires quieted, and the jostling smoothed a bit. I thought we had to be airborne, but the plane's nose kept pointing down. Well past the cliff edge, we continued descending as the aircraft dipped lower than the runway we had just left. All those damn duffel bags were weighing us down.

Our downward trajectory built more speed, though, and soon the nose lifted from sinking to level. Then the plane angled upward, and at last we began to rise.

23

Our plane cruised above the lower Khumbu Valley, and then over the contiguous Solu region. Traversing the Solukhumbu district on foot from Lukla to Jiri had taken Gloria and me a week as we followed sinuous rivers and climbed up and down one ridge after another. By going straight over all those hills "as the gorak flies," our plane covered the same ground in fifteen minutes. The airplane kept gaining altitude to clear the last high point that stood between Kathmandu and us.

As we approached that rocky ridgetop, the steep terrain beneath us rose closer to the aircraft's belly. We flew toward an open pass and shot across the ridge crest about one hundred feet above the ground, rocks blurring by below. The moment we cleared the divide, the windows on each side revealed giant peaks looming a mile off each wingtip. Those mountains soared far above us and filled the window views with more earth than sky.

The cliff on the other side dropped away even steeper. In a minute we were once again two thousand feet above the ground. The enormous river and forest below looked like a thin white rope snaked across a green lawn. My shoulder muscles unclenched, and I leaned back in my seat. I smiled, reached around the seatback in front of me, and clapped Andy on his shoulder. He looked back, grinning, and nodded his head.

By not climbing the heavily loaded plane any higher than they had to, the skilled pilots had saved their airline a little aviation gasoline. Personally, I'd have been happy to kick in another twenty bucks for fuel in exchange for a larger buffer between us and the ridgetop.

With the airplane steady and level, the trip finally felt like a routine flight instead of a terrifying carnival ride. The cabin was too loud for conversation, so we each sat with our thoughts. We would land in about twenty minutes and see for ourselves how bad things had gotten in Kathmandu. Since the quake had hit ten days earlier, only about half of the rumors we heard turned out to be true. I hoped the vague stories about chaos and cholera would prove false.

We passed over the last rolling hills and started across the flat Kathmandu Valley. Green farming fields and brown dirt roads carved the plains into an irregular checkerboard. We flew near the brick factories on the city's east side, where river-bottom clays were baked into bricks. Most of the city's 1.2 million residents lived and worked in buildings made from those bricks. That local use of materials made sense, but brick buildings can collapse easily during earthquakes. Unfortunately, that's especially true in less-resourced countries where wall reinforcements are scarce and construction codes can be lax.

Everyone stared out their windows as our plane lined up for the final approach. A crumpled building flashed by beneath us. The spacious grounds of the Royal Nepal Golf Club sit right next to the airport. Instead of green grass, the fairways of the nine-hole course were covered by a patchwork sea of tarps and tents. Blue, red, and yellow temporary shelters housed a veritable army of displaced citizens.

We landed, gathered our things, and stepped onto the tarmac. Humid air, thick with oxygen at the 4,000-foot elevation, filled my lungs. My heart rate slowed. I was glad we had made it that far, but, like returning to base camp from Camp One, I wasn't sure if our situation had gotten better or worse.

Domestic flights operate from a corner of the Kathmandu airport that usually houses a modest fleet of small, colorful passenger planes. But that morning the pavement was crowded with military transport planes and gray powerful helicopters. A dozen aircraft from five or six countries were shoved tight together, making the movement of supplies a hassle. The roomier international section of the airport was hosting dozens of gigantic cargo planes, so that area had to be even more crowded. The warehouse-size terminal where we waited for our bags seemed quieter than I had ever experienced before. As if respecting a city in mourning, we conversed with one another in hushed voices.

The three-mile drive from the airport to our hotel took longer than usual as we avoided streets blocked by scattered bricks and debris piles. We did not encounter rows of collapsed buildings as I'd imagined. Halfway to the hotel, we stopped to let one of Kathmandu's free-range urban cows wander across the road. While we waited for the sacred animal to move, I noticed an oddly positioned concrete-and-brick building. It was three stories tall and still standing, but the entire apartment house had rotated right off its foundation. The structure had spun about fifteen degrees counterclockwise, causing the building's unsupported corner to protrude out over the sidewalk. Though it seemed intact, the big building tilted unevenly toward the street. I wondered if the structure could be put back on its foundation, or if the whole thing would get razed.

We skirted the usually busy Thamel (a tourist sector) and headed north into the Lazimpat district. In that part of the city I saw only the typical level of Kathmandu disorder. Some streets looked like nothing significant had occurred. We turned down a narrow side street, past the familiar jewelry shops and money-exchange houses. Near the upscale Radisson Hotel we made a final turn and stopped at the Hotel Tibet's front door. A clean and simple place popular with climbers, the hotel sported an elegant decor reminiscent of a Tibetan monastery. Intricate wood carvings encased every beam in the lobby and yak-wool carpets covered the wooden floors. Several tapestries featured the endless knot, a Buddhist cultural marker whose never-ending woven pattern speaks to the intertwining of wisdom and compassion.

At the start of our expedition, we had stayed in the hotel, so I was pleased to see it standing. I had also stayed there during my 1992 and 2009 trips, so it felt like my Kathmandu home away from home. With a big exhale, I flopped down onto a familiar lobby couch.

More taxis arrived with the rest of our team and more luggage. It was only midmorning, so most of our rooms were not yet ready. A few team-mates drifted off to find an open restaurant, while others worked the internet to find flights home.

I went to the lobby bathroom. After marveling at the flush toilet and the running water in the sink, I realized that I was still in the same stinky trail clothes that I had been wearing for almost a week. Being back in a city made me suddenly self-conscious of my hygiene—or more precisely, my lack thereof. I washed up in the sink as a token gesture.

For the first time in five weeks I studied my reflection in a mirror. My face looked thinner, maybe a bit drawn. My black hair and beard had grown shaggy. To document what I looked like, I took a selfie in the mirror, then posted it to Facebook. I was not prepared for the response.

Within minutes people wrote back, concerned about me. I wrote an explanation that I was in Kathmandu and no longer at risk in the mountains. As more anxious comments flowed in, I became confused: What were they worried about?

After a few clarifying comments back and forth with friends, I realized that they were talking about psychological danger. People pointed out my sunken eyes and gaunt look. I studied the photo again. Though I sort of saw what they meant, it was no big deal. A few friends with military experience talked about my "thousand-yard stare." I brushed off their concerns; I was fine. Having been a volunteer first responder to a dozen car wrecks and mountain accidents, I felt that enduring and functioning under challenging conditions was within my comfort zone.

People got blunter. Several wrote me privately, suggesting I seek critical debriefing or trauma counseling. I examined the photo again, trying to see what they saw. To be more open-minded, I scrutinized the man in the picture through the lens of my first-responder training. At first I merely thought he looked wild and maybe a bit scary. But when I zoomed in and studied the man's eyes, I saw it. He looked exhausted and overwhelmed, and it seemed like he was trying to continue through sheer will. He presented a postaccident stare that hinted at significant stress. A month on Everest and ten days in the earthquake zone had taken a toll.

When a hotel room opened, Fraser and I dragged our heavy duffel bags upstairs to our shared room. I returned to the lobby and retrieved the satchel of street clothes that I had left in the hotel's storage room when we departed for the mountains. Fraser took the first hot shower, and soon a clean and classy Aussie stepped from the steamy bathroom. I took my turn under the luxuriously hot water and emerged as a fresher and skinnier version of the Yank Fraser had been traveling with. My once-comfortable blue jeans sagged off me and the waistline drooped far down my hips.

Fraser and I spread out our stuff and selected excess clothes, gear, and food we could leave behind for those in need. The hotel staff could use the goods or pass them along to others who needed supplies. Our pile of leave-behind items covered the desk and spilled onto the floor. With gear scattered everywhere, our room looked and smelled like a trekking-clothes stink bomb had detonated. A pervasive musty odor and the acrid stab of sweat assailed my nose.

Communication with my travel agent sputtered along about the possibility of departing Nepal sooner. But leaving early proved too costly and uncertain, so I stuck with the confirmed plan to fly out in two days. Because it was nighttime in the United States, I had few conversations with family or friends. When I connected with Jill, there was no clear plan yet about receiving and delivering Nederland's donation. We made the joint decision for them to donate it later, once their plans firmed up.

Eventually a recipient Nepali community, the Dhading District, used the money to purchase its first ambulance.

My buddy Alan sent a text inviting me to dinner with two of his friends. Walking alone through the quiet streets, I saw families getting ready to sleep outside in empty lots or tiny urban courtyards. People were nervous about being inside a building when the next aftershock hit.

I met Alan at Kilroy's restaurant. We had not seen each other in eight days, so we hugged and teased each other about not being smelly anymore. He introduced me to his teammates from a previous expedition: Louis Carstens and Phil Crampton. Back in 2013 they had summited Manaslu together, the eighth-highest mountain in the world. As the owner of Adventure Junkies, Phil had led that expedition.

We traded earthquake stories over dinner. Phil, who lived in Kathmandu half the year, had deep knowledge about what was unfolding across the country. He told us how the village of Langtang, in the Langtang Valley, had been devastated. That popular trekking town had been hit by a massive landslide, similar to the one at Everest base camp, but much larger. A tsunami of ice and rock roared down the mountainside and buried almost the entire village. Hundreds of residents and trekkers had died. We all went silent. I stared at the yak steak on my plate and contemplated how fickle natural disasters are, and how unfair life can be.

After saying good night to Alan and Louis, Phil and I walked toward my hotel and his apartment. We ambled down a dark street, discussing the food and fuel shortages expected soon. I asked Phil whether he thought I could be of more help by staying to look for volunteer opportunities, or by leaving so the Nepali people could focus on recovery. Being a straight shooter, Phil said that unless I had a definitive task to do and was self-sufficient with food, water, and lodging, it'd be better to "get the hell out of the way."

I returned to the hotel at about eleven, exhausted. Back home it was daytime, so I had a slew of voice mails and emails. While on the phone talking with Rodney, I received a message that CBS wanted me to appear live in their New York City studio as soon as possible. I discussed the surprise request with Rodney, and he asked, "Of all the people on Everest, why do they keep talking to you? You're not the most famous one there, and you're sure not the best-looking!"

We laughed. Then I said, "Well, I'm not sure. I just try to give them accurate, concise answers."

Upon reflection we figured it was probably the intersection of my skills. Besides the geology knowledge, my fifteen years of being a scientific expert witness allowed me to boil complex situations down to brisk statements. And my work as a speaker and writer let me paint a picture of what it was like on the ground.

Before responding to CBS's invitation, I checked with my office manager, Jeanie Sutter. She had been running my speaking business while I was gone, and when the postquake media requests poured in, Jeanie hustled double-time to manage everything. She said I could get home for two days, and still head back out to New York on Sunday to be on the air Monday, May 11. But she pointed out that Sunday was Mother's Day. Leaving Gloria on Mother's Day seemed an especially bad idea.

We solved the problem by telling CBS I would travel from Colorado to New York only if they made all the travel arrangements and if Gloria could come with me. They instantly agreed. I crawled into bed after midnight, my brain spinning with all that would happen in the next few days.

On the evening of May 7 I sat inside an idling Qatar Airways jet as we prepared to depart Kathmandu for Doha, Qatar. From there I'd fly to Dallas, Texas, and finally, to Colorado. After forty-three days away, I would get to see my family in about forty more hours.

Nighttime covered Kathmandu, so there was not much to see. Still, I kept my head pressed against the smooth window to stay awake and maybe spot the city lights after takeoff.

The pilots throttled up, and we rolled forward. We're leaving. I can't believe it happened like this.

With a shudder the wheels left the ground. No Everest. Nepal's a mess. So many lives wrecked.

A few tents on the golf course glowed from small lights inside. They spread enough illumination to reveal the neighboring shelters. What happens now?

We flew into a cloud bank, and all signs of Kathmandu disappeared. My mind drifted back to the last text message I had sent right before boarding the plane. To Glo, Jess, and Nick, I had written:

I'm coming home.

24

My first meal back in the United States was pepperoni pizza and cold beer, which I bought in the Dallas airport. I took two bites and a small sip, then rested for a moment.

Sometime later I awoke with a plateful of cold pizza next to my ear. I lifted my head off the restaurant table, unsure how long I had been out. With only short bouts of sleep during the two plane rides, I had been awake for most of the last thirty-six hours. I didn't want the airport police to think I was drunk or something, so I shouldered my pack and slouched back into the Dallas terminal. Worried that I might fall asleep if I sat down again, I walked slow laps in the airport for two hours. There was no way I was going to miss my flight to Colorado.

Tired or not, after we landed I speed-walked through the Denver International Airport. Once on the train to baggage claim, I maneuvered my way closest to the exit door so that I could be the first one to enter the terminal when we stopped. The promise of seeing my family in ten more minutes energized me.

My pack bounced on my shoulders as I jogged up the escalator steps. I spotted Glo, Jess, and Nick a split second before they saw me, so I watched their faces bloom into smiles. Unsure who should embrace whom first, we wound up in a four-person family hug. Six loving arms squeezed my torso and patted my back. I spread both arms as wide as possible so that I could hug them as one big bundle. In rapid succession I planted a kiss on whatever part of their heads my lips could reach. I had made it home.

It was almost midnight when we walked into our kitchen. I leaned my pack against the counter and called out: "Jake!" Half-awake when he trotted into the room, he needed a second before he realized that I had returned. When the signals from his nose and eyes came together in his canine brain, his head jerked an inch and his black velvet ears lifted. I knelt and called him again. He charged over and started licking my face. We all laughed.

Crossing a dozen time zones is wearisome enough. Doing it on top of the fatigue and stress from the past two weeks had drained me deeply. Still, being home brought a replenishing sense of safety and peace. When Glo and the kids were free, I hung out with them and tried to catch up on family life.

But there was little time to rest. When Glo and the kids were busy, I spent hours online connecting with expedition teammates and getting updates about Nepal. After a pleasant Mother's Day at home, a CBS-provided town car picked Gloria and me up at the house and took us to the Denver airport. We reached New York City and had a late dinner before catching five hours' of sleep. I had to be on the *CBS This Morning* set by 7:00 A.M. eastern time.

Appearing on national television was a fast-paced experience, and it offered me my first chance to wear makeup. Colorado climber Jon Kedrowski appeared with me, and we talked with the show's cohosts, Gayle King, Charlie Rose, and Norah O'Donnell. Near the end of the segment, Gayle and I discussed the resilience of the Nepali people. Gloria and I returned to Colorado later that day. Jon and I were scheduled to appear together the next morning on two Denver TV news shows hosted by meteorologist Chris Tomer. In addition to being an excellent climber, Chris was also a friend.

After sleeping four hours, I arose to prepare for the Denver appearances. I ate breakfast while watching the international news so that I would be aware of current conditions in Nepal. The reporter mentioned a 7.3 magnitude earthquake there, and I thought he mistakenly used an early underestimate of the April 25 tremor's size. I stopped chewing my cereal and listened more carefully. Then he said the quake happened in Nepal around noon on May 12—that was five hours ago.

Another large earthquake had hit.

Landslides, deaths, and injuries had ravaged Nepal and neighboring countries—again. Everything was worse. A half dozen concerns tripped over one another as they sprinted through my mind. How many people hurt and dead? Was Phortse okay? Any climbers trapped?

The death toll eventually reached 153, lower than the first quake, but still devastating. Early data from the USGS pinned the epicenter forty-two miles west of Namche, much closer to Everest than last time. That proximity meant that the impacts in the Khumbu could be substantial.

While driving to Denver, I frantically scanned the radio for new updates. After hearing the same limited information on multiple stations, I grew frustrated. This made me realize how tough it is to be half a world away, anxious and worried, under the strain of not knowing. The insight gave me an inkling of what it must have been like for my family and thousands of other scared families. I knew how news trickled out from disaster zones, plus night had fallen in Nepal. There wouldn't be much new information for hours, so I shut the radio off. *Those poor people.*

Even before the earthquakes, many Nepalis struggled to get by. Last month's quake had pushed half a million people out of their homes and into tents or temporary shelters. With structures already weakened, the new quake might have caused many more to collapse. And this latest round of continental-plate movement would increase the frequency and intensity of aftershocks.

Climbing Lobuche East in the Khumbu Valley of Nepal on April 16, 2015.

Mount Everest (29,029 feet) rises behind the much lower west shoulder, with Nuptse to the right. The white Khumbu Glacier flows out of the Western Cwm (hidden), curves left, and

PK Sherpa and other climbers crossing crevasses inside the Khumbu Icefall on April 22. Base camp is below and the Pumori-Lingtren ridge looms up on the far side of the valley.

PK Sherpa smiling in the lower Khumbu Icefall at about 18,500 feet, with Pumori (23,494 feet) rising behind.

One of many ladders crossing over a crevasse in the icefall.

Me holding family photos seven hours after the 7.8 magnitude quake that rattled the glacier beneath us at Camp One on April 25, 2015.

Close up of Pumori's north ridge, the approximate starting zone of the deadly base camp avalanche, with Cho Oyu (26,906 feet) in the far distance.

Emily Johnston, Justin Merle, and Damian Benegas (*left to right*) before scouting the upper icefall on April 26.

ABOVE: Teammates (*left to right*) Jason Ahlan, Jim Diani, Fred Bowers, Justin Merle, and Emily Johnston in Camp One on the afternoon of April 26.

RIGHT: Me, Bart Williams, and others waiting our turns for helicopter evacuation out of Camp One early on April 27.

Don Harbart (orange down suit) with Emily Johnston behind (blue suit), as we prepare to board our evacuation flight out of Camp One on April 27.

View of the upper icefall from the rescue chopper. The sunny high ridge in the distance connecting Pumori (*center*) to Lingtren (*right*) is where the deadly avalanche started.

Me sitting on the helicopter floor as we fly close by Nuptse during our short, scary flight from Camp One to base camp.

A black cross under the boulder marks where a body was found after the deadliest day ever on Mount Everest.

My climbing buddy Alan Arnette (*left*) and me at base camp a few days before the Gorkha Quake hit on April 25, 2015.

An earthquake-damaged chorten in Phortse.

Nick, Gloria, Jess, and me (*left to right*) on vacation in the Swiss Alps, 2016.

My longtime climbing partner, Rodney Ley, accompanied me on my final training day before I returned to Mount Everest in March 2017 (Quandary Peak, 14,265 feet).

Me and Dad enjoying the summit of Pikes Peak, Colorado (14,115 feet) in 1999.

LEFT: Sitting atop Gokyo Ri (17,575 feet) and contemplating the summit of Everest to the east on April 5, 2017.

BOTTOM: Phinjo Sherpa trekking the Gokyo Valley along the gray moraine debris of the Ngozumpa Glacier, April 2017.

Moonrise over Everest. Taken from IMG base camp with dining tent illuminated.

Climbers ascending upper portion of Khumbu Icefall just above a major collapse area.

Crossing a short ladder bridge in the Western Cwm at about 20,000 feet, just above Camp One.

Me at Camp Two (21,300 feet) in front of the lower southwest face of Everest (*left*), Lhotse Face (*center*), and Nuptse (*right*).

PK and me at lower Camp Three (23,500 feet) on our first trip up the Lhotse Face, with the upper southeast ridge behind PK. Note the red fixed line and tilted tent to the right.

Entering the death zone at 26,000 feet. The Triangular Face towers above the gently tilted South Col icefield and Camp Four just out of sight to the lower right.

On the summit of Mount Everest (29,029 feet) with PK Sherpa on May 22, 2017, just before sunrise.

The view from 29,029 feet looking southeast. From right to left can be seen Lhotse (fourth highest in the world), Makalu (fifth highest), and Kangchenjunga (third highest) in the far distance.

The massive recovery efforts were just starting to make a difference, and now this. When I pondered what it must have felt like on the ground, adrenaline surged through my arms until my hands ached. Imagining the despair of the Nepali people filled me with sadness.

I recalled a newspaper article I had read before leaving Kathmandu. It described how a distraught mother and child had received a tarpaulin from an aid agency. The mother hung the tarp, and then put her cow under it, prompting some neighbors to criticize her for using the cover to protect an animal instead of her family. In response the mother explained that the milk-producing cow was all they had left, and its milk provided their only food. She said that if the cow died, she and her child would surely die too.

For many Hindu and Buddhist people in Nepal, their faith is a key tenet of their lives. In news reports and on social media, some Nepalis seemed to be asking: What have we done to make the gods so angry?

I struggled to rally myself for the two news segments, hoping viewers would take notice of Nepal's plight and donate to recovery efforts. Gloria and I had contributed, as had so many others. It was a start, but more funds were needed.

Having cleared my work schedule through June 10 before going to Everest, returning home early meant I found myself in the rare position of having free time. I decided to spend the next month doing what I could to help Nepal from afar.

In the first week that I was home, several community groups contacted me, asking if I could share my earthquake story. I realized we could turn these requests into fundraisers for Nepal. So I'd offered to speak for free if the groups donated all moneys collected to the relief efforts. They heartily agreed.

Days and nights became a steady blur of outreach, logistics, and recruiting people to join in. Host locales covered rooms, audiovisual, and other expenses. Local businesses offered products, and a church donated meeting space. Restaurants contributed a portion of people's meal tabs. The momentum was uplifting.

The *Coloradoan* newspaper hosted a forum in Fort Collins where Alan and I shared our earthquake stories. So many attendees signed up in advance that we had to move the event to a larger venue. We raffled off donated items, and I signed and sold books. Every cent collected went to Nepal's recovery. The Fort Collins gym where I had worked out for twenty-six years, the Raintree Athletic Club, hosted a packed-house event where we raised more money.

To promote the events and to keep reminding the public of Nepal's plight, I went on radio programs, made additional TV appearances, and wrote newspaper articles. I worked with Colorado PBS on an in-depth television segment about Nepal.

With more fundraising events scheduled, a key question became where to send the collected funds. Some people remained leery about donating to large international charities. Also, Nepal's government, which has an alleged history of corruption, had demanded that all foreign donations flow directly to it. That meant various agencies and bureaucrats would touch the funds several times before it could reach citizens. There was concern that this opened further possibilities for money to get sidetracked when it was needed the most.

On the other end of the organizational spectrum, funding pleas from individuals popped up on the internet, but there was no certainty about their validity. Willing donors asked me where they could safely send their money to create the most good in Nepal. I found myself in an advisory position for which I had no training.

I researched options and sought counsel from those who knew Nepal even better than I did, including friend and fellow climber Jake Norton. In time I selected what seemed to be the ideal nonprofit for the situation: The dZi (pronounced "zee,") Foundation. Named after the colorful *dZi* charms that Himalayan people wear on strings around their necks, this established nonprofit had partnered with Nepal's most remote communities for more than seventeen years. Together they built schools, water systems, and health clinics. Most of the staff was on the ground in Nepal, with just a few administrators located in Colorado. The salaries for the many in-country employees were themselves an economic infusion to Nepal. Their nonprofit status in America and their prequake operations in Kathmandu allowed them to move funds laterally into the country with ease, which reduced the potential for bureaucratic meddling.

All of the dZi Foundation projects required heavy local involvement like concept approval, volunteer labor, and donated materials. This was critical for designing appropriate projects and for building long-term community ownership. To ensure full transparency with all funds, each project included a large written list of accounts that were posted on the construction site. Before a facility opened, local leaders had to sign their names to the public accounting summary.

The dZi Foundation announced it was focusing its efforts on building earthquake-resilient schools. Those structures could flex when the next earthquake hit, and they would serve as secure community buildings during any disaster. I put my efforts behind the dZi Foundation and encouraged those who asked my advice to do likewise.

My teammates across the United States, and in other countries, held similar fundraisers in their communities. From its guides and climbing clients, IMG eventually collected and dispersed one hundred thousand dollars among ninety sherpa employees whose homes were damaged or destroyed. Sometimes private efforts sparked significant corporate help. My supportive neighbor, Jim Zafarana, was one of the first people to check on Gloria the day of the quake, and his support continued. Jim worked as a high-level executive for Hewlett-Packard, and he helped facilitate the Hewlett-Packard Company Foundation to give more than $271,000 for disaster relief assistance.

Audience members at our presentations always asked about developments in Nepal. To stay current, I connected with Nepali friends, and read online updates about the slow recovery. I uncovered a report titled

"Earthquake Preparedness and Disaster Relief in Nepal: A Position Paper." When I read the editorial note in front of the long document, it was dated May 1, 2015, just six days after the Gorkha earthquake. I was confused. How could the authors produce such a substantial report in six days, let alone while the disaster was still unfolding?

In my twenty years as an environmental scientist, I had worked on several extensive, multidiscipline reports, and they usually required months or longer to research and write. Even after the science is complete, a joint-agency position paper can take a year of review and refinement before all the contributing parties agree.

I scanned the first few pages and was stunned. Indeed, the team of authors hadn't rushed out something in a few days. This substantial study had been under way for five years. Their work started in March 2010, in response to the horrific earthquakes a few months earlier in Haiti and Chile. Their comprehensive ninety-two-page paper integrated the work of about one hundred scientists, many of them Nepalis who lived in America and Canada.

Their position paper presented recommendations for Nepal on "preparedness and mitigation before, during, and after the occurrence of an earthquake." Its findings and warnings were on-target and needed. The report's foreword sagely stated:

> Since the exact timing of earthquakes is impossible to predict, disaster preparedness is the only factor that we can plan and implement now to minimize the loss of lives and property.

Sadly, their report was received by Nepal's government on April 2, 2015, just twenty-three days before the earthquake. There was no time to implement their recommendations.

I burrowed deeper into their work and read some sobering information. One of the most ominous predictions was that a 7.0 to 8.0 magnitude event would cause approximately 100,000 Nepali deaths. April's 7.8

magnitude tremor had killed around 8,900 people in Nepal. The situation could easily have been ten times worse.

In early June, Jake Norton invited me to speak at yet another fundraiser, this time with him and Charley Mace. Though I felt too drained to participate, the event was being spearheaded by Nepali students at Eaglecrest High School in Centennial, Colorado. I figured that if the kids had the drive to lead the way, I should pitch in. So I agreed.

When I told Rodney how I committed to doing another fundraiser, he told me about a conversation that he had just had with his coworker Andy Nelson. Andy had co-led a CSU student climbing expedition to the Mexico volcanoes with Rodney and me two months before I left for Everest. Apparently Andy commented on how many fundraising events I had been doing recently, and he wondered how I was still going. Rodney told me that his response to Andy was, "I've climbed with Jim for almost twenty years. He can hang on tight for a long time. But eventually even he's going to have to let go."

The Eaglecrest school sat eighty-three miles away from our house. I was so tired that Gloria offered to drive both ways. Though attendance at the last-minute event was modest, the Nepali students raised more than ten thousand dollars for their homeland. Gloria drove us north while waning sunset colors disappeared behind the Rocky Mountains. The peaks looked small compared with Himalayan giants. Seeing them made me ponder how a climbing expedition had somehow turned into everything that I found myself doing.

After an expedition, adjusting back to daily life can be trying, even when the trip was safe and successful. The adventurous challenges have ended. Returning home forces the once-footloose adventurer to resume the daily grind of multitasking and endless chores. The awkward readjustment is like a sluggish first day back at work after a long vacation, but more intense. Some climbers call that bumpy time the "postexpedition blues," while others call it "reentry," like an astronaut returning to Earth. This common experience fades away after a few days or weeks, depending upon the individual, the length of time away, and the expedition's intensity.

If the trip is unsuccessful, team members often experience doubt or disappointment. They might have to face the uncomfortable reality of their own newly discovered limitations. These negative outcomes are a natural consequence of embracing tough tasks. While sometimes unpleasant, those difficulties expand a person's comfort zone and provide the raw materials for personal growth.

But if the expedition turns tragic, readjusting to daily life becomes a much greater struggle. Strands of sadness, guilt, and self-doubt get pulled into the convoluted knot of postexpedition life. Those difficulties are even harder to resolve when the tragedy occurs not on the mountain, but at home.

25

2002—Continued

Roped together, Rodney, Terry, and I descend the steep ice slope below Denali Pass. A giant crevasse that we've nicknamed "Jaws" waits far below us, mouth agape, ready to swallow tired climbers who make a mistake while descending from Denali's upper slopes. Each time I place my ice ax for security, I think of one of my loved ones back home and drive the ax in as hard as I can. Glo, then Jess. Nick, then Dad. One move after another, one family member after the next, I focus hard all the way down to make sure I get to see them again.

Rescuing Josh has taken all afternoon, and we're beat. Since it was uncertain if the helicopter could reach the rescue site at 19,100 feet, we'd left Josh with the German and Austrian climbers. Then the three of us dropped down 800 feet to help the Park Service ground team lug up heavy rescue gear. We all got lucky, though, when the helicopter finally arrived with a long rescue line hanging underneath.

On the fly, literally, the chopper plucked Josh right off the mountain. I'll never forget the sight of Josh clipped to the haul line, dangling a hundred feet below the helicopter, with a vertical mile of open air between his boots and the glacier below. Along with our patient, the helicopter carries away my fears and worries. Josh has been handed alive to medical care. We've done our job. Now we no longer had to risk our fingers, toes, or lives to save him. With advanced medical treatment and a bit of luck, Josh will get what he wanted—to go home.

As we near our tent at 17,000 feet, three climbers from another team come out a few hundred yards and offer to carry our packs into camp. It's a nice gesture, but we refuse. They walk next to us in solidarity, asking about the rescue and thanking us for giving up our summit to help a fellow mountaineer. When we stagger into high camp, tired and dehydrated, I dread the hours we'll have to spend melting snow into water and then bringing it to a boil. As a form of communal thanks, another team camped nearby gives us their precious hot water. The rangers and our fellow rescuers trudge safely into high camp behind us.

We awake the next morning, cold and stiff. Rodney and I start a low-enthusiasm discussion about whether we have the energy to make a second summit attempt. Terry tells us his old back injury has flared again and he's worried about even getting down from here, let alone going higher. However, he suggests that Rodney and I should go summit. But when we lead student expeditions, Rodney always says, "The worst decision at altitude is the one to split the team." The climb is over. We're all heading down.

By that afternoon the three of us reach the 14,200-foot camp, and we spend the night there recovering. We hear that a big storm is coming and that if we don't fly out in the next two or three days, we might be stuck on the mountain for a week. After a short discussion we decide to push hard for base camp. As we break camp, I feel discouraged and disappointed about having not reached the summit. It's an odd blend of emotions that the great mountaineering writer David Roberts called "vague sorrow" after he and his partner didn't summit a difficult Alaskan peak named Mount Deborah.

We begin our marathon descent. At the hazardous Windy Corner, just below the 14,200-foot camp, a team going the other way stops us to trade information. Their front climber stands near me and asks, "Did you summit?"

In a low voice I say, "No."

"How high did you get?"

"About 19,000."

"And you didn't summit?"

Before I can answer, he tilts his head and continues, "Oh, wait—are you one of the teams who gave up the summit to help that sick solo climber?"

Word travels fast on a glacier. With little energy, I say, "Yeah, that's us."

It's windy and cold, so I'm puzzled as to why he suddenly takes his glove off. He extends his bare hand. I take it in my gloved one. He pumps my hand vigorously and says, "Thanks for bringing that spirit to Denali."

His kind gesture pokes the lump of mixed emotions I have been carrying in my chest since the rescue started and I knew we were not going to summit. My throat closes tight, so I croak out a whispered response. "You're welcome."

By descending all day and all night, we reach base camp before the big storm. Terry and Rodney pitch our tent while I dig next to our triple-length bamboo marker to recover the food cache we left here two weeks ago. After excavating away the four-foot-thick snow cover, I pull out a basketball-size nylon sack containing two Spanish-rice packets, a can of Spam, and a half-pint of whiskey. I hold it above my head in victory. The boys cheer like crazed pirates who've just opened a treasure chest of gold and gems.

Later that day the legendary Denali National Park climbing ranger Roger Robinson walks into our camp. He tells us that Josh had rushed his acclimatization, and against the park's stern warning, he had also climbed the glacial route solo. No one even knew when Josh collapsed at 19,700 feet. He'd spent the subzero Alaskan night lying in the snow alone. He might lose some brain function, and maybe a few fingers, but Josh was very lucky that Stefan and Thomas spotted him the next day, far off the normal route.

Roger says that after the chopper hauled Josh to base camp, they flew him off the Kahiltna Glacier by ski plane, and then helicoptered him to a hyperbaric chamber at an Anchorage hospital. It looks like he'll recover, though probably with permanent damage. Roger asks a few questions and writes down our names. Then he says, "When people step forward on the mountain, without being asked, and take a risk to help someone else, we like to recognize them."

He pulls a few small items from his jacket pocket and solemnly hands one to each of us. In my palm I study an oval lapel pin that's a bit more than an inch long. The bottom half shows a white, snowy landscape above which protrudes Denali's pointy silhouette. The pin's upper half mimics the Alaskan state flag with a navy-blue sky and seven tiny gold stars outlining the Big Dipper constellation. The far lip of the Dipper points to a single gold celestial object, the North Star. Across the white foreground, in gold letters, it reads: Denali Pro 2002.

Roger shakes each of our hands and thanks us on behalf of the Park Service. That evening we share our rice and Spam with Thomas and Stefan, our fellow rescuers, because our new friends are out of food. While the five of us eat our tiny dinner together, Thomas tells us he and Stefan also received Denali Pro pins. Later in the season the park will also award Thomas Lämmle the singular 2002 Denali Pro Award for leading the bold rescue of Josh.

The warm glow we keep receiving from the climbing community gradually evaporates our small sorrow about not reaching the summit. We feel good that Josh gets to go home and so do we. If the snow stops falling in the morning, we'll help pack down the fresh powder covering the glacial runway so we can fly to Talkeetna.

For our last night on Denali, Rodney, Terry, and I huddle in our tent and pass the tiny whiskey bottle around. We can finally let our guard down. From a thin book of wilderness poetry, Rodney reads aloud Robert Service's haunting poem "The Cremation of Sam McGee." The rhyming verse describes an explorer's struggle to keep his solemn promise of cremating his companion's remains after the man's untimely death.

Our ski plane accelerates down the glacier, fighting for speed. A hundred yards beyond the foot-stomped runway, an enormous crevasse looms large through the windshield. The pilot pulls back on the stick, and we glide into the blue Alaskan sky. Denali slips away below us, and an hour later we land on Talkeetna's gravel runway. We're back in the world of salads and steaks, showers and family.

We walk into the rustic Swiss-Alaska Inn wearing filthy climbing jackets with shiny new pins. Rodney grabs the coveted first shower, while Terry starts spreading two hundred pounds of wet climbing gear around our room. I head to the hotel's dirt parking lot to use the pay phone. Gloria and I have not been able to speak for sixteen days, so I'm excited to talk to her. I'll call Dad next. Just wait until he hears about the rescue!

We're off the mountain a few days early, so I expect Gloria to be surprised. Her greeting seems muted, though. "Oh. Hi, hon."

I chatter about the beauty of the Alaska Range and the vicious cold. Then I launch into an animated summary of the rescue. When I pause to hear her comments, again she responds in a flat voice with what feels like a token statement: "That's nice, Jim."

Uneasy, I ask, "Well, what's up there?"

"Uncle Bob called today. There's bad news from Florida."

I balk. Dad, his sister, Mary, and her husband, Uncle Bob Carr, all retired near one another in Saint Augustine. "Oh no. Did Aunt Mary pass away?"

"No, not Aunt Mary."

My brain stumbles. Hot adrenaline explodes in my chest. In a rising panic I ask, "You mean Dad?"

Glo's voice cracks as she says, "Yes."

I screech, "*What!?* Is he all right?"

"Jim—your dad passed away."

"No! *No!*"

My legs buckle. I slump against the phone booth. Trying to stay upright, I clutch at the metal wind shelter that surrounds the phone on three sides. My hand has no strength. By the time my knees hit the parking-lot gravel, I can't speak.

The phone cord is short, so when it goes taut it forces the handset to rotate upside down. I keep pressing the speaker end of the handset against my left ear, but the mouthpiece bumps the top of my head and rubs against my greasy hair.

As if I were standing twenty feet back from my body, I distantly hear myself sobbing and emitting high-pitched cries. From far, far away, I hear intermittent words from Gloria. "So sorry . . . didn't know how to tell . . . wasn't sure when you'd get down . . ."

The phone's tiny speaker does its tinny best to let us grieve together, even though we're 2,500 miles apart. Upward tension on the metal armored pay-phone cord is all that's keeping me upright. I vaguely sense angular rocks stabbing my kneecaps through my shell pants, but I don't care.

Now my vision's going. I know I'm crying from the water dripping onto my chest, but I'm not sure if my eyesight is blurred from tears or if my brain is shutting down.

I've blown it. I've blown it big-time.

Instead of being in Alaska saving a stranger, I should've been in Florida saving Dad. Denali was just another stupid climb. If I had gone to visit him instead, I could've helped him survive. Right now we'd be drinking beer, eating seafood, and laughing together.

Now I'll never see him again.

I think I hear Gloria in my left ear. Coming partway back to her, I struggle to my feet, rotate the phone's mouthpiece down, and ask, "How? What happened?"

"They found him in his house this morning. We don't know why yet, but they think it happened fast from an aneurysm."

. . .

I stumble back into our gear-strewn hotel room. While Terry towels off his wet hair, he says, "Shower's great, Jimmy. Your turn."

I lean against a wall and in a low voice say, "Something happened. Something really bad."

Terry and Rodney step toward me. I put both hands on my knees for stability, but still begin sliding down the wall. Through tears I blurt out, "My dad died!"

I can't look them in the eye, but I see their bodies jerk at the shock. After being my good friends and climbing partners for years, they know how close I am to my father. They move near and both put a hand on my shoulder. I drop to my knees and cry. They lower to the floor too, staying with me. At some point I look up at Rodney and see him wiping away tears.

During the long van ride from Talkeetna to Anchorage, my head slumps against the window as the green-and-brown wilderness blurs by. I dissect my last conversation with Dad, to memorize it, to squeeze out every second of connection.

On my final night home before flying to Alaska, Dad and I spoke on the phone. Because that day was both Nick's sixth birthday and Mother's Day, I spent much of it cooking, cleaning, and celebrating. After washing the dinner dishes, I slipped out of the kitchen onto the back deck. Soaking in the warm evening air, I dialed Dad in Florida. I only had a few minutes, as I wanted to put the kids to bed. Glo and I alternated nights doing that, but the evening before a climbing trip, I always made sure to read them a story and tuck them in.

Dad and I talked about the Denali plans and compared them with my three previous expeditions. Near the end of the call, Dad said: "I didn't know regular guys could get out of work and go chase adventure all over the world."

He sounded wistful, like he wished he had done it before fifty years of hard work ushered him to the age of sixty-nine. And I think he also meant it as a subtle compliment to me. He didn't dole out praise often, and when he did, he rarely said it directly. But I was pretty sure that he was proud of me for going on expeditions. To let him know that I caught his meaning, and to reflect some credit back to him, I said, "Well, I can do these trips because of the things you taught me and because you showed me how to hustle."

Dad demurred. "Well, I don't know about that . . ."

"Thanks for giving me what I needed, Dad, to take a crack at these big mountains."

Our call didn't last long. The kids were waiting, and there was still packing to do. So we agreed to cut it short. I said, "I love you, Dad."

He answered back, "Luv ya too." It had only been in the last nine years, since Mom died in 1993, that Dad had been able to say even that. Before hanging up, we agreed to talk later, on my way to Alaska. That never happened.

In the Denver airport, then Anchorage, and then Talkeetna, the guys and I would do our packing, traveling, and planning. By the time we finished, it would be late where we were and the middle of the night in Florida. So I hadn't called Dad back.

Now I'll never talk to him again.

I make rushed arrangements to fly home; Terry and Rodney will follow later. As I travel, I call Aunt Mary and my sisters Linda and Joanne. My third sister, Pat, is out of the country but working her way back. When the four of us were growing up, Mom and Dad encouraged us not to worry about other people's opinions, and instead to pursue our own dreams with vigor. Dad would say, "Do your own thing." Mom often tacked on her mantra: "And be nice."

All of us doing our own thing means we live in different states. That meant none of us were with Dad when he died.

· · ·

After the flight to Denver and a long van ride to Fort Collins, I walk up the driveway carrying my pack and a duffel bag of dirty climbing clothes. I drop them on the garage floor and walk into the kitchen. Glo hugs me for a long time, and we don't speak. I think we both know that tears are just a few words away. The kids come running in and hug my waist. I kneel on the oak floor so I can hug them better. I whisper, "It's good to see . . ."

Then tears arrive. The four of us stay in a sad group hug for a long time.

Existence becomes a stormy uphill climb. I stagger ahead, weak and numb, into the raging whiteout of Dad's death.

My three sisters and I decide that we should have a service in Saint Augustine, where Dad retired these last six years, and then a second one in our hometown of Concord. Dad lived there for nearly fifty years, so many of our relatives and family friends are nearby. Because of travel schedules, Pat and I will be the only ones who can attend the small service in Florida. Then we'll fly to Boston with Dad's ashes. Dad had told us that he wanted to be cremated and then to have his ashes cast into the Atlantic Ocean. He and Mom loved the beach, so it feels right.

Gloria and my sisters try to discourage me from taking on the additional burden, but I insist on giving the eulogy at both services. Ever since I was a kid, and worked all those years with him, I felt we had a double relationship. He was my dad, of course. But he was also my work mentor and the man who led us through all those dangerous painting jobs. At work he had told me to call him Joe, like the rest of the crew. And for fourteen years of painting together, I had.

Most of our Lincoln Painting Company crew had passed away by now too. Uncle Bob Davidson died of Lou Gehrig's disease at forty-nine. Then Rocco had a fatal heart attack at age forty-four. That makes me one of the last surviving core members of the crew.

For my boss and team leader, Joe, I had to be strong enough to get this job done. For Dad I needed to give him the send-off he wanted. And for myself I desperately needed to spend every last second with him that I could, before, somehow, I'd have to go on without him.

A pal's last need is a thing to heed, so I swore I would not fail.
—"THE CREMATION OF SAM McGEE," ROBERT SERVICE

Pat and I are on the plane from Florida to Massachusetts. All the family's gathering there for the service tomorrow in Concord Center. The sealed bag containing Dad's ashes is in my daypack on the plane's floor, between my feet. To protect him, I guard the pack between my lower legs. My mind reviews the eulogy I just gave in Saint Augustine. I ponder how I can do better tomorrow. Gloria and my sisters were right: This is almost too much for me. The exhaustion, the emotion. I hope I can hang on to the end, to do this right, to honor him as he so deserved.

The trail was bad, and I felt half mad, but I swore I would not give in.
—"THE CREMATION OF SAM McGEE," ROBERT SERVICE

My sisters and I stand atop the redbrick steps of the Unitarian Church in Concord. We shake hands and share hugs with a hundred friends and family as they leave the memorial service. People head to their cars for the short drive to the West Concord Elks Club, where we'll have a buffet lunch and a celebration of Dad's life.

I move aside to be alone for a moment. Two hundred yards away, on Monument Square, rises the white steeple of Saint Bernard's Parish that I painted with Dad and Uncle Bob nearly twenty-five years ago.

Dad taught me everything I needed to make a living, live my life, and even save a life. With him gone now, how will I carry all that forward into the rest of my life?

26

Ever since Mike died on Mount Rainier in 1992, June 21 has been a day of reflection and remembrance for me. The anniversary of Mike's death, and of my survival, can drag me toward sadness. So I preemptively fight back by going to the mountains every year on or about that date. Typically Rodney and I climb a rock face or summit a peak together to rejoice, give thanks for life, and remember our old friend Mike.

Rodney had just returned from a third Denali trip but was unable to summit due to a sick teammate in high camp. I felt exhausted from doing the Nepal fundraisers, and I had another one scheduled in two days. We connected for the 2015 remembrance on June 18 and decided to make the day simple and low stress. We drove an hour to the mountain town of Estes Park, Colorado, where we had both set off on countless climbs. Under the luxurious sunshine, we hiked an easy trail past Lily Lake, then scrambled uphill through a pine forest to the sport climbing area called Jurassic Park.

We took turns leading each other up casual rock climbs. Granite crystals provided sharp edges for our fingers and plentiful friction for the sticky rubber soles of our climbing shoes. I watched my partner glide up the climb with grace, as if he were slow-dancing to music only he could hear.

As I followed Rodney, warm solar energy reflected off the rock face. The welcome heat seemed like the thermal opposite of the life-threatening cold, which had recently stalked me on Everest and hounded him on Denali. The Colorado sky looked almost as blue as the sapphire-colored Steller's jay that squawked at us from a ponderosa pine. With so much comfort and beauty around us, I relaxed and enjoyed sharing a tranquil climb with a trusted friend.

Back at the car later, I reached into my small red cooler and pulled out two frosty beers. I popped the caps off and handed one bottle to Rodney. He held it skyward and waited. I hefted my bottle up, clinked it against his, and said, "To Mike."

"To Mike," Rodney replied.

We nursed our beers and organized our jumbled rack of climbing gear. Because we were dehydrated, the beer made us chatty. Mike had loved to notice life's ironies, so I wondered aloud what he would have said about my Everest trip ending just nine hours after leaving base camp. I faked his slow, southern drawl and said: "Gee, Jim, that's about the shortest Everest expedition I've ever heard of."

Rodney and I both chuckled. Then he said, "When you were in base camp, you said on the phone that there was only a ten percent chance that you'd ever go back. Where are you now?"

His question surprised me. I paused and looked at the western skyline. More mountains than we could climb in a lifetime stretched north, south, and west. I pulled a slow sip of beer and held it in my mouth. While the carbonation bubbles popped, I searched my heart and gut. When all the fizz had escaped the beer, I swallowed, turned to my climbing partner, and said, "Twenty percent."

Rodney grinned.

. . .

After eight weeks of intense focus on the earthquake impacts, I had to get back to daily living. The fundraisers tapered off, and my first keynote presentation for work arrived. At that conference I shared photos, videos, and stories about the devastating events. Change and uncertainty spawned doubt and fear on Everest, as they do in life. So I distilled what I thought my experiences revealed about facing such challenges.

The climbers on our trip who accepted the dramatic changes and adapted fast seemed to fare best. Those flexible people soon recognized that the original plan to climb Everest was gone, and they quickly shifted their focus to surviving and helping others. Rather than avoiding uncertainty, by embracing emerging challenges like digging at the field hospital, the sherpas and climbers sparked resilience in themselves and in those around them.

All the intense situations we experienced, and those I've encountered on other climbs, showed me that fear is contagious, but so is confidence. By maintaining confident attitudes about our situation, and by believing the massive problems could be resolved, we strengthened our team enough to actually solve them.

In contrast, a few individuals on Everest refused to accept that our climb was over. Their resistance to the changes thrust upon us by the quake appeared to cause them distress. Even worse, it drained energy and conviction from our team. When marching 115 difficult miles to Jiri seemed a possibility, I watched one person fret, complain, and even refuse to walk out. Their adamant unwillingness to engage with the setbacks created stress and fostered discord in our team. When the group's in a desperate situation, it's critical to add to the team's resilience, not subtract from it.

As the summer of 2015 rolled on, many people continued asking me about the situation in Nepal, so I followed the reports out of Asia. Between the 7.8 magnitude earthquake and the 7.3 magnitude aftershock of

May 12, around 8,964 people died in Nepal, 127 of them foreigners. An additional 107 people died in the neighboring countries of India, China, and Bangladesh as a result of the quakes.

The scope of human tragedy also included about 22,000 injured and around 3 million people displaced from their homes. Infrastructure impacts reached mind-boggling levels: Approximately 500,000 houses were totally destroyed, with another 269,000 damaged, according to Nepali sources.

The Himalayas exist because the Indian continental plate smashes into and slides under the Eurasian plate to the north. Just as it has for 50 million years, the Indian plate moves horizontally about two and a half inches every year and lifts the Himalayas about a fifth of an inch. That relentless plate movement causes unpredictable earthquakes along the 1,500-mile-long arc of the Himalayan Range.

Scientific studies of the April 25 quake began appearing, and the news was not good. The ten feet of lateral landslip from the Gorkha quake released about one hundred years of pent-up energy that had accrued in the colliding plates. But that represented only a small portion of the colossal tectonic forces that had accumulated in this area over the last five hundred years.

When the fault zone tore on April 25, it ruptured mostly eastward, as opposed to spreading in other directions too. That uneven tear left fault segments locked up and retaining tension that still needed release. Even worse, because the rupture did not transmit all the way to the ground surface, the tear was incomplete. In essence, the 7.8 magnitude quake was neither large enough nor complete enough to significantly reduce the tectonic risk under Nepal.

Geoscientists sometimes talk about unreleased tectonic energy as a "seismic deficit." This long-term accumulation of unmet demand for earth movement must inevitably be paid in the form of earthquakes. The Gorkha quake provided a modest down payment on that seismic deficit, but a much bigger tectonic bill remains. A larger quake must occur, and its arrival becomes more likely with every passing day.

. . .

Upon my return, friends and acquaintances asked me how bad the trash problem was on Everest. Their inquiries often stemmed from seeing an ugly photo on social media or in the news that showed trash strewn about a portion of Everest's slopes. I saw similar media reports, and they typically had shocking photo captions or inflammatory headlines referring to a "mountain of trash." While attention-grabbing, those sound-bite statements didn't match the awe-inspiring landscapes and mostly clean mountain that I experienced in 2015. In fact, I thought the Khumbu Valley was cleaner than it had been on my two previous trips there.

In 1992 Gloria and I saw trash on the ground and picked some up during our trek, especially plastic items. When Rodney and I went there in 1998, the trails seemed cleaner than six years earlier. Our sirdar, Ang Furi, said trash conditions were getting better every year, as more visitors arrived with stricter personal standards, and as the local people learned that most tourists do not like trash scattered around. Furi told us that in the Khumbu back in the 1980s "the ground had as much garbage as rocks."

Similarly, in 1976, when twenty-one young adults from Australia and New Zealand conducted one of the first cleanup efforts along the Everest base-camp trek, in Namche Bazaar they observed that "paper is blown about as freely as the dust." Their leader's report describes observing trekkers, Nepali citizens, and local business owners alike tossing trash on the ground in the Khumbu. The summary also stated: "It was agreed that reports of the rubbish situation had been exaggerated." Human carelessness, waste concerns, and exaggerating the problem all existed near Everest before commercial climbers arrived in the 1990s.

The ten students on our 1998 expedition were trained in Leave No Trace travel ethics. But, as on the 1976 cleanup trek, we couldn't pick up all the trash we saw. Because local disposal options were limited to burning, burial, or open trash pits in the villages, we had to consider what we would do with whatever we picked up. As an environmental geologist,

I concluded that the best improvement we could provide would be to gather up old batteries to get their dangerous acids, metals, and black powders out of the fragile alpine environment. Our team picked up battery cells discarded on the ground by others. By the time we flew out of Lukla four weeks later, we had a heavy collection of waste batteries. Since some crushed ones leaked their contents, I triple-bagged the whole mess and carried it out to Kathmandu for better disposal.

I was pleased in 2015 to see many trash barrels and recycling bins on the approach trek to Everest. The trails had less litter than they had in 1998, and Everest base camp looked cleaner than the nearby villages. There really was not much trash on the ground at base camp or Camp One, though patches of old expedition waste occasionally melted out from the Khumbu Glacier.

Modern Everest expeditions control their trash and carry it down-valley for local disposal. This process is enforced by the four-thousand-dollar trash deposit that the Nepal government has required of all Everest expeditions since 1993. If a team does not act in environmentally sound ways, they do not get their deposit back. Almost all climbers are nature lovers, so personal compliance is not an issue. I saw no one toss trash on the ground during my forty days in the Khumbu.

During a practice climb halfway into the icefall on April 22, 2015, PK and I traversed a narrow ice shelf with crevasses on both sides. We were clipped to the fixed line, and we stopped at 18,000 feet. I spied a rogue candy bar wrapper blowing across the snow, so I took two quick steps off the safe trail toward it. At my sudden lunge, PK yelled, "What you doing?!"

I grabbed the wrapper, held it up, and said, "Rubbish *ho*." Then I stuffed the trash in my pack's outside pocket for later disposal.

"Okay, good job," said PK. Then he pointed ten feet farther away where a snow bridge had collapsed into a deep crevasse and said, "But no go for rubbish there."

I nodded in firm agreement, and we laughed. Though we couldn't have an in-depth discussion of environmental ethics, PK and I had established our customary approach—we picked up loose trash whenever we saw it. Most of the climbers and sherpas whom I encountered on Everest did the same.

My experiences and observations were markedly different from news reports written by faraway journalists. Their articles sometimes provided ugly trash photos from long ago and inaccurately implied that the pictures represented current conditions. Some of the reporters used lazy journalism practices like providing only a one-sided perspective, or they just repeated what others had previously written. Often the inaccuracy stemmed from taking a single photo of a dirty spot, perhaps where trash from previous decades had melted from the glacier, then misapplying that visual to the entire, enormous mountain. Evocative claims of Everest being a trash heap might fuel indignation, and they might sell magazines, but they aren't accurate.

It's no surprise that social media are even less correct. I once saw an online thread painting all Everest climbers as uncaring louts who throw trash on the ground without compunction. The photo presented as evidence was purportedly taken on Everest, and it showed an open pit filled with garbage. I noted shrubby vegetation behind the hole, so I doubted the picture was from the barren upper Khumbu Valley, but I couldn't be sure. Then I spied the large black circle of an automobile tire in the pit. With the nearest road 115 miles from Everest base camp, the ugly trash pit photo couldn't be from Mount Everest.

Between 1975 and 2016, at least twenty-five expeditions made environmental cleanup a cornerstone of their Everest trip. The earliest efforts concentrated on picking up the accessible waste left at base camp from the 1950s through the 1970s, when ecological standards barely existed around the world. Most expeditions in the 1980s and 1990s policed their litter better and burned it, but trash abandoned during previous generations remained high on the mountain.

Creative social systems emerged in the 1990s to pay high-altitude workers a bounty for any garbage they brought down: six dollars for oxygen bottles and three dollars for every ten kilograms (22 pounds) of other trash. After several years, almost all the deserted oxygen bottles had been removed from the mountain. These days it's rare to see one lying about on Everest.

More recent efforts have tackled the grueling task of recovering trash locked into ice on the windswept slopes. This stubborn residual is frozen onto the mountain and thus hard to pry from the ground, though progress continues. In 2014 Nepal passed requirements mandating that every Everest climber bring down eight kilos (17.6 pounds) of garbage. If everyone removes their own refuse, plus picks up some left behind by others, then, over time, the Everest community can remove all the trash from the mountain.

27

When I swung my right ice tool into the steep slope, the pick sank an inch into the ice. A handful of displaced frozen crystals arced past my head into the cloudy Colorado sky. Like a mild seismic aftershock, a gentle vibration resonated through the ice ax handle. The deep *thud* of the sharp steel pick melding with the mountain told me that my tool placement was good, and the ice was solid. Up I went.

Since it was my fifty-third birthday, I was spending the day as I had a dozen times before: ascending autumn alpine ice with a buddy in Rocky Mountain National Park. The moderate climb provided a fun challenge that still got me home by dinnertime to celebrate with Glo and the kids. Crisp fall air pushed the elk from the high country and drove the summer tourists from the trails. The solitude felt like having the national park to ourselves.

Alan and I started early, so we were hiking through an aspen grove when the morning's first sunlight slanted through the golden canopy. Clouds built thicker all day, though, so we raced to finish the climb before the rain started. We were ascending the middle Ptarmigan Finger on the north side of Flattop Mountain. The deep cleft always held snow through the summer, so by my September birthday, the snowfield solidifies into a firm gully of pliable alpine ice.

With 700 vertical feet of ice below us, only 100 feet of technical climbing remained. I kicked in my crampons and swung a short ice tool in each hand as I led the last pitch. Alan was belaying me from below, paying out rope as I advanced and he stood ready to hold the rope fast if I fell. I stopped to place a final piece of protection before I pushed for the top. After turning an ice screw into the ice field, I clipped the rope to it with two carabiners and a nylon sling, then I exhaled to relax. The intermediate protection would reduce the length of my fall if I slipped off. The final headwall reared up steeper than sixty degrees, so I needed to climb well.

Four months after Everest, some of my hard-won fitness remained, but kicking my crampons several hundred times into the dense ice had tired my calf muscles. I focused hard on each tool swing and every crampon placement, striving for smoothness and efficiency. The farther I got from my last screw placement, the greater my potential fall, so climbing well was my best protection.

I pulled over the headwall lip and stepped onto the flat top of the ice gully.

A rock buttress ten feet ahead offered some cracks where I could stop and bring Alan up. After constructing a solid belay anchor with three metal pieces of rock protection, I tied myself in. Thirty-three years of alpine climbing had taught me never to trust my life, or my partner's, to a single piece of gear.

I yelled down into the gully, "Off belay!"

"Belay's off!" he screamed. His distant voice drifted up from our last belay station almost two hundred feet below.

I slid off my pack and put Alan on belay. After he removed the anchor pieces near him, Alan began climbing. The rope slackened as he ascended, so I reeled him in. I looked around the summit plateau and studied the undulating surface of short grass and black rocks. The smooth peneplain, an erosional remnant from a geologic era long gone, contained the invisible line of the Continental Divide. That subtle watershed boundary separated the flow of rainfall into east and west, toward the Atlantic and Pacific Oceans, respectively.

Raindrops fell from the sky, so I pulled my jacket hood over my helmet. The rainfall turned the basin below us fuzzy gray while the pile of purple rope beside me grew larger. A few minutes later Alan popped over the headwall lip, and I said, "Welcome to the top."

"Nice lead, dude."

We packed up the gear and walked fifteen minutes to the summit marker for Flattop Mountain at 12,324 feet. The rain stopped, so we did too. We broke out our water bottles and snack bags. Our conversation, as it often did, turned to Everest. Alan said, "Nepal just announced that because they closed the mountain, everyone's 2015 permits are valid for two more years."

"Do you think they'll honor that?" I asked.

"Hard to say. Some Nepali government announcements actually happen, and some don't. But, so far, it looks good."

"Bart's going back in 2016. If his permit's still good, that'll save him eleven thousand."

"What about you?"

I pursed my lips and shook my head. "Nope. Jess is graduating from the University of Denver next spring, so I'm out."

"Got ya."

"Even if I could go, I'm not sure it's smart to try in 2016. It'll be the first year back, and no one's even sure that the route's still there. Who knows what the quakes did to the mountain?"

"Since your trip insurance refunded most of your Everest costs, between that and the free permit, you could go back pretty cheap."

I didn't say anything but nodded in agreement.

"I hope you put that trip money aside so that you can go back or go somewhere else."

"Yeah, that would've been a good move, but it's already been spent."

"What?" said Alan on a rising pitch.

"College tuition, a year of hockey, and a new water heater. It's gone."

"Oh no! Can you raise the money again if you want to go back?"

"Won't be easy. Guess I'll watch how the 2016 season unfolds and go from there."

Inner Strength Rock Gym in Fort Collins served as my local climbing gym for seventeen years. When the owners, Mike and Tracy Hickey, asked me in November 2015 to present about Everest and the earthquake, we turned it into another fundraiser with all the money going to Nepal's reconstruction. I updated my slide deck to address common audience questions I had heard over several months. Many people asked understandable questions about altitude, training, and the cost of climbing. But one question baffled me: Is Everest covered in poop?

To me the human waste problem on Everest was like the trash issue: A few limited areas were problematic, but most of the enormous mountain looked clean. The environment is almost perpetually frozen above base camp, so waste hardly biodegrades up there. I saw a little human waste on the ground, but not much. Media reports that Everest was covered in poop seemed inaccurate and even impossible.

In science, hard data are always better than opinions. Because I'd spent two decades evaluating environmental problems, I decided to estimate the extent of human waste on Everest using a scientific approach. So I created the Everest Poop spreadsheet. My witty writing friend, Gordon MacKinney, called it the spreadshit.

First I used the Himalayan Database to determine that about 17,780 people, including climbers, guides, and high-altitude workers, had gone above base camp between 1921 and 2015. The typical healthy human has a bowel movement about once per day. If I knew how many days each person spent above base camp, it would allow me to calculate how many human stools were ever deposited on the upper mountain.

An Everest expedition can require about two months from home to home. Many of those days, though, are for traveling, waiting in Kathmandu, and trekking to and from the mountain. Most teams spend about forty days actually camped on Mount Everest. A significant portion of that time is used for resting and acclimatizing in base camp, so the climbers, workers, and guides spend much less than forty days on the upper slopes. Using an average of twenty days spent above base camp for everyone seemed accurate and reasonable.*

With 17,780 people having spent an average of twenty days above base camp, and with each person having one bowel movement per day, then there might have been around 335,600 poops ever made on Everest above base camp.†

Internet searches about the dimensions of human stool led me to weird websites but yielded little data on the size of the average poop. The available data and personal experience led me to use a dimension of six inches long and 1.5 inches wide. Based on that estimate, each daily poop would cover about nine square inches or 0.0625 square feet of the mountain.

Simple multiplication means that 335,600 poops might collectively cover about 22,225 square feet. Because an acre covers 43,560 square feet, all the poop ever deposited above base camp by humans would cover just a bit over a half acre. While a poop-covered area about four-tenths the size of an American football field may be an unpleasant image, it seemed tiny compared with the vast terrain of Mount Everest.

Next I needed to estimate the surface area of Mount Everest. That can get complicated, so I initially used a straightforward approach, even

---

* Guided clients, like me, climb less than fifteen days above base camp. High-altitude workers often carry loads for two days and then get a rest day. This two-on-and-one-off pattern dictates that over a forty-day expedition, they spend about twenty-five days above base camp. However, many of their carries are day trips from base camp to Camp One or Camp Two and then back down, so they still spend a lot of time at the foot of the mountain. According to the Himalayan Database, over the last twenty-five years about half the people on Everest are locally hired guides and high-altitude workers, and the rest are climbers or guides from other nations. Since about half of the people are above base camp for fifteen days, and the other half for twenty-five days, a value of twenty days per person for everyone works.

† Some unknown percentage of those in recent years were carried down the mountain, and others were removed by the various cleanup expeditions. This meant that the actual number of poops remaining above base camp must be less than 335,600.

though the simple method would underestimate the size of the mountain's undulating surface. On a map of the Everest region, I drew a rectangle around the peak to include all areas above the base-camp elevation of about 17,000 feet. The rectangle enclosed the three major base camps (south side, north side, and the rarely used east side) and included all eighteen major routes ever climbed. That Everest-encompassing rectangle is about six miles long east to west, and two miles wide north to south. So the two-dimensional estimate of Everest's surface area is twelve square miles, or 334,540,800 square feet.

For the final step I used rounded values and divided the 22,225 square feet ever impacted by a human stool by the 334,541,000-square-foot map area of Everest. Thus, using conservative numbers, it appears that all the poops ever taken above base camp might cover, at a maximum, 0.007 percent of the mountain. The other 99.993 percent of the mountain has never been pooped upon.*

These estimates don't mean that the aesthetic and potential health impacts of human excrement on the mountain do not exist. Better waste-management practices are needed. But exaggerated claims about Everest being covered in poop are wildly inaccurate and—well—*grossly* misleading.

During my presentation at Inner Strength, I shared the Everest Poop spreadshit results with the climbers. The anonymity of the dark room—

---

* The mountain is not a flat rectangle like the one I used in my initial calculations, of course. A more accurate geometrical model would be a three-dimensional right-rectangular pyramid, with a base six miles long and two miles wide. The height of the pyramid would be about 12,029 feet, from the base-camp elevation of about 17,000 feet up to the 29,029-foot summit. This improved approximation of Everest's size and shape results in four idealized triangular pyramid sides, which have a total smooth-surface area almost double that of the simplistic two-dimensional surface area value. So the percentage of terrain covered by poop above base camp (still 22,225 square feet) would be even less at about 0.004 percent of the mountain's surface area. An even-more-sophisticated approach that accounted for the terrain's real-world surface roughness would further reduce the estimated percentage of the mountain that has ever been pooped upon to something less than 0.004 percent. No matter which surface-area calculation is used (flat area, smooth pyramid, or rough pyramid), however, the portion of Mount Everest that has never been pooped upon apparently exceeds 99.9 percent.

and perhaps the free beer—triggered at least a half-dozen juvenile poop jokes from the audience, and maybe one or two from me. When the laughter subsided, I explained how less than one ten-thousandth of the mountain above base camp could possibly have poop on it. I saw surprised looks and nodding heads across the darkened rock gym.

As I did during every fundraiser, I urged the attendees not only to contribute to the evening's charity, but also to visit Nepal. The country doesn't have many valuable commodities, like oil or gold, but it's rich in beauty, so tourism is a significant industry. Visiting Nepal as it rebuilds not only injects much-needed money into its economy, it puts people back to work, lifts their spirits, and encourages them to continue recovering. The Nepali citizens needed to know that the world had not forgotten them.

I shared that message from the stage about thirty times in 2015 and repeated it during countless conversations and interviews. Increasingly, I began to consider a return to Nepal myself.

Going back would let me do my share of creating the social benefits I had encouraged others to initiate by visiting there. Of all the countries that I have been to, Nepal had the most gorgeous, awe-inspiring landscape I had seen; that's part of why I kept going back. Visiting the country didn't require me to climb any tall mountains, though. Being a tourist or trekker would let me experience the country's natural treasures, with minimal risk from crevasses, earthquakes, or avalanches.

But, there was Everest.

I had spent three decades dreaming and scheming my way toward the mountain. Then the expedition ended so fast. My drive to climb Mount Everest, to make myself capable of climbing Everest, remained strong. But so did the bad memories. I still recalled the terrible sound of those avalanches rushing down while we had nowhere to run. Scary photos and videos from Camp One reminded me of our anxious days trapped on the glacier. The heartache of watching two tarp-wrapped bodies being flown from base camp stayed with me.

If I went back to Everest, all those memories could percolate to the surface. Would that be healing or harmful? All the geologic information pointed toward another big quake, perhaps soon. Could I risk going back when I knew what was inevitable? I recognized the risks, but I yearned for the rewards. I couldn't find out what awaited unless I went back and tried again.

The biggest question for me was: Would returning to the mountain make a mess of my life or add meaning to it?

28

My climbing pack tips the scale at about fifty pounds. But the weight of what's about to happen makes me feel as if I'm carrying twice that amount. After twenty years spent wondering what it would be like to see the killer up close again, I'll find out in ten more minutes.

I keep slogging up the snowy hill toward the top of the glacial moraine. My four friends march close behind me, letting me set the pace. In another hundred feet I will get my first close-up view in two decades of Mount Rainier's Emmons Glacier, the ice monster that killed Mike.

Half a dozen times since the 1992 accident, I have stood in Rainier's shadow. With various companions I've hiked, backpacked, and skied the forested slopes along the base of the volcano. And twice I gathered with hundreds of fellow climbers at the nearby Rainier Mountain Festival. Even those low-to-no-risk brushes with the peak made me anxious. Now returning to Rainier to climb one of its glaciers to the summit feels terrifying.

The shifting ice slopes and plunging crevasses make me plenty nervous. That's why we assembled a large, strong team. Rodney and Alan agreed immediately to come with me; then we strengthened our rope team with two other climbing friends: my college roommate, Scott Yetman, and his mountaineering partner, Stan Hoffman. Scott and Stan live in Seattle, near Mount Rainier, and they've summited the mountain several times. All four of them are veteran climbers; they understand my history with Rainier; and, most important, they are smart and loyal friends. I call them my A-Team.

The intervening years have lessened my fears, doubts, and guilt. Sharing the story of what happened to Mike and me through my speaking and writing has helped reduce those traumatic burdens. But deep in my gut, a small spring of those gripping emotions still bubbles away. My biggest fear about returning to Rainier stems from looming psychological threats. Some long-buried unpleasant memories of the crevasse accident might get dredged up. Can I really climb up the very glacier that ended Mike's life and almost took mine? What if I'm too racked with terror even to step onto the ice?

Somehow I sense that going back has the potential to provide more healing. If I can summon the courage to once again walk upon that deadly slope, perhaps I can grind another step forward in my life.

I once fought hand-to-hand with the Emmons Glacier when I had to escape from one of its deep crevasses. Using pointed weapons of ice axes and crampons, I struggled up the vertical, and even overhanging, ice wall. I climbed for hours back up the crevasse's black throat toward the sunlight above. When the fight ended, my good friend Mike was gone and I was changed forever. The mountain remained unchanged.

That physical battle ended long ago. Perhaps by now the mountain and I are like two old soldiers from opposing sides. Twenty years after the combat ended, they are no longer enemies. The intervening years can nurture wisdom and mutual respect; returning to a place of tough memories can bring healing and forgiveness.

I understand that Rainier is not sentient; it's only an elevated cone of rock and ice. The mountain would remain unaffected by my presence or my emotions. But for me, perhaps spending time with my old foe might bring more tranquility.

When I crest the top of the moraine, I unbuckle my pack's waistbelt and let the backpack slip to the ground. The edge of the Emmons Glacier is just thirty feet away. I scan my eyes across the glacier and, by triangulating off several landmarks burned into my memory, I zero in on a prominent area called the Corridor. That's where the hidden snow bridge collapsed beneath my feet and dropped Mike and me deep inside the crevasse. Its smooth white stripe of snow runs up the fall line a few hundred feet toward the distant summit. Most climbers consider this compression zone of the glacier relatively safe. But a rare longitudinal crevasse lurked under the snow in 1992. That's what got us.

Below the Corridor, a low-angle slope provides a direct descent to the solid rock prow of Camp Sherman. If Mike and I had made it past that one hidden crevasse, we could have descended the slope in less than an hour. I blurt out, "We were so close to being safe. Oh, we were so damn close!"

My voice cracks, and I drop my gaze to the ground. I see volcanic rocks next to my boots, then the view washes away behind the tears flooding my eyes. The sound of feet scuffing rocks tells me the guys are hurrying over. One friend stands close by my left hip and places his arm over my shoulder. Another squeezes tight on my right side and wraps his arm around my waist for support. I feel two other hands pat my shoulder and the back of my head. In a tight cluster, my four buddies stand with me to grieve.

Twenty minutes later we tie into a single rope about forty feet apart from one another and prepare to climb. Five on a rope can be cumbersome and slow, but having four skilled teammates backing me up provides just enough assurance for me to step back onto the glacier that almost killed me. I say, "If it's okay with everyone, I'd like to lead us out there."

Rodney says, "Whatever you want, Jim."

"It's your call, Jimmy," says Scott. Alan and Stan answer the same.

We conduct a safety check on one another, then all move apart along the moraine to eliminate slack rope between us. I look over my right shoulder and, using a booming voice to bolster my own confidence, I shout, "Look sharp, guys! We're moving out!"

I drive the spike of my ice ax into the surface snow to probe for hidden crevasses. Feeling only solid ground, I lift my right boot high and stomp my crampon into the glacier surface with more force than needed. When doubt is high, momentum is everything. So, without pausing, I stab my ax again and take another step with all the authority I can muster. I've returned to the Emmons Glacier.

By angling left, I lead the team around a few visible black holes, but we all know I'll have to face a crevasse soon. That moment arrives five minutes later. The opening is only two feet wide, so stepping over it should be easy. Still, my tension rises. I give my rope mates a warning. "Small crevasse here. Stepping across."

Back along the rope, the entire A-Team ready their ice axes to self-arrest and catch me if I slip in. We all know that we're being overly cautious, but they're doing everything possible to enable me to push myself forward. That's what great friends and partners do.

I step across the modest gap. At midstride my eyes twitch rightward at the inky depths lurking below. Once safe on the other side, I lift my ax overhead in a small salute and yell, "No problem, boys!"

Loud, joyous whoops rise up from behind me. Alan shouts, "All right, Jim!"

After a few hours of sleep we spill from the tents just before midnight and rope up again. The rangers at the Camp Sherman hut told us that several collapsing snow bridges just above the Corridor had made the standard Emmons Route quite dangerous. They considered it closed. Though disappointed that we will not climb the exact route that Mike and I had descended twenty years earlier, I also feel relieved. I'm not sure I could handle climbing right over the spot where we plummeted into the glacier.

Instead we'll climb a parallel route farther west and ascend the Winthrop Glacier. My partners give me the choice of going first, last, or in one of the safe middle positions. I choose the lead for now. The white-yellow beam of my headlamp lights up the surface as I step onto the ice. Frozen crystals refract the light into colored stars that dance around my boots as I move past.

We traverse a few hundred yards west; then the glacier steepens. The wide ice sheet buckles into a series of round hills surrounded by large crevasses. When I point my headlamp beam at the raised white mounds, dark shadows hide the crevasse openings that I know are there. To me the hilltops look like the humped backs of a dozen dragons prowling around us.

When we ascend above 10,000 feet, the thinner air and lack of sleep make me breathe too fast. I slow to a more sustainable pace since we still have 4,000 vertical feet left to climb. Thirty minutes later we enter a jumbled section of broken ice blocks. Our five-man rope team becomes a hassle as we zigzag around several crevasses. At any moment two of us might be moving west, while the other three traverse east. We do our best to keep all four segments of the rope tight between us as we thread our way through the maze.

A hundred feet higher, two crevasses intersect, and the gap will force me to step atop a precarious ice pillar. The pillar top is the size of a welcome mat, and black slots yawn open on both sides. Stepping onto the tiny ice island doesn't seem inviting, but it's the best way through. The guys in the back are threading an S-curve around another crevasse, so I turn to Rodney right behind me on the rope and say, "Watch me."

I envision a clean stride onto the pillar, and then off the other side. After releasing a long exhale, I place one crampon-clad boot upon the small platform. As I rock forward to exit the airy perch, an urgent call comes from the other end of the rope: "Stop!"

I halt with my weight committed onto the pillar. Black space surrounds me. Scott yells, "We need slack! Back up!"

What timing! I push harder than I want off the pillar and step backward to where I had been a moment before. I look off to where the rope-management problem is, but in the dark I see only three headlamp beams slicing through the air like a laser show. I stand inches from the crevasse edge and wait. After they solve the rope puzzle and give us the okay, I prepare to repeat the committing move. I tell myself, It held once, so it'll hold again. *Right?*

I'm frazzled, so once we move past the broken section, I yield the lead. Over the next four hours everyone takes a turn out front kicking steps into the snow and finding safe passage among the crevasses. At sunrise the vast snow slopes above and below us turn pink, then orange. We climb slower to about 13,700 feet and stop for a water break. I look northeast down the full length of the Emmons Glacier. It stretches almost four miles long and descends more than 8,000 vertical feet before the melting terminus merges into the forest.

Like all glaciers, everything that falls onto and into the Emmons gets transported downhill. As I have many times over the last twenty years, I think about how if I hadn't been able to ascend that crevasse wall and direct the rangers where to recover Mike's body, my friend and I would have become part of the glacier. Over the decades our stiffened gear and frozen bodies would have been ground into microscopic bits of nylon and flesh. In a few dozen centuries, our granular remains would have emerged from the glacier's toe, somewhere down near the pine trees.

We step off the glacier about eight o'clock and scramble onto the volcanic crater rim, a safe berm of volcanic rock and ash. After we untie, the cold wind urges us to add more clothing layers. A bright blue sky stretches west to Seattle and extends over the Pacific Ocean. With no storm threat, we take our time walking counterclockwise along the curved crater toward the summit.

Ten minutes later only five easy strides remain. I pretend for a moment that my four companions are not behind me. I feel like I'm with Mike. Last time we were overjoyed to stand on top together after our multiday struggle up the challenging Liberty Ridge. We were fit and young; our futures seemed to stretch to infinity.

I take the last step, and once again I'm atop Mount Rainier. Trying to smile, I look up into the sky. Hey, Mike! I'm here! I am on the summit with Mike.

The wind taps my jacket hood against my right cheek. I turn and see my other friends lined up just two yards away. I open my arms wide and, as they each take those last steps, we all link into a tight circle. Arms drape over shoulders, hands pat whichever back they touch. Tears and laughter intertwine. I am on the summit with the boys.

I would have never made it off Rainier without Mike, and I could never have come back without Rodney, Alan, Scott, and Stan. My friends have propelled me far.

29

In the spring of 2016, Bart and several other former teammates returned to Everest. I read their blogs and social media posts every morning to track their progress, and to see if Nepal and Everest were safe after the quake. Two weeks later, on a sunny April morning, Gloria awoke late after working her night shift at the hospital. I exited my home office and joined her in the kitchen to prepare my third cup of tea while she made coffee. I gave her a brief update about the Khumbu Valley weather and who had reached base camp. As I spoke, I walked brisk laps around the kitchen. Jake followed close behind, probably hoping we'd take a walk. Half-awake, my wife said, "You're pacing."

I stood still and switched to blowing air across my teacup. Gloria asked, "How do you feel that they're all there, and you're not?"

After I blew two more unnecessary puffs at my tea, I said, "Like all my friends are at a big party and I can't go."

. . .

As a climber and geologist, I had a clear-eyed understanding of the risks. Some people might consider my 2015 companions and me lucky to have escaped the earthquake, and dumb for considering a return.

But my return to Mount Rainier in 2012 had taught me that there was great healing in going back. Standing respectfully upon the glacial dragon again had made the monster less formidable. Reaching the summit once more showed me that while the mountain was still dangerous, it was not so scary as my traumatic memories had led me to believe. I had shouldered the mountain's weight for twenty years, but after we stepped off the volcano, I felt lighter.

The presence and power of my family and friends, both dead and alive, gave me the courage to grapple with mountains, glaciers, and crevasses again. It was not so much the act of climbing that helped me, though. Staring at my fears long enough to make them shrink back had made me stronger and brought me more peace. Perhaps returning to Everest could do the same.

Studies on resilience and post-traumatic stress indicate that, over time, many traumatized people can draw positive aspects from their negative experiences. The slow, hard work of struggling through the mess can lead trauma survivors to find meaning. That transformation can encourage the development of greater strength or wisdom. Though survivors cannot make the traumatic event go away, they can distill from it more vision, purpose, and resilience. This is called post-traumatic growth—literally growth from trauma.

Climbing Rainier again didn't bring Mike back, and post-traumatic growth does not make terrible traumas go away. Nor is post-traumatic growth a magic antidote to post-traumatic stress. It's more akin to how a human creates antibodies after being exposed to a virus. Though the illness may have been painful or difficult, in the end the experience can initiate an internal response that makes a person stronger. In short, enduring past trauma can better prepare someone for the next change, challenge, or uncertainty ahead.

. . .

With nothing serious to train for, I had gained fifteen pounds since returning from Everest. I was displeased with myself. If I went back to Nepal in 2017, I needed to stop gaining weight and start losing it. Since I
wasn't committed to going back yet, it was premature to start an intense
conditioning program. But I quietly started training.

Trail running always helped me lose weight and build endurance. But
since wrecking my right knee while skiing in 2010, I had not been able
to run. My cracked tibial plateau bone healed in six weeks, but the sev-
ered anterior cruciate ligament (ACL) posed a much tougher problem.
First I had to endure five weeks of painful rehab to forcibly regain knee
flexion before the surgeon would operate. When the doctor offered several options to repair my ACL in February 2011, I told him I wanted the
strongest repair possible. I said: "I plan to climb Everest someday and if
my knee gives out up there, I could die. Even worse, a bad knee could put
my teammates in grave risk if they try to drag me down."

He explained how the best option was to take part of my patellar ten-
don from my good knee and install it as the ACL in the bad one. That
required cutting both legs and then long rehabs of both knees afterward.
It was going to be a tough trail, but if that was the choice that would make
me strongest, then that's the path we were going to take.

On the morning of the operation, Gloria kept me company as I sat
on the gurney wearing a cotton hospital gown. They gave me a spinal
to numb my legs and doped me up with anesthesia. My memory of the
morning stops there, but Gloria later told me that as they wheeled me to
surgery, I kept saying, "I can't feel my feet. They're frostbit. We've got to
warm my feet or I'll lose them."

The surgeon did his job well in the operating room. Then, under the strict
guidance of my excellent physical therapist, Tia, I did my job in the rehab
gym. Over the next year I regained my capacity for hiking, climbing, and

skiing. But running even half a mile caused severe knee pain. I had not been able to run when I trained for the 2015 Everest trip, and I wanted to change that if I was going to try again.

I decided that a gradual but relentless buildup might let me regain the ability to run. Besides improving my physical fitness, following a strict regime would enhance my discipline and refine my commitment to Everest training, and to the mountain itself. So I did my first trail run—for one minute. Then I added one more minute every time I ran. No more, no less. By the time my friends were on their summit pushes in late May, I had built up to running two pain-free miles.

On May 23, 2016, my morning check of the climbing news revealed a spectacular photo of Bart standing atop Mount Everest. He, PK, and most of the IMG team had summited around sunrise on a gorgeous morning. The intense sun at 29,029 feet illuminated Bart's familiar down suit into an iridescent shade of orange. I jumped up from my chair, thrust both fists into the air, and cheered aloud. My exuberance startled Jake, who barked and ran in circles. I was so pleased for them, and so inspired, that I increased my run that day by a daring two minutes. The tiny step up didn't hurt, so adding two minutes to each run became my new increment of progression.

IMG and other teams had a safe and good year on Everest. The southeast ridge route from Nepal seemed mostly unchanged and appeared no more dangerous than before. The successful 2016 season also showed that Nepal had recovered enough to handle visitors. These verifications provided another green light for my deliberations about returning to Everest.

I compiled a long list of how I could be better prepared if I returned in 2017. After reviewing my training logs from the 2015 trip, I designed an even more intense program. While gradually increasing my workouts, I also tightened my dietary discipline. I had long ago made obvious changes like no doughnuts, junk food, or french fries. The next step required cutting out more sweets and reducing portion sizes. Though the numbers moved slowly, my scale readings decreased, and my running mileage increased. The foundation for another round of Everest training was solid so far, but a lot of time-consuming hard work remained.

Though the risks of high altitude worried her and the money used was not available for other family needs, Gloria's biggest concern about me joining an expedition was time. When we had discussed my plans for a six-week expedition to Cho Oyu in 2009, she'd said, "It's not even the days you're gone, it's all the training time." She was right.

In the year before Everest, I trained about nine hundred hours, and I also went on two international trips to get altitude exposure. I climbed Pico de Orizaba (18,491 feet) in Mexico with the CSU Outdoor Program, and I hiked to the top of Kilimanjaro (19,340 feet) with Jess when she studied abroad in Africa. Though I needed to avoid injuries from overuse, I always tried to do as much training as possible before each expedition. I figured that every hour spent training made it more likely that I would stay safe and succeed, and less likely that I would get hurt or killed. It's better to find and fix your weakness early than to suddenly discover it later.

As my expedition goals got bigger through the years, the time demands became greater too. I initially created extra time by training late at night or before sunrise when the kids were little. To focus myself on expedition climbing, I dropped other fun pursuits like ski touring and backpacking.

I also adopted time-saving personal habits. In 1982 I grew a beard because my then-new girlfriend, Gloria, said she thought it would look good. I soon noticed that not shaving saved me five minutes every morning. Thirty-four bearded years saved me about a thousand hours. I once read about a hard-core Colorado alpinist who didn't bother washing his car, because it would just become dirty again. I admired his logic, so I stopped washing my car in 1996 (besides, the rain cleans it eventually). Being willing to drive a dusty vehicle eliminated the weekly half-hour chore. This accumulated as five hundred hours of time for more meaningful activities. Those two habits alone saved me enough time for a sixty-day Everest expedition.

Family, work, and passionate pursuits each demand energy and time. Juggling all these requires intricate time management. I simplified the balancing act by reducing my hobbies and interests. I never golfed, hunted, gambled, or watched sports on TV. This saved me considerable time.

The only sporting events I attended were those with one of our kids on the field or next to me in the stands. I only went fishing or downhill skiing with Gloria, Jess, and Nick. By being purposeful with the most treasured resource we have, time, I created the space to pursue my mountain passions with vigor.

Jess graduated on June 4, 2016, and her big accomplishment was a proud and joyful occasion for our family. Graduation day itself was exhausting though, as right after the ceremony, we helped her move out of her apartment and sell her old car. That evening we had a smiling but teary goodbye, as she caught a red-eye flight to Washington, D.C., where she was starting a White House internship. With a significant family milestone reached, we rested for a few days. The next weekend I said to Gloria, "Glo, let's talk about Everest."

"What? *Again?*" she asked in a high-pitched voice. She reacted as if I had just admitted to carelessly crashing the family car a second time.

"Yeah, I know."

"Well. Where are you at?"

"You know the situation. Bart and the guys summited, so the route's good. Nepal honored their permits, so it really is eleven grand less than last time."

"What about the rest of the money?" she asked.

"I'm working on it. Pretty sure I've got it figured out."

We were both less intense than the previous time we'd had this discussion. Glo looked a bit annoyed, but I didn't sense any pushback. She almost seemed resigned to it. I was prepared to plead my case, to point out how the kids were older and so was I. How, unlike other husbands, I didn't spend money on boats, motorcycles, or fancy cars. I had crafted a series of defensive and (hopefully) persuasive points. But I didn't need them.

Gloria let out a big sigh and gave me a pensive look. Two seconds later she said, "All right. But this is the last time."

Rodney and I departed for an overnight alpine rock climb in Rocky Mountain National Park. We carried our big packs up on June 20 so we could reach the summit on June 21. After five miles we neared our objective, a pointed granitic protrusion called the Sharkstooth. Snow still lingered on the higher cliffs, so we rolled our sleeping bags out on a gravel patch at about 11,000 feet and prepared dinner. With only four pitches of easy rock awaiting us in the morning, our confidence was high. The tiny cookstove purred away, working to boil water. I updated my partner on the momentum building for me to try Everest again in 2017. He said, "Sounds like the mountain's passable and Glo's on board. So what else is there?"

"The money. I can pull enough together, but I feel kind of guilty spending that much."

Ever pragmatic, Rodney asked, "Well, what're you willing to give up to pay for it?"

My eyebrows rose, and I stared him right in the eyes. "Almost anything. I'll drive an old rust bucket for twenty years, live a simpler retirement, or work longer. Whatever it takes."

"Okay, then you can afford to go."

I was stunned by how calm he seemed. Last time, we had long, excited, and anxious conversations about the many risks and rewards of going to Everest. This time, it was like we were merely pondering minor logistics. Sure, I had the gear, knew how to train, and understood the mountain better, so there were far fewer unknowns. But Rodney's reaction felt almost matter-of-fact. I said, "You don't seem very surprised that I'm seriously talking about going back."

"What? Surprised that you'd dust yourself off, come up with a new plan, and try even harder for the biggest mountain in the world? No. I'd be more surprised if you didn't go back."

Time was running out to commit to Everest for 2017. To receive the early discount of fifteen hundred dollars from IMG, my paperwork and deposit had to be in their hands by July 31, just a week away. Training kept progressing, Gloria remained supportive, and the money was put aside. Yet I hesitated.

I still felt leery about the risk of more earthquakes and landslides. Instead of working, I cruised the internet looking for new geologic analyses and seismic data that could provide insight into the tectonic risks. I found an online database at Nepal's National Seismological Centre that compiled records about all tremors of 4.0 magnitude or larger—about the level at which humans can feel the ground moving. When I sorted the data to determine how many such tremors Nepal had recorded since the big Gorkha earthquake, the answer shocked me. In the past fourteen months there had been about five hundred.

Five hundred! I said aloud, "Oh, crap."

Instead of calming my fears, this information fed them. With all those, a great quake was going to happen sooner or later. The time to decide about Everest had almost arrived, yet I didn't know what to do.

I slept poorly that night, but in the morning I loaded thirty pounds of gear into my pack and went on a training hike. To focus on my Everest decision, I walked uphill at a slow and steady pace. The gradual rate provided an opportunity to practice moving relentlessly, so I didn't stop at all. I ascended toward the distant summit in a single, measured push. To the other hikers I encountered, it might have looked like I was on a mellow stroll, but inside my head, chaos churned.

Once again I analyzed the dollars and time that Everest would demand. I tried weighing the likelihood of safety and success against the
possibilities of failure or death. Managing work and minimizing family
impacts for a two-month absence would be tricky but doable. However,
I knew that the decision had moved beyond logic.

When planning my earliest expeditions, I tried to determine when
I might have sufficient amounts of the three critical resources: time,
money, and energy. Young people often have time and energy, but no
money. Middle age usually provides energy and money, but no time. And
for the lucky ones who make it to old age, many have time and money,
but no energy. This irony of life meant that if I was ever going to do anything significant, it would probably have to be done when there was a
shortage of one or more of those resources.

The early deaths of Uncle Bob, then Rocco, then Mike, and, finally,
Dad, all made me very aware that not everyone even reaches old age, let
alone has the opportunity to grab for their dream. Going to Everest again
would not be fast, cheap, or easy, but in my current circumstances it was
possible. None of those guys ever got such a big chance.

On the summit I checked my altimeter watch and saw that my ascent
rate had averaged 1,500 feet per hour—not bad. I dropped my pack and
dug out one of the quart-size bottles I had filled with water for training
weight. After a deep pull of cold water, I sat on the summit stone and
ate raisins. My eyes saw the Rockies, but my mind thought only of the
Himalayas.

If I didn't go back to Everest, would I lament that decision later?
Would I regret it on my deathbed? What would Mike advise me to do?
What would Dad think?

I had the knowledge and experience. I knew the risks, and I could
still make myself strong enough to try, even at age fifty-four. If there's an
afterlife, and I meet Mike and Dad there later, how would I ever explain
not trying to climb again?

There'd probably be no self-delusion or polite white lies in the afterlife. I'd have to tell them the blunt truth: I had everything I needed to seize my big dream, but it felt like too much work. It seemed too hard and too scary, so I didn't even try.

I couldn't face them and say that!

Those guys had propelled me so damn far, and now I had the opportunity to climb the highest peak on the planet, to make an enormous dream come true.

It's time to step up.

I could do this not just for me, but for them too. Their lessons and support had kept me alive and gotten me this far. I was so close now. All I had to do was work hard, not quit, and get this done. For all of us.

I'm going.

My heart raced, and both hands tingled. I stood on the summit block. Knowing that no other hikers were nearby, I shouted, "I'm going back to Everest!"

30

Three decades of climbing had taught me how to prepare for the mountains. Previous trips to Cho Oyu and Everest had made it clear how fit I had to be for an 8,000-meter peak. My conditioning for those expeditions went well, but now I was older. This time I needed more of everything: aerobic capacity, strength, endurance, and, most important, the mental toughness to keep going. I started my most rigorous conditioning program ever.

Because long mountain days demand a strong aerobic foundation, I kept increasing my running frequency and intensity. By October 2016 I had progressed to three runs per week, mostly on the hilly trails near our house. My favorite challenge was to run up a steep Fort Collins road called Maniac Hill. Since training for my first Himalayan climb in 1998, my rule for Maniac runs was that no matter how hard it felt or how slow I went, I could never stop. When my improved fitness let me cruise up at a smooth pace, I added a second lap.

Running not only built my aerobic capacity, but it also instilled valuable lessons I could apply to other aspects of my conditioning. Over the years several half marathons and one marathon had shown me how to progressively increase the aerobic load. I also learned, by trial and error, when to schedule "step back" periods of lesser difficulty to let my body recover and adapt. This fine balance would let me build my aerobic capacity while preventing burnout and, hopefully, avoiding injury. Multi-hour mountain runs over 12,000-foot passes and up 14,000-foot peaks imparted critical insights about hydration, nutrition, and pacing for long endurance days.

All that provided an excellent base, but I would be fifty-four on Everest. As we age, aerobic capacity and muscle mass decrease. Unless a person works hard to stay fit, most people hit their physical peak in their late twenties or early thirties. That was so long ago for me that I could barely remember my twenties.

Gloria and I sat down with the kids to tell them I was returning to Everest. Being a gung-ho twenty-year-old, Nick said, "Go for it, Dad. It's your Stanley Cup!" Jess added her support but was less enthused, saying, "It seems like you were lucky to escape last time, and now you're putting your head back into the lion's mouth." She had a point.

The data about climbers who try 8,000-meter (26,000 feet) peaks show an alarming trend. The more extreme-high-altitude attempts a climber makes, the more likely he or she seems eventually to die on a mountain. Mountaineering literature is filled with cautionary tales about such sad, if unsurprising, outcomes. If you keep going back up there, sooner or later something goes wrong. And when things go wrong at high altitude, they go wrong big and fast.

My physical fitness for Everest in 2015 seemed fine, but I knew I could do better. So I began an advanced twenty-four-week strength program designed for expedition climbing. I combined my own mountain-tested training with the progressive program delineated in the book *Training for the New Alpinism,* by Steve House and Scott Johnston. Every gym session contained more than twenty exercises, and I did multiple repetitions and sets of each. As I adapted to the workload, I added another day of weight lifting to each week, increased the weight, and did more sets. Twelve weeks later the early workouts I'd initially struggled with seemed easy.

To scientifically refine the training, I subjected myself to metabolic testing. I ran to exhaustion on a laboratory treadmill while a medical technician sampled my blood. Afterward a physiologist interpreted the results and gave me advice on improving my approach and shifting my diet.

I later added hill sprints to raise my anaerobic threshold. Starting with one all-out dash up a steep hill, I gradually increased to eight laps up and down, one after the other. My gasping on the last repetitions made me look and sound more like an asthma patient than an Everest climber. The exertion hurt so much that I needed a psychological trick to force myself to the end: I imagined I was in the Khumbu Icefall during an avalanche. I ran like my life depended upon it.

During each final uphill sprint, my heart monitor often recorded me hitting my maximum rate of 175 beats per minute. A day of recovery would let my tired heart muscle return to a resting rate of forty, sometimes lower.

I dissected my previous Everest trip to identify crucial movements that I'd have to repeat thousands of times during the climb. Then I added workout elements that simulated those specific moves. I conducted these "Everest exercises" while visualizing key places on the mountain. To prepare for pulling myself up steep ropes with a mechanical ascender, I did hundreds of one-arm cable pulls during each gym session and envisioned myself ascending fixed lines on my way to Camp Four at 26,000 feet.

One of the best exercises was "box steps"—repeated one-leg step-ups onto a high wooden box. While doing them I wore a heavy backpack and held dumbbells in each hand. I increased the weight over several months until it reached a total of ninety pounds. During the brutal last repetitions onto the knee-high box, I pictured myself ascending the final summit ridge. Pushing my physical and mental boundaries helped me build the mindset required to attempt Everest.

Every gym session ended with lots of core exercises. After working hard to hit the day's numerical goal, I pushed myself to do one more sit-up while I thought of Mike. By the end of the twenty-four-week program, I had doubled the weight of every exercise and tripled the number of reps. In December 2016, the incremental running plan let me complete a half marathon with no knee pain. The race felt good, and I was happy to finish in under two hours.

As had always been my habit, I read mountaineering books about my next objective. I believed that each book contained some knowledge, lesson, or tip that could help me summit or keep my partners and me safe. Ed Webster's excellent *Snow in the Kingdom* distilled a wealth of knowledge from his three Everest expeditions and included a remarkable photograph showing an unusual downward view overlooking base camp. That 1985 photo clearly showed that a major landslide of dark rock had fallen from Pumori-Lingtren and bulldozed right across the camp's usual location, just like the deadly avalanche triggered by the quake. The debris field of rocks in the photo extended more than halfway across the Khumbu Glacier, even farther than in 2015. Were rock avalanches common near base camp?

Ed's book contained many historical Everest photos, including a Swiss one taken in 1952 during the first south-side expedition. The black-and-white image overlooked base camp and showed two large fields of rock debris running transverse across the Khumbu Glacier—another possible landslide. Alarmed by this evidence, I dug into geology articles about Everest and its ice fields. In a 1999 glaciology paper, Japanese scientists reported a major rockslide near camp that "formed by a big landslide event, according to local people." Major avalanches like the 2015 one had overrun the Everest base-camp area before.

I tentatively concluded that in the last sixty years, three avalanches might have hit near base camp, maybe more. With humans only present there several months each year (two months each spring and sometimes two more each fall), perhaps landslides were somewhat common along the Khumbu Glacier, but we only saw the evidence intermittently. The inevitable occurrence of more earthquakes amplified the landslide risk. We planned to spend another six or seven weeks camped in that exact spot the following spring. I wondered when the next rockslide might hit.

Unfortunately I didn't have any answers. I wouldn't have time for deeper research over the next two months either, which meant I was going to go back to Everest without knowing. I hadn't even packed my bags yet, and already a shadow of uncertainty loomed over my trip.

The best training for climbing is climbing. So in January 2017, I took my increased strength and endurance to the mountains. Work had to slip down in the priority ranking to leave the top spots open for midweek training hikes and weekend climbs. I trudged up local peaks weighed down with fifty to seventy pounds of unneeded climbing ropes. On snowy days I wore my high-altitude boots to get used to them and make the hikes more challenging.

Colorado has more than thirteen hundred mountains higher than 12,000 feet, and fifty-eight of them exceed 14,000 feet. Hiking, snowshoeing, and ice climbing on these peaks in winter serve as excellent training for the Himalayas. A long day in the hills is always better than a few hours in the gym, so whenever possible, I got outside with friends, usually Alan or Rodney. When necessary I went alone, though I stuck to peaks I knew well in case something went wrong.

My body kept shedding fat and gaining muscle. During a week with multiple hard training days, Gloria said, "You're working out awfully hard. I hope you don't overdo it."

I replied, "Everest isn't going to get smaller, so I have to get stronger."

When I wasn't training for an expedition, I would often skip my workout the day before a climb to rest; then I would take another day after the summit to recover. But such a leisurely approach doesn't prepare you enough for big mountains. To make my training mimic the usual expedition schedule of three days of climbing followed by a day or two of rest, I began stacking two mountain days in a row. Stacked days wore me down, but they taught my body to respond even when it was already tired. My goal was to be fit enough and skilled enough that if I turned around at 28,000 feet and all the fixed ropes and my teammates were somehow gone, I could get myself down.

With two months until departure, I visited my doctor. He conducted a quick wellness check, signed the medical permission form that IMG required, and sat down to discuss my extensive medication requests. The first time I'd walked into his office years ago and asked for a laundry list of pills, my doctor was understandably cautious. But after half a dozen pre-expedition visits, he now understood my requests. He even seemed to enjoy discussing the extreme medical issues that could crop up in remote areas and at high altitudes.

He wrote prescriptions to resolve respiratory distress, gastrointestinal infections, and violent coughing. Then he gave me scripts to address the deadly threats of high-altitude pulmonary edema, in which water pools in the lungs, and high-altitude cerebral edema, wherein fluid accumulates in the skull and squeezes the brain.

Along with these standard medicines, I requested something that would boost my energy in case of emergency. I needed it to keep me alert for twenty-four hours, no matter how exhausted I was. As he considered my request, he cautioned me about side effects and risks. I said, "Doc, if I reach for those pills, it's because I'm caught high on the mountain in some very serious situation. If I don't keep moving and get down soon, I'll be dead. So, I don't care about side effects."

He agreed and wrote me a four-pill prescription for the stimulant methylphenidate, which is often prescribed for controlling symptoms of attention deficit disorder. Next the medical assistant took a blood draw from me—my blood glucose levels had been creeping upward for a few years, so we were watching them. My long-term blood sugar level was also rising. We had discussed the issue before, and I'd made lifestyle adjustments. Because I had lost twenty pounds during Everest training, I felt confident that my numbers would improve.

The doctor's office called me the next day. Both test results were not only higher than before, but they'd also risen into scary new territory. I had officially crossed the line from prediabetic to diabetic. I was devastated.

My mom, Jean, was prediabetic, and her mother, whom we called Nana Rice, had had advanced diabetes. In the early 1960s my grandmother had had two toes amputated due to the disease. Nana stayed with us to recover from the surgery. Family lore says that I was learning to count then, and I would sit by her feet and say, "One, two, three, four, five, six, seven, eight—that's all!"

Now I had diabetes. How could this be? I worked out six days per week, either in the gym for two hours or in the high mountains for six to twelve hours. My body fat was about 13 percent, and I was only four pounds above my optimal expedition weight of 170 pounds. But numbers don't lie.

When Gloria came home from working at the hospital, I peppered her with medical questions, ranted my frustrations, and eventually revealed my fears.

"Gloria, I have frickin' diabetes!" I said. "My climbing career will be over. They'll start chopping off my toes!"

The light of a new day brought some calmness. I signed up for nutritional counseling and a diabetes prevention group, both of which started soon. My training schedule for that day called for me to carry a heavy pack up a high peak. I wasn't very enthused, but a day in the hills always lifted my spirits and cleared my mind. Besides, I had to keep getting ready for Everest.

As the highway curved into the mountains, I drove on autopilot and reviewed my habits around food and sugar. Years of running and climbing had helped me refine my eating habits to stay fueled during long endurance days. A regular intake of carbohydrates kept me energized, and that often meant ingesting simple glucose in sports drinks and gel packets. Since sugar was now my enemy, I decided to eliminate every bit of it that I could. I'd fight back hard.

The day was cold, but I managed to summit Flattop Mountain. I hardly ate, so I moved slowly and did not get back to the car until seven hours later. After a light breakfast the next morning, I went to the gym for my regular workout. The session started poorly and went downhill from there. Every muscle ached, and I could barely make it through the stretches. My body screamed for food, but I ignored it. Food meant carbs, carbs meant sugar, and I wouldn't have that. An hour later I could hardly walk.

After I ate a meal, the fog lifted and I realized my blunder. I had always been proud that—by studying sports science and understanding my body—I hadn't crashed from a lack of energy in more than thirty years. When the body runs out of one fuel, it switches to secondary sources, and the transition is quite unpleasant. Profound weakness and confusion can take a person down, both physically and mentally. Runners call this "bonking" or "hitting the wall." By hiking and then lifting weights on little food, I had not only hit the wall, I'd crashed into it headfirst. Apparently, starvation wasn't a valid method to prevent diabetes.

I needed to learn new ways to adapt my diet so I could manage my blood sugar. Nutritional counseling showed me how to substitute protein for carbohydrates and how to spread my carbs strategically throughout the day. Staying fueled that way during intense training was challenging, but possible. Reducing carbs on Everest seemed impossible, however. The huge difficulties of getting protein, fruits, and vegetables to remote mountain locales meant that expeditions fueled climbers mostly on carbs and simple sugars. On Everest it's considered a good thing to wake up in the middle of the night and eat a candy bar, just to get more calories on board.

Frankly I worried that eating like that on Everest for two months would worsen my diabetes. During a follow-up visit my doctor said, "On Everest you should eat whatever you know will fuel you and keep you strong, regardless of carbs and sugars. Being weak and dying on Everest is the gravest risk to you for the next few months. We can tackle this diabetes problem when you get back."

I went back to fueling myself for endurance, though with fewer simple sugars and more thoughtfulness. To the extent that I could, I put the nagging uncertainties about future health risks aside. There was still a lot to prepare, and my plane to Nepal was leaving in a month.

31

My pre-expedition to-do list grew longer as the time until departure shrank. Training remained a top priority, although I tapered the gym workouts to moderate levels—it was too late to get any stronger, and I needed to avoid injury. Over the years I'd seen other climbers get hurt just before an expedition, some from pushing too hard and others by doing optional activities like volleyball. A few even injured themselves in the early days of their dream trip by playing soccer with local kids or bouldering near base camp. With all I had invested, anything that might derail my plans made me nervous.

I focused my final training days on climbing high mountains. Summiting Grays Peak (14,278 feet) from the winter trailhead required a hefty 4,700 feet of ascent. I completed the long round trip ninety minutes faster than I had right before Everest in 2015. Next, Rodney and I climbed Quandary Peak (14,265 feet). I wore 8,000-meter boots and carried a heavy training pack, yet the trip felt fun and casual. Ten feet short of the top, I waited a few minutes for Rodney to join me so we could summit together. He arrived breathless, and, as he'd done for me many times during our twenty-year partnership, clarified the situation in just a few words: "I can't keep up with you anymore. You're ready!"

During my last week at home, my days were filled with wrapping up work and running errands. I spent evenings with my family and then sorted expedition gear late into the nights. Throughout the previous months, I had field-tested every single item I would be bringing along. Every piece of equipment had to work right, every item of clothing had to fit correctly, and it all needed to integrate into a seamless system. I'd learned my guiding principle for always pretesting my gear and routines from my uncle, Bob Carr, who'd been an accomplished marathon runner and running coach for forty years. When Coach Carr prepared me for my marathon and other big races, he always said, "Nothing new on race day."

Three days before departure Gloria said I looked skinny. I stepped onto the scale, and it read 169 pounds. I was happy to hit my mark. I would soon lose plenty more weight on the expedition, so I started adding some last-minute pounds of insurance fat onto my lean frame. For a few indulgent days ice cream and chips made cameo appearances on my training menu. During a small bon voyage party at a restaurant with family and friends, I even ate french fries.

Three years had passed since the first time I officially began training for Everest back in March 2014. The focus and energy I had expended, and sometimes asked my family and friends to contribute to, were incalculable. One clear tally of my effort did exist: my training log. After making the final entry, I saw the grand totals. Over three years I had spent more than fifteen hundred hours training and covered seventeen hundred miles on foot. I had summited 107 mountains and ascended more than 400,000 vertical feet. That was equivalent to climbing Mount Everest's entire 29,029-foot height more than thirteen times, just for practice. It was time for the real thing.

. . .

When the sun rose on March 22 I had already been up for hours, stuffing the final items into enormous duffel bags. I ate breakfast with Nick, and Gloria snapped photographs of us with an arm over each other's shoulders. Nick was about to finish his final junior hockey year and would soon embark on college, or maybe work—he wasn't sure. Since there was a small chance I might not come back, I wanted to leave him with a helpful message. I said, "Nick, you can take the dedication, focus, and tenacity you've developed so well in hockey and apply them to the next phase of your life. You will be successful."

We both choked up at bit when we hugged good-bye, and then he left for work. I'd already spoken with Jess on the phone and had brief farewell visits with Alan and other friends over the past few days.

An hour before we left for the airport, Rodney came over. We stacked my luggage—two duffels, a carry-on bag, and my daypack—into a stomach-high tower and took a photo of us next to it. Echoing a line from Mark Twight's climbing book *Extreme Alpinism*, Rodney called the pile of bags "one hundred and forty pounds of the lightest climbing gear known to man."

After helping me put the bags in the car, my best friend and I said good-bye. We were both a little teary-eyed when we hugged.

"You've earned this," Rodney said.

"I would've never gotten this far without you," I replied.

Gloria and I both knew we'd chat on the drive and say a short good-bye at the Denver airport. But we said our real farewell at home. We went to the living room. Gloria asked, "Where's your medal?"

From my pants pocket, I pulled out the small black box that held my most treasured keepsakes. Inside the cloth-lined box were Mike's Outward Bound pin, my Denali Pro pin, an ancient Tibetan coin gifted to me by a Buddhist lama, and the Catholic medallion Gloria had given me. The dime-size medal featured the likeness of Pope Paul VI, and Gloria had owned it since 1968. During our first year of dating, she passed it to me to protect me during my first attempt on Mount Rainier back in 1983. I've worn it on every big climb ever since.

I held open the box, and Gloria teased the tarnished metal chain out from my other amulets. We stood face-to-face as she kissed the medal once and I bowed my head toward her. She slipped the chain around my neck, and we kissed. As we hugged, Glo whispered, "Stay safe."

Thirty-six hours later I landed in Kathmandu. When I exited the international terminal pushing a loaded baggage cart, I spied a Nepali man holding up a paper sign printed with my name and the IMG logo. Mohan worked for BEYUL Adventure, the Nepali guiding company IMG had partnered with for years. We knew each other from my two previous 8,000-meter trips. After welcoming me by placing a necklace of yellow marigolds over my head, Mohan laughed and said, "You look skinnier!" As we drove from the airport, I glimpsed a fairway on the Royal Nepal Golf Club; there were no refugee tents pitched there.

Kathmandu had 1.2 million people and six operating traffic lights. (The city actually had 365 traffic signals installed across the valley, but a recent official count stated that 359 of them weren't functioning.) Our driver wove through traffic with one hand on the steering wheel and the other on the horn. A citywide no-honking law was to take effect in three weeks, and it seemed as if every driver wanted to honk as much as possible before it became illegal.

Though bleary-eyed, I gazed out the window, anxious to detect how Kathmandu might have changed since the quake. I saw a few buildings under reconstruction, but there were no obvious signs of the disaster. I knew that other parts of the city, and many places across the country, remained in ruins, however. As we approached the hotel, we drove past a gray concrete wall that had been spray-painted with ten-inch-tall white letters reading We will rise again. This declaration of resilience lifted my spirits.

Hotel Tibet looked just as it had before. A former Gurkha* still served

---

* The Gurkhas are fearsome soldiers of Nepali ancestry who fight for the British army.

as the watchman, and upon our arrival he raised his arm in salute as he did for all guests. My hotel room was identical to the one I stayed in last time. I soon found Greg Vernovage; his room was crammed full of last-minute supplies he and the other six IMG guides had brought with them. We gave each other a big hug, though his ten inches of height above me always made our embraces awkward.

Greg said, "Well, here we go again!"

I shrugged, and we laughed.

This climb was the third 8,000-meter expedition we'd begun together from this hotel since 2009. For Greg this trip also marked his eighth consecutive time serving as IMG's Everest expedition leader. He shared the responsibilities with our deputy expedition leader, Ang Jangbu Sherpa, from BEYUL. Greg told me he'd scheduled a team meeting on the rooftop patio that afternoon. We talked logistics for fifteen minutes until a rising tide of exhaustion washed over me. Instead of conversing with Greg, I nodded and said nothing. As a savvy world traveler, Greg understood my jet lag. He said, "Hey, you look beat. Better grab a nap while you can."

Two hours of sleep helped, but I was still groggy as I trudged up two flights of stairs to the flat rooftop patio. About three dozen fit climbers and guides stood talking in small groups. Among many new faces, my eyes locked on the ones I already knew. I exchanged energetic hugs with five teammates from the 2015 trip: Matt Tammen, Jim Diani, Gigi Aakar, Andrew Towne, and IMG guide Luke Reilly. None of us had seen one another since departing Kathmandu after the quake.

Greg's voice boomed above our chatter, asking us to take a seat. After introducing himself and several of the guides, he had us each say our name and share a little information about ourselves. Our group had people from nine countries. Most of the clients intended to attempt Everest, though a few were in Nepal to trek. Greg explained how we would break into three subteams that would fly to Lukla and then trek up the Khumbu Valley two days apart. This staggered schedule made our logistics more manageable and our arrivals less chaotic at the lodges we would stay in during the ten-day approach.

After the meeting my new roommate, Dean, and I unpacked and sorted gear for a few hours. Then IMG sponsored a fun send-off dinner party. I met IMG guide Dallas Glass, who would lead Team One, the group I was in. Dallas was an easygoing guy, and I liked him right away.

Team One would be the first group to depart for Lukla, and we scurried about Kathmandu the following day purchasing final supplies and snacks from local stores. I focused on eating smart, staying healthy, and enjoying the luxuries of city life before heading into the mountains for the next eight weeks.

Even with official airline cotton balls sprouting from my ears, the plane engines roared at deafening levels as we flew toward Lukla the next day. We were only five minutes from landing, and the sloped runway still looked minuscule. Because tall mountains surround Lukla, once a flight commits to the final approach, there's no possibility of a go-around. The aircraft must land no matter what. Then, once it touches down, the plane needs to brake to a stop soon before the short runway ends. At the far edge of Lukla's tiny airport property is a steep slope covered with occupied buildings; immediately behind those is another mountain face. The plane will stop, one way or the other.

The tires chirped as they contacted the pavement. I watched the scenery flash by through the right-side window as we rolled uphill and lost speed. When the plane halted at the upper end, there were twenty yards between our airplane and the stone retaining wall: Plenty of extra space! As always in Lukla, I stepped off the crazy flight more than happy to walk for a while.

Within ten minutes I ran into a friend from previous expeditions—Mingma Dorje Sherpa, from Phortse. We greeted each other three ways: a Nepali namaste, a Western handshake, and a quick embrace between old teammates. It was good to be back in the Khumbu.

My companions and our luggage were dispersed into several different aircraft, each from different airlines for the trip from Kathmandu. As with many things in Nepal, why that happened remained unclear to me, and how it all got sorted out afterward posed a deeper mystery. A new plane landed every ten minutes, however, and within the hour all our people and bags were reunited. Yak drivers began wrangling our forty duffel bags onto their animals. Bubbling with energy, we started the approach trek to Mount Everest.

We strolled along on stone-cobbled walkways, past shops selling local handicrafts and imported trekking gear. As we exited the west side of town, I saw the wall that had been plastered with paper signs about people missing after the quake in 2015. The desperate notes were gone. I wondered how many of those people hadn't turned up.

By design we spread the hike to Namche Bazaar over two easy days. Moving up the valley faster was possible, but it would increase the chance of getting stricken with acute mountain sickness (AMS). My plan for every day of the trip was not to wear myself out by racing to be first, but never to arrive last either. Putting myself in the middle of the pack would hopefully let me reach each daily destination with energy in reserve.

We stayed three nights in a pleasant Namche lodge to rest, eat, and hydrate. Probably no one in our fit group was tired from the modest hike, but our bodies needed time to adapt to the 11,290-foot altitude. The mountaineer's adage "Climb high, sleep low" was old, but valid for proper acclimatization. For our two trekkers from Florida, Namche Bazaar was the highest they had ever been. During their one night at Namche, they suffered headaches, nausea, lethargy, and poor sleep—AMS. They ended their trek the next day and left the Khumbu.

On a crisp morning we hiked north from Namche along the west bank of the Dudh Kosi River. A rubbish can and recycling bin flanked the trail as we left town. There was very little trash on the ground, and the modest landslide damage to the path had been fixed, so the trail was in good shape. Walking into Phortse brought back memories from our days there after the earthquake. The school and library had both been repaired, though subtle differences in the patched mortar allowed my mind's eye to draw jagged lines where the holes in the walls once gaped open. We stayed in the same lodge as last time, while many of our sherpa friends went to their family homes around the village.

After two nights in Phortse, IMG planned to continue up the Khumbu Valley for a few days and then on to Everest base camp. I would part ways with the team for a week, however—I had trekked up and down the Khumbu three times already, and I wanted to see new places. With Greg's help and encouragement, I had chosen an alternate approach to Everest. I would hike up the Gokyo Valley, west of the Khumbu, with a sherpa guide and one porter. The area was reportedly pretty and far less traveled. I would rejoin my team in a week at Lobuche East base camp before we all attempted that peak as a warm-up for Everest.

Greg assigned Phinjo Sherpa to lead my side trip. We were acquainted from our 2015 Everest expedition but didn't know each other well. A quiet, gentle man, Phinjo lived in Phortse with his wife. Taller and stouter than most Sherpa men, he exuded calmness. We chatted amicably during our shared meals and tea breaks, but he mostly stayed silent when we walked. Our tranquil trek up the Gokyo Valley gave me time to relax after the busy months leading up to the expedition. Instead of sleeping five hours per night, as I did at home, I slept nine hours every night in the lodges where we stayed.

For three days we hiked north, scrambling up 15,000- and 16,000-foot peaks along the way that overlooked the glaciated valley. We reached the last town, Gokyo, and checked in to a modest trekkers lodge. While the porter, Raz, stayed behind, Phinjo and I slipped from our rooms before dawn on April 5. We cruised up the 17,550-foot-tall Gokyo Ri with just one short water break. The training hikes all seemed easier than last time. Other than the typical bout of traveler's diarrhea, I felt strong.

From Gokyo Ri's summit, we had a stunning view of Cho Oyu's soaring south face, just six miles away. I craned my neck to look at Cho Oyu's summit, more than 9,000 feet above my head. I'd stood upon that lofty point eight years earlier. Trying to build my confidence, I noted that the top of Everest was only 2,100 feet higher—not much more. Yeah, but that's almost as high as jets fly, and it's 2,100 exhausting feet higher at extreme altitude.

I turned to the right and gazed at Everest. Its entire upper pyramid loomed before me. Even from thirteen miles away, I could make out the north face, in Tibet, and the soaring southwest face, in Nepal. The southeast ridge, our intended route, formed the right skyline, and it stood out crisply against the deep-blue upper atmosphere.

To the right of Everest I recognized Lhotse and, farther away, the steep west face of Makalu. We could see four of the world's six highest peaks all at once. My eyes shifted back toward Everest to examine the ragged snow plume blowing off the summit and stretching eastward into the sky. The jet stream winds were savaging the upper mountain. I sure hoped the winds would ease off in May like they're supposed to.

Next to me I sensed Phinjo staring at the mountain too. To share the moment even more with him, I referred to the mountain's other names, using Nepali as much as I could.

"Sagarmatha, *ho*?" I asked.

"*Ho!*" replied Phinjo, confirming its Nepali name.

"And to the Sherpa people, Chomolungma?"

Phinjo turned to me and said: "Yes!" He seemed pleased and surprised that I knew the sacred peak's Tibetan name as well. In English, Phinjo explained Chomolungma's meaning to me as "Goddess Mother of the World."

"*Ho*," I said, nodding.

Our eyes locked, and we smiled. Then we both turned our heads back east and continued gazing upon her.

32

Phinjo, Raz, and I walked along a sinuous ridgetop of dirt and rock. This enormous lateral moraine had served as our rough highway through the Gokyo Valley for five days, but now we needed to exit and find a safe way onto the glacier. At twenty-two miles long, the Ngozumpa Glacier is Nepal's longest. Yesterday Phinjo and I had admired the upper glacier's full glory when we hiked up-valley to within three miles of the Tibetan border. While sitting on adjacent boulders, we studied a complex, wrinkled icefield that stretched two miles high and twelve miles wide. It draped off the shoulders of the Himalayas like a giant white shawl.

After spending a third night in our Gokyo lodge, we started our descent in the morning. Rejoining our teammates for the next acclimatization peak required a two-day walk, but first we had to cross the glacier. We followed an old trail along the moraine's crest until it ended abruptly at a vertical mud cliff. The compact soil had sheared away as cleanly as solid bedrock.

Phinjo said, "Trail gone. We must go there." He pointed to a faint new path that diverted around the small collapse.

The terrain near glaciers was always changing: Boulders fell, streams shifted, permafrost melted. And even though the flat valley floor slowed the glacier's movement, underneath everything the ice kept creeping downhill. In this midportion of the glacier, a continuous layer of dirt and rock covered the Ngozumpa. Travelers had etched a trail into the glacial rubble over the years, which provided a reliable route across the glacier. Ten miles farther down the valley from us, near Phortse, the melting glacier was stagnant, dying.

The three of us scrambled down the muddy trail and then took a big step across an eighteen-inch-wide crack filled with dirty water. We had stepped onto the glacier. Like the surface of the moon, a thick mantle of light-gray silt and dark-gray rocks covered the landscape in three directions as far as I could see.

After five minutes of wandering Phinjo found the main trail again. We hiked the rough path, following the cairns—hand-stacked towers of loose stones—that marked the way. The crevasses were almost all pinched shut or filled with dirt, so there was no need for ropes or climbing gear. An occasional open hole or patch of opaque ice reminded me that underneath the debris blanket, a glacier still lived. It was like walking across the dust-covered back of a sleeping dragon.

The trail skirted meltwater ponds that pooled on top of the ice. Farther down the glacier, to our right, multiple ponds had coalesced into a large waterbody called Spillway Lake. As the name implied, scientists had warned that the unstable lake could someday release due to melting ice or collapsing soil, causing a catastrophic flood. These so-called "glacial lake outburst floods" threatened the down-valley residents with yet another natural hazard that loomed over life in Nepal.

We threaded our way along the packed dirt trail. Even though the ground felt solid and we passed only a few small crevasses, I stayed alert. After three-quarters of a mile, we stepped off the Ngozumpa Glacier and I exhaled hard. We reached the tiny hamlet of Dragnag (15,400 feet) and checked in to the pleasant Chola Pass Resort for the night. They had solar-heated water, so I took my first shower in a week.

After breakfast the next morning, Phinjo, Raz, and I started our trek toward the Cho La (*la* is Tibetan for "pass"). One hundred yards from the lodge door, the trail tilted uphill and Phinjo told me it would stay that way for the next two to three hours. Smooth and steady is the way to gain elevation in the mountains, so we plodded our way up the narrow rocky canyon, taking few breaks. We ascended 2,300 vertical feet, and after a short section of hopping from one boulder to the next, we reached the Cho La in midmorning. The air seemed thin at 17,700 feet, but I experienced no altitude problems. Our ascent felt easier than Gokyo Ri had a few days earlier. I was getting acclimatized.

I shared some chocolate with the guys. Phinjo said thanks in Nepali, and Raz said thank-you too, or at least I thought he did—he and I shared no common language. Being of Rai ancestry, he spoke one of their dialects, perhaps Bantawa, but he didn't speak English or even much Nepali.

From the pass the view to the southeast opened up. The three of us admired what many people call the most beautiful mountain in Nepal, Ama Dablam. At 22,349 feet, the ice-shrouded peak soars above its neighbors. Its name means "mother's charm box," referring to a hanging icefield that resembles the necklace that Nepali mothers often wear. Ama's steep and spectacular ridges attract alpinists from all over the world.

We skirted along the edge of a small pocket glacier on the east side of the pass and then descended quickly. After three miles we left the trail and traversed across a grass-covered slope toward the established IMG camp. I expected all my fellow Team One climbers and sherpas to be occupying the Lobuche base camp. Instead, the camp contained Team Two climbers, most of whom I knew only casually. A bit confused, I sought out Mingma Tenzing Sherpa, our base camp sirdar for Lobuche. He and I had been on two previous expeditions together, so we greeted each other warmly. Mingma Tenzing seemed surprised to see us and soon we determined that our trio had arrived a day earlier than scheduled. During our relaxing weeklong trek, we had lost track of what day it was.

Raz set down my trekking bag that he had carried for the past week and stood near my elbow. Soon I caught on that he had completed his job and was ready to depart. I gave him what I hoped was a good tip and thanked him in Nepali, and he took off down the valley to find more portering work.

Mingma Tenzing told me that Teams One and Two would swap places the next day. Team One would return to Lobuche base camp for a summit attempt, while Team Two would go to Everest base camp for the first time. That gave me time for an unexpected and welcome rest. In the last seven days I had hiked to heights between 16,000 and 17,700 feet four times. A few nights at 15,700 feet would help me lock in the acclimatization gains—climb high, sleep low. When I changed clothes in my tent, my calf muscles seemed bigger and my ribs stuck out a little. The Gokyo side trip had let me decompress and provided excellent conditioning for Everest, but I had to eat more to avoid too much weight loss too soon.

That evening I sent Gloria a GPS text telling her where I was and that all was well. Communicating with her had become much easier over the years. On this trip I could contact her by satellite phone, cell phone, text, email, or GPS text, depending on my location. Cheap Nepali calling cards let me dial home directly for two cents per minute. We communicated by one of those methods about twice a day during the trek.

Back in 1998 I couldn't contact Gloria at all from the trek or climbs. Even telephoning the United States from Kathmandu was complex. I had to walk twenty minutes to the busy tourist section, Thamel, and find an international telephone service store. After negotiating the cost with the manager, I would give that person the number I wanted to reach. Then I would sit in a small private booth next to an old phone with no rotary dial or keypad. After a few minutes, if the manager succeeded in making a connection, he would patch the static-filled call to me in the booth. It cost about two dollars per minute.

One particular call in 1998 was not pleasant. Five days before I left Colorado, Jess, then four years old, came down with chicken pox. We suspected that Nick, not yet two, would catch it soon, and I was heading to Nepal for a month. Desperate to arrange some help for Gloria, I called Dad in Florida. I explained how she was about to be alone with two sick kids while I went off to co-lead my first expedition. Dad paused for a moment, then said, "Gimme a day to pack and I'll drive out to help her for a couple weeks."

When the scratchy phone service connected Gloria and me, I asked her about Nick. In a stoic tone she said, "He's got chicken pox now too."

Static hissed in my ear as I scrambled for a response. "Is Dad there yet?"

"Nope."

More static. I apologized, and then rambled for a minute, reminding her, and myself, that as Rodney's co-leader, and the only person who had experience in Nepal, I couldn't quit the expedition or return home. Then I apologized again.

Glo asked, "When will I hear from you?"

"When we get back to Kathmandu, probably in about twenty-three days." After another awkward interlude of crackling noise, I managed to add, "I hope the kids get better fast. Sorry, Glo."

Though we both laugh about it now, that phone call was the most expensive, and the most guilt-ridden, I'd ever made.

After lunch on April 11, my Team One partners and I hiked out of Lobuche base camp and headed to high camp. My pack felt heavier with gear crammed inside and climbing equipment lashed to the outside. Our loads would have been even heavier if the climbing sherpas hadn't carried the tents, stoves, and ropes up the day before.

I stayed in the middle of the group and hiked at a moderate pace. With each step along the trail, I concentrated on efficient movement by applying the lessons I'd learned during so many box steps. Instead of pushing off my foot when stepping up, which wastes precious calf strength, I practiced using the strong quad muscles in my thigh to lift it. I'd then place that foot firmly and use it to pull myself up to the next step. Rest a moment, then repeat.

The measured pace also helped me synchronize my steps with deep breathing. Putting all this together made the ascent feel like I was calmly flowing uphill, as opposed to fighting gravity and struggling with the low oxygen level. After about ninety minutes the trail flattened and we entered the circular rock basin where high camp sat. We had also climbed Lobuche for acclimatization before Everest in 2015, so everything seemed familiar.

Ten yellow tents had been pitched in a line; I picked an empty one and crawled inside. Before doing anything else, I mixed protein powder into water and forced down my recovery drink. Replacing the glycogen in my muscles right after exercise helped keep me fueled for the next day's demands.

My tentmate, Dean, arrived soon after I'd settled in. We stowed our gear and prepared for the predawn summit push. Although mountaineers loosely referred to the climb as Lobuche East (20,075 feet), almost everyone ascended only to the crest of a lower sub-peak, or "false summit." The true summit sits eighty-five feet higher, on the far side of a treacherous snow ridge. Although standing on top often provided an obvious objective for climbers, in this case the extreme risk to get there wasn't worth it. The essential goals for this warm-up climb were to acclimatize and dial in our systems and skills before going where it really mattered—Everest.

I followed the dozen bobbing headlamps of my teammates and our sherpas as we scrambled up rock slabs before dawn. When I looked over my shoulder, about another ten headlamp circles spotlighted the trail below me—the rest of the team. An even bigger glowing orb hung in the western sky as the full moon sank toward the horizon. The scrambling was easy enough not to require ropes, but the thinning air made it hard work.

The sun hit us at about 19,000 feet, and everyone slathered on sunscreen. We donned our harnesses and crampons and moved onto the glacier. A cloudless blue sky stretched for a hundred miles in every direction. Firm snow beneath my boots gave my crampons solid purchase. Our hardworking climbing sherpas had set a few hundred feet of fixed lines the day before, so clipping my harness into the ropes eliminated the possibility of falling. I focused on rhythmic movements, all centered around a momentary rest to suck in a lungful of air.

At about eight-thirty I stabbed my ice ax into the crest of the steep snow slope and pulled myself onto the summit. The senior IMG guide, Dallas, pointed a large camera at me and said, "Good job, Davidson!"

I tried to smile through my labored panting. After Dallas snapped a few frames, I looked down the forty-five-degree slope and saw my friend Mathieu Durand about 150 feet below. To pass along good energy, I shouted, "Almost there, buddy!"

Still working hard, Mathieu gave me a halfhearted wave. I unclipped from the line and walked ten feet into the safe middle of the flat plateau of the false summit. It took a little under five hours to ascend 2,600 feet from high camp—not bad for that altitude. More important, I had climbed Lobuche Far East faster than two years earlier, and the ascent felt easier.

We ate, hydrated, and took photographs. The windless day allowed us to hang out for almost an hour. Even though scores of gorgeous mountains surrounded us, I spent most of my time looking at only one. About half of Everest was visible; the rest remained hidden behind Nuptse. Everest's dark upper pyramid was only seven miles away, yet I could make out the bedrock layers dipping northward into Tibet. I turned my head and located base camp. It sat more than 2,500 feet below me and five miles away, so I couldn't distinguish any individual tents, but I knew they were there. Hundreds of them were pitched on rubble-covered ice along an outside curve of the Khumbu Glacier.

A glance west of base camp wiped the smile off my face: the avalanche path. Beneath my dark sunglasses, I squeezed my eyes tighter, scowling at the ridge crest between Pumori and Lingtren that released the deadly rockslide. It had been two years since I'd seen the area in person, but I'd stared at photos of the unstable slope many times. Just like recalling the face of a criminal, I remembered the dangling ice towers, angled rock slopes, and the large lateral distance between where the landslide started and where it ended atop the tents.

I was excited to start climbing Everest again in a few days, but I was not happy about camping for the next six weeks in the avalanche runout zone.

33

After summiting Lobuche East the day before, we took our time on the nine-mile trek to Everest base camp. We stopped for another water break around four o'clock before hiking the final mile. On every expedition walking into base camp brought me giddy anticipation. After months of planning, training, and talking, we could finally start ascending the mountain.

I felt that energizing uplift when we arrived at Everest base camp on April 13, but being there also made me uneasy. The IMG camp was in the exact same place on the glacier as 2015, on the left soon after entering base camp. Our cook tent, storage tent, and dining tents were all the same ones as last time and placed in an identical pattern. It was like going back in time.

Our cook, Kaji Sherpa, welcomed us with tea, snacks, and a smile. This would be my third expedition with him. I drank my daily recovery drink while waiting for the yaks to arrive. When they did, I found my duffel bag and carried it to my assigned sleeping tent. Since we would spend so long in base camp, the climbers had their own personal tents, both for privacy and to hold all their gear.

After unpacking, I stepped outside and looked toward the mountain. The bulging west shoulder prevented me from seeing the summit, but I had a clear view of the lower Khumbu Icefall. Even from half a mile away, the jumbled mess of ice blocks and crevasses practically screamed danger. I thought, This has got to be the most outrageous place I've ever gone climbing. But to attempt Everest from Nepal, we had to go through the icefall. In sixty-five years of explorations, no one had found a reasonable way around it.

In 2015 Willie Benagas had explained one possible way to me as we stood shoulder to shoulder by the IMG mess tent. Willie and his twin brother, Damian, had climbed a steep route up Nuptse's north face back in 2003. As Willie pointed at Nuptse's west face, he outlined a theoretical alternate route that ascended two thousand feet of crumbly, rotten rock. Then it followed an outlandish half-mile-long traverse beneath hanging ice cliffs at nearly 20,000 feet. His vague description got worse when he said, "Then we'd have to find some way down into the Western Cwm near Camp One."

No one, including him, had even probed a portion of this wild alternative. And so, every spring, hundreds of climbers and sherpas made trip after trip through the gauntlet of the Khumbu Icefall. Because they carried up the heavy ropes, tents, and oxygen bottles, the strong high-altitude workers made at least twice as many trips through the icefall as clients like me. It's dangerous work; they do it to provide for their families. In a three-month spring season, the Nepali high-altitude workers make three to five times as much money as a safer occupation could provide in a year.

The risk-and-reward aspect of their profession reminded me of a job I once did. Back in 1982, Dad hired three other painters and me to climb and paint high-voltage electrical towers. We clambered over metal frame-works as high as two hundred feet off the ground without safety lines. Every tower supported six power lines, and each of those steel cables carried up to 230,000 volts. Dad paid us ten dollars per hour to risk our lives, which was about twice what most painters made, and three times the minimum hourly wage of $3.35 back then. Though the dangers were obvious and substantial, to make that high pay we were willing to take the risk for a few months.

Darkness filled my tent, and the only parts of me exposed to the cold night air were my nose and my wide-open eyes. I needed to sleep, but I kept lifting my head to look westward. All I saw was the tent wall, but I could clearly picture the 5,000-foot rise of Pumori rearing up a mile away, and the ridge that had released the deadly landslide onto base camp. Now it loomed outside my tent like an imaginary grizzly bear. Exhaustion eventually overrode nervousness, and I slept.

Hours later a growl hit my ears. The rumbling sound stabbed a sensitive memory deep in my brain; I sat up and pulled my daypack over my head as protection from the fearful avalanche noise. Before I was fully awake, I'm pretty sure I yelled, "Where is it?!"

I tilted my head to locate the sound's source. The muffled roar was coming from the Lho La, a mile north on the border with Tibet. A glacial serac hanging there released massive ice chunks nearly every day, but they didn't threaten base camp. I shoved down my panic and kept listening as the noise softened, then stopped. There were no rushing avalanche winds or tumbling rocks nearby. We were safe.

After blowing out a big breath, I flopped back onto my sleeping pad. Traces of adrenaline coursing through my body kept me awake for an hour. I couldn't afford to react so powerfully to every distant avalanche rumble—they happen almost every day on Everest, and we were going to camp here for the next month and a half. I had to find a way to make peace with the mountain and all its unsettling habits.

In the morning I spent fifteen minutes alternately pulling on more clothes and pausing to catch my breath. I finally bundled up enough for the bitter cold and stepped out into three inches of new snow. On my way to the mess tent, I ran into Phunuru Sherpa, from Phortse. He was our climbing sirdar, as he had been in 2015. Phunuru had summited Everest nine times, along with dozens of other Himalayan peaks. He treated everyone like they were his best friend, and he always seemed like the happiest person in the Khumbu. In excellent English, Phunuru said, "Good morning, Jim Dai." Then he flashed his big grin.

"Hello, Phunuru Bhai. Did you hear the avalanche last night?"

The smile dropped off his face. He scowled and shook his head from side to side. "Yes, it was very scary."

"It reminded me of the quake," I said.

"Yes, me too."

Big expeditions included a lot of downtime in base camp to rest, recover, and grow new red blood cells to carry more oxygen. I spent the morning hand-washing my smelly clothes and hanging them to dry in the ferocious sunshine. I hoped they'd finish drying before the clouds and cold returned in the afternoon. If they didn't, I would have to drape the frozen clothing inside my tent and resume drying them the next day.

In the late afternoon IMG held the annual ladder practice before any of us went into the icefall. All the client climbers put on their harnesses with two leashes attached for clipping into fixed lines. On our feet we wore high-mountain boots and crampons. Then the IMG guides and senior sherpas had us run a short circuit of ice, climbing up thirty feet and rappelling down a fixed line. After that we crossed an eight-foot aluminum ladder laid out horizontally two feet above the ground.

The small practice circuit helped us fine-tune our systems and lock in the crucial steps as habits. Driving these skills deep into our muscle memory increased the chance of our bodies performing the tasks correctly on autopilot—we might need that edge later at high altitude when our oxygen-starved brains couldn't figure out what to do. Climbing up and down small ice pinnacles on the Khumbu Glacier was fun, and the minor exertion provided "active rest," which encouraged our bodies to acclimate. We were at 17,300 feet and wouldn't go any lower for more than a month.

Though IMG downplayed it, ladder practice was also a way for the Western and Nepali guides to see where each climber was on the experience and fitness scales. This helped them choose the right guide for the client's needs. Fast, skilled climbers often got paired with young, fit guides. Less advanced climbers were usually assigned to older sherpas who possessed more experience, patience, and teaching skills. It was like base-camp speed-dating, matching everyone up for the big dance.

Matchmaking didn't apply to me or PK, however, as I had already requested him as my sherpa guide. We'd only climbed together for a few days in 2015, but knowing you're compatible with someone counts for a lot. PK served as one of IMG's rope fixers, which meant he was strong, fast, and skilled. Also, he'd led Bart to the summit in May 2016, so PK had summited twice already. Greg must have considered my request appropriate, as he and Ang Jangbu, the director of all our Nepali staff, made it happen. My only concern was that, with PK being twenty-seven years old and me fifty-four, I didn't have the speed he possessed, and never would. I harbored no delusions about setting any speed records on Everest. Instead I planned to keep putting one foot in front of the other for as long as it took to reach the top.

I went to bed at 7:00 p.m. to rest for our first trip into the Khumbu Icefall the next morning—we planned to ascend the lower two-thirds and then return to base camp before lunch. This practice run would show everyone what the route looked like so that when we moved up to Camp One wearing our heavy packs in a few days, we could move faster and with more confidence. Historically, one day of climbing among the shifting ice blocks unnerved some people so much that they quit the expedition and left the following day. I understood.

When my watch alarm beeped at 1:45 a.m., I was already awake. I sat up and added clothing layers as fast as possible to trap in my body heat. Before heading to breakfast, I ambled to the neighboring tent and said, "Gigi, are you up?"

"Yes, James. Merci!"

Gigi's native languages, Arabic and French, enriched her fluent English with a musical lilt. Having endured the quakes and avalanches together at Camp One, she and I were permanent friends, and we'd each promised to make sure the other always awoke on time for our middle-of-the-night alpine starts. For three years in a row, circumstances had blocked Gigi's attempts on Everest. The icefall collapse in 2014, the earthquake in 2015, and a fluke broken ankle during the approach trek in 2016 had all stopped her before she could ascend any higher than 20,000 feet. She was back for a fourth attempt, and if she topped out, Gigi would become the first Moroccan woman to summit Mount Everest.

I was the first climber in the dining tent at 2:25 a.m. Dallas came in and grabbed a mug of coffee, and within ten minutes fifteen climbers were drinking caffeine, filling water bottles, and forcing down a semicold breakfast of scrambled eggs and toast. Although I needed every calorie I could swallow, previous alpine starts had proven that if I overate, I would bog down within an hour. The body can't serve two masters, and I needed mine focused on climbing uphill, not digesting a bellyful of food. I shoved down half of what the cook team put on my plate, promising myself to make up the food deficit during lunch.

We all scrambled to finish a dozen minor preparation tasks before the scheduled departure. By 3:00 a.m., we stood in a small circle outside the mess tent. Everyone was dressed against the cold and wearing helmets and harnesses. Greg modeled good leadership by getting up to see us off, and by being enthusiastic. Some team members seemed nervous, while others expressed excitement. I felt a mixture of both.

Our fifteen Nepali guides hustled over from their portion of base camp, an area someone had nicknamed "Sherpaland." Darkness, punctuated by an occasional light blast in the eyes from a powerful headlamp, made it hard to see. We wore similar gear and packs, but after a minute of shouted names and raised hands, all thirty of us managed to find our climbing partners, like birds finding their mates in a squabbling flock of look-alikes.

"PK, *ho!*" I shouted when he stepped out of the darkness.

"*Ho,*" PK said with a smile. "You ready, Jim?"

As pairs of guides and climbers pulled out of camp, PK and I stepped to the side to activate our avalanche beacons. IMG offers them to all the guides, and all of us climbers could afford one, but only a minority of people wore them in the icefall. Those who went without had various reasons: The chest straps holding the beacon snug against the torso restricted their breathing; the transceiver wouldn't help if you got buried by a million pounds of ice, etc. But having seen what avalanches can do on Everest, PK and I both wanted every sliver of protection.

I set my beacon to Send, and PK confirmed that he received me. Then we reversed our signals so we both knew that I could detect him. Carefully I switched my beacon from Receive back to Send. Doing this beacon check delayed our departure by a few minutes, but having a fighting chance to find each other after an avalanche was worth it. The small reassurance lessened my fear of being buried alive.

With my headlamp on low to save batteries, I followed PK out of camp. We walked by a stone altar the sherpas had erected for making offerings to the gods. By circling counterclockwise around the sacred structure, we kept our right sides, our clean sides, toward the altar out of respect. Dozens of headlamps from other teams moved along the trail and showed the way into the icefall. We skirted frozen meltwater pools, and when the gray rock debris gave way to white ice, we put crampons on our boots. The familiar feeling of metal spikes biting into frozen water calmed me.

Jagged ice pinnacles formed a maze, so we followed the trail of crampon scars left on the ground by previous climbers. The spires we walked among increased in height to twenty feet, then thirty. When the slope angle increased, we encountered the start of the fixed lines. I grabbed one of my harness leashes and clipped onto the line with a carabiner. Though the community climbing rope was skinnier than the tip of my pinky, it could hold more than two thousand pounds of force if it was tied to solid anchors. Some sections were fixed, though, with cheap, two-strand, twisted nylon line—we called it water-ski rope.

PK went first to set a steady pace, and I trailed five to ten feet behind. If I followed him too closely, I might run into his sharp crampons, especially in the steep sections when his feet were level with my face. PK and I used the fixed line as a casual handhold, sliding our leash carabiners along the rope as we progressed. Every thirty to fifty feet, the rope was anchored to the mountain by an ice screw or an aluminum snow stake. At each anchor point I stomped a stable platform for my feet, unclipped my carabiner, and clipped it onto the next rope segment above the anchor. Even though it was unlikely that something would fall on me, or that the ground would drop out from under me at that exact moment, being unclipped from the line even for a few seconds still made me nervous.

We scrambled up one ice mound after another. Every few minutes the fixed line led us into a depression and then we had to reascend the far side of the dip. I groaned to myself each time we had to give up any hard-won altitude. We stepped across small crevasses and skirted around big ones as the trail wove a precarious path through the ice towers.

The middle of the Khumbu Glacier flows downhill at a speedy average of three to four feet per day. When portions of the icefield move at different rates, the frozen landscape buckles and shatters into disarray. As we moved deeper into the icefall, the giant glacial shards leaned downhill at more outrageous angles, and the crevasses grew larger. We were climbing through chaos.

Soon the crevasses became too wide to step across and too complex to divert around. The skilled Icefall Doctors had laid down short aluminum ladder sections horizontally to span the gaps. When we arrived at the first ladder bridge, PK kept his carabiner safely clipped to the fixed line in the unlikely event that he lost his balance or the ladder gave way. Remembering how we'd worked together in 2015, I grabbed the loose fixed line and leaned backward—loading the rope with my body weight tightened it into a more rigid and secure handline. PK gingerly stepped from rung to rung, using the fixed line for physical and mental support. When he reached the other side, he turned around and pulled the rope tight with his weight so I could cross.

Holding the handline raised my confidence a bit. However, when I looked down to place my feet on the horizontal rungs, the yawning chasm below gaped up at me. The blue-black hole plunged at least eighty feet inside the glacier. As I crossed the ladder, the dangerous depth kept trying to draw my attention like a campfire compels a person to stare into the flames. I did my best to ignore the mesmerizing view and kept my eyes on the ladder. When I reached the far end and stepped onto relatively stable ground, PK dropped the rope and started uphill again.

I wanted to rest, but we couldn't. Minimizing our exposure time in the icefall was crucial. The last few weeks of scaling gradually higher peaks had helped me adapt to altitude, but the exhausting whole-body effort demanded by climbing the icefall revealed that I wasn't acclimatized enough. PK kept pushing hard from one tricky spot to the next, but my pace began to lag.

By 5:30 a.m., my altimeter watch indicated that we had reached 18,300 feet. We still had a while to go before reaching our turnaround point. The route ahead went up several steep walls, so instead of using a loose carabiner, we connected ourselves to the fixed line with a rope ascender. The device's mechanical-toothed grip on the rope would keep me from falling more than a few feet if I peeled off the steep ice wall. Attaching and then removing the ascender over and over consumed more time and demanded more care, but it added necessary safety.

After ascending three short vertical sections in a row, I was wiped out. My muscles weren't sore, but I had little power. I panted hard whenever we moved, and my heart hammered in my chest. During a short stop to rest, I checked my pulse and estimated it at about 140 beats per minute: too high to sustain for long. We were pretty close to Nuptse at that point, and PK said, "Bad ice above. We must go quick."

When I looked up, I saw the underside of the ice cliff hanging off Nuptse's west face. Crap, we need to get out of here! But I was already going as fast as I could.

After one more steep section, the route began traversing back to the left. I welcomed the flatter terrain, but the way ahead looked sketchy. Freshly broken ice boulders the size of dishwashers and refrigerators littered the way, and we had to travel beneath an overhanging ice chunk the size of a house. A jagged crack wide enough to fit my gloved hand inside cut through the block. PK hustled eighty feet across and had to jump from one ice boulder to the next in two places. I followed with less grace, but with all the speed I could muster.

For another hour the fixed line snaked up until we cut back to the middle of the Khumbu Glacier. I hadn't said anything in a while; I needed all my oxygen for climbing. Discouragement was giving way to doubt. Finally I saw about half of my teammates standing with their packs off at a flat spot I remembered from 2015. We had met our objective for the day, the Football Field, and we'd reached our turnaround point.

I stepped onto the flat block and dropped my pack. With a smile, Dallas said, "Nice work, Jim." I nodded my head in recognition. Even though it was 7:00 a.m. and the sun blazed in the sky, this narrow section of the glacier remained in the cold shadow of the soaring rock walls. I knew I'd chill fast, so I slipped my enormous down coat on right away. The group seemed to be waiting for more of our team to arrive, so I pulled out my water bottle and snack bag. My altimeter read 18,900 feet.

By the time most of our team plodded onto the Football Field, the earliest arrivers were cold and anxious to leave. They started down, and after we rested five more minutes, PK and I followed. Heading downhill went much faster as gravity was now working for us instead of against. The lower we went, the stronger I felt, and I even had an urge to rush. That desire confirmed I was suffering from the low oxygen level; the body knows what it wants. Since we'd just come up the route, the scary ladders and tricky spots were familiar. Everyone hesitated a little less.

We descended the steepest sections by rappelling down the fixed line. This required me to securely anchor myself in, thread the rope through a friction-producing rappel device, and then clip the metal tube and rope to my harness with a locking carabiner. While holding the rappel rope secure inside one fist, my brake hand, I slowly fed slack into the friction device. I walked down the cliff backward as I lowered myself down the rope.

Though not technically difficult, rappelling offers many ways to make small but deadly mistakes. Climbers can thread the device incorrectly, grab the wrong rope strand, forget to anchor in, or make a dozen other missteps. All these subtle errors become more likely when the climber is tired, rushed, or dull-brained from altitude. I was all three.

Ever since I started reading climbing books from the Concord library in the 1970s, I noticed that rappelling had killed many of the world's finest climbers. So, I always double-checked my rig before weighting the rope, and I used a backup system whenever possible. But speed was such a necessity in the icefall that everyone, including me, skipped the backups.

Once we cleared the last rappel and the final ladder, the rest of the down climb was straightforward. We took the spikes off our boots at the same spot we'd put them on earlier: Crampon Point. After a twenty-minute trudge downhill to the lower end of base camp, we returned to the IMG dining tent. We'd been gone only six hours, but the icefall had taken a toll on me. I texted Gloria:

Tough day here . . . tired & a bit weak.

Nurse Gloria replied:

You are building lots of new red blood cells.

At lunch Dallas told us we'd take two rest days before heading back up "the Hill," as we sometimes called Everest. I hoped I could recover in that time. On the next trip we'd be climbing much higher.

34

I was discouraged at how sluggish climbing above 18,000 feet had felt the previous day. Because Alan had been through the Khumbu Icefall dozens of times on his previous expeditions, I called him in Colorado and told him I'd reached the Football Field in under three and a half hours. He said my time was fine for a first acclimatization trip and not to worry.

Greg held brief private chats later that day with each climber to let them know how they were doing. Like anticipating a performance review at work, I thought I was doing fairly well but remained anxious to hear what the boss would say. Greg's command post sat at the edge of camp, just twenty yards beyond my tent. When I saw he was alone, I walked over and talked with him. As I wrote in my journal later:

> My chat with Greg was ten seconds long. Greg said, "You're good to go." I said, "Yes, I think so." He said, "I just checked the 'Fine' box next to your name." That was it.

My concerns abated, I turned my attention to resting and communications. I sent emails to friends and family, posted icefall photos online, and wrote a blog post. After spending hours on my laptop in the dark comms tent, I went to sit in the sun next to my tent. Greg walked past with someone following him—the professional climber Ueli Steck. Known worldwide for his impressive climbs and solo ascents, Ueli had earned the nickname "the Swiss Machine" from the title of the 2010 movie about him, which showcases Ueli's outrageous-speed solo climb of the Eiger's gigantic north face in his native Switzerland.

Greg saw me staring, so he stopped on the trail. "Ueli, this is Jim Davidson."

Ueli smiled, extended his hand, and said in soft-spoken English, "Nice to meet you, Jim."

As we shook hands, I said, "Great to see you, Ueli. I'm sure you don't recall, but we met briefly at the Ouray Ice Festival a few years ago."

Ueli was forty years old and had short brown hair and a pointed chin. His modest size and lean physique were ideal for climbing high and fast. We chatted a moment about the annual Colorado ice-climbing event, and then Greg hustled Ueli along to his tent. They had been colleagues and friends for several years.

Climbing media had been reporting that Ueli intended to climb the difficult West Ridge to the top of Everest and then continue to Lhotse. That feat alone would be amazing enough, but base camp's hyperactive rumor mill alleged that he might add Nuptse too, thus enchaining all three peaks of the triple crown.

For the rest of the afternoon I focused on two critical tasks: fine-tuning my gear and forcing down liquids. The cold, dry air and rapid breathing rates at high altitude combined to make climbers lose a quart or two of water per day through respiration alone. Staying hydrated on Everest required drinking five or six quarts of water every twenty-four hours.

Enhanced hydration also meant plenty of bathroom breaks. Although a minor nuisance during the day, frequent nighttime pee breaks became a serious inconvenience. Even at home, leaving a warm bed to answer nature's call wasn't pleasant—doing it during the coldest hours of a Himalayan night was an ordeal.

Going outside to urinate required five or ten minutes to put on clothing layers and boots, all while fighting off the urgent need for relief. Once a hat, headlamp, and gloves were on, the anxious climber could hustle along the snow-covered trail to the pee spot behind a boulder. (The seat and bucket inside the toilet tent were reserved for bowel movements.) Once finished, the relieved climber had to return to the tent, wrestle off all those outer clothes, and settle back in. But by then the cold night air would have chilled the sleeping bag. Getting rewarmed and returning to sleep could take a while.

To avoid all those tedious difficulties, most climbers instead stayed inside the tent and used a pee bottle. The container was usually an old plastic water bottle with a few key attributes: widemouthed to prevent missing, leakproof for obvious reasons, and clearly marked to eliminate any potential for mistaking a pee jug for a drinking water bottle. Many people put a warning sticker on their pee bottle that read "Danger" or "Biohazard." On previous trips I'd marked mine with a hand-sketched skull and crossbones, along with duct tape for tactile identification at night.

For this trip I had bought a soft-sided bottle with a different design from my drinking bottles. It held a voluminous one and a half quarts. On their first trip using a pee bottle, some people mistakenly bring a one-pint bottle. Rookies. They learn fast, though, the first time they run out of empty bottle space before they run out of pee.

Peeing inside a tent required only a headlamp, some planning, and a little practice. Most men kneel in the tent, though a few can manage the process lying down. Female climbers sometimes brought plastic funnel-shaped appendages to help them. A full pee bottle could be stored standing or lying down, if you trusted the lid. The bottle could be put outside the tent, left inside, or stored in your sleeping bag if you desperately wanted a short-term heat source to hug. The overnight storage decision needed to factor in whether the pee would freeze solid: Trying to melt a full, frozen pee bottle presents an interesting problem the next morning.

All the possible pee-bottle mishaps explained a viewpoint I had heard expressed during my first 8,000-meter climb, on Cho Oyu. IMG had told us to bring one warm sleeping bag to leave in base camp, and that we would share IMG group bags in the upper three camps. But my teammate, Horst, a doctor from Germany who resided in Florida, told me that he brought a second sleeping bag of his own for the high camps. When I asked him why, he declared, in a heavy German accent, "If I am going to sleep in a piss-soaked sleeping bag, I prefer the piss to be *my own*."

Expedition climbers regularly run into mountaineering friends in far-flung corners of the world, and Everest base camp is a major crossroads. During our rest days of April 17 and 18 I had three visitors—a Nepali climber and an Indian mountaineer who stopped by to introduce themselves after we connected through social media, and my Canadian friend Al Hancock, who shouted a greeting to me as he walked past our campsite.

Al didn't stop because he knew IMG had a "closed camp" policy to discourage visitors. Inhibiting people from dropping by might sound unfriendly, but the approach reduced exposure to illnesses and germs carried by friends and strangers who had just traveled in from all over the world. Also, curious trekkers sometimes wandered through base camp to look around, meet Everest climbers, and shake their hands. Some cautious base-camp residents regarded these transient travelers as "disease carriers." With so much at stake, Everest hopefuls put a strong emphasis on staying healthy.

Near the summit of Everest the air contains only 30 percent as much oxygen as it does at sea level. Supplemental bottled oxygen helps some, but we would only use it for about a day and a half on our summit push. And bottled "Os" wouldn't get you to the top or keep you alive if you weren't already well acclimatized.

Ever since the first expedition to Mount Everest in 1921, climbers knew that slowly adapting to the thinner air was the way to eventually reach the top. That's why everyone with summit aspirations arrived at base camp a month before their summit push. To progressively urge our bodies toward better acclimatization, we would go partway up the mountain, stay for a few days, then descend to base camp. Each rotation would last three to six days, and over a month we would do two or three trips up and down to ever greater heights.

PK and I left base camp at 2:25 a.m. the next morning and started toward Camp One with our teammates. Even though my pack weighed about twenty pounds more than on our practice run, familiarity with the route allowed me to move a bit faster. We worked our way through the lower icefall for two hours. I noticed minor changes over the past three days: A crevasse had widened here, an ice block had shifted there.

When we reached the point closest to Nuptse, we turned left for the traverse back toward the glacier's middle. PK stopped, and I closed the two-stride gap between us just in time to see him unclip his leash from the fixed line. He turned to me and said, "Rope gone."

Gone? I looked near his boots; the thin fixed line led down into the ground. Panning my headlamp ahead illuminated about twenty-five yards of terrain covered by a thick bed of jagged ice shards. I spotlighted the place where the line reemerged from the ground. The rope hadn't been cut or removed—it was buried. Instinctively I turned to my right to examine the cliff above us, and after a few seconds I realized that the ice tower with the major fissure cutting through it was also gone. It had collapsed onto the trail within the last three days and buried the fixed line.

Together we pulled hard on the protruding fixed line, but it didn't budge. The rope was buried under several feet of dense debris.

PK said, "We go fast." Then he scurried across the ice shards like he was walking on hot coals.

We had no idea what caverns or instabilities lurked beneath the recently collapsed debris, so watching him move across it unroped horrified me. Adapting the group technique we used to cross an avalanche path one person at a time, I never took my eyes off him while he was exposed to the danger. Once he was past the debris, he clipped back into the line and moved to a more sheltered spot. Then he beckoned me to him with three quick waves of his forearm. My turn.

I tried calming myself with the fact that the other climbers ahead of us must have just crossed without a problem, so it was no big deal. But this justification only half assuaged my fear as I unclipped my leash from the rope and hustled toward PK. One panicked corner of my brain screeched, You're unroped in the icefall; what are you *doing*?! But urgency made me ignore the voice.

When I scrambled as fast as I could at 18,400 feet, my heart rate spiked to its maximum. My mind flashed to running hill sprints back home. I reached PK and clipped back into the fixed line. Then I placed both hands on my head to open up my chest as I gasped for breath: should've done more sprints.

Redlining your cardiovascular system always takes a toll. Waves of weakness flushed through my legs as I tried to relax and bring my heart rate down. After I recovered enough to follow PK, I set out at a more measured pace, but I didn't feel very good.

Once past the traverse, we started gaining altitude again. We switched our harness leashes from a fast-sliding carabiner to a slow but safer mechanical ascender. After one more steep ice face, we pulled onto the Football Field at about 5:45 in the morning. We'd made it there faster than last time.

I slipped off the pack and pulled on my down coat to trap body heat. The vicious cold meant we couldn't rest for long, so I wolfed down a handful of salty peanuts and a few ounces of sugary sport drink. We stripped off our puffy jackets, stowed them in our packs, and started up into new terrain. The general landscape seemed familiar from our trip through in 2015, but the fast-moving glacier meant that the frozen landscape and the fixed-line route both varied every year.

Crevasses broke the Khumbu Glacier into a series of tall ice blocks. We climbed thirty feet up the front of one, walked six feet across its top, and descended thirty feet down the backside. For the next twenty minutes, we did the same thing on three more pinnacles. After all that work, we'd advanced only about one hundred lateral feet and had gained almost no elevation.

When the Icefall Doctors built the route a few weeks ago, they avoided the most dangerous and impassable zones. The fixed lines cut back and forth, trying to link the less chaotic areas. At about 19,300 feet the route cut far left and brought us close to the west shoulder. We were underneath the hanging seracs that had fallen on the sixteen Nepalis in 2014. I wondered how far downhill the glacier had carried those three missing bodies by now.

Camp One sat only five hundred vertical feet above us, but progress slowed. The shattered terrain resembled an unstable heap of broken cinder blocks, with sharp-edged remnants leaning one against the other. We wound our way over, under, and through the debris as gravity imperceptibly pulled the whole pile down toward base camp.

As we angled up, we crossed the open top of an ice tower, and I snatched a glimpse of the twisted path ahead. Two dozen climbers followed one another like ants as the fixed line led back below the surface, threading among ice blocks and dipping in and out of debris-clogged crevasses. We spent more time inside the glacier than on its top surface.

Two bus-size glacial blocks pinched the trail so tightly that when PK squeezed through the alleyway, his pack scraped against the frozen walls behind him. I followed him, listening to my sleeping pad scuff the ice and hoping the glacier wouldn't decide to shift in the next few seconds.

The narrow slot brought us to the edge of an open canyon. We were thirty feet up one sidewall, and below us stretched an icy pit the size of a hockey rink. But instead of a smooth ice sheet, the floor was a rugged moonscape of glacial holes and ice boulders—the remains of a massive icefall collapse. On the pit's other side, six climbers stood still beneath a tall ladder, waiting their turn to ascend.

Rather than stand with them on the recently subsided pit floor, we stayed on the elevated shoulder and waited. When the last climber started up the lashed-together aluminum ladder, PK and I descended, crossed the crumpled zone, and scampered to the base of the ladder. As PK started up, I held the side rails and footed the ladder for him. He stepped onto the collapsed canyon's upper edge, clipped in, and then held the ladder top steady for me as best he could. Though the ladder bounced, I relaxed into the motion. These sections played to my strengths.

We traversed rightward, moving out of the direct-impact zone beneath the west-shoulder seracs. After one more steep ladder, we escaped over the upper lip of the Khumbu Icefall. The tension in my chest loosened as we stopped for a rest. After five hours of laboring under darkness and shadow, we finally stood in the sunshine. Warmth penetrated my clothing, so I took off a layer and slathered sunscreen on my neck and face. My altimeter read 19,600 feet; we'd be at camp soon.

The boot path in the snow zigzagged as it gradually ascended the last two hundred vertical feet. Ahead of us the elongated Western Cwm basin stretched three miles to the Lhotse Face. The horseshoe-shaped frozen walls soared more than a mile above my head, confirming that my wild recollections from two years ago weren't imagined. Their beautiful heights lifted my spirits. But more than seven square miles of mountain walls plastered with semiattached rock and ice chunks triggered my fear of earthquakes and avalanches.

Our camp was pitched in the same place on the glacier. Those of us on the team who rode out the 2015 quake there called it our lucky spot. PK and I slowly walked the last hundred yards and arrived at about 8:30. I was back in Camp One.

After crawling into an empty tent, I mixed my recovery drink. Most days I had to force myself to swallow the lumpy protein slurry, but this morning I gulped it down, anxious for the liquid. A headache was setting in, a rarity for me, and my body was drained from the climb. I texted Gloria that we were safe in Camp One.

The white walls surrounding camp reflected the midmorning sun, and soon I was overheating inside the tent. My tentmate for this rotation, Jim Diani, arrived later. "Big Jim" had been at Camp One with me in 2015; he'd also been on Everest during the terrible icefall collapse of 2014. That made this Big Jim's third Everest expedition, even though he had yet to make it past Camp One. His quiet nature made some people think Jim was a low-energy guy. But he was a veteran climber and a smart engineer. I trusted his calm and thoughtful approach.

Jim looked pretty wiped out. Once he recovered a bit, he settled in. The rest of the day was focused on recovery, so we both took a morning nap.

I awoke around eleven to find my tentmate asleep and camp quiet. Everything seemed just as it had on April 25, 2015. As I lay in the hot tent, my mind churned up memories of that morning. I remembered the first avalanche rumble and the sick feeling of dread when the second slide added its ominous roar. I recalled my stomach lurching as the seismic waves rippled through the glacier and heaved our tent skyward.

Continental plates don't function on annual cycles; nor do they pay any heed to superstitious anniversaries. But people do. I kept checking my watch as 11:56 a.m. approached. Logically I knew that no earthquake or avalanche would occur at that precise moment just because the place, setting, and time all felt eerily the same to me. But at 11:55 a.m. I sat up slowly and listened anyway. A gentle breeze fluttered a loose tent flap nearby. Muffled Nepali conversation drifted from our cook tent. The mountain remained quiet.

At 11:56 I held my breath and placed my right hand on the tent floor to check for vibrations. Cold sharp crystals stabbed at my palm through the nylon. The glacier stayed motionless.

Still suspicious, I pushed my fingertips hard into the glacier's surface, as if to take the earth's pulse. The continental plate didn't move.

Late in the afternoon, I sent a GPS text to Alan about the trip to Camp One:

Took six hours. Some very sketchy moves in icefall. Feel pretty good. Headache but fine.

Alan replied:

> **6 hours is great for 1st trip to C1. Well done. Try to stay cool,**
> **hydrate and look forward to your next milestone—C2 Baby!!!!**

The first night at a new altitude was always rough, but I slept pretty well. After breakfast on April 20, Dallas told us we would take a day hike up the glacier to reach the 20,000-foot elevation mark. The activity would advance our acclimatization and also show us part of the route to Camp Two.

We left camp without packs and hiked up the Western Cwm. Every two hundred feet or so, an enormous crevasse cut across the entire width of the glacier. The cracks were about 150 feet deep and a third of a mile wide—roughly the distance of two or three city blocks. Climbing into and then out of one giant slot after another slowed us down, as did the altitude. From our high point at about 20,100 feet, the remaining two-mile stretch to the next camp looked almost flat, but that was deceptive—we knew the glacier gained another 1,200 feet before reaching Camp Two. We returned to Camp One, ate a simple freeze-dried dinner, and prepared to move up in the morning.

Later that afternoon Dallas told me that he expected everyone to reach Camp Two in under four hours, maybe four and a half at the most. He also informed me that PK had been pulled into his other job of helping install fixed lines on the Lhotse Face. So Dallas asked me to travel to Camp Two with Karim Mella and his regular guide, Karma Rita Sherpa. They were both skilled and pleasant to be with, so I was fine with the change. Karim was the first citizen of the Domincan Republic to summit Everest. He did that back in 2011 when he was a teammate of Alan Arnette, so Karim and I connected through our mutual friend. I had visited Karim's home country in 1987, so we enjoyed chatting together.

To avoid the roasting midday sun, we left Camp One the next day at 6:00 a.m. We struggled down into and back out of a dozen large crevasses for the first hour and a half. At about 20,300 feet, the glacial cracks appeared less often, the ice surface smoothed, and the fixed line ended. I unclipped from the last rope segment and trudged behind Karim and Karma Rita.

As we slogged farther up the Western Cwm, I scanned my head and eyes across the landscape, looking for cracks, sags, or linear features in the snow that hinted at a crevasse lurking below. I remembered Nick's advice to keep my head on a swivel. To reduce the risk, I tried stepping precisely where the guys just had, or at least on other climbers' crampon prints in the hope that they'd already tested the ground.

These actions were prudent but no guarantee. A scary story from Alan about this section of the route kept running through my mind: On his first Everest trip, in 2002, Alan was above Camp One on his way to Camp Two. Most teams travel the area unroped, but Alan was tied into the middle of a climbing rope with one teammate in front of him and one behind. Out of nowhere, a snow bridge collapsed beneath Alan's feet and dropped him into a deep-blue crevasse. Fortunately his skilled rope team caught his fall and anchored Alan until he could climb out. The experience shook him back then, and he still got uncomfortable when he told me the story a decade later. After the Mount Rainier accident, fears about falling inside a glacier lurked in my psyche the way a crevasse hides just beneath new-fallen snow. I kept swiveling my head.

As we walked up the valley, my crampons crunched every time they bit into the Khumbu Glacier's outer skin. I tried accelerating but couldn't sustain it for long and had to settle back into my plodding pace. My leg muscles weren't sore or tired, but the low oxygen level reduced my power. I clomped out twenty steps, then needed to stop for a break. After a minute my body didn't want to start again, as if instinctively protecting itself from exertion when there was barely enough air to function.

I forced my legs forward again, staring at my boots and listening to my steps. *Crunch. Crunch. Crunch.* To urge myself along, I would pick a random snow patch about fifty feet ahead and try not to stop before getting there. A few times I made it, but not many.

To take my focus off suffering, I reminded myself to look up. The

Western Cwm spanned less than half a mile wide. One of the harder ways to climb Everest, the West Ridge, ran parallel to us, high on the left. Nuptse's steep north face rose nearly 5,000 feet straight out of the glacier to my right. The entire upper horseshoe basin of the Cwm looked avalanche-prone. We stayed in the middle of the valley, trying to avoid all the potential slide paths. The previous winter had had lower-than-average snowfall, which reduced the avalanche hazard but would make our route up the steep Lhotse Face even icier.

With so many rest stops, the last mile to camp took me an excruciating two hours. Karim was patient with me, but Karma Rita seemed annoyed at having to wait. Our average half-mile-per-hour pace and four hundred feet per hour of ascent in that segment didn't make me proud or Karma Rita happy. But three hours and forty-five minutes after departing Camp One, I dropped my pack on the lateral moraine where IMG had placed Camp Two.

Our fastest person that day, an überfit professional bike racer from Germany named Mo, made it to Camp Two an hour ahead of me, while our slowest arrived half an hour behind me. Although chagrined about being toward the back of the pack, I was pleased to have reached a new personal high point on Everest. Considering I hadn't been at 21,300 feet in more than seven years, I cut myself some slack and focused on recovery. I moved into a tent with Big Jim, unpacked my gear, and rested.

More than an hour before official sunset, the high rock walls surrounding us blocked the sun's rays from reaching the Cwm floor, and biting cold settled onto camp. I dressed in proper dinner attire: a down suit. In the unheated mess tent, the only way to stay warm was by covering ourselves from ankle to head in three inches of feathers.

I crawled from our tent and surveyed the frozen landscape. Camp Two sat on the highest dirt patch on Everest. One hundred feet past our camp, the rest of the mountain's upper pyramid was ice or icy bedrock. Measured straight-lined on a map, the summit of Everest was only one mile away, but the land rose 7,700 vertical feet in that mile. In the fading evening light, the southwest face of Mount Everest turned yellow-orange, like a New England sugar maple in fall.

35

Sleeping at 21,300 feet was rough. My heavy openmouthed breathing had woken me up eight or nine times, and the need to pee had
roused me three more. I'd started a low-dose regime of acetazolamide, a
common high-altitude medicine that promoted acclimatization but included the annoying side effect of enhancing urine production. The pills
worked well on both counts.

Big Jim fared no better. When he lay horizontal his plugged sinuses
limited his breathing, so he'd sat up half the night clearing his nose and
throat.

As we both got dressed for breakfast, Jim said, "Ugh, that was miserable."

"Yeah, I feel hungover," I said.

He glanced at my face. "You *look* hungover."

I chuckled, then wiped my hand across my head to smooth down the
greasy hair strands sprouting at wild angles. "Better?"

"Much."

We laughed. When I dragged myself from the tent, the view swept away my grogginess. A 4,000-foot-tall crystalline ice basin encircled us on three sides. The gray-and-yellow rock buttresses of Everest's southwest face stretched high into the deep-blue sky. My neck soon ached from staring upward.

On an Everest training climb, Rodney and I had speculated how stupendous the mountain view might be in the upper Khumbu Glacier. I immediately texted him:

Woke up today at head of Western Cwm. Surreal ice world.

He responded:

This is so unreal. You are right where you belong. Everything you've done the last 20 years has pointed to this moment. I'm proud and jealous in equal measure.

As my teammates and I hunched on small campstools at breakfast, the folds of our down suits sagged like overlapping fat rolls. But beneath those feathers we were skinny and getting skinnier. I forced down some of the warm oatmeal and solidified fried eggs the cooks had worked so hard to prepare. But high altitude suppresses the appetite, so I struggled to eat half a plateful. High elevation apparently also diminishes intelligence and class, as our breakfast conversations centered on sleep, snot, and toilet-tent visits. My mom would have been appalled.

Once the morning sun hit camp, we went on a short acclimatization hike to examine the Lhotse Face. The uppermost section of the glacier was traditionally not outfitted with fixed lines, so we hiked unroped, one behind the other, for half a mile. The pale-blue ice was low angled, maybe ten or fifteen degrees steep, and we stepped over a few narrow glacial cracks. I watched the ground for evidence of larger crevasses and focused on my breathing as I placed one crampon-clad boot above the other.

Later in the day I wrote about our two-hour unroped hike in my journal:

> We crossed dozens of crevasses, small to medium . . . I do not
> like this cavalier crevasse attitude.

I also recorded a story that my Norwegian teammate, Inge, told about Babu Chiri Sherpa. Babu was a famous guide who had summited ten times and held two Everest records: one for the fastest ascent at the time, and one for spending twenty-one hours on the summit without supplemental oxygen. In 2001 Babu was walking unroped on the glacier near Camp Two. He fell one hundred feet into a crevasse and died.

The rapid drumming of a metal spoon against an empty cook pot called us to lunch. Big Jim exited our tent, and I followed. Outside, three of our teammates gestured up at the West Ridge—a small black dot was ascending a white icefield about a thousand feet above us. The climber was soloing with no rope; it had to be Ueli. As he climbed the steep ice ramp toward the West Ridge, he tucked underneath a vertical cliff and stopped, probably for protection from falling debris. Ducking back into my tent, I grabbed my wide-angle GoPro and snapped two frames of a tiny dark figure clinging to an enormous ice slope.

For a moment I imagined myself up there at 22,000 feet, climbing unknown ground with only two ice axes and crampons for security. A falling rock, a collapsed snow step, or any minor problem could knock a climber off his feet and send him rocketing down the ice face. Shuddering at the thought, I couldn't quite comprehend the skill, poise, and self-control required to venture up there unroped.

Mesmerized, I watched Ueli Steck solo even higher. But being late for meals was considered poor form, so I hustled off to join my team in the mess tent. I planned to take telephoto pictures with one of my other two cameras after lunch, but when I returned twenty minutes later, afternoon clouds had rolled in and I couldn't see Ueli anymore. I felt lucky to have watched one of the world's greatest climbers before he disappeared into the mist.

My tired body urged me to stay horizontal in our tent, but my bored brain prompted me to do something. I hauled myself outside and wandered among the other expedition sites, taking a short walk to aid acclimatization. Camp Two stretched for a few hundred yards along the narrow lateral moraine beneath the West Ridge. IMG occupied the uppermost end of this strand, so I ambled downhill, careful to avoid slipping on the muddy ice. Big teams, like Himalayan Experience and Adventure Consultants, used fifteen to twenty tents. Smaller groups had only a few shelters and simplified things by eating their meals in a modest cook tent.

My slow stroll through Camp Two revealed a mess. On our approach to Everest, the trails appeared nearly trash-free, as they were in 2015. I'd worried that since so many people fled after the earthquake, base camp might have become strewn with refuse. I'd been pleased to see that it remained tidy—most teams had assigned staff to stay behind and pick up their campsite. Also, I'd heard that the Indian Army and the Sagarmatha Pollution Control Committee had conducted additional cleanup after the quake. But the sudden evacuation of Camp Two on April 27, 2015, had impacted the landscape.

With insufficient time and manpower to disassemble camp and no excess helicopter capacity to haul materials out, most of the tents and equipment at Camp Two had to be abandoned in place. Many teams had covered their equipment with tarps and tent fabric, but a year of wind, weather, and hungry goraks had scattered everything about before anyone could return. Tent pieces, personal items, and food wrappers littered camp, and most of it was frozen to the ground due to repeated thaw-and-freeze cycles.

When Everest climbing resumed in 2016 and continued into 2017, Camp Two residents collected loose refuse into piles and informally carried it down. But whenever I spotted a piece of trash and tried grabbing it, the scrap was usually embedded in the ice. I could pick up only about a fourth of what caught my eye. With residual trash melded to the mountain, Camp Two remained messy. At IMG we picked up what we could and brainstormed more aggressive cleanup tactics.

The descent from Camp Two all the way back to base camp could be accomplished in half a day, but the downhill run required an early departure to clear the Khumbu Icefall before the late-morning sun loosened everything up. We were packing to depart at 5:00 a.m. when a radio call from below informed us that the route had been closed due to a collapse. The Icefall Doctors would need time to repair the rope-and-ladder system, and by then it would be too late in the day to run the icefall gauntlet. Dallas decided we should stay another day at Camp Two and try the next morning.

While exasperating, staying longer was not a problem. Three nights in a row at Camp Two would help us adjust to the altitude. I measured my resting pulse at fifty-eight beats per minute, a good sign of adaptation, but walking up even a small hill sent my heart rate soaring.

My GPS had only 35 percent battery left. I needed the power to track our descent, so instead of texting Gloria, I called her on the satellite phone. During our short chat, Glo told me that she and the kids had gone out for a nice restaurant dinner. I cheerily discussed the details with her and then talked to Jess and Nick for a few minutes. After our call, thinking about my family back in Colorado and me stuck at Camp Two made me homesick.

When direct sunlight hit our tent around ten in the morning, the temperature rose so fast that I stripped off three layers of clothing in twenty minutes. A lunchtime radio call informed us that the route had reopened, but now a rain-and-snow mix falling in base camp might require us to spend a fourth night at Camp Two. The possibility made me unhappy; this intense high-altitude environment was exhausting. I recorded in my journal how conditions vacillated wildly. After a frigid early morning, it became too hot at 10:30 a.m. under the sun, too cold at 12:30 p.m. beneath the clouds, and then back to too hot at 2:30 p.m. By 4:30 p.m. there was the odd combination of being hot inside our tent while it snowed outside. I concluded: The stresses are high, and the comforts are low.

Before leaving Camp Two, we each had to decide if we would stay at Camp One on our next rotation or push from base camp all the way to Camp Two in one day. We needed to make the decision days in advance because we had to leave our sleeping bags, down suits, and other gear at whichever camp we intended to return to. It was a tough call to make so far ahead of time, especially when we were all still struggling to adapt to the altitude at Camp Two.

Many in the group committed to doing the long climb up from base camp in one push, but that could easily become exhausting. I believed the slow and steady approach was better this early in the trip, so I leaned toward sleeping at Camp One for a night. I swapped messages with Alan about this important decision, and he strongly advised stopping at Camp One to avoid burnout. When Dallas asked about my plans, I told him I would drop my gear at Camp One on the way down and stay there for a night on the next rotation.

We started our descent at 5:45 a.m. on April 24. With crevasse concerns still fresh in my mind, I felt nervous about the first mile of unroped glacier travel. The early-morning light helped me detect subtle dips in the glacier's surface that suggested possible crevasses underneath. A few hundred feet above Camp One, we clipped back into the fixed lines, and my tension eased. PK and I zoomed from Camp Two to Camp One in an hour and twenty minutes, about a third of the time it had taken me to climb up.

I stashed my sleeping bag and upper-mountain gear in an IMG storage tent, where it would remain until I returned in a few days. Our Camp One cook gave PK and me cold lemonade, and then we descended into the icefall. The hockey-rink-size collapse had expanded over the last few days. From our position it now stretched two hundred feet north toward the west shoulder and at least six hundred feet south toward Nuptse. The canyon floor now looked like four rubble-covered hockey rinks lined up end to end. We climbed through the unstable ruins as fast as we could—the rest days at Camp Two had given my legs the strength to push hard, and the thickening air beckoned us on.

There were many sections of moderately steep terrain to descend where falling could get a climber hurt or even killed. But rappelling them all would add hours to our exposure time in the icefall, so we employed the infamous arm, or sherpa, rappel; instead of using a belay device to secure ourselves to the rope, we simply wrapped a loop of fixed line around a forearm and grabbed the line for some control. Facing down-hill, we then scurried straight down the steep slopes with fast, aggressive steps. We counted on nimble footwork, rope friction against our arm, and grip strength to keep us from falling. Varying how hard we squeezed the rope through our thick gloves let us manage our speed—sort of.

This worked fine unless someone lost their grip, ran into an icy rope section, or misjudged the steepness. We stayed attached to the fixed line with a sliding carabiner leash in case we fell into a crevasse. There was lots of room for error, but the arm-wrap technique was fast, and in the icefall, speed counted. We descended more than 2,300 feet of complex icefall terrain in two and a half hours.

After five days up high, base-camp air felt thick. The warm sunshine drove us to line up for showers under the gravity-fed system our kitchen staff had rigged inside a floorless tent. The modest water flow and the cool breeze whistling through the shower tent prevented me from considering it luxurious, but a small bar of soap and several gallons of warm water trickling over my body made everything better.

With our first full rotation under our harnesses, we all looked forward to a few days of much-needed recovery. The thin, dry air had given most of us a hacking cough. Mild cases of this "Khumbu cough" ruined our sleep, strained our voices, and made exercise difficult. Severe coughing fits can become so violent as to painfully tear intercostals (muscles between ribs), or break rib bones—one of our Team Two climbers cracked his ribs coughing and left the expedition days later.

For some on our team, things seemed uncertain. Inge had come down with pneumonia during our rotation and flew by helicopter down to Namche Bazaar to recover. My friend from 2015, Matt, had developed a painful toothache, so he descended to Namche to see the only dentist within one hundred miles.

Health issues forced several of our teammates to drop out completely. Karim's friend Omar had labored to ascend to Camp One and seemed ill. Upon his evacuation to Kathmandu, medical tests discovered that a significant problem had emerged. He did not return to Everest. Another teammate, Tony, had been struggling to acclimatize, perhaps because he hailed from the lowlands of Texas. He became stricken with a sudden case of high-altitude pulmonary edema and was immediately evacuated. The mountain was starting to take a toll. For those who had to leave, all the time and effort they'd invested, as well as roughly $45,000, were gone.

The rest period in base camp gave us time to write, read, and recover. Kaji and his cook team labored long hours every day to make our big group three meals plus a nightly dessert—the kitchen staff even baked chocolate cake when someone had a birthday. But the variety of ingredients was limited, so the meals grew repetitious. A few climbers hiked down to Gorak Shep to buy lunch in a lodge, just for something different. That sounded tempting, but I didn't want to be exposed to germs from dozens of travelers, so I stayed in base camp.

April 25 was a sad anniversary day for the climbers and guides who'd been on Everest when the quake hit. The day must have felt even sadder for all the Nepalis; much of their homeland had been impacted, and their struggle to recover continued.

The big toe on my left foot had rubbed itself raw during our descent from Camp Two, so I went to the Himalayan Rescue Association medical tent. Doctor Meg Walmsley was there, and she remembered me from borrowing my GPS to text her family after the 2015 quake. We shared memories about trying to excavate medical supplies at the destroyed HRA site. After examining my toe, Meg concluded it wasn't infected, gave me friction-reducing bandages, and sent me on my way.

To keep our bodies from getting lethargic, we went on brief walks nearby. On April 28, I hiked partway up Pumori with Karim, Dean, Brad, and Big Jim. A rocky hilltop at about 18,000 feet gave us an excellent view of the Khumbu Glacier as it flowed out of the churning icefall. Towering high over the ice was the 23,800-foot triangular buttress of the west shoulder. Past the shoulder, the upper pyramid of Everest loomed more than a mile higher.

On our hike back to base camp, we ran into Min Bahadur Sherchan. The Nepali climber and former Gurkha soldier once held the record for the oldest man to summit Mount Everest. He'd accomplished the feat nine years earlier, when he was a spry seventy-six years old. Since then, he'd lost the record to a Japanese climber, Yūichirō Miura, who was also the first man to ski down Everest, back in 1970. Mr. Sherchan was back on the mountain to attempt the record again at the age of eighty-five.

I took my pulse every morning inside the sleeping bag to monitor my recovery. Over the past four days in base camp, my resting heart rate had dropped from sixty-five to sixty, then to fifty-three, and finally, to forty-nine beats per minute. My body seemed ready to go back up, but my mind wavered. I admitted in my journal to feeling uncertain after hearing avalanches every night and being hesitant about returning to the deadly icefall. I listed concerns about untrustworthy ladders, tenuous ice blocks, and multiple collapses. To shift toward a more resilient mindset, I then listed many things in my favor.

We were supposed to start our rotation to Camp Three soon, but the weather looked questionable. IMG had hired a professional weather modeler every year to send Greg detailed predictions for Everest. With reams of wind, temperature, and moisture estimates for every elevation,

Greg then applied his eight seasons of Everest knowledge to determine if we should wait or go. Better communications and more accurate weather models had helped make the mountain safer over the years, but technology couldn't reduce the strain of having to decide whether conditions looked good enough for dozens of friends, clients, and employees to risk their lives. At dinner on April 29, Greg told us that the winds at Camp Three might soon reach fifty to seventy miles per hour. We would wait another day before heading up for our final rotation.

April 30 started off cool and cloudy in base camp, but clear on the upper mountain. In the late morning I received a text message from Alan asking me to get in touch ASAP. His urgency unsettled me, so I called him on my cell phone. After a quick greeting, I said, "You sound anxious, buddy. What's up?"

"Well, I'm not sure yet, and I hope the early reports are wrong, but have you heard anything about Ueli?"

A tingle raced through me. "I saw him a few days ago, and then I heard he went up the Hill. Why?"

"Two of my contacts in base camp say he fell off Nuptse. And that he may be dead."

My hand holding the phone dropped down next to my thigh. I tilted my head backward and looked up at high gray clouds, then glanced sideways at Nuptse as if trying to discern an answer. After a few seconds I placed the phone back to my left ear. "What can I do to help?"

"The world media is already sniffing around, and no one wants to report this wrong. Can you ask Greg?"

I looked toward Greg's command tent. "Yeah. I'll call you back in a few minutes."

We hung up, and I resumed gazing at Nuptse while I pondered how to ask Greg about his friend. One minute of slow walking brought me to his tent. After a brief hello, I said, "Greg, I don't want to start rumors or create worry. I'm trying to verify what I just heard. Did something happen to Ueli?"

Greg stared at me blankly. "How the hell did you find out so fast?"

"Alan told me. Someone in base camp called him. Greg, I'm so sorry about Ueli."

Greg shared what he knew so far. Ueli had been soloing the north face of Nuptse earlier in the morning, probably for training, acclimatization, and maybe to scout the peak for a triple-crown attempt later. Some sherpas near Camp Two later saw him fall from near the top. With no rope or partner to catch him, Ueli fell about 3,000 vertical feet. A helicopter had recovered his remains and returned to base camp.

I called Alan to confirm the terrible news—one of the world's best mountaineers was dead. Alan said he'd just spoken with someone on the recovery team; Ueli's body would be flown out of base camp at any moment. I looked toward camp's upper end and told Alan, "I see a chopper lifting off right now."

Alan said something, but I couldn't hear him as the helicopter flew toward me, about fifty feet off the ground. Standing on the trail between Greg's tent and mine, I craned my neck as the helicopter soared right over me. I watched as Ueli Steck left the mountains one last time.

Base camp became somber. After a quiet lunch, Dallas told us they had arranged for the nearby teams to join us on a community project: We would pitch in to rebuild the raised helicopter landing pad at the south end of camp. The shared infrastructure could potentially save any one of our lives in the weeks ahead. Close to sixty guides, climbers, and sherpas from several teams showed up to work; even Russell Brice pitched in. Though the idea had probably been taking shape before Ueli's death, after losing him, the project seemed to become a proxy memorial.

For several hours mountaineers and mountain workers toiled together moving boulders, helmet-size rocks, and damp glacial soil. When the forty-foot-diameter circular mound reached three feet high, we packed the mountain detritus down tightly by having everyone walk on it.

That afternoon, beneath storm clouds sagging with moisture freshly gathered from the glaciers, I realized that the helipad had been more than just an infrastructure project. It had pulled us all from our tents and our sadness. Side by side we worked, laughed, and grieved. When the project was done, the Everest community was a little closer and a little safer.

I think Ueli would have liked that.

36

May 2 arrived, and the weather forecast looked clear, which meant it was time to head up toward Camp Three for our final rotation. After making sure Gigi was awake, I walked to the mess tent under a big, starry sky. It was difficult to be enthused about eating breakfast at 1:30 a.m., especially as I was growing sick of the menu. But food was fuel, so I ate as much as I thought my stomach could handle in the middle of the night. Then, loaded up with our gear, PK and I walked away from the mess tent at 2:10 a.m. I followed PK along the rocky trail through Sherpaland and up a small hill to the IMG camp altar.

The square altar was made of stacked angular stone. It covered an area about six feet by six feet and stood four feet tall. A five-inch-thick wooden prayer pole protruded from the middle of the cubelike rock pile and extended fifteen feet into the sky. From the top of the pole, five long strands of multicolored prayer flags draped down. They stretched fifty feet in different directions and were anchored to the ground with glacier-polished rocks. On the altar's top surface lingered traces of the food-and-drink offerings our Buddhist staff had placed there to pay homage to the Buddha and ask for safety for us all.

Making sure to keep our clean sides toward the altar, we circled around it. A small tendril of pleasant smoke flowed from a burning incense stick—sandalwood, I think. PK chanted softly under his breath as we walked out of camp. I silently repeated the one mantra I knew: *Om mani padme hum.*

We followed our teammates' headlamps on the icy trail that skirted base camp. Our group had shrunk by several members and their climbing guides. Matt Tammen's tooth pain had worsened, and he'd gone all the way to Kathmandu in a last-ditch effort to resolve the problem. Inge had recovered enough to join the final rotation, but his fellow Norwegian, Knut, had unfortunately caught pneumonia and descended to Namche. When we geared up at Crampon Point, Dean felt terrible and returned to base camp. His trip was over.

Though I felt groggy from insufficient sleep, we made good time in the lower icefall. My crampon kicks felt firm, and my carabiner clips in and out of the fixed lines were crisp. We reached the Football Field in two hours and forty minutes, which was faster than last time. Upon our arrival there, someone told us that the route above had closed due to a new collapse. We might not be able to go any higher, but returning to base camp meant we'd slip behind schedule and maybe miss the good weather. So we waited.

We bundled up and passed the first half hour eating, drinking, and talking with our teammates. But as our sweat-dampened clothes chilled, the predawn cold gnawed into us. We bunched together to share warmth and block the wind for one another. As we waited, more IMG members joined our cluster, and we snuggled closer. Someone in the middle joked about being cozy while those on the outer edge shivered. We began taking turns standing in the circle's warm core and rotating out to the cold perimeter. Scientists would describe our approach as social thermoregulation; we called it a penguin huddle.

After another hour, the guides up ahead had gotten the route open, and we moved out. My thigh muscles had stiffened after standing in the cold for that long. Being crowded together now caused human traffic to slow our progress, which increased our risky time in the icefall. While frustrating, it was simply too dangerous to unclip from the lines and pass slower people.

Higher up, we walked across the glacier's top surface for a minute until the ice block ended at a vertical drop-off. A six-foot-wide gap separated us from the next big tower we needed to reach. The crevasse walls near the surface of the chasm shined a pale blue-white. Farther in, the ice progressed to deeper shades of blue. After about ninety feet, the indigo depths of the mine shaft–like abyss revealed nothing more. Though the crevasse had a bottom—they all do—I couldn't see it.

The Icefall Doctors had spanned the gap with a ten-foot ladder laid horizontally between the ice towers. Both ends were anchored in place by an aluminum snow stake hammered vertically into the glacier. The ladder looked fairly stable, even though it tilted to the right. For added safety, the icefall team also installed two skinny handlines, which hung loosely along each side of the ladder bridge. Clipping into these lines with one or two harness leashes provided backup in case any climbers lost their balance—or their nerve.

The icefall route included dozens of these horizontal ladder crossings. After multiple trips through the maze, I'd grown used to the haphazard setups, but every time I looked at one, my safety instincts and rigging knowledge warned me not to set foot on it. First, ladders weren't constructed for horizontal applications. Dad told me more than forty years ago never to use a ladder like a plank. They're designed to serve as one leg of a triangle that includes a strong building and solid ground; neither the side rails nor the rungs should be loaded horizontally with several hundred moving pounds.

Second, the flimsy ladder sections on Everest were chosen for their light weight, not their strength. I could tell at a glance that they were the cheap Type III ladders* designed for homeowners to clean out their gutters once a year. For walking across a possible ninety-foot drop, I

---

* In the United States, ladder strengths are rated from light duty (Type III) up through Construction and Industrial Heavy Duty (Type IAA) by the American National Standards Institute.

would've picked a Type IAA ladder, which was rated for much bigger loads. If this bent aluminum remnant ever had a duty rating sticker, it had long since been scratched away.

PK clipped the nonlocking carabiner of one harness leash to a handline and then scampered across. I stepped to the edge and attached two safety leashes, one to each handline. Because I used a locking carabiner on one leash, I spent five seconds twisting the locking ring tight.

"Not necessary," PK said.

I waved a hand to let PK know I'd heard him, but I didn't reply. With both leashes attached, I exhaled once to clear my mind. Then I walked across with each crampon spanning two rungs: the front points on the rung ahead, and my heel on the one behind. I moved across in one smooth effort; stopping, hesitating, or thinking about the possible consequences wouldn't help.

As I stepped over one gap after another, I concentrated on the next rung ahead, not the nine stories of open air beneath my feet. I consciously ignored all the dark space to my right and left. When I stepped onto solid ground, I clipped my nonlocking carabiner into the next section of fixed line. I spent another five seconds unlocking the carabiner of my second leash. As I removed that carabiner, PK poked it and said, "Too slow."

"*Thik cha*," I replied to state that I thought it was okay.

If the ladder shifted or the ice edge collapsed, my caution with the leashes could save my life, and I'd be correct in taking the time. But if slowing down put us in the wrong spot when an ice tower fell over or an avalanche hit, PK would be proved right. There was no way to know.

Speed and safety are always at odds with each other in the mountains. In mountaineering, as with painting, cutting corners on safety saves time but increases risk. The Khumbu Icefall, like nowhere else I'd ever been, forced those two needs into direct conflict with each other. Climbing through the icefall meant making hundreds of small risk-management decisions. And while all those compromises were being made, the sun overhead kept shining, the seracs on both sides kept leaning, and the glacier underfoot kept creeping downhill.

Besides the variations in how much risk seemed acceptable to each person, cultural differences played a role too. Being fast was not only a plausible risk-reduction approach, but for high-altitude workers it also offered other benefits. A reputation for speed can bring a Nepali guide praise, recognition, and enhanced employment. On Everest, speed was social currency.

We traversed back to the glacier's midline, where the ice moved fastest and crumpled the most. My altimeter read 19,600 feet, so I expected us to reach Camp One within the hour. But then we got word that another collapse had cut off the route just ahead of us. It felt like the near misses were getting closer.

Our teammates were stopped in a row with their packs off, so we lined up behind them. Back on went the down coats, and out came the snacks. I split one of my precious candy bars from home with PK and Inge. With the sun up but still hidden behind Lhotse's high profile, we walked in place and danced little jigs to stay warm. Dallas and four sherpa guides surged forward to help open the route. I stole glances upward at the west shoulder icefields hanging above us. Based on the probable fall line, I concluded that we were standing in the impact zone of a warehouse-size block. If it let go soon, as it would someday, we were stopped in a terrible place. Yet we waited there for two hours while the guides struggled to repair the fixed-line system.

I was starting to think we would have to return to base camp. In addition to all the wasted effort, going back meant descending the icefall under the dangerous midday sun. Fortunately Dallas radioed back that they had patched the route and we could continue up. In a burst of energy, we all put our packs on, but no one moved very far. There were about forty climbers in front of us, and it took thirty more minutes of waiting until the backlog cleared and we could push forward.

When our turn came, PK and I entered the rubble-filled "hockey rink" canyon once again. The ladder system up the far side looked even crazier than before. After the morning cave-in, the ladder was short of reaching the lip, so the guys had placed it atop a precarious ice boulder. The extra height helped, but the twenty-five-foot ladder steepened to dead vertical and still ended six feet short of the top. After ascending the ladder to its uppermost rung, we had to climb the last body length of vertical ice by kicking our crampons in and muscling an ascender up the free-hanging fixed line. I was panting hard when I reached the upper lip.

We crossed a few more horizontal ladders and pulled into Camp One at about 10:10 a.m., eight long hours after leaving base camp. By subtracting the three and a half hours we'd spent standing still, I had climbed up in four and a half hours. My time was much faster than before, and well under the six-hour requirement that Greg and Dallas had set.

IMG's established time standards for traveling between camps were set up so that the times shortened—and the enforcement intensified—on each sequential trip up the Hill. During our first rotation the times were suggested goals; for this second trip they were requirements. If you exceeded one, you'd still better meet all the rest. On our summit push in about ten days, the standards would be rigid cutoff times. Miss one and your trip was over, no exceptions.

Our guides told us that these harsh criteria had to be met for everyone's safety. I agreed. During the 1996 Everest disaster, moving too slowly and not turning around soon enough on summit day contributed to the many deaths. We had a duty, as individuals and as a community, to distill hard-won lessons from past tragedies and apply them to improve our approach and to refine ourselves.

Inge and I were the only two client climbers planning to sleep at Camp One. Everyone else planned to continue to Camp Two, even though the long icefall delays would put them in the Western Cwm during the stifling heat. The remaining trip was going to be difficult, but with their sleeping bags and gear waiting at Camp Two, they had to go. I later wrote in my journal: *I made the right call to spend the night here.*

Big Jim arrived about forty minutes after me and decided to wait out the hottest hours at Camp One. Because he and a few other climbers planned to move higher in the cool afternoon air, Jim hung out in my tent. I spread my sleeping bag over the roof to create shade, but soon we were roasting in the seventy-degree tent. We lounged until Dallas, Jim, Gigi, and Markus left for Camp Two at 3:15 p.m. It felt strange, and not very gung ho, to stay behind when almost all the other climbers pushed on. But as I noted in my journal that night, when Rodney and I talked by phone two days earlier, we had discussed my decision to spread the ascent to Camp Two over two days. He had said, "Since you're not going to the top this time, leave some energy in your tank, even if it means you're a little slow."

I enjoyed the quiet time alone and sent some text messages home via GPS. When we climbed, I set my GPS to Track mode so my position was posted every ten minutes to an online map of the mountain, allowing family and friends to track my position. Alan texted me that watching my location dot not move for hours in the icefall today had worried him. The real-time tracking map also allowed curious strangers around the globe to watch our progress. My writing friend, Emily Chappell, once told me that in her sport of transcontinental bike racing, such internet followers are called "dot watchers."

After a good night's sleep, we left camp at dawn to head to Camp Two. Inge and his guide, Pasang Sherpa, traveled with PK and me. Just above Camp One, we came upon a ladder bridge spanning a chasm so wide that it required three aluminum ladders tied together end to end. Lashing multiple ladders together to form a twenty-five-foot-long wobbly plank took safety-rule compliance to new lows. Using such an outrageous contraption in the United States would get someone fired, and their company would be slapped with a hefty penalty from the Occupational Safety and Health Administration. But America was far away; on Everest there wasn't any OSHA. I sometimes joked that if they had one in Nepal, they'd call it NOSHA.

Inge moved toward the long horizontal ladder. He'd skied to the South Pole, traversed Greenland, and he was in Camp Two during the 2015 quake. Inge was a solid mountaineer. I watched him clip his harness leash onto a handline and attach a second leash to the line along the ladder's other side. He walked on the rungs with steady steps. As he reached the midpoint, the ladder assembly sagged an inch or two. Once he cleared the ladder bridge, I clipped in both of my leashes, wondering what the sherpas thought. I began crossing the ladder. When a cross-breeze pushed some cold morning air through the crevasse, I felt a chill on my right cheek, as if an ice dragon were breathing on my face.

During the next water break I stood by Inge and said, "You use two leashes on the ladders."

"Yes, always," he replied in crisp English.

"I do too, but not everyone does."

"I have young sons, seven and nine. Two children, so two leashes."

I smiled. "Thank you, Inge." His example helped lock in my decision about how to handle the ladder crossings.

We climbed to the end of the fixed lines, unclipped, and plodded up the glacier. A little later we encountered IMG's Team Two descending from their first Camp Two rotation. We all stopped for a moment to get caught up and I chatted with Mathieu, who told me his stay felt terrible and his acclimatization wasn't going well. I reassured him that we all felt awful the first time up at 21,300 feet, but he confided that as soon as he reached base camp, he planned to visit the HRA doctors.

As we traversed below Nuptse's north face, I kept looking up and wondering where Ueli had fallen. His steep solo climb had been far riskier and more severe than the normal route we ascended with the security of fixed lines. Still, knowing that this high basin had just killed one of the world's best mountaineers made me realize how easily Everest could flick me away too.

Reaching Camp Two was easier and a little quicker than last time. I moved in with Big Jim, and as I unpacked my gear he told me that their ascent up the Western Cwm the previous day had been hot and slow. Both his late-afternoon group and the earlier group required more time to reach Camp Two in the heat than our cool-of-the-morning subgroup did. Yet PK told me, "Tomorrow, you must move faster. If too slow to C3, they turn people around every year."

I was dismayed by his statement. While I knew I wasn't fast, I'd beaten every time requirement and had been pleased with my steady approach and the reasonable condition I was in when I arrived at each camp. To me the expedition was a marathon, with the goal of reaching the halfway point—the summit—in good-enough shape to get back to the finish line: home. Sprinting hard and getting exhausted early seemed counterproductive. At the close of our conversation about the climb to Camp Three, PK said, "Tomorrow is examination."

We spent the rest of the day hydrating, eating, and practicing patience. Expeditions always include many unknowns and extensive downtime, so patience is a key attribute. During an afternoon snow squall, we sorted gear and napped. Big Jim kept coughing and sitting up in repeated struggles to breathe through his plugged sinuses.

By dinnertime the weather reports predicted that the winds up high would decrease soon, so we finalized preparations for a morning ascent. Cold settled upon us as I lay in my sleeping bag contemplating the climb to Camp Three. Two-thirds of the 2,400-foot ascent would be on steep, hard ice that shot up the Lhotse Face without interruption. In my journal, I tried firing myself up:

> I've been an ice climber for a long time—not a great one, but a
> solid one. I can do this!

Based on my previous ascent to 24,300 feet without oxygen on Cho Oyu, and on my recent pace, I estimated that the tough climb might take me seven or eight hours. Dallas told us earlier that the goal was to reach Camp Three in seven hours, with some leeway as long as you made it there in eight. After the brutal climb, however, we then had to tough out another eighteen hours overnight at 23,700 feet without bottled oxygen. Several times when we had discussed Camp Three, Alan had warned me, "Be ready for the roughest night of your life."

37

When we stepped onto the glacier at 4:00 a.m., the sky was clear, but only a few stars were visible. The nearby walls of Everest, Lhotse, and Nuptse loomed so high they blocked the lower half of the sky around us. During our first break, I shut off my headlamp. When my eyes adjusted to the darkness, I looked up. The shrunken star field directly overhead was peanut-shaped and stretched lengthwise above the Western Cwm. What the limited sky lacked in breadth, it made up for in intensity. The stars and galaxies burned white-hot in the cold Himalayan night.

The one-mile approach passed beneath our boots slowly and steadily. We cramponed up seven hundred vertical feet of gently sloped ice and reached the upper edge of the Khumbu Glacier at about six o'clock. I put my headlamp in my pack and sipped water while studying the route ahead. An open, frozen moat, called a bergschrund, separated the active glacier from the stationary ice face above. The fixed lines up the Lhotse Face began there at 22,000 feet, and the initial steep ice bulge made the safety line hang almost dead vertical. Though it might look as if mountaineers pull themselves up the ropes, such an approach would never work for long. As I advised beginner climbers, don't pull yourself up with your tiny arms. Instead, use your big leg muscles to *push* yourself up the climb.

PK went first. Being twenty-seven years younger than me—and maybe that many pounds lighter as well—he zoomed up the ice cliff. Between fixing lines and hauling loads to the upper camps, he'd climbed this section several times recently, so I watched his footwork. As smoothly as I could, I followed at a pace that matched my oxygen intake: *Don't go anaerobic.*

Placing each boot off to the side kept my weight on my feet and let me sneak in a quick hands-free rest halfway up. I did fine, but on the last move clearing the bulge, I slithered over the top like I was hauling myself out of a lake onto a slippery raft. My old mountaineering partner Patrick used to say about such ugly moves, "Graceless, but effective."

Once I stood and caught my breath, I scanned the route ahead. I knew that the hard ice in this section rose uninterrupted for more than three thousand vertical feet. It tilted up at about forty degrees, with the occasional flatter bench of dense snow. Two dozen climbers ahead of us slowly followed the fixed lines toward Camp Three, which was perched about halfway up the face. It was going to be a real grind.

I swung my leg hard to drive my crampon into the ice. Using my higher leg, I raised myself onto the next highest footstep and immediately locked my knee. This put all my weight on the leg bones and gave my muscles a brief reprieve. Using the mountaineer's rest step was critical if I was going to repeat these moves several thousand times over the next few hours. *Breathe.*

Extending my arm, I slid the ascender up the fixed rope to provide balance and safety. Then I picked my next foothold—a flat spot stomped in by previous climbers. I aimed, kicked, stepped up, and shifted my weight onto the new higher foot. *Lock the knee.*

It took two hours of brutal work to ascend one thousand feet of dense ice. I was taking too many breaks, and each one was getting longer. But if I ignored the burning need to rest, my chest heaved as if I were sprinting at top speed. I tried estimating my rapid heart rate by counting the sharp pulse stabs in my left temple, but I lost count.

Climbing the Lhotse Face demanded an unwavering desire to reach Camp Three, no matter how hard it felt. But I knew that arriving there on time and in decent condition required self-control. Go too slow, and my Everest expedition was over. Go too fast, and my body might collapse. Like a race-car driver, I had to push my vehicle to its limit but not blow the engine or crash.

Every fifty to one hundred feet, we reached an anchor at the top of a rope segment. Most anchors consisted of just one ice screw, with no backup. The gear and knots used were adequate but not good, and certainly nowhere close to standard. If I'd installed such subpar anchors when I taught ice climbing for CSU's Outdoor Program, Rodney would have fired me. Yet there I was, trusting my life to these marginal pieces at 23,000 feet. *Keep your weight off the rope.*

Depending on how close we were to other parties, sometimes five or six of us would be attached to the same one-piece anchor. If the anchor point failed or the skinny fixed line got cut, we'd all hurtle down the ice face and launch over the bergschrund cliff. *Try not to think about it.*

Much of this year's rope on the upper mountain was only six or seven millimeters in diameter, which made it thinner than most ascenders were designed to grab. In places, tattered sections of weatherbeaten lines from previous years emerged from the ice and intertwined with the newer rope. The aged lines sometimes had deep cuts and core shots—places where the protective sheath had been ripped away, thus exposing the vital inner core—which made them untrustworthy. The old line in this section was white and red, while the new line was red and white. *Don't mix them up.*

At every anchor station I paid strict attention to staying clipped in by at least one of my two leashes at all times. The safest sequence was to move my sliding leash carabiner past the anchor onto the next line segment. Then I would release my ascender's grip from the lower rope and move it above the anchor too. If I mistakenly reversed the sequence, the potential existed for a fifty- to one-hundred-foot fall back onto a questionable anchor below. If altitude-induced spaciness made me really mess up and I unclipped them both at the same time, I could plummet 1,000 feet, all the way back down to the Khumbu Glacier. It had happened to Everest climbers before.

We reached the tents of lower Camp Three around eight-thirty that morning. Several IMG climbers and sherpas had stopped on the flattish snow section for a break, so PK and I joined them. I dropped my pack to the ground and sat on it. After gulping water and forcing down food, I checked my altimeter—23,200 feet. IMG always placed its tents in upper Camp Three. This sound practice helped ensure clean drinking-water snow for our team, and the higher positioning gave us a small head start on the lines toward Camp Four during the summit push. But in my tired state, the extra five hundred vertical feet to our tents seemed like another whole mountain to climb.

Though the weather report predicted that the wind would fade away, it hadn't. Steady winds of ten to thirty miles per hour hampered us all morning, and they were increasing. As we moved out of lower Camp Three, I envied the people resting inside their tents. The ice slope tilted to its greatest angle, probably fifty degrees in one short section. My pace slowed, and the frequency of breaks increased. The winds accelerated to twenty to forty miles per hour, which made my hands and feet sting with cold. Even stronger gusts pushed us around on the ropes like puppets on a string.

Portions of the face were outfitted with a second fixed line, with one strand designated for ascending and one for descending. This split allowed traffic to flow in both directions at the same time. As we crept past 23,500 feet, someone appeared to be stuck on the rappel line, about thirty feet ahead of us. Though we had not spoken much during the last hour, PK said, "New sherpa with problem. I will help—you stay here."

I gave him a thumbs-up, then yanked my down hood over my helmet to wait. PK continued up our fixed line and huddled with the young man. This was a chance to shoot some photos and video, so I took the risk of removing my outer glove and fired up my GoPro. The roaring wind drove bouncing snow pellets across the glazed ice in violent waves. During a lull, the video cam recorded me coughing as if I had been a lifelong smoker.

The windchill was about minus thirty Fahrenheit. Spending one minute with my right hand clad only in a liner glove left my fingers tingling with prickly cold. With three fingertips almost frostnipped, I shoved my forearm inside my down suit and nestled my fingers into my left armpit. The young sherpa walked backward down the rappel line, which meant the problem was resolved. When PK waved me up, I pulled my outer glove back on and resumed the torturous ascent.

Instead of being rested after the stop, I felt weaker, as if the cold inactivity had sapped my momentum. The oxygen level had decreased to about 40 percent of what was available at sea level. I breathed so hard and fast that my diaphragm muscles ached. My body fought against each upward step, and our ascent rate shriveled to two hundred feet per hour. Concerned that I might hit the wall and grind to a stop, I frantically searched my mind for something to drive me forward.

Before I left home, Gloria gave me a plastic bag containing three sealed envelopes. They contained personal letters from her, Jess, and Nick. I decided to save the precious notes for the later part of the trip when my enthusiasm would be low and the workload high. Because I knew this last rotation would be rough, I'd opened the first envelope, the one from Nick, just before leaving base camp. Among the uplifting messages he wrote, one stood out in my mind. He'd taken an old hockey adage and adapted it for Everest. When players get tired, hockey coaches order them to "keep your skates moving" in order to make something big happen. As I battled my way up, straining to ignore my body's screaming instinct to stop, I repeated the mantra my son had written for me: Keep your boots moving!

One painful hour later, my helmeted head was just below IMG's Camp Three. On a cramped platform laboriously chopped out by the strong climbing sherpas, about nine yellow tents huddled tight against one another. They were only five vertical feet and ten lateral yards away. Two

IMG climbers watched our final approach. Trying to look good at the finish line, I wanted to reach the tents in a single push, but I couldn't do it. Exhaustion forced me to stop five yards short. After panting for a minute, I plodded the last five strides into camp.

Our tent platform had been carved out of the face, so the ledge was no larger than it had to be. With the tents taking up almost all the space, there was hardly room to stand outside. The downhill edge of our tiny perch was unguarded by rope, and there was a 1,700-foot drop down the ice face after that. If a climber slipped over the crumbly edge, it would be a fatal toboggan ride to the bottom.

Though hypoxia from the low oxygen levels made me feel drunk and detached, I followed PK as we squeezed between several tents. He pointed one out for me, so I dropped my pack inside and crawled in after it. I sat in the doorway and caught my breath. After pushing the left sleeve of my maroon down suit aside, I studied my watch face. I closed my eyes to concentrate on the math. It was 10:35 a.m.; we had climbed to Camp Three in six and a half hours. I made the cutoff.

I shared the tent with James, from the UK, who was part of IMG's Team Three. He'd already spent a night at Camp Three because he was acclimatizing for a possible summit attempt without bottled oxygen. The wind increased all afternoon, so we hardly talked. I shot a few short videos in the tent but didn't even try to speak over the roaring winds. We lay in our down suits, sleeping bags pulled up to our necks, and watched wind-blown snow build thicker against the tent walls. PK had told me, "Do not leave tent unless bathroom. C3 very dangerous."

After getting a recovery drink and water into me, I texted Gloria:

Safe at C3. Raging winds for hours. Brutal. 20 to 40 Mph, Gusts higher.

She replied:

I knew you could do it. So proud of you!!!

I wrote:

**In brutal conditions I made lower c3 in 4.5 Hrs and upper in 6.5
Took all i had. recovering now. Pulse 94.**

She replied:

This is a big accomplishment!

The only thing to do was rest and recover, so I lay still. I felt like I had
the flu and a hangover at the same time. To endure the hours, I convinced
myself that every minute of suffering meant more red blood cells would
grow, and that each one of them increased my chances of summiting
soon.

At about four-fifteen our tent door zipped open. A rush of wind and
snow swirled inside as a climber slumped in through the doorway, as-
sisted by two other team members. It was Big Jim.

"Oh, I figured you were staying in another tent," I said.

"So tired," he muttered.

"Holy crap. Are you just getting in?"

"Yeah. Cold."

He'd been climbing the Lhotse Face in a windstorm for more than
twelve hours.

Ice crusted his hair and hood; frozen water and snot splattered the
front of his down suit. When I started helping him out of his pack, I noticed how lethargic he seemed. Jim's face was drawn, and his eyes looked
distant. I helped him get his harness off and worm into his sleeping bag.

His guide, Mingma Sona Sherpa, from Phortse, soon brought warm
water and food, and I spent a while working with Big Jim to get him to
consume half of it. After an hour he stopped shaking from cold, but his
profound fatigue became clear, and Jim said he might have suffered food

poisoning the previous day and that the resulting diarrhea and dehydration had weakened him. I was sandwiched in the middle of the tent,
which put me next to my sick friend. I did most of the nursing, and James
supported when he could. Screaming winds made it tough to communicate with one another, but we didn't want to talk anyway. Dallas came
by just before sunset to check on us and remind us not to leave the tent
at night.

Whenever I moved fast, my temples throbbed and I got a dull pain in
the back of my left eye. I kept reminding myself to move slowly, and to
take care of myself as well as Big Jim.

Though I should've been asleep, the loud wind, Jim's coughing, and
my rapid heart rate kept me awake. Lying on my back forced rock-hard
ice lumps beneath the tent floor to stab my spine. When I rolled to my
side, I'd doze off, but then the violent pounding of my heart against my
chest wall would wake me. The uncomfortable night passed one restless
minute at a time.

I awoke gasping for air, my pulse racing. Half panicked, I sat up fast,
which made my head throb. Thinking the night might be over, I checked
my watch—11:30 p.m. In the darkness I noticed Big Jim sitting up next
to me.

"You all right?" I asked.

"Yeah, but I'm going to be late."

"What?"

"I'm leaving soon, so I hope they'll still be there," he said.

"I think you're dreaming. Lie down."

He lay back, his sleeping bag swishing against the tent wall. The wind
had slowed, and the air felt viciously cold. I flopped back, twisted my
body to avoid the sharpest ice chunks, and fell asleep. Over several hours
I had many vivid and aggravating dreams—I call them stressmares—and
I woke up often. During foggy periods of wakefulness, I heard Jim cough-

ing, blowing his nose, and talking out loud. Around three in the morning, I realized Big Jim was talking rapidly, as if arguing with someone.

"No, that's not right," he said and paused. "If you're not there, then how am I supposed to get the bus?"

Thinking it was a dream, or maybe that I was the confused one, I sat up and asked, "What are you talking about?"

He looked at me and said, "We'll never catch the bus."

Big Jim prattled on. Between coughs, he would make sense for a few seconds and then veer wildly into nonsense about buses, schedules, and people who weren't there. When I asked him basic questions to judge how alert and oriented he seemed, he'd give me half an answer, then ramble off into delirium.

I considered the possibility of a stroke, but the signs didn't match. High-altitude cerebral edema was possible. The key field-assessment technique was to have him walk a straight line, but we sure as hell weren't going out onto our tiny ice platform at night to test his balance. As a substitute, I asked him to close his eyes, spread his arms wide, and then arc them toward each other until his fingertips touched. He missed a little bit but did okay.

James woke up and asked what was going on. I softly told him that our tentmate had a problem. Then I turned to Big Jim and said, "Tell James what you just told me."

Jim launched into an elaborate story about buses, people, and other things I couldn't follow. While he spoke, I studied his eyes under the light of my headlamp. They were wild and distracted.

When Jim stopped rambling, I looked at James, who was now sitting up. "That's not proper," he said.

Big Jim grew less responsive as his vivid hallucinations drew his mind away. My friend was in serious trouble.

38

1982

Dad likes unusual painting projects because they make us more money and they're more interesting. He'd outdone himself this time by finding us a job to sandblast and paint the inside of sewage treatment chambers. Rocco keeps calling them shit tanks. Great.

The metal tanks belong to the city of Lowell, Massachusetts, about twenty miles from our home in Concord. They've been drained and rinsed with clean water, but a dusty residue of dried human waste lingers everywhere. We need to descend into the underground steel tanks, blast the old lead chromate paint off, and then spray on two new coats. The smallest settling tank measures three feet by three feet across and sixteen feet deep. Just looking down into the confining hole sends a ripple of claustrophobia through me.

Dad is fifty years old with a bad back from decades of construction, so he's not crawling around in there. With his bulging beer belly, Rocco would hardly fit inside, let alone be able to move around and work. I'm twenty and in pretty good shape from painting. I recently started rock climbing, too. I like the challenge and my improved fitness, and I'd be taking my first climbing class soon. But on this job, being in shape means I'm the one going down into the shit tanks.

Along with heavy pants and boots, I'm wearing a thick sweatshirt to protect me from the sand when it rushes out of the blast hose. I grab a pair of protective gloves and a heavy canvas blasting hood, which drapes onto my chest and back. The hood has a clear plastic window six inches wide by three inches high. A fine wire mesh across the viewport makes it hard to see, but it protects my eyes from any misdirected blasts of sand. Looking through the hazy window is like trying to see distant mountains half an hour after sunset.

Dad will stand at the top of the tank opening as my watchman, and to relay signals to Rocco. To make sure exhaust fumes don't fill the sewage-treatment building, Rocco will operate the compressor and sand pot from outside. I suit up while Dad lowers a ladder into the narrow mine shaft. After I climb over the chest-high tank lip and step onto the ladder, Dad hands me a hammer.

"What's this for?" I ask.

"That's your emergency signal," he says. "Once we hit the juice on the blaster, I won't be able to hear you, and you sure as hell won't hear me. If we need to kill the sand, whack the wall three times."

It's time to switch to hand signals, so I motion okay with my right hand. The oversize glove makes my gesture sloppy, but after all these years, we can read each other's nonverbal messages from fifty feet away. We have gestures and body stances for "Start the blaster," "Stop it," "Get more paint," and a dozen other commands.

I scramble down the ladder to the bottom of the four-sided metal shaft. Standing in the darkness, it feels like being inside a tall, vertical coffin. Dad lowers to me the nozzle end of a black rubber blasting hose thicker than my wrist. He's wearing a hat and safety glasses as he leans over the hole twelve feet above my head. As my safety man and the crucial communication link between Rocco and me, I know he won't take his eyes off me for a second.

Because I've blasted for years, I know that when they turn the air on, the rushing force of the sand will make the hose kick back hard. The confining pit makes me feel trapped and a little helpless. I'm thankful Dad's watching over me.

I lower my hood. Except for the tiny window, the world goes black. Both the hood and the cheap paper dust mask I'm wearing inhibit my breathing. I haven't even started, and I'm already panting.

When I look straight up, Dad cups a hand to his right ear to tell me he's listening, paying attention. I make a thumbs-up and jerk it skyward in two vigorous steps. He repeats the gesture back at me, and then through the thick canvas I hear his muffled yell to Rocco: "Hit it!"

Air hisses from the ceramic nozzle, and the hose jumps as the first slug of sand races toward me. Here it comes!

Everything happens at once.

A dense stream of screaming sand blasts from the tiny nozzle at more than three hundred miles per hour. The pit goes pitch-black as swirling sand dust fills my cramped space. All four metal walls reverberate the roaring blast noise as if a jet engine is revving full-throttle next to my head. When the hose kicks back, a coil deflects off one wall and wraps around my ankle like a python.

Though I can't see, I point the nozzle and start tracing a back-and-forth pattern across the tank wall. I assume I'm stripping off paint, but I don't know. Sand grains ricochet off the walls and rain down on me from every angle. When I point the nozzle in a different direction, the slithering hose kinks and curves around me. I need both arms to control the beast. Sweat runs off my forehead and into my eyes, but I can't spare either hand to wipe the sting away. My heart beats faster than it should for the work I'm doing. I'm hot, and my chest heaves as I suck hard at the dusty air under the hood.

My breathing rate increases. I have the urge to rip the blasting hood off my head, but I know that's a bad idea. Suddenly tired, I want to sit down and rest but there isn't enough room. The thrashing snake hose almost escapes my grip.

I'm dizzy. To steady myself, I lean against the wall and point the blasting nozzle at the steel floor. I know enough not to point the blast stream at my boots, as it would eat away the leather in seconds and then get my feet. I stay motionless as I pant and try to think.

My chest tightens. Instinct tells me to flee, but there's nowhere to go. What was I supposed to do with the hammer?

Suddenly the sand flow stops and the noise fades. I look around, confused. There's a muffled sound, like someone's yelling. I look up the dark tunnel, and through a dusty haze, I see Dad waving at me. I think he's talking, but I can't hear him over the ringing in my head. Raising a hand to my ear, I shake my head from side to side.

Now he's waving his forearm in circles toward himself like a cop directing traffic. He's giving me the signal for "Come here," but I'm not sure why. We have work to do. Aren't they going to give me more sand?

With his index finger, Dad forcefully points at me. "You."

He jerks his hand toward his face and pokes two fingers toward his eyes: "Watch me."

In a big flourish he sweeps his whole arm in a giant circle: "Come here now!"

The vigor of his gestures tells me I must comply, even though I don't understand why he wants me up there right away. He's not asking me, he's telling me. Maybe somebody up there is having a problem and needs my help.

I move to the ladder, grab a face-high rung, and glance upward. He's nodding his head yes, so I guess I'm doing the right thing. I heft my heavy boot to the first rung, but it slips off. That sends me a tipsy step backward onto the uneven sand, and I bump the tank wall behind me with my shoulders.

I step forward, determined to climb. After a few rungs, my heart hammers against my chest. Tired, I stop halfway and rest my forehead against a ladder rung. The ladder jostles hard and startles me. I look up and see two hands holding the ends of the side rails. Though I can't see the details in the darkness, I recognize the outline of Dad's face. He rattled the ladder on purpose. Why?

My legs are leaden, but I push on. After a few more feet, I look up to see how I'm doing. Rocco's head looms over the hole now too. He's holding the ladder top against the sidewall to steady it. Even with his help, the damn swaying ladder is giving me trouble.

Though Dad still seems a long way away, his face is visible now. He looks intense, like he's mad or something. He hardly ever gets like that. Dad keeps waving one arm wildly, calling me up. I trust him, so I do what he says.

I'm almost there. Dad leans way in, grabs the back of my sweatshirt, and yanks. It's like he's trying to pull me right up the ladder. The move also pins my chest against the rungs so I can't fall back. My head is level with the tank's top edge as a hand grabs the crown of my blasting hood and rips it off my head. Cool fresh air splashes onto my face like sweet spring rain.

Dad says to someone, "Grab him!"

A thick tattooed arm goes past my head and a hand seizes my belt.

Dad yells, "Pull!"

I'm lifted up as if gravity has been reversed. Dad and Rocco pop me out of the dust-filled tank like two Boston cops I once saw yank a man headfirst out of an open car window. I crash to the ground, my legs tumbling down behind me.

Dad orders, "Let's get him outta here."

They hoist me to my feet and drape my arms over their shoulders. In a stumbling cluster, we hustle toward the sunlight pouring through the open doorway. We burst outside, and they let me slump to the ground. An ocean of clean air envelops me. The relief is luxurious. I lie in the grass with my eyes closed and pant.

Rocco says, "What the fuck was that, Joey?"

"Not enough oxygen," Dad replies. "The dust displaced all the air."

"You all right, Jimmy?" Rocco asks.

I wave my hand at him, but my forearm flops to the grass.

Dad says, "Keep breathing and you'll be all right."

39

Big Jim's delirium didn't match the classic signs of cerebral edema, but he sure wasn't thinking right. I had seen this kind of mental confusion in an altitude-sick teammate before when Rodney and I led an expedition to Bolivia. Though simpler than my Wilderness First Responder training, old mountaineering advice dictated that the three best cures for altitude sickness were descend, descend, and descend. But we sure weren't going to take him down the Lhotse Face at night. We could get him lower after the sun came up in about three hours, but we needed to do something for him right away.

It was time to tell Dallas. He was sleeping in a tent about thirty feet away, but I couldn't call out to him over the wind—the whole team might panic if they heard me yelling loud enough to alert him. The more controlled alternative was to go get him. I had to go out onto the icy tent platform at night, alone.

My temples throbbed as I wriggled out of my sleeping bag. I turned on my headlamp and waited for my heart rate to decrease. Putting on the first boot in one push made me breathe twice as fast. For the second boot, I broke the process into three small steps and rested between them. I pulled on my thick gloves, crawled over Big Jim's long legs, and, before exiting, said to him, "You stay here."

Then I turned to James and said, "Don't let him follow me."

Even in my down suit, stepping into the night at 23,700 feet was like walking into a liquor store beer cooler in a wet bathing suit. Cold wrapped around me and gnawed through my clothing.

Experience told me to put on my crampons for traction, but taking off my outer gloves to fiddle with the straps was risky. So was walking across the ledge without spikes, but I decided to skip the crampons. I grabbed my ice ax for security, driving it into the firm snow with all my strength. I stepped forward, then breathed three times. All the tents were pitched just a foot or two away from one another, and each one had eight or ten skinny guy lines anchored off in every direction. In the darkness it would be easy to trip over a cord and slip off the edge. Before each step I studied the next yard of terrain with my headlamp to find a place for my big boot among the cat's cradle of tent lines. The awkward traverse took only a few minutes, but I was relieved when I reached the far end.

"Hey, Dallas, wake up," I said through the tent wall. "We have a situation."

"Huh? Who is it?" he asked.

"It's Jim Davidson. Hey, Jim Diani's got a problem. He's hallucinating, and it's getting worse. I think he needs medicine or oxygen. Sorry, but you need to come check on him."

"I'll be right over—just let me suit up."

I carefully returned to our tent and felt safer once I crawled back inside its nylon walls. When Dallas arrived ten minutes later, we all crowded closer to make a spot for him. He talked to Big Jim, and I could see Dallas's advanced medical training by the way he spoke to the patient. Jim gave reasonable answers to the medical questions. Then I gave my friend a prompt: "Jim, tell Dallas about the bus."

When Big Jim finally stopped chatting, Dallas and I exchanged a silent glance. Then he used a fingertip pulse oximeter to measure Jim's heart rate and the oxygen saturation of his blood. His pulse was a bit high, about eighty-five, and his oxygen saturation was 70 percent, a shockingly low number at sea level, but not too bad for being three-quarters of the way up Everest. To make sure the instrument was working, Dallas tested me too. My pulse was seventy-two, and my oxygen level was 74 percent.

Dallas decided to put Jim on bottled oxygen and he gave Jim several high-altitude medicines, including dexamethasone to reduce brain swelling. We all returned to our sleeping bags, but Jim and I didn't get back to sleep. Minute by minute the miserable night finally came to an end. Around five, daylight began filtering through the yellow tent fabric. We'd made it through the night at Camp Three.

Everyone was anxious to descend; Big Jim had improved, but he needed repeated reminders to keep getting dressed and load his pack. I worried about his ability to handle dozens of dangerous anchor-station change-overs on the fixed lines. But Dallas, of course, had a solid plan to keep Jim on oxygen and to have Jim's sherpa guide, Mingma Sona Sherpa, manage him closely. Melting snow, cooking, and even eating were huge hassles in the cramped confines of Camp Three, so we all skipped breakfast, anticipating a hot meal down in Camp Two.

PK and I clipped into the line at 5:35 a.m. We started out slow to let our bodies wake up and find the rhythm of sliding down the lines. As my confidence built, my arm rappels grew more assertive. I judged my control and fine-tuned my speed by the feel of the skinny line racing through my gloved hand. Every few minutes, a subtle bump or flat spot on the rope slid between my fingers. These were damaged spots, probably caused by some hypoxic climber who'd accidentally stomped on the rope with their sharp crampons. My anxiety spiked every time one of these dangerous flaws passed by: I'm trusting my life to a weakened line attached to marginal anchors.

The mountain's upper pyramid loomed above my right shoulder, and the long sidewalls of the Western Cwm framed Cho Oyu in the distance.

Looking down at Camp Two about 2,400 feet below, I could barely make out the yellow dots of our tents. With a deep-blue sky overhead and miles of white ice on either side, I could see three of the world's highest summits. We faced downhill and, in the biting cold, raced down the tilted ice sheet. The spectacular view and tremendous exposure made the descent exhilarating. This was exactly what I'd imagined for four decades. I was in my element. I was on Everest.

PK and I faced inward and used classic rappel technique on the steeper sections of blue ice. My backpack and down suit inhibited flexibility, and my giant down hood limited my ability to look behind me. During one rappel I stepped backward onto a snow patch and it collapsed beneath my left boot. I punched through a snow bridge and sank into a crevasse up to my knee. Having my leg dangling into a slot scared me, but as long as I maintained control of the rappel, I wouldn't plummet inside. *Keep your brake hand tight.*

It took a minute to wiggle and thrash my way out, and then we continued descending. Our last rappel took us down the short, overhanging face of the bergschrund. Altogether we rappelled about 500 vertical feet and arm-rappelled the other 1,200 feet of the face.

Less than two hours after leaving Camp Three, we stepped onto the gently sloped ice of the Khumbu Glacier. Our trudge downhill was technically easy, but slow due to having no food in our systems. The fifteen-foot uphill scramble into camp challenged me. At 8:25 a.m., I dropped my pack outside the Camp Two mess tent.

"You did good," PK said. I wrote in my journal that it was my first compliment from him.

To let Gloria know I was safe, I sent her a text:

I am fine but beat. Behind in everything. Recover now.

She replied:

Yes. Recover. Rejuvenate and refresh. Love you. Been worried.

I ate an enormous breakfast and drank cup after cup of cold water. As expected, it was too late to depart for base camp, so we planned to rest for the day and descend in the morning.

Jim trudged into camp about two hours behind me. He seemed more alert, but worn down. I could tell that his mental abilities were returning because he said: "I took twelve hours. They'll never let me go back up."

He was right, and my heart ached for him. I replied, "Don't worry about that right now, Jim. Let's get some food into you."

The next morning I helped Jim pack up his stuff. Dallas told me he'd make sure Big Jim got down okay and that I should head out soon with PK. We left Camp Two at 5:40 a.m. and cruised toward Camp One. The day was cold but pleasant, and I stopped several times to take photos. A giant snow plume ripping from the summit ridge proved that the wind continued to scream across the top. In a few more days, hopefully, the arriving monsoon would push the jet stream north into Tibet and drop the wind low enough for a summit attempt.

As we descended, the air grew thicker with every step and the hike seemed effortless. I followed PK's quick pace and listened to the crunch of our crampons on the ice. With no other climbers nearby and no wind in the protected valley, our footsteps were the only sounds. The Camp Three rotation had been as brutal as everyone said it would be, but it was over and it had gone pretty well for me.

I stopped, let PK get fifty yards ahead of me, and turned around to admire the upper mountain. With no one else visible, I felt alone in the Western Cwm. There was no movement and no sound. Other than a few transient humans each spring, the Valley of Silence contained what it always had: ice, rock, and time.

We reached Camp One in an hour and fifteen minutes and walked right past. Descending through the icefall seemed easier this time, but we couldn't go very fast because there were climbers going the other way. Since the ascending climbers were working so much harder than us, we often stopped to give them the right of way. We waited at a cliff edge while a heavily laden climber took cautious steps across a four-ladder bridge spanning a deep crevasse. He almost seemed to be suspended in midair.

Parts of the icefall had changed over the previous five days. A house-size chunk of ice leaned downhill at a steeper angle, and debris from recent collapses covered the route in some places. The longer and warmer days were speeding up the glacier.

Once safely at Crampon Point, we removed our spikes and peeled off a layer. I sipped some water, and—as we did on every descent—PK and I wandered among the ice pinnacles and picked up loose trash that had recently melted out of the ice. Then we hiked twenty minutes toward IMG. Fifty yards short of camp, PK stopped and looked me over. He tucked in my loose jacket flap and went to square up an uneven collar. I pushed his hand away, laughing. "What are you doing?"

"Must look good."

"PK, I don't care what I look like."

"But if look good, climb good."

I realized that if we wandered into camp with me looking disheveled, it might reflect poorly on him. I let him tuck in a dangling gear strap and straighten my helmet half an inch. He looked me over again, nodded, and turned toward camp.

"*Ek chin*," I said. Wait a minute.

He turned back to face me. In an exaggerated manner, I pretended to pick a tiny speck of dust off his sleeve and toss it away. We both laughed and walked into base camp.

Spring had arrived at 17,300 feet. Shrinking snow piles created new meltwater streamlets that gurgled around camp. As I settled into my tent, it hit me: There was no more preparation. After weeks of acclimatizing, years of training, and decades of dreaming, I was finally ready to climb Mount Everest. I texted Rodney:

Back in ebc. Trip to c3 was rugged, fast, healthy & succesful.
I've checked the very last box there is. Standing by to climb
Everest.

Five days in a row of climbing had left me tired, but I felt good. Big Jim arrived later at camp exhausted but lucid, and we all spent the afternoon eating and hydrating. After dinner that night, most of our teammates went to watch a movie in the musty communications tent. I stayed with Big Jim to keep him company while he prepared for his helicopter ride off the mountain. We were quiet as Jim stuffed items into his duffel bags. Then he sat for five minutes and did nothing.

"The chopper's coming," I said. "You have to be ready in fifteen minutes."

"Yeah, I got it," he said. But he just sat there.

I kept prodding him, and eventually he finished packing. We hauled his bags outside and dropped them near the mess tent.

"I'm so damn sorry to see you go," I said.

"Thanks for helping me up there, Jimmy. Stay safe and go climb that mountain."

"I'll do my best, buddy."

We hugged good-bye as two climbing sherpas grabbed Jim's duffels. The three of them walked a hundred yards to the helicopter landing pad we'd rebuilt. About twenty minutes later the chopper arrived, landed, and took off again. I watched it fade away down the valley.

Jim leaving wasn't the only sad incident of the day. We heard that Mr. Sherchan, the eighty-five-year-old Nepali climber, had died the previous day in base camp. A heart attack was suspected, but no one really knew.

With our last rotation behind us, the mood at breakfast the next morning was upbeat. A few people speculated that our summit attempt could start as early as May 10, in three days, and then we could all head home early. That sounded nice, but on several big peaks I'd seen myself and others get our hopes dashed when a summit push was delayed. Since then I had avoided making or embracing any overly optimistic predictions. The mountain always dictates when, and if, we get lucky enough to attempt the summit.

At lunch Greg told us we would have four rest days, and possibly more, as the weather looked unsettled. About a third of our team decided to go down-valley to rest, heal, and soak in the plentiful oxygen. While I yearned for a break from base camp, I didn't want to risk getting ill, so I stayed put. PK took advantage of the lull by hiking back to Phortse to visit his family.

With part of Team One gone and Teams Two and Three on their final rotations, our camp grew quiet. I spent the days recovering, wondering about the weather, and thinking about the summit. Intermittent snow in base camp made some of the days dreary.

Over the years I'd learned not to get upset about bad weather. Eventually all storms end. During tough conditions the trick is to use the time wisely by getting ready for when the storm has passed. My pants sagged off my skinny hips, so I ate and drank all I could stand. Then I mapped out which snack items I would eat, in what sequence, for the maximum benefit during our summit push. I checked every piece of equipment and sharpened my crampons. Dad always said, "Take care of your gear and it'll take care of you."

When the weather was decent, we hiked to high points near camp to help preserve our hard-fought acclimatization and keep our bodies active. Too little activity leads to lethargy, and when the time came to climb, we'd have to fight inertia to get moving again. It was better to stay engaged.

May 10 brought the full moon. I'd hoped we would be putting that helpful light to use on our summit push, but stormy weather kept rolling in and out of the Himalayas. The sky cleared enough after sunset for me to photograph the moonlight illuminating the cloud-filled Western Cwm.

During his final rotation my friend Mathieu became ill and experienced a very low oxygen-saturation level of 60 percent. He made the difficult but necessary decision to end his trip. With Tony, Omar, Dean, Big Jim, and Mathieu all evacuated over the last month, five of our fifteen original Team One members were gone.

Over on Team Two, Matt Tammen couldn't resolve his dental problem and was forced to end his third attempt on the mountain. The harsh environment on Everest is ruthlessly efficient at creating and exploiting physical, mental, or acclimatization problems. Fatigue, low oxygen, and other stressors can inflate the difficulties until they become life-threatening or even life-ending. Being on Everest clarifies just how hard humans must struggle to endure nature's incessant pressures.

On May 11 the stalwart rope-fixing team finished installing lines from Camp Four to the summit. As has become the custom in recent years, a Nepali-only team of climbing sherpas reached the top together as the first summiters of the season. The route to the top was officially open.

Back home, May 12 was Nick's twenty-first birthday; on Everest clouds covered the mountain again. Greg said no one was going for the top. After lunch several of us lingered in the mess tent and chatted for hours. Hopes for an early summit day had faded, and several people were anxious about business commitments and family needs back home. We nursed cups of tea and lamented all the personal problems that would pile up if the weather didn't improve soon. It was the fifty-second day of the expedition and our sixth day of waiting in base camp.

Several guys started strategizing how they might still catch the early flights home they had scheduled long ago. Karim and Dave asked me if I wanted to join them in prearranging a helicopter to fly directly to Kathmandu from base camp after we'd reached the top and returned. With no definite start date for our seven-day round-trip climb, setting a departure time felt too speculative. Even discussing it lowered my drive to head back up the Hill.

Knut walked into the dining tent looking fresh and healthy after his extended stay in Namche to shake off pneumonia. He stood at the far end of the dining table as the four of us continued our departure discussion, slumped over our mugs of cold tea.

"You're talking about going the wrong direction," Knut said.

We turned toward him. Somebody asked, "What do you mean?"

Knut pointed down-valley and said: "Home is that way." Then he pointed over his shoulder toward the icefall. "The mountain's over there." He turned and straightened his arm with a flourish toward the summit of Everest. "You should be talking about going there!"

A moment of silence filled the big tent. I stood up and took two steps toward Knut, like a kid changing sides in a soccer game. "He's right," I said. "Knut's right." For the first time in days, I felt energized. I walked over to him and shook his hand. "Thanks, Knut. Welcome back."

When students on our climbing trips asked what the weather was going to do, Rodney always said, "Don't ask what the weather's doing. Instead, ask what you're doing *in* the weather." One of my teammates, Markus, and I promised each other that we would go on a training hike the next day, regardless of conditions. We departed in the morning under high, wispy clouds. As we hiked the trail across the rocky glacier, a spectacular rainbow encircled the sun. This halo phenomenon occurs when light refracts through atmospheric ice crystals, and it often indicates that a storm front will arrive soon.

We hiked up a 900-foot-tall hill and lingered for an hour as the sky grew cloudier. When we returned to camp in midmorning, we heard that about twenty people had summited earlier in the day. The good news made us anxious to try soon as well, but the marginal conditions meant that a few of those summiters had rough descents and suffered frostbite. Most years, a multiday spell of stable weather gives climbers the confidence to start their five-day ascent and two-day descent. Everyone was hoping for the usual window of good weather, but the fickle storms were yielding only short periods of marginal conditions. Greg said, "Instead of a big, open window to go through, all we're getting is keyholes."

The rainbow halo and Greg's weather report were both right: Stormy conditions prevented anyone from summiting the next day. Even though we still didn't have a departure date, Greg called our remaining climbers back from Namche so we'd be ready when the weather gods smiled upon us. A day later, on May 15, Markus and I chose a bigger acclimatization hike. Under a mostly clear sky we walked down-valley along the glacier's edge, and when we reached the dusty outskirts of Gorak Shep, we turned right and began hiking up Kala Patthar. We flowed uphill with ease. Apparently climbing Mount Everest to 23,700 feet provides excellent conditioning for hiking an 18,000-foot hill.

Memories of visiting Mike's spirit on the top of Kala Patthar two years earlier and our *puja* ceremony there a quarter-century ago swirled in my mind. Those experiences had woven a winding path that brought me here again. Though my purpose for ascending Kala Patthar seemed different this time (preparing for the Everest summit push), perhaps the reasons for all three visits were much the same. My quest for awe, joy, and peace meant honoring the lessons from the past while embracing the future with as much resilience as possible.

Once again I sat among the wind-stirred prayer flags atop Kala Patthar, gazing at Everest and thinking about Mike. Markus and I shared snacks as I told him about the *puja* that Gloria, Prem Lakpa, and I had held for Mike. After explaining how we hung prayer flags, I pointed to a boulder five yards away and said: "When we tossed the sacred rice, I stood over—" Then I burst into tears. Some old injuries never fully heal.

Cloud banks gathered thicker around Everest and the other peaks flanking the Khumbu Valley. As we sat eating among hundreds of colored prayer flags, a small brown-and-gray bird landed nearby and began singing. Life of any kind is rare in the high Himalayas, especially songbirds, so we listened with pleasure. The sparrow-like crooner was unafraid, coming to within two feet of us while he sang at length. I shot two videos, and he flew away.

Two minutes later, the bird returned, landed, and hopped to within a foot of my boots. The bird and I studied each other, and I said, "Mike, is that you?"

Markus and I laughed. The bird flew behind us and resumed singing. Fifteen minutes into the encounter, I shot another video as he hopped right past me and then flew away. We began talking about how magical the visit had been when the little fellow playfully whooshed by our heads and landed so close to me that the thin white rings beneath its eyes were visible. This time I snapped several photos of our companion resting on speckled bedrock among the blue, white, red, green, and yellow prayer flags. A partially cloud-covered Everest served as the backdrop. I later identified the visitor as an alpine accentor, one of the few songbird species found above 16,000 feet in the Himalayas. The bird took wing and soared north toward Tibet.

Wet snowflakes fell from the sky as we hiked back into base camp that afternoon. We learned that another ten climbers had sneaked through an acceptable keyhole to the top; a few on our team grumbled that maybe our leader was playing the weather game too conservatively. Waiting was tough, but I agreed with the cautious approach. On smaller peaks, climbers can try for the top, and if unsuccessful, they can make another attempt. But on big mountains, it's rare to have enough energy or time for a second summit attempt. We would probably get only one shot, so we had to get it right. And when we climbed into the death zone, above 26,000 feet, we were betting our lives.

40

Karim's positive outlook made him one of my favorite teammates. He was usually an animated conversationalist, but when he sat next to me at dinner, he scowled and stayed quiet. Everyone has the occasional tough day on an expedition, so I didn't press him to chat. But when I saw him poking a fork at his meal without eating, I asked, "What's up, Karim?"

He dropped his utensil and it bounced off the edge of his tin plate with a clatter. "I can't eat this food anymore. I'm so sick of it."

"I know. But we have to eat for the summit. Pick one thing and just gobble it down," I said.

"I can't, man. I just can't."

Karim was a military man and a previous Everest summiter—if we were bumping up against his tolerance limits, things were bad. I, too, struggled at mealtimes. When I didn't want to eat but knew I should, I sometimes recalled the scene from the first *Rocky* movie when Sylvester Stallone's character drank five raw eggs from a glass for the nutrition. That gritty willingness to do whatever it takes to reach a big goal inspired me. I would stare at the tent wall, conjure the movie's triumphant theme song in my mind, and shovel the bland food into my mouth.

With insufficient protein in our diet, our bodies resorted to using muscle as fuel; I'd lost roughly fifteen pounds since the trip started. My teammates and I sometimes compared how baggily our clothes now fit. Ryan, a lean and muscular climber on Team Three, said he thought he'd lost more than thirty-five pounds already.

On May 16 conditions up high started out decent, which allowed many climbers at Camp Four to reach the top. But the weather report said the jet stream had split in half, which made the predictions for the next few days uncertain. So we waited. It was day fifty-six of the expedition and my tenth day of waiting in base camp.

I'd sat out mountain storms before, but nothing like this. Looking for a boost, I called Alan back home. I told him I was willing to do whatever was necessary to climb Everest, but there was nothing to be done.

"I'm not sure I can take much more," I said. "I just want to get out of here."

"What? Not you," Alan replied.

"I don't think I even care about going back up there."

"Come on now . . ."

His support calmed me, but after the call my morale remained low. It was time to deploy one of my remaining secret weapons: another letter from home. I sat up, sipped some water, and carefully tore open the envelope from Jess. Along with love and encouragement, my twenty-three-year-old daughter had written:

> It is one of the most important things you've ever taught me:
> to feel the fear, and do it anyways. I often don't think in limits:
> I think of a lofty goal, and come up with a plan to achieve it. I
> thrive on it, and I think that's because it is how you raised me.
> It is how you live. To dream big, and let nothing stop you from
> achieving those dreams. . . .

I've been thinking a lot about our conversation on the way down to Denver a few weeks ago. This big question: What are you willing to suffer for? This goal of reaching the summit of Mount Everest is one you've been willing to suffer for almost your entire life.

You will suffer more before it is over. But each and every minute of this suffering in order to reach your goal (which you will, very soon), is suffering that, as you said, makes you a better person. And ultimately, that is the change we seek by doing difficult climbs.

I wiped away tears and looked around my tent. Half-frozen socks dangled from carabiners. Labeled bags of energy gels and recovery drinks sat atop the pile of equipment for the summit push.

I'd invested significant time, effort, and resources to get this far. More important, many of my friends and loved ones had put a lot in too. I couldn't let all that go to waste just because I was tired, or scared, or homesick. Leaving—quitting, really—would be so damn easy. But the easy path rarely offers a significant reward. I considered what my kids would learn from me leaving now: Do you want to teach them that it's okay to quit when things get tough?

The thick clouds covering base camp began whipping ice pellets against my tent. I lay inside and listened to the ebb and flow of precipitation hissing against the nylon. What if the weather doesn't break in time to even try for the summit?

Staring at the yellow tent ceiling, I contemplated the schedule. All expedition permits ended on May 31, which meant the last possible day to head up would be May 24, eight days away. Could I wait that long?

I had a burning urge to *do* something, to solve the problem somehow. But it was weather—I couldn't clear away clouds with drive, energy, or determination. These traits had always been my strong points, but when facing external conditions I couldn't change, these action-oriented habits were futile: How can I persevere when there's nothing to do?

Rushing toward the top during unfavorable conditions would be risky and undisciplined. We needed to muster the restraint and self-control to endure the long wait. The answer, of course, was patience. But sitting patiently seemed like the opposite of standard perseverant actions like doing more or working harder.

And then it hit me: Patience *is* perseverance. It's passive perseverance. All storms end. If we waited long enough, the weather would clear.

The realization made me sit up and grin. Ice pellets still fell from the sky, and our departure was no clearer than before. But my resolve was strengthened, and I felt a calm certainty. I would wait as long as it took. Then we would head for the summit.

About a week earlier Dallas had given us detailed instructions on how the bottled oxygen systems worked and how to use them. For our impending summit attempt, he gave us a short refresher in the communications tent. I'd used oxygen for a day on Cho Oyu eight years earlier, so I was familiar with how to connect the regulator, operate the valve, and clear ice buildup from the mask. But I still listened to every word Dallas said as if my life depended upon it—because it might.

IMG used custom-built bottles made from lightweight carbon fiber. Each empty cylinder weighed about ten pounds and was the size of two large bread loaves placed end to end. A bottle held 1,850 liters of compressed oxygen. At the recommended three-liters-per-minute usage rate for climbing, a full bottle would last about ten hours. We would also utilize a low flow of one liter per minute while resting in the tents at Camp Three and Camp Four, so each climber needed four bottles total. A few older climbers wanted higher flow rates of five or six liters per minute for the summit push, so they bought an extra oxygen bottle. To have that one bottle supplied, carried up, and waiting at 27,700 feet cost an extra five thousand dollars. Even though Bart had suggested it just in case I struggled on summit day, I hadn't purchased an extra bottle. I hoped I hadn't made a mistake.

The Western guides and the climbing sherpas performed better than most of the client climbers at altitude, but they still used supplemental oxygen to stay strong, smart, and warm. So the expedition would also send up two or three bottles for each of them. Altogether IMG had brought more than three hundred bottles of supplemental oxygen for our extended team, and they all got carried to Camp Three or higher on the backs of high-altitude workers.

The precious oxygen made breathing easier and let us climb faster during the last two days of the summit push. Just as important, oxygen kept the body warmer, which helped prevent hypothermia and frostbite. The most important consideration for my family was that climbing Everest from the south without supplemental oxygen was three times more deadly than climbing with it.

At the common three liters per minute, bottled gas still didn't make high-altitude climbing feel anything like sea level, or even the top of a Colorado fourteener. The consensus among mountaineers was that bottled Os, as we called them, made a given elevation feel about 3,000 feet lower. This meant that moving at 27,000 feet on supplemental air was as hard as 24,000 feet had felt to me on Cho Oyu before I started using the Os. That crushing day had been so difficult that I'd considered abandoning my expensive camera in the snow just to lighten my pack by a pound. I had a sobering sense of how brutal the final legs of our summit attempt would be, even with supplemental oxygen.

Greg and Dallas held a short meeting with each climber to check in before the summit attempt and review our high-altitude medicines. I brought my drug kit to Greg's tent and sat down with them.

"How are you feeling about heading up?" Greg asked.

"Nervous, but ready. From your perspectives, how am I doing?" I asked.

Greg looked at Dallas, who said, "You're in the middle of the pack like a car cruising at fifty-five miles per hour for fuel efficiency—the perfect spot."

"Anything I can do better?" I asked.

"You're always moving steadily uphill," Dallas said. "And whenever I see you at a rest stop, you're changing layers, drinking, or eating—taking care of yourself. Keep it up."

"Your times are good," Greg added. "You're all set. Just stay healthy."

Their analysis didn't surprise me, but I was glad to hear it out loud. Then Greg said, "Show us your meds and explain them."

I placed my light-blue stuff sack on the packing crate that served as a table. Greg asked, "Is that the bag you keep them in?"

"Always," I said.

Greg wrote that into a notebook. I tipped the sack upside down and dumped out three brown-plastic prescription bottles. Then I reviewed them out loud: dexamethasone for high-altitude cerebral edema, nifedipine for high-altitude pulmonary edema, and acetazolamide for acute mountain sickness. The vicious cold and extreme altitude on summit day meant that the only first aid we could realistically administer to get a sick climber down would be to "drug them and drag them."

After I read the dosages aloud, I passed each bottle to Greg. He verified what I said and wrote it all down in his notebook. Greg pulled out three permanent markers and colored the three white bottle lids: one green, one blue, one black. He recorded the color-coding system next to my name.

During our summit bid, Dallas would lead us into the upper reaches of the atmosphere while Greg remained in base camp. By staying in the relatively thick air at 17,300 feet, Greg would serve as the chief thinker and final decision maker for our entire team. If someone high on the mountain found one of our climbers ill, Greg could use the notebook to provide specific instructions. He could tell them what color bag to look in, what color-coded container to open, and how many pills to give. These steps reduced the potential for confusion and errors when altitude-impaired rescuers administered medicine to a dying mountaineer. This kind of forethought, experience, and multilevel safety systems exemplified why I climbed with IMG.

. . .

Even though we'd been waiting in base camp for eleven days, our breakfast table buzzed with energy on May 17. The previous evening's weather report indicated that conditions might open up soon. Greg was supposed to get a morning update, and everyone was hoping for good news. I prepared by gorging myself on pancakes soaked in imitation maple syrup.

Greg walked in carrying the printed weather report in his hand. "Good morning."

The tent fell silent. Our leader had the same pleasant grin he often sported, but I thought I sensed a restrained smirk at the corners of his mouth. I clenched both hands into fists and listened.

Greg said, "We're heading up tomorrow!"

Cheers filled the tent. High fives and fist pumps erupted. After letting the noise and energy boil over for a minute, Greg waved the weather report over his head. Everyone hushed one another, and we quieted down so fast, it was as if Moses himself had held aloft a stone tablet inscribed with the Commandments.

Greg gave us more details and a few cautions. The keyhole had gotten larger, but not as big as we wanted. We would have to head up under nonideal conditions on May 18 and hope things continued to clear as we moved to each higher camp. For our possible summit day of May 22, the winds were projected to be low but then increase again soon after. The weather window was not ideal, but with shifting jet-stream patterns, it was the best we were going to get. Besides, with so few days remaining, there wouldn't be enough time for a later attempt. This was our only shot.

As my teammates and I moved around camp completing our final preparations, no one strolled—we hustled along the trails like hard-driving commuters racing to catch a train. Our summit train departed in eighteen hours.

Illness and forced evacuations had altered the makeup of our teams. IMG regrouped us into two waves, with Team One going first and the remaining members of Team Two and Team Three starting three days later. As the climbers from Teams Two and Three returned from the low-lands, one of them generously brought a giant box of doughnuts from the Namche bakery. Someone steered me toward the small dining tent to grab one.

I pushed aside the yellow door flap and walked inside. The tent was empty except for me and a tempting selection of puffy baked goods. I sat down and eyeballed the illicit treats. Years earlier I'd given them up for weight-control reasons, and my recent blood glucose levels made dough-nuts forbidden. Yet the smorgasbord of fried dough and white sugar beckoned.

My training instincts and health awareness stood on their mental soapboxes and spouted off a litany of concerns. But in the next week I would lose five pounds, probably more. Though it was hard to calculate and impossible to measure, I'd read that on summit day alone, Everest climbers burn 10,000 to 12,000 calories—the same as running four mar-athons. A 300-calorie snack wasn't going to hurt, and it might even help.

I picked out a large chocolate doughnut with thick frosting and mul-ticolored sprinkles, or "jimmies." I eased into the back of my chair and gazed with reverence at the sacred donut. Then I closed my eyes and bit into the massive sugar bomb. It was glorious.

I packed my gear by midday. Because less-prepared teams will sometimes copy the actions of carefully implemented expeditions, our departure time was a secret. We didn't want to prompt other groups to climb on the same schedule as us and crowd the route. This caution kept me from posting any public information, but I needed to tell those closest to me. In an email to sixteen family members and good friends, I wrote:

> It is hard to believe that there are no more training, workouts, skills development, practice sessions, ramp-up peaks, inter-mediate goals, or rotations left until I get to try climbing Ever-est. The time to climb Everest is actually here!

Though I didn't want to scare anyone or be morbid, I knew there was a 1 percent to 3 percent chance of me dying on Everest. So if something went wrong up there, this might be the last they heard from me. Just in case, I continued:

> You guys are my never-ending source of strength, resilience, and love. I would not be who I am, or where I am, without each of you in my life. So, when I head out of base camp soon with my boots on and my pack full, the most important thing I carry with me is you. I am going to do my damnedest to get up this mountain. I will give it all I've got.
>
> And, as always, I will keep enough energy in my deepest reserves to get back down safely. That reserve can never run out as you all are that reserve for me. When I get as high as I can, I will smile and send out a greeting to you from my heart.
> With a smile and a hug from Everest base camp, Love, Jim

I stood outside the mess tent at 2:10 a.m., shifting my weight from one leg to the other. As each climber and guide pair departed base camp, they shook hands with several expedition crew members who lined up to see us off. Wishes of "Good luck" and "Namaste" were exchanged. As I worked my way down the reverse receiving line, Phunuru shook my hand and said, "I will go to C2 to support everyone, so see you there soon, bro."

Kaji smiled wide and clasped my hand in both of his. "Good luck, Jim Dai."

"Thank you, Kaji Bhai," I replied. "Namaste."

Towering above everyone, Greg anchored the end of the line. I grinned at him and stuck out my hand. He smiled back, shook my hand, and gripped my forearm with his left hand. "Have a great climb, Jim!"

"I will. Thanks for everything, Greg."

I followed PK past the last tent, and we turned left toward the altar. Alongside the many prayer flags, several new offerings appeared. Small plates of food, bowls of uncooked rice, and a photo of His Holiness the Fourteenth Dalai Lama had been placed atop the altar.

For this important day, juniper branches had been carried a dozen miles up-valley and placed upon the altar stones. Juniper is known for its resilience and hardiness in tough conditions. The unburned branches released a sticky-sweet resin smell into the night air. Several small juniper piles had been set ablaze and left to smolder. Many Tibetans and Nepalis believe the aromatic smoke purifies and protects travelers.

We began our circumambulation around the altar, emulating the path of the sun. PK took some dry rice from a bowl and tossed it into the air as an offering. He chanted in a low, murmuring voice. It sounded like Sherpa or Tibetan rather than Nepali, but I wasn't sure. Certain that his words were Buddhist prayers, I joined in as best I could by repeatedly saying, "*Om mani padme hum.*"

Following PK's lead, I grabbed a small handful of rice and cast portions of it as we circled the altar. I tossed some toward the Khumbu Icefall and some toward Everest's summit. Thinking of my family, I threw some toward Colorado, eight thousand miles away. Remembering to avoid ego and to express compassion toward others, I flipped rice forward to bless PK; the long pellets bounced off his pack and shoulders. Then I blindly tossed the last of it high over my shoulder so it would fall upon the team members behind me. From somewhere, airborne grains fell through the beam of my headlamp like tiny shooting stars released from the night sky. A few kissed my jacket sleeves and fell to the ground for the camp birds.

As we completed our circle, we walked into the acrid cloud of juniper smoke. Invisible ash made my eyes clamp shut, and the smell of burnt wood filled my nose. We walked through the cleansing plume and emerged into the clear air, hopefully purified enough to approach Chomolungma, the Goddess Mother of the World.

We moved in silence and angled across the rugged moraine toward the icefall. It was time to climb into the sky. In five days either my lifelong dream would come true, it would slip away unfulfilled, or I'd be dead.

41

The route had changed—the icefall had flowed and tumbled about a hundred feet downhill since we'd first entered the shifting block pile thirty-three days earlier. Solid acclimatization and practiced technique helped us move through efficiently. PK and I progressed well for the first two hours, but crowding slowed us at several ladder crossings. We were going all the way to Camp Two, so it would be a long day.

About halfway through the icefall, the fixed line led us down into a twenty-foot-deep crevasse. We clambered inside and stood on the snowy floor. The exit required a steep climb up the other side. PK and I were mixed in with IMG members as well as climbers from other teams; several guiding companies had chosen the same schedule as us. While we waited for the man in front of PK to ascend the cliff, eight other people backed up behind me, including Karim and Karma Rita.

PK ascended, cleared the top, and headed along the next section of fixed line, beyond my view. After attaching my ascender, I followed him. I'd just reached the halfway point when the glacier beneath and behind me emitted a loud *crack!*

I snapped my head around to where the sound emanated from. The eight climbers behind me were glancing around the crevasse, trying to figure out where the noise had come from and if any blocks were shifting.

Whompf! In unison all eight of them looked at the crevasse floor under their feet. Then the front person stared up at me with wide eyes and bared teeth. "Go!" he yelled.

They all wanted out of here *now*. I turned to the ice face and raced up the remaining fixed line. I attached a leash above the anchor and tried to remove my ascender, but just as I did, someone below me yanked the rope down hard. The tight line pinched my ascending device against the ice face, making it impossible to remove. I was stuck tight, and they were all stuck behind me.

I pressed the release trigger and twisted the ascender, but I couldn't loosen it. I looked down, intending to tell whoever was yanking the rope to let go so I could free myself and get out of their way. To my surprise, a sherpa was climbing toward me fast by swarming up the fixed line hand over hand.

When his head reached my foot, he grabbed my pant leg and then pulled down on my harness as his next handhold. He crawled right over me as if I was part of an obstacle course. Without clipping in, he passed by and raced ahead to flatter ground. Getting his weight off the rope, and him off me, allowed me to finally detach my ascender. I bellowed, "Clear!" and zoomed ahead. Over the next few minutes, Karim and the other climbers emerged from the crevasse, scared but fine. We'd all heard the glacier settle, but no one saw anything move and nothing fell on us.

Safely atop the next block, I paused at an anchor and panted. PK looked back from five yards ahead, and I waved my hand twice to tell him I was okay. Once my heart rate settled toward normal, I proceeded, the glacier dragon's snarl still echoing in my mind.

An hour later we were in the upper icefall at about 19,500 feet. I was plodding up a steep ice ramp, locking my knee after each step and pausing for breath before the next stride. Lost in the measured rhythm and satisfying crunch of crampons on ice, I was startled by a voice from close behind.

"Davidson, you've got a perfect rest step."

It was Dallas, ten feet behind me.

"Thanks, Chief," I said.

We smiled and gave each other a thumbs-up. I took another step, grabbed a breath, and turned my head to talk over my shoulder. "We're reeling this big monster in."

"We sure as hell are!"

Around seven-thirty we reached Camp One, which was almost empty, and continued higher. The air above 20,000 feet didn't seem as thin as before, but after eleven days with little activity, my body was sluggish. The Western Cwm began heating up, making the second part of our ascent an overheated slog. Along the way, we walked across a large field of disturbed snow filled with jagged ice chunks: fresh avalanche debris. PK and I arrived at Camp Two at about eleven-twenty with seven IMG climbers ahead of me and three behind. I was tired but glad to have completed the 4,000-foot ascent in good order.

I settled into a tent with James, and we chatted about the plan. The schedule called for a full rest day at Camp Two before moving up to Camp Three, but if the winds didn't settle down, we might wait an extra day before going higher. We needed the wind to be less than thirty miles per hour on summit day; anything higher increased the risk of frostbite and all the other problems that arise fast at high altitude.

After lunch we rested and sorted gear. An old saying warns mountaineers that "ounces turn into pounds." I reviewed the necessity of every item I intended to take on the summit push. If it wasn't critical, it wasn't going higher.

To improve my efficiency and reduce errors brought on by high-altitude spaciness, I organized my equipment in color-coded nylon stuff sacks. Food went in a green bag. Emergency supplies and storm gear were in a bright-red sack. Medications stayed in the light-blue drug kit. To prevent forgetfulness after climbing all night on the summit push, I had a yellow stuff sack for sunrise. Everything inside had to be utilized when I saw the yellow sun lift above the horizon: sunglasses, lip balm, sunscreen.

Dinner was okay, but most of us struggled to eat. Even though we should've been hungry after a long climbing day, at that altitude our bodies were simply not interested in food. In the thin atmosphere it seems like the body doesn't want to use up precious oxygen to metabolize a meal. It prevents you from eating by creating nausea, making your stomach feel full after ingesting a mere handful of food, and by blunting your taste buds so that even your favorite treats taste bland. I forced down what I could and went to bed early.

Reduced oxygen levels often turn mountain nights into marathon sessions of sleep apnea and crazy dreams. I slept pretty well but was wide awake when the sky turned light around four-thirty. James and I waited in our sleeping bags for camp to warm up before crawling out for breakfast.

I ran into PK outside the mess tent. We both gazed at the clouds scuttling over the Lhotse Face. Though climbers had tried for the summit the previous day, bad weather had forced them to retreat. Conditions still looked marginal up high, but were slowly improving.

PK said, "I think C3 not possible."

"The wind?" I asked.

He was silent for a moment. Then he said, "Cutoff is seven hours."

It took a second, but then I realized he was talking about me. He thought I was too slow to beat the time limit for reaching Camp Three. But that didn't make sense.

"I already went there last time in six and a half hours," I said.

"I think you, Gigi, and Brad too slow for South Col."

He was suggesting that I shouldn't go any higher. I was stunned and angry. He was lumping me in with the two slowest climbers—they'd taken twelve or thirteen hours to reach Camp Two a day earlier, compared with my nine. Greg and Dallas had given no indication that anything was lacking in my times or performance. It felt like this was all coming from PK. Over my thirty-five years of mountaineering, I was used to having mutual trust and confidence with my climbing partners. Now, on the Everest summit push, it appeared that my climbing sherpa didn't have full confidence in my abilities.

Our conversation stumbled and stopped. Emotions were flooding through me; pushing through this important discussion would be the wrong thing to do at the moment. I needed to step back, calm down, and think. We ended with a vague agreement to talk later.

I retreated to my tent to process what PK said. Certainly I wasn't as fast as the superfit young guns out front. But I'd met every time cutoff, had arrived at each camp in pretty good shape, and had never needed assistance on any aspect of the challenging terrain. I couldn't see any basis for him suggesting I was incapable of trying for the summit.

Like all the clients, I was indebted to my climbing sherpa for his guidance, support, and load carrying. But his judgment here seemed incorrect. I journaled about it for a while. To make sure I wasn't ignoring a blind spot, I solicited the input of someone with in-depth Everest knowledge: Alan Arnette. I texted him my travel times and told him what Dallas and Greg had said versus what PK was now saying. Alan responded:

You are 100% fine. Greg would have told you otherwise.

I replied:

Yeah im worried PK will try to pull plug on me. we will talk with Phunuru and guide today.

Once I found Dallas, I explained the situation and voiced my concerns. Dallas thought I'd taken nine and a half hours on the trip from base camp to Camp Two, and he was fine with even that time. He also told me that the hard cutoff to turn someone around at Camp Three on our next trip was eight hours—one and a half hours more than I took on our last rotation. To me there seemed to be confusion or a disconnect between what IMG needed and what PK wanted. I requested a meeting with Dallas, PK, me, and Phunuru as the climbing sirdar and translator.

An hour later the four of us sat on a boulder pile twenty yards from camp. I started by complimenting PK as my guide, and then I asked Dallas to review my past times and the cutoff limits. After Dallas repeated the eight-hour limit for the next day, I insisted that Phunuru translate it all into Nepali to ensure there was no misunderstanding. Phunuru and PK spoke for a few moments. They nodded in agreement, and I requested that Phunuru ask PK how I was doing.

After a short discussion Phunuru reported, "He says all your rotations were good. Your eating and drinking are good too."

I was relieved when Dallas confirmed again that my pace was fine. Even though PK's English was pretty good, I insisted that Phunuru translate what Dallas had just said. He did and then everyone nodded. I was glad that PK had heard it from both Phunuru and Dallas.* But I remained uneasy that PK might still look for an opportunity to turn me around. He seemed more agreeable during our meeting than he'd been earlier, but I also understood that he might not be pleased that I'd requested a meeting with his two bosses. I wasn't looking to put him on the spot; we needed to work well together over the next four or five days. But I wanted to make damn sure that I wouldn't get turned around unnecessarily, and that there were no incorrect expectations. We were heading up to make the highest-stakes decisions of our lives, in an environment with no margin for error.

I hoped for a good day on the Lhotse Face to boost everyone's confidence, including mine. I had a great one. After leaving Camp Two, we pulled into Camp Three in less than five and a half hours. Comparing the climb to my previous Camp Three trip, I wrote to Alan:

it was easier by 20 Percent!

He responded:

---

* Greg Vernovage later told me that he too never had any concerns about my speed or abilities.

Excellent. You are stronger faster better! Bionic Climber Jim!!!!!

A clear sky and strong morning sun made Camp Three pleasant, and I felt good. Instead of crawling into the tent and fighting to breathe like last time, I stood on the platform to cheer for and photograph my arriving teammates. I snapped one shot of Inge smiling with the entire Western Cwm below him and another of Gigi posing jauntily for the camera.

Unfortunately not everyone on our team was feeling so well. Two of our strongest climbers had suddenly fallen ill at Camp Two. Patrick got slammed by a violent stomach disorder, and my Canadian friend Greg caught a bad cold. They dropped off the first summit wave in the hopes of recovering enough to join the second group in a few days. Out of the fifteen original Team One climbers, eight remained.

To maintain our strength, we all went on low-flow supplemental oxygen. The one liter per minute uplifted my body and spirits a modest amount. I ate and drank what I could while sharing a crowded tent with Brad and James. With all my nonessentials left at Camp Two, I had no books, music, or journal for pleasant distraction, so I concentrated on envisioning the summit push.

I recalled images and facts about the route ahead from the Everest books and videos I'd studied. Then I tried to estimate when we would reach key landmarks over the next two days. I needed to climb as efficiently as possible so that on summit day I could sustain the extreme effort for eighteen or twenty-four hours—or however long it took.

As long as everything was reasonably safe, I had no intention of quitting just because I was scared, cold, or exhausted. This was Everest—I expected to feel all that and more. I intended to leverage everything I had, everything I knew, and everything I could muster to make the summit. Over the years I'd learned that the mind could drive the body longer, harder, and higher than seems possible.

I unfocused my eyes as I looked past the tent wall to perceive the

summit vision beyond. I kept picturing myself just below the top, pushing upward.

Back home, Rodney once asked me what it would take to force me to turn
around on summit day. If I were in danger of collapsing or dying, I would
certainly give up the summit to save myself, as well as those around me
who would be endangered if they tried to bring me down. I had no intention of disregarding thirty-five years of mountaineering experience or
throwing caution away. Pushing for the top when you know you shouldn't
is a prime symptom of summit fever, and summit fever can be fatal.

I planned to climb until I either reached the summit or conditions
forced me to stop. Even if I knew I wouldn't make it to the top, I still
wanted to experience as much of the mountain as I could by climbing as
high as possible. If I had to turn back, I at least hoped to see the sunrise
from high on the mountain.

A few months ago, Rodney had also asked what I'd do if I knew I could
summit but would get frostbitten. I had to think about that one. Based
on vague logic and fuzzy math, I was willing to lose one toe, but not ten.
If I did freeze one, it would be the second toe on my right foot. I'd once
frostnipped the end of that digit,* so its circulation was impaired.

Rodney knew almost more about my cold-damaged toe than me—on
several of our coldest climbs together, when my right foot went numb,
he had bravely offered to let me put my chilled and numb right foot on
his warm stomach. No greater friendship can be extended than lifting
four layers of insulation off your torso to let your unwashed partner put
his stinky, icy foot against your bare belly. I recalled the Bolivian dawn
at 19,000 feet when Rodney saved my toe, and our summit. When my
blanched, bare toes touched his pink stomach skin, he clenched his eyes
shut and snapped his head back. Coldness surged from me to him while

---

* Ironically, that frostnip did not occur when I was climbing a high, snowy mountain, but rather
while winter biking in the flatlands of Ohio.

warm life flowed back to me. He gathered the loose folds of his down jacket around my foot and clutched it tight to his torso like a running back cradling a football.

Just before Everest, when I admitted I was willing to sacrifice that weakened toe for the summit, Rodney complained in jest, "Hey, not so fast. I've got a lot invested in that toe!"

Thinking about Rodney prompted me to text him:

At c3. I did great today. On oxygen now. looking good.

He responded:

My heart is soaring to hear your words and know you are in position.

Radio calls informed us that about three dozen climbers had summited earlier in the morning, as had ten others the previous day. Alan texted me that conditions continued to look good for the next two days, but winds would pick up midday on May 22, just a few hours after what we hoped would be our summit time. Our modest weather window was staying propped open.

I managed to nap in the afternoon. After an hour I awoke to a screaming noise and a shaking tent. I thought I was dreaming about an earthquake, but I soon realized it was a helicopter. As it flew by, the nylon tent walls shuddered and flexed. The chopper continued upslope a few hundred feet. Helicopters seldom went higher than 22,000 feet on Everest; it was extremely dangerous even to try. Yet the noisy one above our heads was at almost 24,000 feet. It had to be a rescue attempt—a desperate one. James and Brad each looked out one of the two tent doorways. Stuck in the middle between them, I asked, "What do you see?"

"It's dangling a long line," James said. "Here it comes."

As the roaring chopper passed over us, its rotor wash squashed our dome tent's roof down and battered it against our heads. I hoped the chopper wouldn't crash onto us.

After one more circle around Camp Three and a final attempt to climb higher into the sparse air, the chopper rocketed back down the Western Cwm empty-handed.

To soak in the last of the afternoon warmth, I sat in our tent doorway, watching the clouds below drift through the valley like a wispy white tide. From a tent twenty feet away and ten feet below us, a head poked out through an open doorway. "Hey, Jim!"

"Charley! I didn't know we were neighbors," I said.

From the other end of their yellow tent, a second head popped out. It was Wendy Gustin, a fellow Coloradan and Charley Mace's private client. We chatted and joked. I snapped two photos of them sticking out of their tent like some kind of two-headed mountain turtle.

My teammates and I were eating an early dinner at about four-forty-five when a red helicopter flew up. It made several attempts to move above us, perhaps trying to take advantage of the cooler and thicker evening air. After a few circles above our heads, it flew away. We never learned what the chopper was trying to achieve, or what happened to the person they were trying to rescue. It was another one of the mysteries that sometimes occur at extreme altitude.

As the evening light dimmed, I knew it was time for the last, best item that I had been saving through the entire expedition: Gloria's letter. I unzipped the plastic bag and removed the third sealed envelope she had given me. After carefully tearing off one end, I pulled out two pieces of paper—one in her handwriting and, much to my surprise, one in mine.

Gloria had not only enclosed the note she had written for me two months ago but also a much older letter. I had mailed it to her in June 1983 right after my first major climbing trip. With the dramatic energy of a twenty-year-old who had not reached the top of his first big mountain, I railed about the weather and circumstances that prevented my three partners and me from summiting Mount Rainier. Reading further, I felt the passion and energy of this first-year climber leap off the page as he detailed how he and his team managed to summit their consolation climb of Mount Baker, in northern Washington. I laughed out loud when I read this newbie pontificating about how high and scary the mighty mountain had been, all 10,781 feet of it!

Hidden among all the fun nostalgic details was a keen insight. I had scribbled, "Who knows, maybe someday I'll even climb Mount Everest!"

That old letter was just one of a hundred that we had written each other in the first two years of our long-distance relationship. Gloria's note to me exuded upbeat energy and enthusiasm to strengthen me for the challenge ahead. I needed my headlamp to read both letters a second time. Holding pieces of our distant past and our present lives in my hand, I tried absorbing all the love and energy I could for the summit push awaiting the two of us just one day into the future. I reread her closing lines one more time:

Go get your dream, enjoy this experience and summit Mt. Everest. Just promise to come back. Love, Glo

My second stay at Camp Three was merely uncomfortable, instead of miserable, like last time. Some climbers can't sleep well with a plastic oxygen mask strapped to their heads; I did okay by focusing on the benefits of the oxygen and ignoring the drool-collection cup pressed against my face. PK came to our tent in the morning with hot water. Packing my gear went slowly, but my head wasn't plagued by pounding temples or mental spaciness like last time.

Outside the tent we switched my regulator to a fresh oxygen bottle for the climb to Camp Four. I hefted my bulging pack on and sensed the extra sixteen pounds of tank, regulator, and mask. PK and I stepped off our flattish tent platform right onto the middle of the tilted Lhotse Face. The 1,700 feet of instant exposure below us grabbed my attention. Though there were quite a few climbers moving up from the lower part of Camp Three, we were ahead of most of them. We clipped into the fixed line and started toward the South Col.

Our fast transition from standing still to climbing uphill at 23,700 feet rocketed my heart rate. My body awakened to the hard work, and I settled into a rhythm. To conserve energy, I took small steps and paused to breathe after each one. Then I would slide my ascender up until my leash was tight, and I'd take another short rest. By matching my pace to the three-liters-per-minute oxygen flow, I hoped I could sustain the ascent rate for a long while.

The burrito-size mask strapped sideways over my mouth blocked my lower peripheral vision, and I couldn't see my feet unless I tilted my head forward. So I concentrated on careful boot placement and smooth movements. The temperature was about zero degrees Fahrenheit, and there was little wind hitting us, thanks to Lhotse's hulking shoulder. But that wall also kept the sun from reaching us.

After an hour we approached the famous Yellow Band. This regional bedrock layer occurred on several high peaks nearby, including Everest and Cho Oyu. To clear the cliff, the fixed line threaded up a series of low-angled gullies. Scrambling over rock provided a fun break from the snow climbing, and my steel crampons emitted a metallic screech as they scuffed against the bedrock. The terrain might not have warranted a rope if I encountered it on a Colorado peak, but at over 24,000 feet, and wearing cumbersome boots and a bulky down suit, I welcomed the security of the fixed line. When my head popped above the cliff top, I thought about how amazing Rodney would find the place. I gave the bedrock an affectionate pat on behalf of my climbing buddy.

We ascended another 800 feet as the route continued its rising traverse. Down to my left, I had a clear view of the upper Khumbu Glacier about 4,000 feet below us. PK and I didn't speak much as we made steady progress; my altimeter watch soon indicated that we had passed 25,000 feet.

Lhotse's upper cliffs released the occasional loose rock from somewhere above. As a spinning rock shot past about ten yards away, it buzzed like a hummingbird swooping toward the valley floor.

Around nine o'clock we encountered a small cluster of descending climbers. Since they were going down the same rope we were ascending, we had to pass one another. They knew that climbing uphill is harder than going down, so they kindly stepped aside as much as they could to let us by. PK leapfrogged his two leashes around each of the stationary climbers to stay attached to the line. I did the same flurried sequence of unclips and reclips to stay safe as I squeezed past the four bulky people. We repeated this risky, awkward dance dozens of times as we encountered more descending climbers.

The intense focus and hard work that everyone was putting forth meant we rarely talked to anyone going the other way. Once, when I'd stepped off the narrow trail to let some fast-descending climbers move through, I wound up face-to-face with a masked stranger. I sensed that we were looking into each other's eyes through our dark glacier glasses. With my voice hoarse from altitude and muffled by the plastic mask, I asked, "Summit?"

He or she, I couldn't tell which, nodded vigorously. I laughed with joy and patted his or her down-suited arm. Laughter escaped the climber's mask, and my shoulder was patted in return. After crowding past me, the person pointed at me and then the summit with up-and-down nods of the head. I nodded in return and flashed a sloppy thumbs-up with a gloved hand. I started back up the trail energized.

Not all the descending climbers were in such good condition. We ran into two people assisting a man who plodded along the fixed lines with halting steps. As I clipped around the three of them at an anchor station, the exhausted man slumped down and sat in the snow. His two helpers rousted him back onto his unsteady feet and prodded him to keep trudging downhill. Whether the tired person was altitude-sick, exhausted, or both, I couldn't tell. But they needed to descend as fast and as far down the mountain as they could.

On the right four yellow tents huddled in the snow about one hundred feet above us. The tents served as the high camp for those trying to climb Lhotse via the steep couloir, or gully, nearby. Ahead of us rose a protruding ridge of gray rock called the Geneva Spur. Named by the Swiss, of course, the steep bulge provides the last major rise before the South Col.

We crept our way along the snowy footpath, gaining altitude as we contoured up and around the spur. A few times we again had to wait for descending climbers to precariously work their way around us, or us around them. Including the twenty-seven of us from IMG, around ninety climbers and guides were moving to Camp Four that morning. Since we were dispersed, the small traffic jams probably added only thirty minutes to our ascent. The delay—and the danger—could grow tomorrow, however, when we all departed Camp Four to climb single-file along the narrow summit ridge.

At the crest of the Geneva Spur, the slope angle flattened considerably. PK and I dropped our packs and sipped slushy water. Behind PK the summit of Nuptse looked lower than us, and, sure enough, my altimeter read 25,900 feet. There are only fourteen summits in the world higher than we were right then.

The last fixed-line anchor behind us was pretty sketchy. After we'd passed it by about fifty feet, PK said he wanted to go back and improve it—a good idea. With my mask dangling from my chin, I asked, "Do you want me to go with you?"

"No, I can fix. You go Camp Four."

PK went back. I put on my oxygen mask again, shouldered my pack, and unclipped from the last section of line. The remaining two hundred yards to Camp Four was a casual trail of broken rock. Oddly, the flat terrain was the easiest piece of ground we'd been on for the last 9,000 vertical feet. I walked along the scuffed footpath at a comfortable pace with a windless, deep-blue sky above me. The moment seemed downright pleasant—which was even odder because, at 26,000 feet, I was officially walking into the death zone.

42

Climbers call the upper part of the world's fourteen highest mountains the death zone not because some of us *might* die, but because if we don't descend quickly enough, all of us *will* die. Fit, healthy mountaineers who are acclimatized enough to reach 26,000 feet can live there for two days, maybe three. If they're poorly acclimatized or stricken by an altitude-caused medical emergency, they don't last even one day, bottled oxygen or not. A few genetically gifted and hardy mountaineers can survive four or more days, but it's quite rare and extremely risky to stay that long in the death zone.*

Because no one knows in advance where they'll fall on the survival spectrum, and because things go wrong big and fast above 26,000 feet,

---

* The death zone was originally named the "lethal zone" by climber and physician Dr. Edouard Wyss-Dunant, in the 1953 publication *The Mountain World*. After working with the autumn 1952 Swiss Everest expedition, he wrote that when climbers entered the lethal zone, they were in a "land of giants where man seems to be an ant with insane pretentions." He also noted: "*Survival* is the only term suitable for describing the behaviour of a man in that mortal zone which begins at about 25,500 ft. Life there is impossible and it requires the whole of a man's will to maintain himself there for a few days. Life hangs by a thread, to such a point that the organism, exhausted by the ascent, can pass in a few hours from a somnolent state to a white death."

everyone wants to summit and get out of the death zone as soon as possible. I arrived at Camp Four around noon on May 21. The clock was ticking.

After scanning sixty or seventy colorful tents, I found the IMG campsite and lumbered over. One of our climbing sherpas pointed me to an empty tent, and I dropped my pack next to it. The atmosphere was about 60 percent thinner than at sea level and my body moved as if I were underwater—sluggish and uncertain, just like my brain. Removing one crampon required several steps, with a rest needed after each minor task. Getting ready to crawl into the tent took twenty minutes.

Once he reached camp PK stopped by to tell me that he would come back later with warm water. I crawled into my bag and rested. Every few minutes I removed my oxygen mask to consume my recovery drink, sip water, and stuff pieces of granola bar into my mouth. My altimeter read 25,928 feet, which seemed right. The South Col was actually about sixty feet short of the 26,000-foot mark, but it was close enough.

Someone was rustling gear around just outside. When I zipped open the door, Gigi was standing there. I helped drag in her pack; she and Brad would be my tentmates for our short time at Camp Four. We planned to stay in camp for about ten hours and then leave for the summit around ten or eleven at night. After Gigi settled in, she photographed me holding up a picture of my family. She asked me to snap a photo of her putting on mascara as a joke.

When Brad showed up, I moved over to make room for him and wound up in a spot with fist-size rocks poking up from underneath the floor. Lying down was painful, but we probably wouldn't fall asleep anyway. Our bodies were so starved for oxygen that eating and drinking were repugnant and sleep felt impossible. The best we could hope for was to rest our muscles and minds.

I was happy when the urge to empty my bowels arrived that afternoon; answering nature's call would be far easier on flat ground during daylight than it would be later, hanging off a cliff edge in the cold darkness. Wrestling on my big boots wore me out. To simplify gear complexities while squatting, I went outside without my oxygen system and trudged to camp's eastern perimeter.

After finishing, I put the used toilet paper in a plastic bag and waited five minutes for the waste to freeze. I picked it up with one of the biodegradable waste bags made from soy that IMG had issued all of us and required us to use on the upper mountain. I then placed both small bags into a larger sealable bag I'd brought to haul down my waste. The poop-scooping process didn't bother me—I'd done it a few thousand times while following around Jake the Wonder Dog.

Standing beyond the edge of camp let me study the South Col. The flat saddle, covering an area of about two city blocks, separated Everest from Lhotse. Rock piles poked through along the edges, but most of the pass remained covered with a permanent icefield. Most Everest books I'd read over the last four decades mentioned this famous plateau. Generations of climbers had stayed here the night before their summit push, and now it was my turn. Just past the col's eastern edge, the slope dropped 8,000 vertical feet down the mountain's steep and rarely visited east side.

From photos and maps, I recognized the saddle's far northeastern corner, where nine desperate climbers had huddled, lost, during a raging nighttime storm in May 1996. Their terrible plight after summiting was described by Anatoli Boukreev and G. Weston DeWalt in the book *The Climb*. A small part of me wanted to walk two hundred yards to see the infamous survival spot up close, but a high-altitude history tour wouldn't be a smart use of my limited strength just hours before the summit push. Besides, I felt nervous being even a short distance away from the tents. The South Col's bleak and wind-beaten landscape more closely resembled an uninhabited ice planet than part of the green-and-blue Earth.

Sunlight reflected off the icefield we would cross to start the climb. The ice began at a low angle and then steepened at the bottom of the Triangular Face, a pyramid of snow and rock that rose 1,700 feet. Atop its crest huddled a tiny perch called the Balcony, which, at 27,700 feet, marked the approximate halfway point on summit night. The Balcony was where we would find the extra oxygen tanks our climbing sherpas had already stashed for us. The lower half of the route looked challenging but doable. The upper part onto the south summit, the Hillary Step, and the true summit remained out of my view, but I knew the route got narrower and more exposed the higher we went.

I tottered back toward camp. With my eyes cast downward, I noticed that the ground was splattered with trash—shredded tents, old food containers, and camping debris. Though the tedious slur about Everest being totally covered with garbage was inaccurate, for the hockey-rink-size area of Camp Four, it seemed valid.

Holding a trash sack and seeing the mess triggered my instinct to pick up litter. I bent over to snag a plastic noodle packet, but found it glued to the ground by ice. I tore off what I could and stuffed it into my trash bag. I meandered from one item to the next, but most of them were frozen in place. After about ten attempts, I'd only shoved three or four pieces into the bag. I searched for garbage sitting on top of the ground rather than being embedded in it. This helped, but bending over compressed my torso, which made breathing even more difficult. After five more toe-touch moves to grab trash, my head throbbed violently. I dropped to one knee to pry a Mars-bar wrapper from the ground's icy grip, and then I had to sit on a boulder and pant.

I looked around, wondering how this mess had formed. Though I was too foggy-brained to really think then, I later concluded that most of it occurred for two reasons. First, teams sometimes inadvertently abandon their entire camp at the col when they descend. They intend to return, but storms, injuries, or illnesses sometimes prevent them from going back. Second, as humans become hypoxic zombies at Camp Four and drift closer to death, no one is as careful or caring about the environment as they are five miles lower. Like stunned survivors after a car accident, everyone's efforts are focused on surviving and fleeing from danger, not tidying up. Down at sea level, municipal crews cleaned up after car wrecks, but no organized cleanup system existed in the death zone.

As I continued my way to camp, I paused after each step to pull in three deep breaths. I had to match my efforts to the input of oxygen I could gulp from the feeble atmosphere. By the time I reached our tent, I'd been wandering around without supplemental oxygen for more than twenty minutes. Though I felt spacey, my ability to do that was a sign of good acclimatization. In contrast, field studies during World War II showed that, without bottled oxygen, unacclimated military pilots fell unconscious in four to six minutes at 26,000 feet.

My two tentmates and I spent a slow-motion afternoon resting and preparing for our summit push. We all inhaled a modest one liter per minute of oxygen while in Camp Four, and most of us would use three liters per minute during the climb. PK had explained to me earlier that at a few difficult sections, he would momentarily turn my flow rate up to four, or even five, liters per minute. Short power boosts like that had to end fast, however, to make sure each oxygen bottle lasted nine to ten hours. It felt weird to let someone else adjust my flow rate, but he knew both the route and the oxygen system well, and doing so would be easier than me repeatedly taking my pack off.

Our large tanks helped minimize the difficult and dangerous oxygen bottle changeovers. We would each use one bottle from Camp Four up to the Balcony, a trip that would take four to six hours. There we would remove the half-full tank and leave it to use for our descent later in the day. By putting on a fresh tank at the Balcony, we would have five to six hours to climb the remaining 1,300 feet to the summit and then four to five hours to make it back to our waiting half bottle.

Altogether the two big tanks would provide me with enough oxygen for ten to twelve hours going up and about eight to ten hours coming down. If I wasn't back at Camp Four, or lower, in eighteen to twenty hours, I risked running out of oxygen and facing a dramatic physical collapse, which happened to a few climbers every year. Of course, if we weren't back inside a tent after twenty hours of hard climbing in the death zone, we'd be in serious trouble anyway.

Sitting in our tent, I rigged up heated footbeds in my boots. After practicing with them at home, I'd added extension cords between the batteries and the electric footbeds. The four-foot-long extensions let me keep the battery packs in my chest pocket for closer monitoring and adjustment. If I used the lowest heat setting, the batteries would last about sixteen hours, which should get me through until the sun rose and I was descending. If the night was windy or especially cold, say minus thirty degrees Fahrenheit, higher heat levels would drain the batteries in eight hours or less.

In midafternoon we heard that an American climber had died the night before while attempting the summit, and that his body still lay alongside the trail. We were all saddened, and Gigi got upset that we would pass right by his body. I told her that we would have to steel ourselves for that grim encounter, and possibly others.

More than 280 climbers had died on Everest since the first expedition in 1921, and many of the deceased remained there. Recovering a frozen two-hundred-pound body was awkward, difficult, and dangerous for any recovery team; if encased in thick ice or frozen to the ground, a recovered corpse might weigh three hundred pounds or more. Most bodies were moved behind boulders, buried under rock piles, or lowered into crevasses. Knowing that a fellow climber had just died where we were headed in a few hours made the death zone feel even more ominous.

The uncomfortable tent and our looming departure made us fidgety. One of the three of us always seemed to be jostling around.

Dallas unzipped the door, poked his head in, and asked how we were doing. Everyone gave him a positive report. "Good. We're moving our start time up," he said.

"Why?" Brad asked.

"There's a big group going out tonight. We don't know their leaders, and none of our sherpas know any of their Nepali guys, either. So we want to leave before they do."

I understood what Dallas meant. If our leaders and sherpas weren't familiar with the other group's staff, then maybe that guiding company wasn't very experienced. Less knowledgeable guides tended to attract and allow less skilled climbers onto Everest. We needed to be in front of them.

"What time do we leave?" I asked.

"I want you standing outside, ready to go, at 8:00 p.m."

I looked at my watch; it was already after 4:00 p.m. Hydrating and eating would take an hour or two. Getting dressed and rigged up would take another hour or more. There wasn't any time to spare. I texted Gloria:

We r starting climb early at eight pm. Summit 430 Am or later.

PK and the other sherpas had been bringing around warm water and soup all afternoon whenever the oxygen-starved stoves managed to melt some snow. Since our departure had been moved forward several hours, they no longer had time to make enough water to top off everyone's bottles. I was short by one quart.

The three of us worked around one another in the crowded tent as we dressed and loaded our packs. A full oxygen bottle was the only big item I'd carry. Everything else was small but essential: goggles and sunglasses, headlamp and cameras, storm mitts, spare hat. Not only was the hat super warm, but it had also belonged to Mike, so I took it with me on every big mountain. I put my family photos and protective amulets in a zippered pack pocket to make sure they couldn't fall out when I fumbled around later with gloved hands.

My altimeter read 25,875 feet, about fifty feet less than when we arrived seven hours earlier. We hadn't moved downhill, so the apparent lower altitude reading meant that the barometric pressure had increased, a sign of good weather.

Outside our tent a female voice called, "Hey, Jim Davidson!"

"Over here," I said.

I unzipped the tent and found Ellen Gallant kneeling in our doorway. Tall and fit, she was an energetic climber as well as a medical doctor. We were both on Everest in 2015, though with different teams.

She said, "I heard you guys were heading up, so I wanted to wish you luck."

"You're not going tonight?"

"No, we're resting a day. We'll try tomorrow night." She gave me a quick hug, wished us luck, and said, "It's your summit time, Jim!'

The sun set around six-thirty, and inside the tent we turned on our headlamps. Our three moving light beams set the accumulating fog of our exhaled breath aglow. Excitement swelled in my chest, and a knot formed in my gut. Everything seemed favorable, but any problem like stomach cramps or weather changes would end our summit attempt. To suppress my worries and lift up my teammates, I amped up the enthusiasm.

In a voice loud enough to escape my oxygen mask, I said, "This is it, you guys. We're heading to the top!"

Brad nodded, and Gigi giggled as she packed. Taking great care to thread the regulator well, I switched from my half-empty Camp Four cylinder to a full oxygen bottle. I turned on my footbed warmers, activated my GPS tracker, and posted a message on my social media:

The summit push begins!

At 7:45 p.m. I pushed my pack outside and crawled after it. When I looked across the South Col, two dozen headlamps from climbers who had already started ascending lit the way. Their yellow beams of light danced upon the snow and morphed from circles to ovals and back again as they turned their heads. Draped in darkness, the Triangular Face looked scarier than it had in the light of day.

I attached my crampons, taking care not to frostnip my fingers. PK would be ready any minute. I walked twenty feet from our tent and shut off my headlamp to gaze at the heavens. As predicted, the high clouds had dissipated, and stars populated the blackening sky. I turned away from the other climbers' headlamps and saw no lights all the way out to the horizon. The noise level grew as my teammates emerged from their tents, so I joined the group.

PK and I found each other and he asked, "Feel good?"

"Yes, very good."

He checked my harness, and I checked his. Then PK looked over my shoulder to examine the oxygen gauge of the bottle protruding from the top of my pack. The valve clicked as he set it to three liters per minute.

"During climb, I will adjust oxygen for you. Much faster," he said.

I nodded. "I'm ready!"

PK walked out of camp, and after waving at Dallas, who would head out soon, I followed. My crampons crunched upon the ancient ice as we began our rising traverse of the South Col. In spite of my nervousness, I grinned beneath the stiff plastic mask.

Hard work wiped the grin off my face fast. PK kept looking back to judge my condition and adjust the pace. I concentrated on smooth movements and steady breaths: *Be efficient.*

Where the ice slope steepened, we clipped into the first fixed line and started up the lower Triangular Face. We soon passed a stationary climber who seemed to be struggling with a crampon. I checked my altimeter watch frequently to monitor our ascent rate. So far we were averaging about 450 feet per hour, which was quite good. I would've worried if we were less than 300. We caught up with a cluster of climbers trapped behind a slow person.

After ten minutes of being stuck going their pace, PK asked, "We pass?"

I hesitated, then shook my head no. PK's eyes narrowed a bit. I understood that he wanted to get in front of the slow person; so did I. But passing five or six people would force us to go all out for several minutes, and sprinting early in a marathon is never a good plan. We'd have to wait for a better time.

Soon enough we moved around them, and a few other climbers passed us too. I tried to assign no importance to any of those changes and instead held myself at a pace I could maintain all night.

In the top lid of my pack, the GPS tracker pinged out our location every ten minutes. Glo said she'd be watching the whole time. I sent her a mental message that so far everything was looking good. She'd also told me that as the summit push progressed, the whole gang would be joining her for a dot watch party: Nick, Giordan, Rodney, Alan, and his wife Diane would all be there. Jess would be watching my tracker's progress from her apartment in Washington, D.C.

The terrain grew rockier and steeper as we followed the fixed lines up the face. For a short section, the route squeezed through a narrow gully filled with loose snow that had blown in there. The climbers ahead of us had mostly packed the soft snow down, but the occasional step collapsed. Pulling my boot out of the shin-deep snow holes was tiring, and every time I had to repeat the action, I wasted a few precious calories.

About two hours into the ascent, my altimeter indicated we'd reached 27,000 feet—higher than Cho Oyu's summit. I'd officially broken my own altitude record. Every step upward now set a new high mark for me.

We encountered several small delays due to crowding—five minutes here, ten minutes there. As with any travel, going to a spectacular place during peak season means that traffic, motorized or human, is inevitable. Since there was no simple way to avoid it (I was part of the problem; we all were), I decided long before the summit push to embrace these stops as a chance to catch my breath and enjoy being in a rarefied place. Whenever PK and I came up on a short line of people, I tried to look around and appreciate the amazing terrain.

The density of climbers slowed us to an ascent rate of about 375 feet per hour. This was still fine, but I would be watching my altimeter closely. My left foot began feeling cold. At first I thought the chill had sneaked in during one of the traffic stops, but over the next half hour, the cold deepened. Between every step with my left leg, I wiggled and flexed my toes to encourage blood circulation. Still, the icy feeling crept farther back along my foot. I started stomping my boot down hard during each short rest.

PK noticed and asked, "What is wrong?"

"My foot's cold."

"If foot cold, we must go down."

What? I was stunned by his response and suddenly worried. My foot was a concern, but not a serious one yet. Being so quick to suggest we abandon the summit attempt seemed like a drastic overreaction—we hadn't even tried to solve the problem yet.

To downplay the issue, I said, "No, we don't have to do that. I'll add more heat."

We stopped for a moment, and I pulled the battery pack from my chest pocket. I increased the left footbed's heat output, even though the expenditure could cost me hours of warming capacity later. I would need to turn the setting back down as soon as my foot recovered.

As we continued, I wondered why PK had suggested retreating so quickly. I stared at his heels, moving up a step when he did. He suddenly put his palm in front of my eyes to get my attention.

He pointed forward and said, "Dead body."

One yard ahead and a few feet off to the side lay a deceased climber. I panned my headlamp along the remains. The person lay on their back in a contorted, almost curved, position. They were clipped into a previous year's faded fixed line, not the new one we were ascending. The head pointed downhill, with the boots resting upslope. Dense wind-slab snow covered most of the body, including the person's face. The climber's once-bright yellow down suit had faded like last year's dried sunflowers due to the ultraviolet rays in the intense high-altitude sunlight. The body had been there for a while.

It was partially embedded in the mountain's frozen surface, which perhaps prevented anyone from being able to move it aside. I instinctively responded with a gesture from my Catholic youth and made the sign of the cross on my forehead and chest. As we ascended, I pondered where the person was from and how long the corpse had been lying there.*

The graphic scene had momentarily distracted me from my foot.

---

* Months later, I learned through news reports that the climber was Goutam Ghosh, a fifty-year-old from India. He and two other climbers from his team died while descending from Everest's upper slopes on May 21, 2016, exactly one year to the day before we encountered his remains at about 27,300 feet. His body was later exhumed by a hired sherpa recovery team, taken off the mountain, and returned to India. Like me, Mr. Ghosh had been on Everest during the April 2015 earthquake and had returned.

When we climbed higher, I wiggled my toes and was scared to discover that my entire forefoot was now numb. This made no sense; the higher heat level should have worked. Also, my more vulnerable right foot seemed fine. If my foot didn't recover, I might get bad frostbite. This was no longer a philosophical debate over beers with Rodney—the possibility of frostbite now seemed real. If I told PK, he might enforce a retreat. So, should I tell him that my foot felt fine, and just continue? Our round-trip climb might take another twelve or fourteen hours. How bad would my foot get in that time?

PK stopped, and I looked up. Three feet off the trail was another corpse. The climber's gear was so new and untarnished that I wondered for a second if the person might still be alive. But the awkward position, the windblown snow piled against the limbs, and a small glimpse of an ashen cheek told me they were dead. I realized it was probably the American who had died a day earlier. Instead of some long-ago unknowable accident, this person had died only yesterday, doing exactly what I was doing now. Their clothing and gear resembled mine, and, like me, they had a career, a family, and an Everest dream they wanted to reach: This climber had been just like me.*

Conceptually I understood that people died on Mount Everest every year. But being an arm's length away from a fellow climber's body made that fact more real, more human. I wondered if there was something I could or should do, but since their teammates or guide company must've taken care of any personal effects they were carrying, I couldn't think of anything I could do to help. I mumbled the Lord's Prayer as we moved on.

My legs seemed heavy, as if they were made of stone from the Yellow Band. A glance at my altimeter revealed that we were now at 27,400 feet. We would reach the Balcony soon and be halfway to the summit. I looked around, my headlamp beam skittering across jagged boulders. I half expected something deadly to leap out of the darkness at me. I felt like an ant trespassing in a land of giants.

---

* I later learned that this body was that of American doctor Roland Yearwood (age fifty), who died May 20, 2017. Like me and Mr. Ghosh, he'd also been on Everest during the April 2015 earthquake and had returned to try again.

43

We climbed slower as steeper terrain, more crowding, and fatigue hindered us. Worried about the time and our oxygen usage, I checked my altimeter watch again. Our ascent rate had shrunk to three hundred feet per hour.

One hundred feet higher, we encountered another body. Its wind-battered clothing and partial burial by rocks indicated that it'd been there for years. Nothing could be done now. At a loss, I murmured, *"Om mani padme hum."*

We soon encountered eight to ten climbers clustered together, most fiddling with oxygen bottles and a few kneeling and drinking water: the Balcony.

I arrived at the flat, kitchen-size perch not with an exuberant stride, but with a weary flop. Glad to stop and anxious to check my foot, I sat on the edge of the snow platform and slipped off my pack. I'd spent the last half hour analyzing the possible reasons my left footbed wasn't working: drained battery, switch turned to Off, broken heating wire, disconnected cord. The first two couldn't be the cause because the indicator lights atop the battery glowed bright red. The heating-element wires were sometimes known to break; if that was the problem, it was unfixable now. My toes and the climb would be in grave danger. To figure it out, I had to put my foot at even more risk.

My suit's thick insulation bunched at my waist, making me inflexible. I bent my lower leg at an odd angle and began grappling with my cramponed boot, panting from the effort. I needed to make sure the sharp spikes didn't tear into my hands or my down suit. I rested for a moment, reengaged my wrestling partner, and, at 27,690 feet, pulled off my outer boot.

"What are you doing?" PK asked. "Must put boot on!"

"I'm fixing my cold foot."

Electric needles of icy pain stabbed through the inner boot separating my already chilled foot from the savage midnight cold. I had about thirty seconds to solve the problem. Leaning backward, I lifted my left leg into the air. A loose footbed plug dangled from the rear of my inner boot—it had disconnected from the extension cord. Reconnecting the plug into the cord end by my ankle would require both hands, meaning that I needed to put down my outer boot: *Don't knock it off the Balcony!*

Taking the boot in both hands, I slammed it down to drive the crampon points deep into the firm snow. Then I peeled off my outer gloves and stuffed them inside my suit so I wouldn't drop them or let them get cold. Like the world's least limber man, I grabbed the cuff of my left leg and yanked my foot toward my face. Under the bright light of my headlamp, I plugged the extension cord back in. I pushed myself up into a more natural position and caught my breath before pulling on my gloves again.

Once I set the left-side footbed to its maximum heat level, I waited.

I studied the route below us. A line of about forty headlamps traced the 1,700 vertical feet we'd already climbed. The lights resembled streetlamps leading the way down a curved mountain road. They barely moved—it took me a few minutes to detect a slight shift in their positions. Despite their slow progress, those climbers were working hard. They needed to summit before low oxygen, insufficient time, or their failing bodies forced them to turn around. To cover the one and a quarter miles between Camp

Four and the summit, the fast climbers would take six hours and the slow ones twelve. The slowest of all wouldn't reach the top.

Like a soft fingertip gently poking my skin, a warm spot pushed against my left foot. I wiggled my toes madly and pressed my forefoot hard against the footbed. The warmth grew. From underneath my mask, I shouted, "Yes!"

"All good?" PK asked.

I gave a thumbs-up and then shook my fist rapidly.

"Okay, I will change your bottle."

I nodded but held up a single finger: "*Ek chin.*" One minute.

I needed a well-oxygenated moment to pull on and tighten my outer boot. Once I'd done that and recovered, PK shut the valve and removed my regulator from the half-full bottle. I avoided exertion while off supplemental Os and chugged down a half pint of water. Heat spread through my left forefoot and drove away my concern. Pleased that I'd been of sound-enough mind to figure out and fix the problem, I took it as a good sign that my brain was working. PK finished the critical tank change, and I shoved a third of a candy bar under my mask and into my mouth. He waved and pointed uphill.

Suddenly I felt edgy about something I couldn't identify. I scanned the ground to see if we'd left anything, and then my right hand touched my chest pocket—the battery. If I didn't lower the left footbed setting, the heat would disappear long before the sun rose. I poked a gloved finger at the battery-pack control button to reduce the output from a comfy level three to a sustainable level one. We'd achieved a lot in fifteen minutes, and I felt confident as we pulled out of the Balcony around twelve-fifteen.

We turned left and traversed a gently sloped section of the southeast ridge, my crampons squeaking against the dense snow as if I were walking on Styrofoam. Darkness had prevented me from taking any photos or videos so far. My energy level was high, and we were trudging on the heels of a slow team, so I activated my GoPro. I could only record for less than a minute before my hand chilled and I had to put the camera away.

The route steepened as we moved up snow slopes along the spine of the ridge. I slid my ascender ahead and breathed. Then I lifted a boot to the next kicked-in foothold and grabbed another breath. Two more moves and two more inhalations later, I'd risen about one vertical foot. A modest breeze blew at us from the left—with an air temperature of about minus fifteen degrees Fahrenheit. The windchill stung my left cheek and burned my forehead.

I pulled on my thick down hood to conserve heat. When that wasn't enough, I raised my left arm and held it tight against my head to block the wind. I pressed my bicep against my numb left cheek and draped my forearm over my brow to warm my stinging forehead. Everest climbers' corneas sometimes freeze temporarily on summit night, and I considered digging out the clear goggles I'd brought all this way to prevent the problem. But stopping in such an exposed spot seemed unwise, so I hoped a terrain change would protect us soon. My altimeter read 28,000 feet.

The slope steepened, the work grew harder, and no one spoke. With my giant boots and bulging down suit I could hardly see my feet, and the Earth's surface felt distant. Sound from the wind and crunching crampons couldn't reach my ears through my hat and thick down hood. Inside the mask, there was no taste or smell; my only functioning sense was vision. The swaying beam of my headlamp illuminated snow and the backs of PK's yellow boots—they both looked the same as they had for the last forty-five days. I almost felt like I was floating up the ridge in a bubble, isolated from my partner, my team, my planet.

I looked right and studied the enormous star field over Tibet. With no clouds present, the atmosphere so thin, and the night so cold, the white-blue stars didn't shimmer. Burning bright and steady, they looked hot, but I felt no heat from them or anything else. All I sensed around me was dark, deadly air filled with a billion unreachable stars. It was the closest thing I could imagine to being an astronaut on a space walk.

In Nepal, to my left, hundreds of high mountains, some of them 20,000 to 26,000 feet tall, poked out of the ground like small, rough triangles. As my vision shifted lower, then lower still, I gazed deep into an elongated canyon tucked right against Everest—the Western Cwm. The three-mile-long Khumbu Glacier looked tiny.

Alongside the glacier, nearest to me, I thought I saw several dozen points of light. Most were yellow, although a few red, orange, and green ones appeared too. I worried that I was seeing things and perhaps my brain was oxygen deprived. Then I realized that the tiny lights were the illuminated tents of Camp Two, 7,000 vertical feet below.

The stunning perspective jolted me alert, and I tried to figure out where we were on the route. After a moment's thought, I realized we had to be above the enormous southwest face. I looked at my altimeter: 28,500 feet. All the difficult thinking had roused me from my detachment. More alert, I noticed lights about a quarter mile away to my right. They were at about the same elevation as us, and they moved: headlamps. Other climbers were pushing for the summit from their high camp in Tibet. Their northeast ridge route met ours right at the top. Between them and us was a broad, steep slope of snow and ice, which had to be the colossal eastern side of Everest, the Kangshung Face.

There was an odd pain behind my left eyeball. Though I blinked and rubbed my eye, the dull ache wasn't going away, and it grew sharper whenever I worked extra hard. Contemplating the possible causes—stroke or cerebral edema—worried me. A Colorado climber I knew had experienced a transient ischemic attack, basically a ministroke, when he attempted Everest. As a preventive measure, I'd been taking a baby aspirin daily to thin my blood for the past six weeks.

To check my mental capacity, I did multiplication tables in my head. My cognitive capacity seemed good, though if it were subpar, I wondered if I would even know. I didn't sense that anything serious was about to happen, so I kept climbing.

The fixed line steered us to the right, and the ground flattened for the next twenty yards. About fifteen people lined up beneath a steep rock cliff that stretched about fifty feet up into the darkness. The climbers bunched tight along the rope, and everyone moved slowly. We were caught in our first serious traffic jam.

Since I had time, I pulled out my GoPro to take some video. I pushed the Power button, and the screen came on for a second and then went black. Although I tried two more times, it wouldn't activate. Cold had killed the battery. I had a spare battery, but swapping them out required me to remove my gloves down to bare skin so I could open the camera's delicate access door. Handling the small batteries was finicky work too. Bare skin and cold equipment were a bad combination on a high mountain at night.

Contemplating the need to take off my gloves, I recalled a story shared by Everest climber and photographer Ed Webster. During a cold Everest dawn, Ed had removed his mittens to take photographs at 28,000 feet. He'd lost eight fingertips to frostbite. With his story running through my mind, I concluded that no photo was worth freezing my fingers. Though disappointed to lose the use of my best camera, I decided not to change the battery. I still had two other cameras for when the sun came up.

Though I was anxious about waiting twenty minutes, we were still in good shape. I was working and breathing hard, but my energy was high and my legs weren't tired. Every minute or so, the line advanced and I stepped forward. The rock face steepened to about fifty degrees in one section, and I looked for the best footholds. In some places I had to trust the fixed rope with all my weight.

Just below the cliff top, we encountered two climbers off to the left who weren't ascending. They'd stopped midcliff, and everyone had to go around one of them, which was causing the delay. The climber nearest to me wore a yellow down suit. He huddled by a fixed-line anchor point looking at his companion ten feet farther away. Wearing a blue down suit, the second man fiddled with his harness rig. I noticed they weren't wearing masks, so I assumed that their oxygenless attempt had gone too slowly and they were turning around.

As he moved past them, PK said something in Nepali to the yellow-suited man three feet away, but I didn't hear the climber respond. I continued ascending the fixed line, and when I got close to the man, I asked through my mask, "How are you?"

He was looking away and did not answer. Under all his thick layers, he might not have heard me, or maybe we had a language difference, but his silence seemed odd. I looked up the line at PK about six feet above me and said, "I don't think they're well. Should we do something?"

"No, let's go. I told them to go down."

The man farther away paid us no attention and kept fussing with his harness and gear like he was rigging to rappel. They were headed down, which was good, but they didn't seem very sharp.

"PK, I think we should radio Greg," I said.

He nodded and spoke in Nepali over the radio. After a moment he said, "Okay. I told Phunuru and Greg. Dallas will check them soon."

Dallas could be anywhere behind us, depending on what was happening with our climbers in the back.

"Where's Dallas?" I asked.

PK pointed at the base of the cliff we'd just ascended. "Right there."

With the two climbers headed down and Dallas nearby, PK's plan made sense. Dallas was in charge, had advanced medical training, and was carrying a first-aid kit and a radio. Besides, I couldn't do much for them in the middle of the cliff with twenty other people bunched up below me. I nodded to PK, and we moved higher.

The route turned due east and rose over a buttress of rock and snow. I needed two breaths after each step as I plodded to the crest. Because I expected the route to keep rising, I was surprised to see the ridge descend fifty feet and then lead into a long traverse. Trying to match the terrain pattern ahead to the route description I'd memorized, it hit me—we were on top of the south summit.

To confirm, I looked at my altimeter: 28,700 feet. We were higher than any other mountain in the world, including K2, the second highest, about 800 miles northwest of us. Only one mountaintop rose higher than us now, and its dark outline jutted skyward in front of me, just a quarter mile away and 300 feet higher. Unless I got slammed by altitude sickness, or maybe hit on the head by a falling meteorite, we sure as hell weren't turning around now. After dreaming about it for decades, I couldn't quite comprehend that I might be summiting Everest in the next hour or two.

44

From the south summit, the route threaded an unlikely path along the Cornice Traverse—a sharp rock ridge plastered with jutting fins of windblown snow. These giant snow rolls, called cornices, projected sideways off the mountain into empty air. They can accumulate fifteen feet thick and grow fifty feet laterally off the ridge. A climber might think he or she is walking on flat, compact snow, but underneath the thin snow ledge lurks empty space. Many great mountaineers had lost their lives when a fragile cornice collapsed beneath their feet.

Most of the tenuous cornices jutted off the ridge's right side, into Tibet. Our route avoided many of them by staying mostly in Nepal. Having the fixed line to follow and protect us helped, but with a nearly eight-thousand-foot drop to the left and an eleven-thousand-foot plunge to the right, crossing the airy Cornice Traverse in the dark looked intimidating.

Headlamps appeared and disappeared as other climbers wove their way across. PK and I took a short rest break. I slammed down some water and an energy gel. The pain in my eye was still there, but it wasn't getting worse. It was a few minutes after 3:00 a.m. If we kept climbing at our current rate, we were going to summit in the dark. We were moving too fast!

Eight years earlier I'd reached the top of Cho Oyu an hour before sunrise. The night was too cold to stand around, so I left the summit without seeing the hard-earned view. I didn't want that to happen on Everest.

Pointing at my watch, I said, "PK, we're going to summit before the sun comes up. We must go slow. *Bistare janne.*"

He shook his head. "No. Up fast, down fast is best."

With plenty of hard work ahead, there was no need to debate. We descended the south summit for five minutes and started across the Cornice Traverse. The slope change gave my tired muscles a rest, but soon we started ascending again. A dry tackiness in my mouth meant I was way behind on hydration and nutrition, but the complex terrain and big drops beneath our feet made taking my pack off too precarious.

I glanced over my right shoulder and looked back along the first third of the Cornice Traverse. Two miles away and far below us, I recognized the dark pyramid of Lhotse. Four lights moved slowly up the couloir: climbers pushing for the summit. Watching the dots move from afar made me wonder if everyone back home was watching my GPS tracking dot online. I mentally sent Gloria a message: "I'm okay, Glo. We're getting really close." I tried pushing the words out to her from my brain, but the sensation flowed from my chest. Then I thought of the others: Jess and Nick, Rodney and Alan. I feel good. I think we're going to make it.

The ridge grew narrower as we threaded our way between bedrock outcrops and snow blobs barely glued to the mountain. Where footholds had been kicked into the snow, the traverse was fun and exhilarating. But on the rock slabs our crampon points sometimes skated about.

As we ascended a steep snow slope, I sensed an enormous drop-off to my left. I pointed my headlamp into the void, illuminating the uppermost seventy feet of a rocky cliff. My gut said the blackness plummeted much farther.

We reached the top of a snow dome, and the flatness provided a rare place to pause. I looked farther west into Nepal, where we'd trekked six long weeks ago. The shadowy silhouettes of two mountaintops poked up into the night sky, and points of starlight glowed in the open notch between them. With my head tilted down to view the mountains, it seemed like the stars were below me.

Farther along, we followed the fixed line through a rocky section of the ridge crest that took us from Nepal into Tibet and back again. My headlamp revealed gray-and-white limestone. From geology papers I'd read, I knew that this bedrock contained traces of ocean life that lived 470 million years ago—swaying sea lilies and scurrying trilobites. Continental collisions over the last fifty million years had uplifted their fossilized remains to the roof of the world. The little sea creatures in the rock had summited Everest long before me.

We caught up with a pair of climbers a few minutes later, and the second one was struggling with a tricky rock section. There was no way to pass them on the exposed terrain, so PK and I had to wait. I pushed my ascender three more inches up the fixed line to tighten my leash; the added security let me relax my muscles and rest for a moment.

PK turned to me. "Hillary Step."

I perked up. The famous forty-foot-tall rock bulge had been known for decades as the final barrier before reaching the summit. Mountaineers with limited rock-climbing skills sometimes struggled to scale the cliff, which had caused dangerous bottlenecks on crowded days. But last year, in May 2016, when climbers resumed ascending Everest after the earthquake, it appeared that the Hillary Step was gone. Several guides concluded that the rock step had collapsed as a result of the quake. Other people argued that the step still existed beneath the unusually thick snow cover in 2016. A debate flared between the climbing community and the Nepal Tourism Board about whether the well-known natural feature had been destroyed. Despite the promoters' desire for the landmark to still exist, the consensus among climbers was that the Hillary Step was gone.

As a geologist I wanted to look for evidence. I asked PK, "Where was the Hillary Step?"

He pointed to the north, about twenty feet above us, where a steep slope of jumbled boulders now stood. There was nothing that a climber or geologist would call a rock face or cliff; the tallest visible rock on the slope was less than ten feet high.

To make sure we understood each other, I asked, "Where did the Hillary Step go?"

PK pointed down a wide gully on the Nepal side that stretched about eighty feet below us before disappearing into the blackness. I asked if the step no longer existed by saying in simple Nepali, "Hillary Step *hoina*?"

"*Hoina*," PK said, as he flourished his arm toward the gully.

I shone my headlamp down the slope again. Just broken rocks and darkness. When the slow climber cleared the way, we advanced forward ten feet and found ourselves perched atop a smooth rock slab where the Hillary Step once stood. I panned my light beam across the slab and looked for grooves, scars, or the crushed bedrock dust that geologists call rock flour. But I didn't see any noteworthy damage to the remaining rock slab. Like a climber missing high on Everest, the Hillary Step had disappeared without a trace.

The route angled to the right over a section of slippery rock and led us up a jutting prow of steep snow. As I followed the fixed line up the exposed snow rib, there were no constraining boulders or walls on either side of me, just open air. I looked down to my right and realized that we were at the very top of the eleven-thousand-foot-tall Kangshung Face. An enormous slope of snow and ice plunged uninterrupted down Everest's east side more than two vertical miles to the Kangshung Glacier below.

The snow steps looked okay, and the fixed line provided a mostly secure backup, but the immense exposure and openness all around suddenly gave me a creepy feeling. Perhaps altitude, exhaustion, and sleep deprivation had finally caught up with me, or maybe it was the frightening potential drop, but my confidence waned. Fear rose. I leaned into the slope awkwardly and spread my hand on the snow, looking for security. Not good!

From the back of my mind, Dad's words resonated over my shoulder, "Focus on the climb, not the drop!"

I stood straighter on the snow steps and relaxed. After exhaling hard, I looked up and contemplated the climb ahead. I focused on kicking solid foot placements and moving up with confidence.

The slope angle soon eased, and I stopped to rest. I checked my altimeter watch: 28,850 feet, 3:50 a.m. The watch face was easier to read now, and my headlamp beam seemed dull. I looked up and realized that the eastern sky was turning lighter—a thin accent stripe of bright orange stretched just above the Tibetan horizon. Above it the sky graded from light blue to deep royal blue before giving way to black. Fewer stars were visible now, but Jupiter and the crescent moon glowed in the east.

Without thinking, I whispered, "Look, Dad."

A minute later PK moved out and I followed. The crampon trail stayed five to ten feet back from the dangerous cornice lips. Soft blue light set the cornice sides aglow, and I moved a step toward the edge to see why. I peered down the upper east face and saw more glowing snow below us. The curved Kangshung Face was acting like a white parabolic collector, which stretched two miles high and four miles wide. It gathered the early dawn light and shot it up underneath the cornices.

There were no clouds above us and no wind. A smooth slope of firm snow arced one hundred yards ahead. At the high point, about thirty feet above us, three headlamps wobbled in place, illuminating red and yellow down suits. Those climbers dropped their packs on the ground: I think it's the summit.

The trail squeezed by the last bedrock outcrop before the top. As I walked past, a wind-scoured alleyway between the rock face and a head-high snowbank became visible. Six people stood there. I stopped for a moment to make sure they were okay. Since they seemed fine, I turned to follow PK. Suddenly there was a shout from someone in the alley.

"Jim!"

I looked back, confused, and raised my oxygen mask. "Who is it?"

"Karim."

"Karim, what're you doing?"

"We're waiting for sunrise. It's Dave, Mo, me, and everybody. Join us."

How brilliant! I looked five yards up the line to where PK had paused for me to catch up.

I faced uphill and called out, "PK—it's Karim and our group. Let's stop and wait with them for the sun."

He pointed at the narrow strip of color to the east: "There is sun. Let's go."

The sun's rays can hit high mountaintops well before official sunrise, but the sunshine wouldn't directly reach us for at least another thirty minutes. I was torn. PK wanted to keep moving, but we were in great shape, so waiting seemed safe. I thought Karim was right.

"Let's wait and summit with our friends," I said.

PK waved me to him. He wanted to go now.

I had to decide. After two seconds I waved PK back to me, turned around, and walked three yards into the alley. I squeezed in among the multicolored down suits of my teammates, both members and climbing sherpas. Muffled laughs came from behind their masks, and someone patted my shoulder. PK arrived a moment later. I grabbed his sleeve and pulled him close, between another puffy teammate and me.

The happy camaraderie felt warm, but the cold air was angry. Just seconds after I stopped, my scalp tingled with icy pain. It had to be twenty below zero, maybe less. I flipped my hood over my head, cinched it tight, and began walking in place like my friends. We checked our watches and glanced at the colored sky, which kept easing toward daylight.

Someone asked, "Should we go?"

"Not yet," Karim answered.

We all deferred to his veteran judgment. Frigid minutes passed, and the stars kept disappearing.

PK tugged on my sleeve. "We go."

I looked across the world's highest penguin huddle to Karim. "Should we move?"

"Okay, it's time! But go slow." he said.

Since we'd entered the narrow alley last, PK and I exited first. Everyone in the group had been ahead of me on the mountain, so I stepped back, intending to let them get in front and summit before me. But the trail was narrow, and the steep slope behind me offered an icy launch chute to the almost eight-thousand-foot drop back to Camp Two. It wasn't a good place to be clipping around each other. With an apologetic wave to the next person in line, I stepped behind PK, and we moved ahead.

The stars had disappeared and the sky grew lighter. PK was fifteen feet ahead, and Karim followed me thirty feet behind. I looked back along the summit ridge below me.

Karim pulled the plastic mask away from his face, smiled wide, and said, "Brother, make it the slowest hundred meters of your life!"

Under my mask I grinned too. I stepped uphill, took a deliberate pause, and looked ahead. Smooth white snow offered an easy path into the colored sky. To my right the rising sun pushed waves of orange and pink ahead of its arrival. Off to my left the western sky was releasing its gentle grip on nighttime and starlight.

A deep satisfaction flowed through me. After each step I stopped to stretch out the final minutes of summiting and to savor my dream coming true. I wanted to feel all the joy and experience every second of awe.

My head rose higher than the final snow mound and I saw over the mountaintop, far into Tibet. After two more gentle strides, at 4:19 a.m., I stopped and embraced PK.

I'd summited Mount Everest.

45

Even though the air around me contained 70 percent less oxygen than normal, and I needed supplemental oxygen to survive, I could finally breathe freely. Calmness filled me. For thirty-five years I'd wondered if I was dedicated enough to attempt the highest peak on the planet. Now I no longer wondered.

As an Everest aspirant, I fretted over skills, strength, and speed. Those worries had evaporated. Since leaving home two months earlier, I kept hoping everything from intestinal microbes to Indian monsoons would align well enough to let me summit. They had.

Two yards away a dozen climbers hooted, hugged, and held their arms aloft. I smiled with them but felt the urge for a quiet moment. PK and I stood aside by the glowing cornice.

I soaked in the spectacular view I'd come so far to see. Off to my left, the eastern Himalayas stretched into neighboring India and Bhutan. I turned my head and scanned Nepal's southern Terai plains. Then I shuffled my feet in place and rotated my body clockwise to survey western

Nepal, where white mountains extended to the horizon and beyond. Finally I studied the vast, elevated plains of Tibet before returning my gaze to the brightening eastern sky.

During my 360-degree panorama, I'd recognized the familiar silhouettes of Kangchenjunga, Makalu, Lhotse, and Cho Oyu. Though I couldn't pinpoint Manaslu and Shishapangma, I knew I'd glimpsed them as well. All six of these 8,000-meter peaks were far below us.

I glanced down at the snow between my boots to see the highest mountain of all. Buddhists regarded Chomolungma as the Goddess Mother of the World, and they considered the summit her head. Because they also deemed the soles of one's feet unclean, standing on the highest point of the summit could be considered disrespectful. Like some climbers before me, I refrained from stepping on the highest snow mound, which was level with my shin, just one stride away. There was no conquering to do or any vainglorious thrill to seize by taking the last step. I'd climbed as far as I needed.

We'd stopped only a minute earlier, but the cold already cut into me. We were lucky there was no wind. Being careful not to frostnip my fingers, I took several photos of PK with my second camera, and he snapped some of me. We passed the camera to a climbing sherpa, who captured a close-up of PK and me together.

All night I'd stored the satellite phone inside my down suit to keep the battery warm, so I could call Gloria and the gang from the summit. After turning it on, I dialed home, but the call dropped. I made three more attempts but they all failed, and soon my fingertips ached with cold. Disappointed, I put the phone away.

I pulled out my GPS. At 4:36 a.m., I pushed a few buttons and sent out my prewritten message:

I'm standing on the roof of the world!

With communications finished, I started refueling for the downclimb. My frozen candy bar was rock hard, so I let the pieces warm up in my mouth before chewing, lest I break a tooth. More climbers had summited from both sides of the mountain, and another dozen were approaching from the southeast ridge. In case of a photographic mishap, we took a few photos with my third camera, a ten-year-old clunker. Then PK said, "My hands are cold. We must leave."

"Wear my down mitts," I offered.

"I have mitts. No good. We must go now."

I didn't understand why neither his mitts nor mine would work. In six weeks of climbing together, PK had never complained about the weather, and he didn't seem to struggle with cold hands. I wondered if he just wanted to descend soon. The sun hadn't yet cleared the eastern horizon, and I wanted to see it happen. Was I right that we should stay longer to experience a glorious summit sunrise? Or was PK correct to have us leave sooner to get in front of the descending summit crowd?

There was no way to know, but the summit was no place for disagreement. I figured that climbers should take each other at their word.

"All right, we'll go," I said.

We packed up, and I began focusing on the descent. The climb was only half finished; the dangerous part still lay ahead. Descents often posed more danger than ascents because of exhaustion, mental disengagement after the summit, and other factors.

Before we left, PK talked with another sherpa, which gave me a final moment on the summit. The sky was enormous—I looked down to see Earth in all directions. On a day as clear as we had, visibility from 29,029 feet stretched about two hundred miles in every direction. Though Everest wasn't quite high enough to reveal the curvature of the planet, with a turn of my head my eyes took in more than a hundred thousand square miles of the world's grandest terrain. Within that stunning expanse waited more snowy mountains than I could climb in a hundred lifetimes.

My life had presented many sensible opportunities to stop climbing:

school, work, marriage, parenthood. Life had also thrown harsh obstacles in my way so it would've been safer or simpler to give up: Mike's death, Dad's death, injuries, the earthquake. Despite all the change, challenge, and uncertainty along the way, I'd kept going until I reached this summit. I was proud I'd stayed on the winding path long enough to get to this moment. And I was very grateful to have made it.

"Okay, let's go," PK said.

He started descending the narrow snow strip in the sky. I exhaled hard and followed. My legs and body felt strong, but my mind was a little spacey: *Don't make any mistakes!*

As we moved down the fixed line, I slid my carabiner along the rope and marveled at how much easier going downhill felt. We reached the first anchor station, and I carefully worked my two leashes from one section of line to the next. With an anchor point about every seventy feet all the way back to Camp Four, there were at least one hundred more transfers to go: *Double-check every clip!*

Eighty yards along the ridge, the cornice sides to my left began glowing soft orange. A moment later, they flared even brighter—sunrise. Amber light radiated off the east side of Lhotse directly ahead, which meant that the whole Kangshung Face underneath us had to be aflame too. The urge to peer over the edge and see the eleven-thousand-foot wall glowing beneath me was great. But if I moved to the edge to look down, the risk of breaking off a cornice and falling over the lip of the two-mile-high wall was greater. I stayed clipped in and kept back from the brink.

Farther down, the scalloped edge of a small cornice wavered toward me so that I was only two feet from the lip. I reached over and dipped my left hand into the sea of orange light. The feeble warmth couldn't penetrate my glove, but I imagined myself soaking up the energy.

We stopped to let ascending climbers work around us. To the west the giant triangular shadow of Everest stretched a hundred miles across Nepal. I pulled my second camera out from inside my sweaty clothing. Holding the wet camera in my hand, I framed a beautiful shot and pushed the shutter button. It made a weak whirring noise and stopped.

Multicolored bars of light danced on the screen. Next the entire screen turned fire-truck red, and a message appeared: UNABLE TO READ. REFOR-MAT MEMORY CARD.

Then the screen went black. I pushed the Power button again and again, but the camera didn't respond. It was fried.

I had a sickening feeling that all the photos on the memory card might be gone. My stomach squeezed tight; I wanted to find out if I'd lost all those gorgeous pictures, but fiddling with a comatose camera on a knife-edge ridge was a bad idea. I slipped the dead weight back inside my suit pocket and tried not to think about it.

We descended the exposed snow slope that had spooked me on the way up. A quick peek down the massive east face made my stomach lurch. I understood why some climbers said that crossing the Cornice Traverse in the light of day was more terrifying than when nighttime hid the huge exposure. As we worked our way through the tricky rock section where the Hillary Step once stood, we ran into Charley and Wendy going the other way. They congratulated us, and I wished them good luck.

Soon we reached a small flat spot just below the south summit. The sun's rays hit us directly now, so I stopped to address the items waiting in my yellow sunrise kit. I slathered sunscreen on my face and, most important, slipped on my glacier glasses. I knew several Everest climbers who'd become snow blind because of insufficient eye protection. While snow blindness eventually reverses, descending without sight could prove disastrous.

The forty-foot ascent back to the south summit forced me to rest again. We'd been working hard in the death zone for ten hours, and my strength was fading. When we reached the steep rock cliff where those two climbers had struggled, a snarl of ascending people delayed us by fifteen minutes. During the wait, my mind drifted and I sensed fatigue creeping in. I stared out from our perch at 28,500 feet until the rope moved and startled me: *Come on, focus!*

I double-checked my rappel setup and lowered myself down the rope. Below the cliff we switched to an arm-rappel descent for the moderate part of the southeast ridge. The angle eased even more, and at around 28,200 feet, we encountered a group of four sherpa men moving another Nepali climber downhill. We stopped. The man wore a blue down suit and was apparently being rescued. Climbing rope had been wrapped around his body and limbs to truss him up tight, and he was attached to two short lines being pulled by the rescue team. They were dragging him down.

He wiggled his forearm and made a sound, so he was alive. One rescuer spoke in Nepali to PK while the others chatted calmly to one another. PK turned to me, pointed at the blue-suited patient, and said, "This is man from last night."

It took me a few seconds to process what he'd said, and then it hit me—the blue suit. He was one of the two slow-moving climbers we'd passed on the cliff. Although our brief encounter had occurred just five hours earlier, it seemed like long ago to me, and perhaps even longer to the man being dragged downhill.

I asked, "Where's the other climber, the one in yellow?"

PK pointed down in the direction we were headed and said, "South Col."

I tilted my head toward the rescue team and asked: "Do they need our help?"

"No. Strong sherpas. Route all downhill to Camp Four."

PK said some departing words to their leader. I waved at one of the rescuers, who gestured back. Then we continued descending the gentle snow slope. We reached the Balcony at about seven o'clock, and PK changed both of our oxygen systems back to the half-full bottles we'd left there. We both slipped our mostly empty summit bottles into our packs to haul them down. I chugged down my remaining water. I hadn't needed a pee break in about six hours.

The Balcony seemed less scary in the daylight, and being there reminded me of my cold-foot problem on the way up. I wiggled my toes to check. They all felt fine, but the electric footbeds no longer emitted any heat. The sun was out though, and they had lasted through the night, so they'd done their job.

We turned right and started descending the Triangular Face. With all the steep sections behind us, we picked up speed. Perhaps the thicker air lured me downward, or maybe my mountaineering instincts urged me to escape the death zone. Either way, I didn't look around much, and the same word kept repeating in my mind: *Descend.*

I transferred my leashes quickly and didn't linger at any of the anchor stations. I moved my legs as fast as I could while maintaining control. We shed 1,700 feet of elevation in forty-five minutes.

Once we cleared the ancient blue ice at the South Col, the fixed ropes ended. PK and I drifted apart by about fifty feet. Maybe cramming close together on the narrow route for so long had made us both want some space for a few minutes. Though we had differed on how best to climb, and how long to linger on top, we couldn't discuss it during our summit push. There wasn't enough energy, oxygen, or shared language for a debate. Besides, we needed to work together to get back down.

The strong sun warmed me, and I listened to the steady crunch of my crampons as I walked across the saddle. Twenty yards short of our tents, PK and I joined up again and walked side by side into Camp Four. I dropped my pack outside my tent at 7:55 a.m.—we'd descended the entire 3,000 feet from the summit in less than three hours, and the round trip had taken just twelve.

Gigi and Brad were still on their way down, so I was alone in our tent. With the summit behind me, the tent seemed welcoming instead of ominous as it had been a day earlier. I tried the satellite phone, and it worked. When I dialed home, Gloria answered.

"Glo, I'm safe in Camp Four."

"Yeah! You summited Everest!"

"I know. I can't believe it. I tried calling from the top, but the phone didn't work. Dammit."

"It's okay. We watched your tracker, so we knew you made it. Everyone cheered."

We talked for about ten minutes, but I didn't remember much of our conversation. Gloria told me later that on the call I'd sounded "out of it."

I'd been awake for twenty-seven hours, and I really wanted to sleep.

PK pushed hard to depart within the hour, but I needed more time. Like a robot with low batteries, I packed my gear.

Gigi returned to our tent, and she and I hugged and congratulated each other. On her fourth attempt, she'd summited Mount Everest.* As I finished packing, Brad returned, exhausted but happy. Though the three of us must have passed each other on the ropes, none of us noticed when it happened. Interacting with other people at high altitude in the dark is like being drunk and wandering through an outdoor party at night.

All twenty-seven members of our IMG team who left Camp Four on May 21 reached the top, including ten clients, two guides, and fifteen climbing sherpas. As each client and sherpa pair were able, they started the tiring descent from the South Col. Dallas wanted all of us to at least get down to Camp Three, with Camp Two much preferred. Because climbers my age sometimes have heart attacks and strokes after summiting, I needed to reduce those risks by descending as far as possible.

I stepped outside our tent around nine-thirty. Several sherpas were standing behind Dr. Ellen Gallant as she treated a man on the ground who wore a yellow suit—the second climber from the pair who had struggled on the descent.†

PK and I walked out of the South Col, followed the trail around the Geneva Spur, and kept angling down. When I had to tilt my head upward to see the summit of Nuptse, I knew we were lower than 25,500 feet. We'd made it out of the death zone.

---

* Another Moroccan woman, Bouchra Baibanou, had reached the top a day earlier, making Gigi the second woman from her country to summit Mount Everest.

† In the following days we partially patched together what had occurred with these two climbers, and we learned more from media reports later. Apparently Dawa Sange Sherpa (age nineteen) guided his Pakistani client, Colonel Abdul Jabbar Bhatti (age fifty-nine), to the summit on May 20–21, using bottled oxygen. They reportedly moved slowly, experienced rough weather, and ran out of oxygen. When we encountered them at about 28,500 feet on May 22, they were uncommunicative, probably due to exhaustion, hypoxia, and language differences. Although we thought they'd been climbing up for five or six hours like the rest of us, they'd actually left the South Col on the night of May 20, more than twenty-four hours earlier. Since their reported summit at the very late hour of 3:00 p.m. on May 21, they'd only descended about 400 feet in eleven hours. Both men survived, although Sange suffered severe frostbite and the amputation of all his fingers and the majority of both thumbs.

46

PK and I completed our traverse of the upper Lhotse Face and reached about 24,400 feet. The fixed line turned right and began its 2,400-foot descent of the ice wall, where scores of climbers were ascending on their summit push. We reached IMG's Camp Three around eleven-thirty. With plenty of daylight left and the weather holding, there was no doubt we should continue. I wanted to take a nap in one of the IMG tents, but I knew that the best guarantee of health and life was to keep descending.

Even though we were acclimated enough to stop using oxygen, I still had to carry the equipment down. I figured that if I was lugging the weight, I might as well use the oxygen to stay as safe and strong as possible, so I kept breathing the Os. My legs felt fine, and my techniques still seemed good, but exhaustion and lack of sleep made me weary. At one point I couldn't recall anything from the last ten minutes. I think I sleepwalked in broad daylight as I descended the ice face at 23,000 feet.

As my mind drifted, my thoughts kept returning to the broken camera and the probability of lost photos. I dwelled on how many pictures had been lost and whether they were recoverable. Alan was an engineer and an electronics whiz; maybe he could help me retrieve them. I began explaining the problem to Alan in my mind, carrying on a full conversation. My hands and feet continued the mechanics of descending, but my brain fixated on the imaginary discussion. Then a new thought popped into my mind: Maybe Rodney knows where to find my photos.

To my surprise, rather than join the mental debate, Rodney interjected: *You're on the damn Lhotse Face. Pay attention!*

He sounded perturbed. In all the years we'd been friends and partners, we'd never had cross words with each other. I took his sharp tone to mean that the camera was less important than arm-rappelling with a 1,000-foot drop beneath me. So I stopped thinking about the photos and refocused on getting down.

To make amends for my lapse, I paid strict attention during my leash transfers at the next anchor. The steps looked correct, but my movements seemed sloppy. Rodney was right: I needed to be careful. To avoid any rigging mishaps, I resumed double-checking everything, every time. Calling on thirty-five years of embedded habits, I closely managed the rappels and stomped my crampons with authority. *No mistakes!*

An hour of intense focus got us almost to the bottom of the ice face. The oxygen bottle and all my high-mountain gear made my pack heavy and bulky, so I held my brake hand extra tight as I walked backward down the last steep rappel. When I cleared the bergschrund crack, and my crampons touched the ground, I was back on the uppermost Khumbu Glacier. I stepped underneath an overhang to get away from any ice PK might knock loose as he rappelled down.

The glacier's tilt seemed pedestrian compared with the wild terrain we'd been on for the last few days. Still, the accumulating tiredness made me slow on the downhill trudge. I kept a wary eye open for crevasses as PK and I walked unroped toward Camp Two. Twenty yards from the tents, we needed to ascend a fifteen-foot hill of moraine debris. I had to rest between every small step to reach the top.

Ten climbers and sherpas from IMG's second group cheered as PK and I approached the mess tent. After handshakes and hugs, I drank a big mug of sugary lemon drink before I even took off my pack. Eight and half hours after standing on the summit, we were safe.

Wearing a down suit in the midafternoon sunshine overheated me. I went to change clothes but then recalled that I didn't have any—two days earlier I'd accepted Phunuru's offer over the radio to send my excess gear bag to base camp on a half-empty helicopter that was departing Camp Two. Not having to lug the weight down to base camp sounded like a good idea at the time, but now I had no lighter clothing. I would have to live in my smelly suit for another day. I didn't care.

During our Camp Four satellite call earlier, Gloria expressed worry about me descending. Though bleary-eyed, I texted her:

I made it down saef to camp tvwo.

She replied:

Yes I was watching. Please rest sleep eat and drink. You did it!!!!!

After staying awake for thirty-four hours and being on the move for twenty-four of them, sleep came fast when I lay down. Soon, though, I woke up to Phunuru shaking my leg.

"Jim Dai. I need to check you for frostbite."

"I'm good," I said with a drowsy slur.

"No, I must see your feet, bro."

As a veteran sirdar, Phunuru checked on the health of each returning member, and he knew better than to trust the judgment of an exhausted summit climber. I struggled to sit up and slip my legs from my sleeping bag. When I started removing the first sock, a glimmer of social etiquette crossed my mind.

"My feet stink."

Phunuru chuckled. "I don't care. Just let me see them."

I peeled off my damp socks and presented him with my wet, wrinkled feet. Phunuru examined my soles, then turned his attention to the toes. He studied each one, pinched the sweaty digit, and watched for the pink flush of returning blood.

After ten individual tests, he looked up with a big smile. "No frost-bite!"

We laughed hard and high-fived like we were in a casino and I'd just won a bet against the house. In a way, I had.

I flopped back onto the sleeping bag as Phunuru zipped the tent door closed. Half inside my bag and half splayed on the lumpy tent floor, I fell asleep, still holding the pair of wet socks.

Several hours later I awoke to the sound of rapid boot scuffs on the rocky moraine outside my tent. The familiar clink of aluminum climbing gear being sorted mixed with fast-paced Nepali chatter. I stuck my head outside the tent; Phunuru stood there directing six sherpas who were gearing up.

"What's going on?" I asked.

"Ryan collapsed on the Lhotse Face," Phunuru said. "We're going to bring him down."

"Do you need my help?" My croaky voice and disheveled look probably didn't give him the impression that I would be very helpful.

"No, we're rested. We got it, Dai," he answered.

Getting him down took hours, but by the middle of the night, everyone on our summit team, including Ryan, was safe in Camp Two. Our fatigue was so profound that no one ate much dinner.

Even though I'd missed an entire night's sleep, I awoke at 2:00 a.m. when I heard our wave-two climbers preparing for their summit push. I dressed for the nighttime cold and went out to wish them luck. My friend Sharon looked nervous, so I gave her a little pep talk, telling her she could definitely make the top. After they left, I packed my gear for our descent and sent a text message to my best friend:

Hey Rodney. I summitted Everest.

After explaining my hallucinations and how his voice kept me focused, I also wrote:

Thnks for being with me on my exausted descent of Lhotse
face yesterday.

He replied:

I am honored to be in your heart esp when it mattered the most.
SO PROUD OF YOU.

As I moved about camp, I sensed a vague discomfort in my chest. More a dull ache than a specific pain, it hurt the most when I pulled in and let out a big breath. I concluded that my diaphragm muscles were tired and sore from so much heavy breathing.

At breakfast I learned that a few people were too tired to finish the descent right away, so they would rest for a day before heading down. PK and I left Camp Two at 6:20 a.m. Even though I was tired, the thick, rich air down at 20,000 feet let us move fast. My spirits were high as we cruised through the Western Cwm in the crisp morning air. We had no worries, save one: the Khumbu Icefall. By May 23 springtime had a firm grip on the glacier, and the extra heat and liquid water would loosen and weaken the icefall. One last trip through the gauntlet still stood between us and a safe, successful climb.

We halted at 19,700 feet for a rest. Like a race-car driver during a final pit stop, I considered how much fuel I needed to go flat out for the last lap. I chugged down eight ounces of water and ate two caffeinated energy gels. As I looked around, I realized we were sitting within a hundred feet of where the helicopters had evacuated us after the quake.

I gazed deep into the Western Cwm. The spectacular basin of mile-high walls and moving ice that had seemed so mysterious to me decades earlier now felt familiar, but familiarity didn't lessen its majesty.

The deep crevasses fifty feet ahead and the steepening slope marked where the glacier began its accelerated plunge into the icefall. We slipped on our packs and checked our harness rigs.

"Last trip through. Let's climb well," I said.

"And fast," PK said.

We hustled along the ropes and sped across ladders as the sun crept higher. Around nine o'clock a slow-moving team snarled us. We waited in line at a wobbly three-ladder bridge. During the delay I studied the house-size glacial block leaning over us. In my mind I asked it to stay motionless for a bit longer, please. The bridge cleared ten minutes later, and we hurried across. Since my polite request had worked, I began preemptively thanking other precarious-looking ice towers for letting us pass. A low-grade nervousness ran through me as we pushed past more frozen pinnacles. I tried to be gracious and respectful, as if we were squeezing through a crowded biker bar, hoping to make an exit without getting clobbered.

PK and I walked out of the lower icefall under a blazing blue sky. To cool off we rolled our suit tops down to our waists. We wandered around picking up trash for a while, then carried it to the temporary drop-off point at the base of the icefall, where a member of the Sagarmatha Pollution Control Committee had a blue tarp spread on the ground. We placed the garbage we had just picked up into the appropriate piles: recyclables, burnables, and other trash. Then we walked around the meltwater pools proliferating on top of the ice and joined the muddy trail through base camp.

At the edge of the IMG camp, we circled clockwise around the altar and walked the final steps to our cook tent. Kaji and the guys cheered and embraced us. Greg burst from the mess tent sporting a big grin. He closed the gap between us with three long strides and gave PK and me hugs and congratulations.

Before PK and I went to our own tents to change clothes, we shook hands again and slapped each other on the back. I asked him to come to my tent in an hour for his summit bonus.

PK and I had differed sometimes on how to balance speed and safety, and that caused some frustrations over the last few days of the trip. But as we were two skilled climbers so close to the top, I think PK and I both knew that we could work well enough together to complete our climb of Mount Everest safely. And we did. We both wore smiles, we both still had ten toes and ten fingers. Soon we would return to our families. It was more than enough.

I staggered off to remove my steaming down suit. A little stunned to be back in my tent, I sipped my recovery drink and stared out my open tent door. The climb was over, and I could go home.

After changing into cleaner clothes, I stepped outside to dry my damp suit in the sunshine. Greg walked past on the way to his tent. He smiled and said, "Congratulations again, Jim. Great job!"

"Greg, thanks for . . ." My voice cracked. I placed my dirty hand against my trembling lower lip; dangling flakes of sunburned skin poked my index finger.

Greg turned around, walked over, and stood before me. He grabbed my upper arms with his hands and waited.

I laughed a little, and then, in a quivering voice, blurted out, "Thanks for helping me make my dream come true."

EPILOGUE

The Denver International Airport train pulled to a stop. When the automatic doors slid open, I hustled to the escalator. I climbed the moving stairs two at a time and, at the top, turned in to the terminal. Gloria, Nick, and Rodney stood twenty feet away, holding a colorful sign: EVEREST SUMMIT 2017.

Glo and I hugged for a long minute and kissed several times. I stepped over and embraced Nick. He slapped my back with both hands and said, "I *knew* you'd summit, Dad. I knew it!"

"Thanks, Nicky!"

Rodney stood behind Nick with a beaming smile. I moved to him, and we laughed while we hugged. "So good to see you, amigo!" I said.

"I'm so happy for you. Way to go, man!"

Everyone commented on how skinny I looked, and Gloria kept rubbing my scraggly beard. She told me we were having a small cookout party on our deck in a few hours. I was thrilled but needed to clarify some rigid culinary rules I'd developed while on Everest. Wagging my finger with exaggerated energy, I rattled them off: "There are no fried potatoes, no fried eggs, and no pancakes allowed in the house!"

They all laughed. After gathering my two duffels, we started home. Even though I was exhausted from the thirty-eight-hour trip and another sleepless night, I energetically answered their questions. We were all stunned at how fast I'd made it home—a helicopter ride to Kathmandu and excellent flight connections allowed me to travel from base camp to Denver in just four days. When I walked into our house after sixty-six days away, Jake the Wonder Dog barked and ran in circles.

Gloria, Nick, and Rodney started making dinner. When I went to grab a shower before Giordan, Alan, and Diane arrived, I stepped on the bathroom scale. I'd lost twenty-two pounds.*

Our evening-long celebration included everything I wanted: home, warmth, good friends, and fresh food. While Rodney recorded a video, Alan made a touching champagne toast and we all clinked glasses. Then Gloria said, "I have a toast too."

I slid close to her, and we put an arm around each other's waists. Gloria said, "We met when we were nineteen, and he was reading these books about summiting Mount Everest. And I thought: This guy's actually going to do this someday. I know he will. And here we are."

Of the many questions people asked me after Everest, the most common was: "So what's next?" The first time I heard it was during the brew-pub party Gloria and I threw to thank friends and supporters who'd helped me along the way. Since I'd only been home a week and hadn't even recovered physically, I dismissed the inquiry with a wisecrack: "My next goal is to finish this beer."

Later we organized a community event where I shared my Everest

---

* My trainer friend, Sandy, gave me a body composition test a few days later. Though I weighed 150 pounds, my body fat had increased from 13 to 18 percent. Of the twenty-two pounds I had lost, two were fat, and the other twenty were muscle. Because we can't eat enough food up there, or the right types, in two months Everest ate up all the muscle it had taken me years to build.

story and photos* to raise money for Nepal's continuing earthquake recovery. During the question-and-answer session, a fellow climber asked what my next expedition might be. I didn't have specific plans yet, but I mentioned a few interesting places in South America.

Seven weeks after summiting, the issue of what might be next took on a greater significance. I'd just finished speaking at a corporate conference for safety professionals. During the coffee break I chatted with a middle-aged woman who said: "I wonder how you'll pick your next adventure. After all, you can't climb anything higher than Mount Everest."

I paused for a moment. Then I said: "Well, there's no mountain taller, but life will have challenges bigger than Everest."

That set me wondering. What was my next Everest?

I chose to climb Mount Everest in part because committing to it would engage and energize me. I knew that going there would refine me into a better version of myself. Tackling tough goals like climbing a mountain, running a marathon, or earning a degree had always compelled me to do and become more. Embracing those challenges helped me build a resilient mindset, which better enabled me to accept change, face adversity, and endure uncertainty.

The few moments I spent standing atop Mount Everest didn't change me, but cultivating the resilience I needed to reach the summit did—and that extended to all aspects of my life. Though I'd faced the beginnings of diabetes before Nepal, after returning, my blood sugar values were the lowest they'd been in years. The rigorous physical demands of Everest helped me pull back from the disease. My improved fitness now allows me to stay active, avoid medication, and improve my health.

Looking back at my climbing career, I can see how engaging with greater and greater challenges steadily prepared me to climb Mount

---

* The camera that fried right after the summit never worked again. I recovered most of the photographs on the memory chip, with the exception of about twenty summit photos. Although disappointed to lose those pictures, I do have a few pictures of PK and me on the summit, and of the gorgeous sunrise from 29,000 feet. Along with thousands of other Everest photos, I brought home powerful memories of the awe that I experienced.

Everest. For me, it was essential to pick high goals and then transform myself into becoming capable of reaching them. Taking on big challenges made me more focused, disciplined, and resilient for the next mountain ahead.

There's *always* a next Everest.

AFTERWORD

May 30, 2020

Mount Everest has grown about an inch higher since I climbed it three years ago. While the mountain has changed very little since then, a great deal has changed for mountaineers—and for all of us.

As I finished this book in the spring of 2020, Mount Everest, and much of the world, was nearly closed down in response to the COVID-19 pandemic. In March 2020 the China Tibet Mountaineering Association canceled all permits for foreigners planning to ascend Everest. Within days Nepal barred climbing and trekking across the country. These two decisions almost shut down Mount Everest completely, except for one expedition. A national team from China was allowed to proceed after quarantine, and forty-nine of the climbers summited in May 2020. (That team also resurveyed the mountain. In conjunction with Nepali surveyors, who conducted their own field survey in 2019, they recalculated the summit elevation as 29,031.86 feet [8,848.86 meters].)

Far more important than any climb, this horrible pandemic has killed many people and sickened many more. The virus has fostered ambiguity in almost every aspect of life. It's as if the virus has press-ganged all of us onto an awful expedition of unknown duration to an unclear destination. So how can we survive and perhaps, somehow, even thrive when confronting so much uncertainty?

While I don't have any medical or societal answers, there are some expedition approaches and attitudes that might help. We can rally the willingness to adapt and the tenacity to endure. We must take care of ourselves and each other because we will need to recharge and then summon the resilience to face the unknown time and time again. Social shifts, including some lockdowns, mean we'll also need patience and perseverance in Everest-size amounts. There will be more suffering and loss to come. We must steel ourselves.

To me, my journeys have revealed that engaging with great difficulties often compels us to become more competent and capable. Over time, even traumatic events have the potential to improve us. Psychological studies show that we can eventually extract meaning from almost any mess. We can distill lessons, wisdom, and strength that we then carry to the next tough climb in life. This gradual process of post-traumatic growth cannot remedy past tragedies or restore life to the way it "used to be." But, post-traumatic growth does make us more resilient for the changes, challenges, and uncertainties that we will surely encounter on the next Everest.

ACKNOWLEDGMENTS

Climbing Everest requires the sustained efforts of many dedicated people, and so does writing an Everest book. I wouldn't have completed either one without the unending support and encouragement of my wife, Gloria Neesham Davidson. Since 1982, she has stood with me as we embraced the good things in life and endured the rest together. Thanks, Glo.

Our family expedition has been expanded, energized, and improved by my daughter, Jess, and my son, Nick. Even though my climbing and writing doesn't always make our family life simpler, your love keeps me grounded, and your encouragement lifts me up.

The person I've spent the most time with in the mountains is my trusted friend and rock-solid partner, Rodney Ley. I would never have even made it to the base of most mountains without you in my life, let alone dared to try for the top. *A la cumbre, mi amigo!*

A huge thanks to my long-term friends and climbing partners Terry Parker, Alan Arnette, and John Calderazzo. Your positive energy and willingness to jump in have fueled me onward and upward. I also appreciate Alan sharing his vast Everest knowledge with me and John helping me become a better writer.

I appreciate the continued support of my extended family, including Aunt Mary and my three sisters: Pat, Linda, and Joanne. On many mountain trips, I have been accompanied by great adventure partners, like Scott Yetman, Stan Hoffman, Sam Ley, Greg Ley, Andy Nelson, and so many more. The positive spirit of my old friend and partner, Mike Price, goes with me on every trip.

The experts at International Mountain Guides and the great sherpas and support staff with BEYUL Adventure Pvt. Ltd. made my two Everest trips possible. I thank my many Everest teammates from all around the world. And of course, I am especially thankful for Greg, Emily, Dallas, and PK Sherpa for getting us all up and down safely. I am grateful for the decades of support from LOWA Boots USA, and the friendship of Peter Sachs, Lesley Christoph, and the entire LOWA team. My ten happy toes thank you too for making such fine, warm boots.

On the long journey of writing this book, I learned much by working alongside the fine authors in the Raintree Writers critique group. My work was improved by the sharp eyes and deft abilities of Brigitte Dempsey, Kenneth Harmon, Brian Kaufman, Gordon MacKinney, Laura Mahal, and Patricia Stoltey. Thanks also to Northern Colorado Writers and Lighthouse Writers Workshop for all the excellent conferences and seminars. Several friends, family, and colleagues reviewed early drafts of this work and I am grateful for their valuable input and suggestions.

I deeply appreciate the Mountain and Wilderness Writing Program at the Banff Centre for Arts and Creativity for the scholarship and residency opportunity that allowed me to join the 2018 program. This book began taking shape during three magical weeks hosted by Joanna Croston and the Banff team. I am grateful for the guidance of my editor, Tony Whittome, and for the other fine instructors, Marni Jackson, and Harley Rustad. My fellow writers made it a fun and productive experience. Thanks, Emily Chappell, Chris Kassar, Eileen Keane, Fiona McGlynn, Paul Pritchard, Christina Reynolds, and Ailsa Ross.

Many other writing colleagues provided inspiration, guidance, and support, including LeAnn Thieman, Kevin Vaughan, David Roberts, James Edward Mills, Meghan Ward, Jocey Asnong, Kerrie Flanagan, Teresa Funke, and more. I am especially grateful to Molly McCowan for her helpful edits and to BK Loren, whose groundbreaking writing and teaching showed me new ways to share stories.

I feel fortunate and thankful for my savvy literary manager, Sharlene Martin, and the excellent team at Martin Literary & Media Management. Their hard work brought me and this project to just the right editor, George Witte of St. Martin's Publishing Group. Working with George and the experts at St. Martin's was like being part of a well-run expedition. My gratitude goes to Kevin Reilly (editorial assistant), Sue Llewellyn (copy editor), Joe Rinaldi (publicist), Michelle Cashman (marketer), Mac Nicholas (marketer), John Morrone (production editor), and Janna Dokos (production manager).

My heartfelt thanks to Jeanie Sutter of The Second You, for managing my speaking business while I was away on Everest and other odd places over the last seven years. Finally, I appreciate the hard work of Richard Schelp, Stephen Kirkpatrick, and the Executive Speakers Bureau for finding so many in-person and virtual speaking opportunities for me to share what the mountains have taught me.

AUTHOR'S NOTE ABOUT SOURCES

In this memoir, I have endeavored to present the events that occurred as accurately as possible, based on my memories and sources. The sources used include:

- Six journals I kept from 2014-2017
- Personal letters
- Recordings or transcripts of media appearances that I made
- Hundreds of emails that I sent and received
- Thousands of text messages I sent and received from two cell phones and a GPS unit
- Hundreds of social media posts made on five different platforms
- Thousands of photographs, with time and date stamps
- Hundreds of short videos, with time and date stamps
- GPS tracks for almost every day spent trekking and climbing in 2015 and 2017

- Over two dozen books about Mount Everest and climbing, several of which were referenced in this book.
- Over three dozen articles about geology, earthquakes, the Gorkha quake, accidents, fatalities, etc., several of which were referenced in this book
- The online Himalayan Database records
- Multiple discussions and interviews with guides and teammates with whom I climbed
- Multiple discussion with friends and family involved in these events
- Fact-check discussions and communiques with noted Everest authorities Brent Bishop and Bob A. Schelfhout Aubertijn

The facts, quotes, details, dates, places, and times from these multiple sources were cross-checked and then used to supplement my memories. Some dialogue quotes were taken directly from videos, some were extracted from contemporaneous journal entries, and others were recreated to the best of my recollections.

Despite these fact-checking efforts, personal perceptions vary among individuals. Human memory is also imperfect and variable. These become amplified when those involved were tired, stressed, distracted, or hypoxic, as was often the case above 17,000 feet. Any residual inaccuracies in this memoir are unintentional.

IN MEMORIAM

The author respectfully recognizes the people in Nepal and neighboring countries who were impacted, injured, or killed by the Gorkha earthquake of April 25, 2015. The quake, its aftershocks, and its aftermath killed nearly nine thousand people. Among that enormous loss, nineteen people on Mount Everest perished, including:

Tengien Bhote	Renu Fotedar
Daniel Paul Fredinburg	Marisa Eve Girawong
Chhimi Dawa Sherpa	Dawa Chhiri Sherpa
Lhakpa Chhiring Sherpa	Jangbu Sherpa
Pema Hissi Sherpa	Pemba Sherpa
Pasang Temba Sherpa	Shiva Kumar Shrestha
Krishna Kumar Rai	Milan Rai
Thomas Ely Taplin	Vinh Truong
Hiroshi Yamagata	Ge Zhenfang

And a nineteenth mountain traveler, whose name remains unknown.

Note: Some variability exists in the reported spellings of these names. Any oversights or errors are unintentional and regretted.

LEGEND OF SUMMITS

A. Mount Everest (29,029 feet)
B. Lhotse (27,940 feet, summit off to right)
C. Nuptse (25,791 feet, summit off to right)
D. West Shoulder (23,800 feet)
E. Pumori (23,494 feet, summit off to left)
F. Lingtren (22,142 feet)

LEGEND OF KEY LOCATIONS (APPROXIMATE)

G. General path of 2015 avalanche and
   wind-blasted debris that overran
   base camp (with flow arrows)
H. Upper end of base camp
I. IMG base camp in 2015 and 2017
J. Khumbu Icefall
K. Camp One (hidden)
L. Avalanches off West Shoulder toward
   Camp One (with flow arrow)
M. Camp Four

NORTH

PHOTOGRAPH BY JIM DAVIDSON, 2017